THE PLAYS AND
POEMS OF
Philip Massinger

THE PLAYS AND POEMS OF
Philip Massinger

EDITED BY
PHILIP EDWARDS
AND
COLIN GIBSON

VOLUME II

OXFORD
AT THE CLARENDON PRESS
1976

Oxford University Press, Ely House, London W.1

GLASGOW NEW YORK TORONTO MELBOURNE WELLINGTON
CAPE TOWN IBADAN NAIROBI DAR ES SALAAM LUSAKA ADDIS ABABA
DELHI BOMBAY CALCUTTA MADRAS KARACHI DACCA
KUALA LUMPUR SINGAPORE HONG KONG TOKYO

ISBN 0 19 811894 5

© *Oxford University Press 1976*

All rights reserved. No part of this publication may be reproduced, stored in a retrieval system, or transmitted, in any form or by any means, electronic, mechanical, photocopying, recording, or otherwise, without the prior permission of Oxford University Press

*Printed in Great Britain
at the University Press, Oxford
by Vivian Ridler
Printer to the University*

CONTENTS

VOLUME II

THE RENEGADO
Introduction   1
Text   11

THE PARLIAMENT OF LOVE
Introduction   97
Text   107
Appendix (Malone Society Reprint)   177

THE UNNATURAL COMBAT
Introduction   181
Text   195

A NEW WAY TO PAY OLD DEBTS
Introduction   273
Text   293
Appendix (Wright's excerpts, 1640)   378

THE RENEGADO

INTRODUCTION

(a) *Date*

The only firm evidence for the date of composition of *The Renegado* is provided by Malone's and Chambers' transcript of Sir Henry Herbert's licence for performance, dated 17 April 1624: 'For the Cockpit; *The Renegado, or the Gentleman of Venice*: Written by Messenger.'[1] Bentley (iv. 812) reports a third transcript of the licence, possibly in the hand of Craven Ord, among the clippings in the scrap-books of Halliwell-Phillipps, now in the Folger Shakespeare Library: 'For the Cockpitt company   The Renegado or the Gentleman of Venice by Messenger this 17th Apr. 1624. 1.[li]'

None of the topical allusions in the play to such things as the freedom of English women, Dutch Anabaptists, or court immorality positively contradicts late 1623 or early 1624 as the date of composition, and there is a little evidence that *The Renegado* was written some time after 1621.

At II. vi. 9, Gazet, on seeing his master return from his meeting with Donusa, describes Vitelli as 'One by his rich sute should bee some french Embassador'. The Comte de Tillières, the regular French ambassador at the English court from August 1619 until June 1624, had no reputation for fine clothes, but there was a special French envoy who did have such a reputation. Sir Simonds D'Ewes records that 'many thousands' flocked to see Cadenet, brother of the Duke of Luynes, when he visited England from December to January 1620/1. 'I found him a proper tall man and a gallant courtier . . . his hatband, scarf, and clothes were so richly set out with diamonds, as they were valued to amount unto between 30,000*l*. or 40,000*l*.' James Howell also noted his 'light Garb' and 'his Train of ruffling long-hair'd Monsieurs', and his magnificent appearance was still remembered by Chamberlain in April 1622.[2]

---

[1] Adams, *Herbert*, p. 28.
[2] D'Ewes, *Autobiography*, ed. J. O. Halliwell, 1845, i. 164–8; Howell, *Epistolae Ho-Elianae*, ed. J. Jacobs, 1890, pp. 99–100; Chamberlain, *Letters*, ii. 432.

Carazie's remark that English noblewomen's doctors and chaplains 'are growne of late so learn'd' that they maintain that their mistresses 'should to ease [their] husband Bee allow'd a priuate friend' (I. ii. 40–6), sounds like an early attack on the fashion of Platonic Love, adopted by the court under Henrietta Maria, but well known in England before 1625.[1]

(b) *Sources*

The most important studies of the sources of *The Renegado* are those of Koeppel, Heckmann, and Rice.[2] These have established that Massinger drew his plot from Cervantes's stories of life in Algiers, supplemented by three English descriptions of the Turkish empire: Biddulph's *The Travels of certain Englishmen into Africa, Troy, Bithynia, Thracia, and to the Black Sea*, edited by Theophilus Lavender, 1609; George Sandys's *Relation of a Journey begun An. Dom. 1610*, 1615; and Richard Knolles's *General History of the Turks*, 1603.

The basic elements of the play—the pursuit of a woman carried into captivity at Algiers, a Moorish princess's love for a nobly-born Christian, a captive Christian woman's rejection of a Moorish lover, an escape with the assistance of a repentant renegade—are found in several of Cervantes's works, for he thriftily used a basic narrative drawing on his own experience of slavery at Algiers for a *comedia* titled *El trato de Argel* (Life at Algiers), written in the 1580s but not printed until 1784;[3] the episode called 'The Captive's Story' in *Don Quixote*, Part 1, xxxix–xli, published in 1605, and translated into English in 1612; the story 'The Liberal Lover', published in 1613 as one of the *Novelas ejemplares*, and translated into French in 1615 and into English in 1640; and into yet another *comedia*, *Los baños de Argel* (The Prisons of Algiers), published in *Ocho comedias y ocho entremeses nuevos* (1615), and never translated in full (a partial French version appeared in 1862).

[1] See note to I. ii. 40–6. The earliest English translation of Honoré D'Urfé's *Astrée*, which helped to create the new mode, was published in 1620.

[2] Koeppel, *Quellen-Studien*, pp. 97–103; T. Heckmann, *Massinger's 'The Renegado' und seine spanischen Quellen*, Halle, 1905; W. G. Rice, 'The Sources of Massinger's *The Renegado*', *PQ*, xi (1932), 65–75.

[3] See *Cervantes*, S. J. Arbo, 1955. This *comedia* was not translated into English until 1870, but Massinger might have read a manuscript copy of the Spanish original; his ability to read Spanish is generally accepted (see M. Chelli, *Le Drame de Massinger*, Lyon, 1923, pp. 42–3). Lope de Vega wrote an adaptation of *El trato de Argel*, called *Los cautivos de Argel*, about 1600, which was printed in 1647.

Introduction

However, the most extensive parallels are those between *The Renegado* and *Los baños de Argel*.

Massinger's Donusa combines two of Cervantes's characters: the Lady Zara, courted by King Muley Maluco but in love with Don Lope, a Spanish prisoner,[1] and Halima, wife of Caurali the Captain of Algiers, who actively courts her husband's slave, Don Fernando. Cervantes's Zara has already been secretly converted to Christianity by a slave woman; Massinger chooses to stage Donusa's conversion (IV. iii), reworking material from a scene in *The Virgin Martyr*, in which the heroine Dorothea reconverts two apostate Christians sent to win her from her faith.[2] Paulina corresponds to Don Fernando's young wife Costanza, carried into slavery and vainly courted by Caurali. The bare bones of Massinger's Renegado are in the blood-thirsty Yzuf, Caurali's renegade companion, and Hazèn, a repentant renegade who is condemned to death by the Cadi of Algiers, and (like Vitelli) excites admiration by his steadfast courage. Another renegade, who pretends to be a merchant in order to secure a boat for the fleeing lovers in 'The Captive's Story', may have contributed something to the character, as well as the idea for Vitelli's disguise. However, the English dramatist is as original in developing in Grimaldi a full-scale portrait of a violent man driven to despair and conversion as he is in creating the humane Jesuit Francisco from Yzuf's father of the same name in *Los baños de Argel*,[3] or the ebullient Gazet from Don Lope's companion, the shadowy figure Vibanco.

Massinger's principal alterations to the Spanish narrative consist of the substitution of comic and satirical scenes for a number of episodes displaying Spanish heroism and faithfulness; the scenes in which Donusa meets Vitelli, first at the bazaar and later in the seraglio; a new sequence of events following the discovery of the lovers; and Paulina's part in securing their escape by a pretended conversion to Islam. The idea for the scene in which Donusa visits the bazaar may have come from *El trato de Argel*, and the business of the password which gives Vitelli access to the seraglio seems to

---

[1] Each version of the story insists on his rank as a gentleman; this is plainly the origin of the alternative title of Massinger's play.

[2] *The Virgin Martyr*, III. i. 67–213. Verbal echoes and parallels in argument are noted in the Commentary.

[3] There are incidental references to priests redeeming captives in the other versions of the story; a comic sacristan appears in *Los baños de Argel*, and there is a bishop, Jorge d'Olivares, in *El trato de Argel* (cf. *Renegado*, IV. i. 72 SD. and note). The creation of Francisco as an active agent in the overall action of the play resembles the development of the scheming Francisco in *The Duke of Milan*.

have been suggested by an episode in 'The Liberal Lover'. Donusa's sensual invitation to the Venetian, and his later appearance, richly dressed, to Francisco and Gazet, have analogues in both *El trato de Argel* and *Los baños de Argel*.

The turning point in *The Renegado* is the scene (III. v) in which Donusa and Vitelli are discovered together by Asambeg and Mustapha. In the source play, Caurali and Halima accidentally find Fernando and Costanza together, but are tricked into excusing the couple's amorous behaviour. Later Zara secretly provides Don Lope's ransom, and he returns from Spain to rescue everyone. Massinger wanted a more exciting sequence of events, and turned to other sources. Manto's betrayal of her mistress's love for Vitelli came from Knolles (pp. 557–9), and much of the documentary material for the following trial scene (IV. ii) was taken from Biddulph and Sandys. Paulina's pretended conversion may have been suggested to the dramatist by an episode in *La gran sultana dona Cathalina de Oviedo*, another play in the 1615 volume which contained *Los baños de Argel*. There the heroine procures release for a pair of lovers by giving herself in marriage to Sultan Mourad, while holding to her Christian faith. (That Massinger knew this play is suggested by resemblances between the opening scenes of *The Renegado* and *La gran sultana*.) Sandys has a story of escape by means of a rope ladder from the 'blacke Tower' (p. 41), and all of Cervantes's narratives end with a flight by sea.

As for the richly documented Turkish background of Massinger's play, Rice has drawn attention to verbal parallels and borrowings which indicate that the dramatist read widely in search of authentic information and names (details are given in the Commentary). It is also of interest that the Daniel Lakyn who wrote a commendatory poem for *The Renegado* may have been a doctor who had first-hand knowledge of Morocco and Constantinople (see the Commentary).

(c) *Text*

The Renegado was entered to John Waterson in the Stationers' Register on 22 March 1630, and was printed for him by '*A.M.*'

M[r] Ioh: Waterson   Entred for his Copie vnder the handes of S[r] Henrye Harbert and M[r] Purfoote warden A play called The Runegado by Phil: Messenger   vj[d].

(Register D 197; Greg, *Bibliography*, i. 37; Arber, iv. 231.)

Introduction

The printer is identified by Sayle[1] with Augustine Mathewes, the only London printer with those initials known to be working in 1630. The edition is mentioned in booksellers' catalogues in 1656, 1661, 1663, and 1671.[2] It will be referred to from now on as *30*; the title-page is reproduced on page 11.

30 is in quarto, A–L⁴, M² (46 leaves); H3 and M2 are unsigned: see Greg, *Bibliography*, no. 430 (ii. 580). The contents are: A1, blank; A2ʳ, *title*; A2ᵛ, 'Dramatis Personæ. The Actors names.'; A3ʳ, *dedication begins*, 'TO THE RIGHT HONOVRABLE GEORGE HARDING, Baron *Barkley*, of *Barkley* Castle, and Knight of the Honourable Order of the BATHE.'; A3ᵛ, *dedication ends*, *signed* 'PHILIP MASSINGER.'; A4ʳ, *poem*, '*To my Honour'd Friend, Master* PHILIP MASSINGER, *vpon his* RENEGADO.', *signed* 'IAMES SHIRLEY.'; A4ᵛ, *poem*, 'To his worthy Friend Master PHILIP MASSENGER, on his Play, Call'd the RENEGADO.', *signed* 'DANYEL LAKYN.'; B1ʳ, 'THE RENEGADO.', *text begins*; M2ᵛ, *text ends*, 'FINIS.' The text is set in roman, 20 lines measuring approximately 79 mm. The compositor first set a standard of 36 lines to the page, but changed to a standard of 37 lines from sheet C on (there are 33 lines on B3ᵛ, 35 on G2ʳ, and 38 on C4ʳ and F3ᵛ).

Two skeletons were used in the printing; one for sheets B, C, D, and E–G (o), H–I (i), K–L (o) and M, the other for E–G (i), H–I (o), and K–L (i). The printing is generally careful, with fewer turned letters and literal misprints than occur in many of the plays. There is nothing to suggest that more than one compositor was involved in setting up the text.

Eleven of the twenty-four formes are variant. B (i) and (o), H (i) and (o), I (i), L (i) and M (i) exist in two states, C (i) in three states, D (o) and L (o) in four states, and E (o) in five states. Fifty-eight corrections and two corruptions have been noted, concentrated in D (o), E (o) and L (o). There is clear evidence that Massinger attended the printing-house and made alterations while printing was in progress,[3] though a number of errors were passed over, to be corrected in later stages of proof-reading or written into the completed text.

---

[1] C. E. Sayle, *Early English Printed Books in the University Library Cambridge (1475–1640)*, 1900–7, no. 4543.
[2] Greg, *Bibliography*, iii. 1325, 1336, 1350, and iv. 1660.
[3] Examples are to be found at II. iii. 10–12, II. iv. 104, II. vi. 7, IV. i. 114, and V. iii. 115.

The Renegado

There are several indications that the text was set up from an autograph manuscript, including traces of alteration in the manuscript at I. iii. 159–63, II. iii. 10–12, V. iii. 145–6, and elsewhere, and survivals of Massinger's characteristic pointing in scene headings (as at I. ii, II. v, and V. iv).[1] There is an occasional unnecessary capital C or H (as at V. vi. 11), and the compositor's mistaken 'dispute actions' for 'disputations' (II. vi. 5) may be due to Massinger's formation of the letter 'a', in which the down stroke is sometimes separated from the body of the letter. An occasional stage direction is specific enough to have had a playhouse origin ('*The chamber shot off. Enter Aga.*'), but on the whole it is likely that the printer's copy was the author's fair copy, rather than a manuscript prepared for use in the theatre. There are vague directions for groups of minor characters ('*Saylors, Turkes*', '*Ianizaries*', '*Boteswaine, &c*'), and descriptive musical directions ('*A solemne musicque*', '*loude Musicque*', '*A dreadfull musicke*'). Actions, properties, and wardrobe are described with a fullness that is characteristic of an author rather than a stage annotator. Mustapha '*puts of his yellow Pantophles*'; Donusa '*Giues him her hand to kisse*'; she '*Whispers, and vses vehement actions*'; Vitelli '*Stands amazde*'; Asambeg '*plucks out a guilt key*'; Francisco enters '*in a Cope like a Bishop*'; The Aga and Capiaga enter, '*leading in Donusa in blacke, her trayne borne vp by Carazie, and Manto.*'

There are copies of *30* in the following libraries and institutions: Bamburgh Castle Library; the Bodleian Library (2 copies); the Boston Public Library; the British Museum (4 copies); the Clark Library, University of California; Cambridge University Library; the Chapin Library; the University of Chicago; the Library of Congress; the Folger Shakespeare Library (3 copies); Glasgow University; Harvard University; the Henry E. Huntington Library; the University of Illinois; Kings College, Cambridge; Kings College, Newcastle; the University of Leeds; the University of Liverpool; the University of Manchester; Merton College, Oxford; the University of Michigan; the Newberry Library; the University of Pennsylvania; the Pierpont Morgan Library; Princeton University; the Royal Library, The Hague; the Royal Library, Stockholm; The National Library of Scotland; the University of Texas

---

[1] Massinger's use of full stops instead of commas in a sequence of names within a stage direction is discussed by W. J. Lawrence, *Those Nut Cracking Elizabethans*, 1935, 194–205.

(2 copies); the Victoria and Albert Museum (2 copies); Worcester College, Oxford; and Yale University (2 copies).

The present text has been prepared from the Bodleian Library copy, Malone 236 (5).

There are autograph corrections in the Harbord copy of *The Renegado* (Folger Shakespeare Library, Gosse 5298).[1] Most of the 32 corrections emend simple printer's errors, altering spelling and punctuation or correcting a defective reading, but there are also three cases (discussed in the Commentary) of actual rewriting, at I. i. 11, III. iii. 89, and IV. i. 114.

The Renegado was printed in the collected editions of Coxeter, Mason, Gifford, Coleridge, and Cunningham, but otherwise seems to have been ignored. A. K. McIlwraith prepared the first critical old-spelling edition of the play as part of his unpublished doctoral thesis, 'The Life and Works of Philip Massinger', Oxford, 1931; it was followed by another unpublished doctoral thesis, 'An Edition of Philip Massinger's "The Renegado"', by Alice Senob, University of Chicago, 1939. Both of these editions have considerably helped the preparation of the present edition. Shirley's commendatory poem was included in his collected *Poems &c.* (1646) and has since been edited by Gifford and Dyce (1833), R. G. Howarth (1931), and R. L. Armstrong (1941). Readings from the 1646 text are given in the textual notes with the attribution *Shirley*. Selections from the play, including the whole of IV. iii, were given in *Beauties of Massinger*, printed for John Porter in 1817. A. J. F. Mézières translated brief passages, in *Contemporains et successeurs de Shakspeare*, Paris, 1864.

(d) *Stage History*

In the seventeenth century *The Renegado* seems to have remained on the stage longer than most of Massinger's plays. It was licensed for performance by Sir Henry Herbert on 17 April 1624 (see page 1). Presumably the original production was by members of the Lady Elizabeth's company, which played at the Cockpit (or the Phoenix) until the group dissolved after the closure of the theatres in March 1625, in mourning for James I.[2]

---

[1] For the provenance of this copy, see vol. i, pp. xxxii–xxxiii; modern examinations of the corrections are listed in vol. iii, p. 7.

[2] See Bentley, i. 176; also W. B. Markward, 'A Study of the Phoenix Theatre in Drury Lane, 1617–1638', unpublished doctoral thesis, University of Birmingham, 1953,

Beeston, the owner and manager of the Cockpit, apparently retained possession of many of the company's plays, which became part of the repertory of Queen Henrietta's men, the new company at the Phoenix. Bentley (i. 220-2) points out that the cast list printed in the 1630 quarto derives from a performance given by this company as it existed at the end of 1625 or early in 1626. Some five years after the initial production by Queen Henrietta's men, the quarto title-page refers to frequent performances ('it hath beene often acted by the Queenes Maiesties seruants').

The Renegado was still an attractive property in 1639, when Beeston included it among several plays protected against 'all other Companyes of Actors . . . [who] are not any wayes to intermedle wth or Act any of th'aboue mentioned Playes'.[1] At this time the play was in the repertory of the King and Queen's young company (Beeston's boys), who succeeded Queen Henrietta's men at the Cockpit in 1637. Bentley (iv. 814) quotes a later contemporary tribute to Philip Massinger, 'that the sweet Renegaddo pend', from an enthusiastic reader or playgoer.[2]

After the Restoration, the play was revived by the King's men on 6 August 1662, at the Vere Street Theatre (Adams, *Herbert*, p. 118).[3] Edward Browne recorded in his Memorandum Book a payment of half a crown to see a performance of *The Renegado* 'At the New Theatre in Lincolnes Jnne fields'; this must have been in 1662 or before 6 May 1663, when the King's men moved to Bridges Street.[4] Perhaps Browne saw the performance noted by Herbert, but it may just as well have been another.

In the Bodleian Library (MS. Rawlinson Poet. 20) there is an undated folio manuscript of 47 leaves containing an adaptation of *The Renegado* which has been taken to be the actual text used for the

and T. J. King, 'Staging of Plays at the Phoenix in Drury Lane, 1617-42', *Theatre Notebook*, xix (1964-5), 146-66.

[1] The list is dated 10 August 1639; it is printed in *Malone Society Collections*, II. iii (1931), 389-90, and discussed by Bentley, i. 324-42.

[2] Samuel Sheppard, *The Times Displayed*, 1646, sestiad 6, stanza 15.

[3] Herbert's entry is dated 6 June 1662, but I accept Professor J. Freehafer's view that the performance of *The Renegado* and four other plays was deliberately backdated by two months to enable Herbert to collect the licensing fees rightly due to Hayward and Poyntz, to whom he sold his office on his retirement about 27 July 1663 (see *The London Stage (1660-1800)*, Part 1, ed. W. Van Lennep, Carbondale, Illinois, 1965, 38-9).

[4] British Museum, MS. Sloane 1900; printed in W. W. Greg, 'Theatrical Repertories of 1662', *Gentleman's Magazine*, ccci (1906), 69-72.

1622 revival.[1] It is a transcript from the 1630 quarto, not from an independent manuscript (as proved by several readings in which the writer copies quarto errors before correcting them), at times close and accurate, at times free and careless of the verse arrangement. The adaptor modernizes obsolete expressions, breaks up long declamatory speeches, expurgates coarseness and low comedy (III. iv, in which Gazet begs to be made a eunuch, is omitted), updates topical allusions, and makes a few changes in the plot. The main alterations of this kind are the insertion of an earlier affair between Mustapha and Manto, and the rewriting of the final scene so that Asambeg and Mustapha are trapped in Vitelli's prison by Grimaldi and the sailors when they escort Paulina and Donusa there. This text is clearly intended for the theatre (as further evidenced by the addition of directions for music and new stage directions), but there is no mention of actors, and no indication that the manuscript was ever actually used as a prompt copy.[2] Its connexion with the recorded Restoration performance(s) remains uncertain.

No modern production of *The Renegado* is known.

[1] See W. J. Lawrence, 'The Renegado', *TLS*, 24 Oct. 1929, p. 846; J. G. McManaway, *Studies*, pp. 14–15; Bentley, iv. 814.
[2] The stage directions added to those in the 1630 quarto tend to be expansive and unspecific; a typical one is 'Enter Eunuchs with Arms full of Baggs of gold & Cabinetts of Jewells—& cross on the stage—Manto directing them by signs as to Vitelli's shop' (fol. 17^r).

THE RENEGADO,

A TRAGÆCOMEDIE.

As it hath beene often acted by the Queenes Maiesties seruants, at the priuate Play-house in *Drurye-Lane.*

By PHILIP MASSINGER.

LONDON,
Printed by *A. M.* for *Iohn Waterson,* and are to be sold at the *Crowne* in *Pauls Church-Yard.* 1630.

Dramatis Personæ.

ASAMBEG, *Viceroy of* Tunis.
MVSTAPHA, *Basha of* Aleppo.
VITELLI, *A Gentelman of* Venice
  disguis'd.
FRANCISCO, *A Jesuite.*
ANTHONIO GRIMALDI, *the*
  Renegado.
CARAZIE, *an Eunuch.*
GAZET, *seruant to* Vitelli.
AGA.
CAPIAGA.
[IANIZARIES.]
[GARDES.]
MASTER.
BOTESWAINE.
SAYLORS.
IAILOR.
3. TVRKES.

DONVSA, *neece to* AMVRATH.
PAVLINA, *Sister to* Vitelli.
MANTO, *seruant to* Donusa.

The Actors Names.

Iohn Blanye.
Iohn Sumner.
Michael Bowier.

William Reignalds.
William Allen.

William Robins.
Edward Shakerley.

Edward Rogers.
Theo. Bourne.

13. IANIZARIES.] *Gifford; not in* 30   14. GARDES.] *editor; not in* 30

TO THE RIGHT HONOVRABLE
GEORGE HARDING, Baron *Barkley*, of *Barkley* Castle, and Knight of the Honourable Order of the BATHE.

My good Lord.

To be Honoured for old Nobility, or Hereditary Titles is not alone proper to your Selfe, but to some few of your rancke, who may challenge the like priuiledge with you: but in our age to vouchsafe (as you haue often done) a ready hand to rayse the deiected spirits of the contemned Sonnes of the Muses, Such as would not suffer the glorious fire of Poesie to be wholly extinguished, is so remarkable, and peculiar to your Lordship, that with a full vote, and suffrage it is acknowledged that the Patronage, and Protection of the Dramatique Poem, is yours, and almost without a riuall. I despayre not therefore, but that my ambition to present my seruice in this kinde, may in your clemency meete with a gentle interpretation. Confirme it my good Lord in Your gracious acceptance of this trifle, in which if I were not confident there are some peeces worthy the perusall, it should haue beene taught an humbler flight, and the writer (Your Countrey-man) neuer yet made happy in your notice, and fauour, had not made this an aduocate to plead for his admission among such as are wholy, and sincerely deuoted to your seruice. I may liue to tender my humble thankefulnesse in some higher strayne, and till then comfort my selfe with hope, that you descend from your height to receiue,

Your Honours

Commanded Seruant.

PHILIP MASSINGER.

To my Honourd Friend, Master PHILIP MASSINGER, *vpon his* RENEGADO.

DABBLERS in *Poetry* that onely can
   Court this weake *Lady*, or that *Gentleman*,
      with some loose witt in *rime*;
      others that fright the *time*
Into beliefe with mighty words, that teare
   a Passage through the eare;
      or *Nicer* men,
That through a Perspectiue wil see a *Play*,
   and vse it the wrong way,
      (not worth thy *Pen*)
Though all their Pride exalt 'em, cannot bee
Competent Iudges of thy *Lines* or *thee*.

I must confesse I haue no Publike name
To rescue iudgement, no *Poeticke* flame
   to dresse thy Muse with *Praise*,
   and *Phœbus* his owne *Bayes*;
Yet I commend this *Poem*, and dare tell
   the *World* I lik'd it well,
      and if there bee
A *tribe*, who in their *Wisedomes* dare accuse,
   this ofspring of thy *Muse*,
      let them agree,
Conspire one *Comedy*, and they will say
Tis easier to *Commend*, then make a *Play*.

              IAMES SHIRLEY.

---

title. *To* . . . RENEGADO.] *30*; *To M.* Phil. Massenger *on his Renegado. Shirley*
11. 'em] *30*; them *Shirley*   13. Publike] *30*; glorious *Shirley*   20. *Wisedomes*] *30*; wisdom *Shirley*
21. this] *30*; The *Shirley*   subscription IAMES SHIRLEY.] *30*; *not in Shirley*

To his worthy Friend Master PHILIP MASSENGER, on his Play, Call'd the RENEGADO.

THE *bosome of a friend cannot breath foorth*
A flattering phrase to speake the noble worth
Of him that hath lodg'd in his honest brest
So large a title: I among the rest
That honour thee, doe onely seeme to prayse, 5
Wanting the flowers of Art, to decke that Bayes
Merit has crown'd thy Temples with. Know friend
Though there are some who meerely doe commend
To liue i'th Worlds opinion such as can
Censure with Iudgement, no such peece of Man 10
Makes vp my spirit; where desert doe's liue,
There will I plant my wonder, and there giue
My best indeauours, to build vp his story
That truely Merits. I did euer glory
To behold Vertue rich, 'though cruell Fate 15
In scornefull malice doe's beate low their state
That best deserue, when others that but know
Onely to scribble, and no more, of't grow
Greate in their fauours, that would seeme to bee
Patrons of Witt, and modest Poesie: 20
Yet with your abler Friends, let me say this
Many may striue to equall you, but misse
Of your fayre scope; this worke of yours men may
Throw in the face of enuy, and then say
To those that are in Great-mens thoughts more blest, 25
Imitate this, and call that worke your best.
Yet Wise-men, in this, and too often, erre
When they their loue before the worke preferre.
If I should say more, some may blame me for't
Seeing your merits speake you, not report. 30

                          DANYEL LAKYN.

18. *of 't*] *30*; oft *Coxeter*

The Renegado

The Scene *Tunis.*

Actus primus. Scena prima.

Enter VITELLI *and* GAZET.

Vitelli. You haue hirde a Shop then?
   Gazet.   Yes sir, and our wares
(Though brittle as a maydenhead at sixteene)
Are safe vnladen; not a Christall crackt,
Or China dish needs sodring; our choice Pictures
As they came from the workeman, without blemish,   5
And I haue studied speeches for each Peece,
And in a thrifty tone to sell 'em off,
Will sweare by *Mahomet,* and *Termagant,*
That this is Mistris to the great Duke of *Florence,*
That Neece to old King *Pippin,* and a third   10
An *Austrian* Princesse by her Roman lippe,
How ere my conscience tels me they are figures
Of Bawdes, and common Courtezans in *Venice.*
   Vitelli. You make no scruple of an oath then?
   Gazet.   Fie sir
Tis out of my Indentures. I am bound there   15
To sweare for my Masters profit as securely
As your intelligencer must for his Prince,
That sendes him forth an honourable spie
To serue his purposes. And if it be lawfull
In a *Christian* shopkeeper to cheate his father,   20
I cannot find but to abuse a Turke
In the sale of our commodities, must bee thought
A meritorious worke.

   I. i. 7. off,] *Coxeter;* ~; *30*   11. Roman] *30;* German *conj. Greg*   lippe]
Massinger *MS*; nose *30*

Vitelli.   I wonder sirra
What's your Religion?
    Gazet.   Troth to answere truely
I would not be of one that should command mee
To feed vpon poore Iohn, when I see Pheasants
And Partriges on the Table: nor doe I like
The other that allowes vs to eate flesh
In the Lent though it be rotten, rather then bee
Thought superstitious, as your zealous Cobler,
And learned botcher preach at *Amsterdam*
Ouer a Hotchpotch. I would not be confin'd
In my beliefe: when all your Sects, and sectaries
Are growne of one opinion, if I like it
I will professe my selfe, in the meane time
Liue I in *England*, *Spaine*, *France*, *Rome*, *Geneua*,
I am of that Countryes faith.
    Vitelli.   And what in *Tunis*,
Will you turne Turke heere?
    Gazet.   No! so I should loose
A Collop of that part my *Doll* inioyn'd mee
To bring home as she left it, tis her venture,
Nor dare I barter that commoditie
Without her speciall warrant.
    Vitelli.   You are a Knaue sir;
Leauing your Roguerie thinke vpon my businesse,
It is no time to foole now.
Remember where you are too! though this Mart time,
Wee are allowde free trading, and with safetie.
Temper your tongue and meddle not with the Turkes,
Their manners, nor Religion.
    Gazet.   Take you heede sir
What colours you weare. Not two houres since there landed
An *English Pirats* Whore with a greene apron,
And as she walk't the streets, one of their Mufties,
Wee call them *Priests* at *Venice*, with a Razor
Cutts it of, Petticoate, Smocke and all, and leaues her
As naked as my Nayle: the young Frie wondering
What strange beast it should be. I scap't a scouring;
My Mistres Buskepoynt, of that forbidden coloure,

        36. *Geneua*,] *Coxeter*; ~. 30   46. safetie.] *30*; ~, *Mason*

Then tyde my codpeece, had it beene discouer'd
I had beene caponde.
   Vitelli.   And had beene well seru'd;
Haste to the Shoppe and set my Wares in order,
I will not long be absent.
   Gazet.   Though I striue sir   60
To put of Melencholy, to which, you are euer
Too much inclinde, it shall not hinder me
With my best care to serue you.   *Exit* GAZET.

        Enter FRANCISCO.

   Vitelli.   I beleeue thee.
O wellcome sir, stay of my steppes in this life,
And guide to all my blessed hopes heereafter.   65
What comforts sir? haue your indeauours prosper'd?
Haue wee tirde *Fortunes* malice with our sufferings?
Is she at length after so many frownes
Pleas'd to vouchsafe one cheerefull looke vpon vs?
   Francisco. You giue too much to fortune, and your passions, 70
Ore which a wise man, if Religious, tryumphs.
That name fooles worship, and those tyrants which
Wee arme against our better part, our reason,
May add, but neuer take from our afflictions.
   Vitelli. Sir as I am a sinfull man, I can not   75
But like one suffer.
   Francisco.   I exacte not from you
A fortitude insensible of calamitie,
To which the Saints themselues haue bowde and showne
They are made of flesh, and bloud; all that I challenge
Is manly patience. Will you that were train'd vp   80
In a Religious Schoole, where diuine maximes
Scorning comparison, with morall precepts,
Were daily taught you, beare your constancies triall
Not like *Vitelli*, but a Village nurse
With curses in your mouth: Teares in your eyes?   85
How poorely it showes in you!
   Vitelli.   I am School'd sir,
And will heereafter to my vtmost strength
Studie to bee my selfe.
   Francisco.   So shall you find mee

Most ready to assist you; Neither haue I
Slept in your greate occasions: since I left you   90
I haue beene at the Viceroies Court and presde
As far as they allowe a *Christian* entrance.
And something I haue learn't that may concerne
The purpose of this iourney.
  Vitelli.   Deere Sir what is it?
  Francisco. By the command of *Asambeg*, the Viceroy,   95
The Cittie swels with barbarous Pompe and Pride
For the entertainement of stout *Mustapha*
The *Basha* of *Aleppo*, who in person
Comes to receiue the neece of *Amurah*
The fayre *Donusa* for his bride.
  Vitelli.   I find not   100
How this may profit vs.
  Francisco.   Pray you giue mee leaue.
Among the rest that wayte vpon the Viceroy,
(Such as haue vnder him command in *Tunis*,
Who as you haue often heard are all false *Pirats*)
I saw the shame of *Venice* and the scorne   105
Of all good men: The periurde *Renegado*
Antonio Grimaldy;
  Vitelli. Ha! his name
Is poyson to mee.
  Francisco. Yet againe?
  Vitelli.   I haue done sir.
  Francisco. This debauchde villaine, whom we euer thought,
(After his impious scorne done in Saint *Markes*   110
To me as I stood at the holy Altar)
The theefe that rauish't your fayre sister from you,
The vertuous *Paulina*, not long since,
(As I am truely giuen to vnderstand)
Sold to the viceroy a fayre *Christian* Virgin,   115
On whom, maugre his fierce and cruell nature
Asambeg dotes extreamely.
  Vitelli.   Tis my sister;
It must be shee, my better *Angell* tells me
Tis poore *Paulina*. Farewell all disguises;

---

90. occasions:] *Gifford*; ~ ∧ *30* you] *30*; ~: *Coxeter* 107. Antonio] *Massinger MS*; Antono *30* 113. Paulina,] *Coxeter*; ~ ∧ *30*

Ile show in my reuenge that I am Noble.

Francisco. You are not mad?

Vitelli.   No sir, my vertuous anger
Makes euery veyne an arterie, I feele in mee
The strength of twenty men, and being arm'd
With my good cause to wreake wrong'd innocence
I dare alone run to the viceroys Court
And with this Ponyard, before his face,
Digge out *Grimaldies* heart.

    Francisco.   Is this Religious?

    Vitelli. Would you haue me tame now; Can I know my sister
Mewde vp in his *Serraglio*, and in danger
Not alone to loose her honour, but her soule,
The hell-breed Villaine by too? that has sold both
To blacke destruction, and not haste to send him
To the Deuill his tutor? to be patient now,
Were in another name to play the Pandor
To the Viceroyes loose embraces, and cry aime
While he by force, or flaterie compels her
To yeeld her fayre name vp to his foule lust,
And after turne *Apostata* to the faith
That she was breed in.

    Francisco.   Doe but giue me hearing,
And you shall soone grant how ridiculous
This childish fury is. A wise man neuer
Attempts impossibilities; 'tis as easie
For any single arme to quell an Army,
As to effect your wishes; we come hither
To learne *Paulinas* fate, and to redeeme her,
(Leaue your reuenge to heauen.) I oft haue tould you
Of a Relique that I gaue her, which has power
(If we may credit holy mens traditions)
To keepe the owner free from violence:
This on her breast she weares, and does preserue
The vertue of it by her daily prayers.
So if she fall not by her owne consent,
Which it were sinne to thinke, I feare no force.
Be therefore patient, keepe this borrowed shape
Till time and oportunitie present vs

    145. fate] *Mason;* faith *30*

With some fit meanes to see her, which perform'd,
Ile ioyne with you in any desperate course
For her deliuery.
    Vitelli.   You haue charmde me sir
And I obey in all things; Pray you pardon
The weakenesse of my passion.
    Francisco.   And excuse it.   160
Be cheerefull man for know that good intents
Are in the end crownd with as fayre euents.   *Exeunt.*

Actus primus. Scena secunda.

Enter DONUSA, MANTO, CARAZIE.

    Donusa. Haue you seene the *Christian* Captiue, the great Basha
Is so enamourd of?
    Manto.   Yes an't please your Excellency
I tooke a full view of her, when she was
Presented to him.
    Donusa.   And is she such a wonder
As tis reported?
    Manto.   She was drown'd in teares then,   5
Which tooke much from her beautie, yet in spite
Of sorrow, shee appeard the Mistresse of
Most rare perfections; and though low of stature,
Her well proportion'd limbes inuite affection;
And when she speakes, each syllable is musique   10
That does inchaunt the hearers. But your Highnesse
That are not to be parallelde, I yet neuer
Beheld her equall.
    Donusa.   Come you flatter me,
But I forgiue it; we that are borne great
Seldome distast our seruants, though they giue vs   15
More then wee can pretend too. I haue heard
That *Christian* Ladies liue with much more freedome
Then such as are borne heere. Our iealous Turkes
Neuer permit their faire wiues to be seene
But at the publique *Bannias*, or the Mosques   20
And euen then vaylde, and garded. Thou *Carazie*

    I. ii. 1–2. *rearranged by McIlwraith*; *30 reads* Haue . . . Captiue, / The . . . of?

Wert borne in England, what's the custome there
Among your women? Come be free and merry,
I am no seuere Mistres, nor hast thou met with
A heauie bondage.
    Carazie.   Heauie? I was made lighter
By two stone waight at least to be fit to serue you.
But to your question Madame, women in England
For the most part liue like *Queenes*. Your Countrey Ladies
Haue libertie to hauke, to hunt, to feast:
To giue free entertainement to all commers,
To talke, to kisse, there's no such thing knowne there
As an Italian girdle. Your *Cittie Dame*
Without leaue weares the breeches, has her husband
At as much command as her Prentice, and if need be
Can make him Cuckold by her Fathers Coppie.
    Donusa. But your court Lady?
    Carazie.   She, I assure you Madame,
Knowes nothing but her will, must be allow'd
Her Foot-men, her Caroch, her Vshers, her Pages,
Her Doctor, Chaplines, and as I haue heard
They are growne of late so learn'd that they maintaine
A strange Position, which their Lords with all
Their witt cannot confute.
    Donusa.   What's that I prethee?
    Carazie. Marry that it is not onely fit but lawfull,
Your Madame there, her much rest, and high feeding
Duely considered, should to ease her husband
Bee allow'd a priuate friend. They haue drawne a Bill
To this good purpose, and the next assembly
Doubt not to passe it.
    Donusa.   Wee enioy no more
That are of the *Othoman* race, though our Religion
Allowes all pleasure. I am dull, some Musicque.
Take my *Chiapines* off. So, a lustie straine.   *A Galliard.*
Who knockes there?
    Manto.   Tis the Basha of *Aleppo*
Who humbly makes request he may present
His seruice to you.
    Donusa.   Reach a chaire. Wee must
Receiue him like our selfe, and not depart with

One peece of Ceremonie, State, and greatnesse
That may beget respecte, and reuerence
C1ʳ In one that's borne our Vassall. Now admit him.

    Enter MUSTAPHA, *puts of his yellow Pantophles.*

  Mustapha. The place is sacred, and I am to enter
The roome where she abides, with such deuotion   60
As Pilgrims pay at *Mæcha*, when they visit
The Tombe of our great Prophet.
  Donusa.   Rise, the signe
That wee vouchafe his presence.
                  The Eunuch takes vp the Pantophles.
  Mustapha.   May those Powers
That rais'd the *Othoman Empire*, and still gard it,
Reward your Highnesse for this gratious fauour   65
You throwe vpon your seruant. It hath pleasde
The most invincible, mightiest *Amurath*
(To speake his other titles would take from him
That in himselfe does comprehend all greatnesse)
To make me the vnworthy instrument   70
Of his command. Receiue diuinest Lady   *Deliuers a letter.*
This letter sign'd by his victorious hand,
And made Authenticque by the imperiall Seale.
There when you find me mention'd, far be it from yow
To thinke it my ambition to presume   75
At such a happinesse, which his powerfull will
From his great minds magnificence, not my merit,
Hath showrd vpon mee. But if your consent
Ioyne with his good opinion and allowance
To perfit what his fauors haue begun,   80
I shall in my obsequiousnesse and dutie
Endeuour to preuent all iust complaints,
Which want of will to serue you, may call on mee.
  Donusa. His sacred Maiestie writes here that your valour
Against the *Persian* hath so wonne vpon him   85
That there's no grace, or honour in his guift
Of which he can imagine you vnworthy.
And what's the greatest you can hope, or aime at,

    68. him] *Mason*; ~) *30*   69. greatnesse)] *Mason*; ~, *30*   74. yow] *Massinger MS*; yo *30*

It is his pleasure you should be receiu'd
Into his Royall Familie. Prouided 90
For so far I am vnconfind, that I
Affect and like your person. I expect not
The Ceremonie which he vses in
Bestowing of his Daughters, and his neeces.
As that he should present you for my slaue, 95
To loue you, if you pleasde me: or deliuer
A Ponyarde on my least dislike to kill you.
Such tyrannie and pride agree not with
My softer disposition. Let it suffice
For my first answer, that thus far I grace you. 100
                        Giues him her hand to kisse.
Hereafter some time spent to make enquire
Of the good parts, and faculties of your mind
You shall heare further from mee.
   Mustapha.   Though all torments
Really suffer'd, or in hell imaginde
By curious fiction, in one houres delay 105
Are wholy comprehended: I confesse
That I stand bound in dutie, not to checke at
What euer you command, or please to impose
For triall of my patience.
   Donusa.   Let vs find
Some other subiect, too much of one Theme cloyes me: 110
Is't a full Mart?
   Mustapha.   A confluence of all nations
Are met together. There's varietie too
Of all that Marchants trafficque for.
   Donusa.   I know not.
I feele a Virgins longing to descend
So far from mine owne greatnesse, as to be 115
Though not a buyer, yet a looker on
Their strange commodities.
   Mustapha.   If without a trayne
You dare be seene abroad, I'le dismisse mine
And waite vpon you as a common man,
And satisfie your wishes.
   Donusa.   I embrace it. 120

        101. enquire] *30*; Enquiry *Coxeter*

Prouide my vayle; and at the Posterne Gate
Conuey vs out vnseene: I trouble you.
    Mustapha. It is my happynesse you daine to command me.
                                                                Exeunt.

[I. iii]   *Actus primus. Scena tertia.*

A shop discouerde, GAZET *in it.* FRANCISCO, *and* VITELLI, *walking by.*

    Gazet. What doe you lacke? your choyce *China* dishes, your pure
Venetian Christall, of all sorts, of all neate and new fashions, from
the mirror of the madam, to the priuate vtensile of her chamber-
maide, and curious Pictures of the rarest beauties of *Europa*: what
doe you lacke Gentlemen?   5
    Francisco. Take heed I say, how ere it may appeare
Impertinent, I must expresse my loue,
In my aduise, and counsell. You are young
And may be tempted, and these Turkish Dames
Like English mastiues that increase their fiercenes   10
By being chainde vp, from the restraint of freedome,
If lust once fire their bloud from a faire obiect
Will runne a course the fiends themselues would shake at
To enioy their wanton endes.
    Vitelli.   Sir, you mistake mee.
I am too full of woe, to entertaine   15
One thought of pleasure, though all *Europes Queenes*
Kneel'd at my feete, and courted me: much lesse
To mix with such, whose difference of faith
Must of necessitie (or I must grant
My selfe forgetfull of all you haue taught mee)   20
Strangle such base desires.
    Francisco.   Be constant in
That resolution, I'le abroade againe,
And learne as far as it is possible
What may concerne *Paulina.* Some two houres
Shall bring me backe.   *Exit* FRANCISCO.   25
    Vitelli.   All blessings waite vpon you.
    Gazet. Cold doings, Sir, a Mart doe you call this? Slight

---

I. iii. 7. loue,] *Massinger MS*; ~: *30*   8. In my] *Massinger MS* (in My); My *30*   18. such,] *Massinger MS*; ~; *30*

I. iii. 27-59 *The Renegado*

A pudding wife, or a Witch with a thrumbe Cappe
That sells Ale vnder grownd to such as come
To know their Fortunes, in a dead Vacation
Haue ten to one more stirring.
    Vitelli.   Wee must be patient.   30
    Gazet. Your seller by retayle ought to be angry
But when hee's fingering money.

    Enter GRIMALDI, MASTER, BOTESWAINE, *Saylors*, TURKES.

    Vitelli.   Heere are company;
Defend me my good *Angell*, I behold
A *Basiliske*!   34
    Gazet. What doe you lacke? what doe you lacke? pure *China*
dishes, cleere Christall glasses, a dumbe Mistres to make loue too?
What doe you lacke gentlemen?
    Grimaldi. Thy Mother for a Bawde, or if thou hast
A hansome one thy sister for a Whore;
Without these doe not tell me of your trash   40
Or I shall spoyle your Market.
    Vitelli.   — Old *Grimaldy*?
    Grimaldi. Zoundes wherefore doe wee put to Sea, or stand
The raging windes aloft, or pisse vpon
The fomie waues when they rage most? deride
The thunder of the enemies shot, boorde boldely   45
A Marchants shippe for prize, though we behold
The desperate Gunner ready to giue fire
And blow the decke vp? Wherefore shake we off
Those scrupulous ragges of charitie, and conscience,
Inuented onely to keepe Churchmen warme,   50
Or feede the hungry mouthes of famished beggers;
But when we touch the shore to wallowe in
All sensuall pleasures?
    Master.   I but Noble Captaine
To spare a little for an after clappe
Were not improuidence.
    Grimaldi.   Hang consideration: 55
When this is spent is not our shippe the same?
Our courage too the same to fetch in more?
The earth where it is fertillest returnes not
More then three haruests, whilst the glorious Sunne

Posts through the *Zodiacke*, and makes vp the yeere:
But the Sea, which is our Mother, (that embraceth
Both the rich *Indies* in her outstrecht armes)
Yeeldes euery day a croppe if we dare reape it.
No, no my Mates, let Tradesmen thinke of thrift,
And Vsurers hoord vp, let our expence
Be as our commings in are without bounds:
We are the *Neptunes* of the *Ocean*,
And such as traffique, shall pay sacrifice
Of their best lading. Ile haue this Canuas
Your boy weares linde with Tissue, and the cates
You taste, serude vp in gold; though we carouse
The teares of Orphanes in our *Greekish* wines,
The sighes of vndone Widowes, paying for
The musique bought to cheere vs, rauish'de Virgins
To slauerie sold for Coyne to feede our riots,
We will haue no compunction.
   Gazet. Doe you heare sir,
We haue payde for our Ground?
   Grimaldi. Humh.
   Gazet. And humh too,
For all your bigge words, get you further off,
And hinder not the prospect of our shoppe
Or——
   Grimaldi. What will you doe?
   Gazet. Nothing sir, but pray
Your worship to giue me hansell.
   Grimaldi. By the eares,
Thus sir, by the eares.
   Master. Hold, hold.
   Vitelli. You'l still be prating.
   Grimaldi. Come let's be drunke! then each man to his whore,
Slight how doe you looke! you had best goe find a Corner
To pray in, and repent. Doe, doe, and crie:
It will shew fine in *Pirats.*   *Exit* GRIMALDI.
   Master. Wee must follow
Or he will spend our shares.
   Boteswaine. I fought for mine.
   Master. Nor am I so precise but I can drab too:

    84. looke!] *Massinger MS* (∼?); ∼, 30

Wee will not sit out for our parts.
  Boteswaine. Agreed.
                        Exeunt MASTER, BOTESWAINE, *Saylors.*
  Gazet. The deuill gnaw off his fingers, if he were
In London among the clubs, vp went his heeles
For striking of a Prentice. What doe you lack,
What doe you lacke gentlemen?
  1 *Turke.* I wonder how the Viceroy can indure
The insolence of this fellow.
  2 *Turke.* He receiues profit
From the Prizes he brings in, and that excuses
What euer he commits. Ha, what are these!

         Enter MUSTAPHA, DONUSA, *vayld.*

  1 *Turke.* They seeme of ranke and qualitie, obserue 'em.
  Gazet. What doe you lacke? see what you please to buy,
Wares of all sorts most honourable Madona.
  Vitelli. Peace sirra, make no noyse, these are not people
To be iested with.
  Donusa. Is this the *Christians* custome
In the venting their commodities?
  Mustapha. Yes best Madame
But you may please to keepe your way, heere's nothing,
But toyes, and trifles, not worth your obseruing.
  Donusa. Yes, for varieties sake pray you shew vs, friends,
The chiefest of your Wares.
  Vitelli. Your Ladiships seruant;
And if in worth or Title you are more,
My ignorance pleade my pardon.
  Donusa. Hee speakes well.
  Vitelli. Take downe the looking glasse: here is a mirror
Steelde so exactly, neither taking from
Nor flattering the obiect it returnes
To the beholder, that *Narcissus* might
(And neuer grow enamourd of himselfe)
View his fayre feature in't.
  Donusa. Poeticall too!
  Vitelli. Heere *China* dishes to serue in a Banket,
Though the voluptuous *Persian* sate a guest.
Heere Christall glasses, such as *Ganymede*

Did fill with Nectar to the Thunderer
When he dranke to *Alcides*, and receiu'd him
In the fellowship of the *gods*: true to the owners.
Corinthian plate studded with Diamonds,
Conceald oft deadly poyson; This pure metall
So innocent is, and faithfull to the Mistres
Or Master that possesses it, that rather
Then hold one drop that's venemous, of it selfe
It flies in peeces, and deludes the Traytor.
 Donusa. How mouingly could this fellow treat vpon
A worthy subiect, that findes such discourse
To grace a trifle!
 Vitelli. Heere's a Picture Madame
The master peece of *Michael Angelo*,
Our great *Italian* workeman; heere's another
So perfit at all parts that had *Pigmalion*
Seene this, his prayers had beene made to *Venus*,
To haue giuen it life, and his caru'd iuory Image
By poets nere remembred. They are indeed
The rarest beauties of the *Christian* world
And no where to be equal'd.
 Donusa.   You are partiall
In the cause of those you fauour I beleeue;
I instantly could shew you one, to theirs
Not much inferior.
 Vitelli. With your pardon Madame
I am incredulous.
 Donusa. Can you match me this? *Vnvailes her selfe.*
 Vitelli. What wonder looke I on! I'll search aboue
And suddenly attend you.   *Exit* VITELLI.
 Donusa. Are you amazde?
I'le bring you to your selfe. *Breakes the glasses.*
 Mustapha. Ha! what's the matter?
 Gazet. My masters ware? We are vndone! O strange!
A Lady to turne rorer, and breake glasses!
Tis time to shut vp shop then.
 Mustapha. You seeme mou'de.
If any Language of these *Christian* dogges
Haue call'd your anger on, in a frowne shew it

123. Conceald] *30³*; Conceale *30¹,²*

I. iii. 151–76 *The Renegado* 31

And they are dead already.
    Donusa.   The offence
Lookes not so farre. The foolish paultrie fellow
Shew'd me some trifles, and demanded of me
For what I valew'd at so many aspers,
A thousand Duckets. I confesse he mou'd mee;   155
Yet I should wrong my selfe should such a begger
 Receiue the least losse from mee.
    Mustapha.   Is it no more?
    Donusa. No, I assure you. Bid him bring his bill
To morrow to the Palace and enquire
For one *Donusa*: that word giues him passage   160
Through all the guard; say there he shall receiue
Full satisfaction. Now when you please.
    Mustapha.   I waite you.
   1 *Turke.* We must not know them, lets shift off and vanish.
                     Exeunt MUSTAPHA, DONUSA, 2. TURKES.
    Gazet. The swines Pox ouertake you, theres a curse
For a Turke that eates no Hogs flesh.

                   Enter VITELLI.

    Vitelli.   Is she gone?   165
    Gazet. Yes you may see her handy-worke.
    Vitelli.   No matter.
Said she ought else?
    Gazet.   That you should wait vpon her
And there receiue Court payment, and to passe
D1ʳ The guards, she bids you onely say you come
To one *Donusa*.
    Vitelli.   How! remoue the wares,   170
Doe it without reply. The *Sultans* neece!
I haue heard among the Turkes for any Lady
To shew her face bare, argues loue, or speakes
Her deadly hatred. What should I feare? my fortune
Is suncke so low, there cannot fall vpon mee   175
Ought worth my shunning. I will run the hazard:

    157. the least] *conj. Greg*; least *30*; least the *Massinger MS*   160–2. *rearranged by Coxeter*; *30 reads* For . . . *Donusa*: / That . . . guard; / Say . . . satisfaction. / Now . . . please / I . . . you.   163 SD. *Exeunt* . . . TURKES.] *Gifford*; *follows* you. (l. 162) *30*   165 SD. *Enter* VITELLI.] *Gifford*; *not in 30*

She may be a meanes to free distres'd *Paulina*.
Or if offended, at the worst, to die
Is a full period to calamitie.

The end of the first act.

[II. i] *Actus Secundus, Scæna prima.*

Enter CARAZIE, MANTO.

Carazie. IN the name of wonder! *Manto*, what hath my Ladie
Done with her selfe since yesterday?
  Manto.   I know not.
Malicious men report we are all guided
In our affections by a wandering Planet,
But such a suddaine change in such a person,   5
May stand for an example to confirme
Their false assertion.
  Carazie.   Shee's now pettish, froward;
Musique, discourse, obseruance tedious to her.
  Manto. She slept not the last night: and yet preuented
The rising Sun in being vp before him.   10
Call'd for a costly Bath, then willd the roomes
Should be perfum'd; ransackde her Cabinets
For her choyce, and richest Iewells: and appeares now
Like *Cinthia* in full glory, wayted on
By the fairest of the Stars.
  Carazie.   Can you guesse the reason,   15
D1ᵛ Why the *Aga* of the *Ianizaries*, and he
That guards the entrance of the inmost port
Were call'd before her?
  Manto.   They are both her creatures,
And by her grace prefer'de, but I am ignorant
To what purpose they were sent for.

Enter DONUSA.

  Carazie.   Heere shee comes,   20
Full of sad thoughts: we must stand further off.
What a frowne was that!

II. i. 13. choyce] *30*; choycest *Coxeter*

Manto.   Forbeare.
Carazie.   I pittie her.
  Donusa. What Magicque hath transform'd me from my selfe?
Where is my Virgin pride? How haue I lost
My boasted freedome? what new fire burnes vp
My scortched intrailes? What vnknowne desires
Inuade, and take possession of my soule;
All vertuous obiects vanish'd? Haue I stood
The shocke of fierce temptations, stopte mine eares
Against all *Siren* notes lust euer sung,
To drawe my barke of chastitie (that with wonder
Hath keept a constant, and an honourd course)
Into the gulfe of a deserude ill fame,
Now to fall vnpittied? And in a moment
With mine owne hands digge vp a graue to burie
The monumentall heape of all my yeares,
Imployde in Noble actions? O my fate!
But there is no resisting. I obey thee
Imperious *god* of loue, and willingly
Put mine owne Fetters on, to grace thy tryumph;
Twere therefore more then crueltie in thee
To vse me like a tyranne. What poore meanes
Must I make vse of now? And flatter such,
To whom, till I betrayde my libertie,
One gratious looke of mine, would haue erected
An altar to my seruice. How now *Manto*?
My euer carefull woman, and *Carazie*
Thou hast beene faithfull too.
  Carazie.   I dare not call
My life mine owne since it is yours, but gladly
Will part with it: when ere you shall command mee;
And thinke I fall a Martir, so my death
May giue life to your pleasures.
  Manto.   But vouchsafe
To let me vnderstand what you desire
Should be effected: I will vndertake it
And curse my selfe for Cowardice if I pausde
To aske a reason why.

28. Haue I stood] *30*; I that haue stood *Gifford*   33. fame,] *Gifford*; ~? *30*
34. Now to] *editor*; Now *30*

Donusa.   I am comforted,
In the tender of your seruice, but shall be
Confirm'd in my full ioyes, in the performance.
Yet trust me: I will not impose vpon you
But what you stand ingagde for, to a Mistres,   60
(Such as I haue beene to you.) All I aske
Is faith, and secresie.
    Carazie.   Say but you doubt me,
And to secure you I'le cut out my tongue:
I am libde in the breech already.
    Manto.   Doe not hinder
Your selfe by these delayes.
    Donusa.   Thus then I whisper   65
Mine owne shame to you.—O that I should blush
To speake what I so much desire to doe!
And further—   *Whispers, and vses vehement actions.*
    Manto.   Is this all?
    Donusa.   Thinke it not base
Although I know the office vndergoes
A course construction.
    Carazie.   Course? 'tis but procuring,   70
A smocke imploiment, which has made more Knights,
In a Countrie I could name, then twenty yeares
Of seruice in the field.
    Donusa.   You haue my ends.
    Manto. Which say you haue arriu'de at, be not wanting
To your selfe, and feare not vs.
    Carazie.   I know my burthen,   75
I'le beare it with delight.
    Manto.   Talke not, but doe.
                            Exeunt CARAZIE, MANTO.
    Donusa. O Loue what poore shifts thou dost force vs too!
                                    Exit DONUSA.

[II. ii]   *Actus Secundus, Scæna Secunda.*

           Enter AGA, CAPIAGA, *Ianizaries.*

    Aga. She was euer our good Mistres, and our maker,
And should we checke at a little hazard for her,

Wee were vnthankefull.
  Capiaga. I dare pawne my head,
Tis some disguised Minion of the Court,
Sent from great *Amurath*, to learne from her
The Viceroys actions.
  Aga. That concernes not vs:
His fall may be our rise, what ere he bee
He passes through my guardes.
  Capiaga. And mine, prouided
Hee giue the word.

Enter VITELLI.

  Vitelli. To faynt now being thus far,
Would argue mee of Cowardice.
  Aga. Stand: the word.
Or being a Christian to presse thus far,
Forfeits thy life.
  Vitelli. Donusa.
  Aga. Passe in peace.
Exeunt AGA, *and Ianizaries.*
  Vitelli. What a priuiledge her name beares! Tis wonderous strange!
The Captaine of the *Ianizaries*! If the great Officer,
The guardian of the inner port denie not—
  Capiaga. Thy warrant: Speake, or thou art dead.
  Vitelli. Donusa.
  Capiaga. That protects thee; without feare, Enter.
So: discharge the watch. *Exeunt* VITELLI, CAPIAGA.

Actus Secundus, Scæna tertia.

Enter CARAZIE, MANTO.

  Carazie. Though he hath past the *Aga*, and chiefe Porter
This cannot be the man.
  Manto. By her description
I am sure it is.

II. ii. 13. beares! Tis] *McIlwraith*; beares. / Tis 30[1, 2]; beares? / Tis 30[3]   14. The ... Ianizaries] 30; *omitted Coxeter*   16. Speake, or] *Gifford*; Speake, / Or 30   17. thee; without] 30; thee; / Without *Gifford*   17–18. Enter. / So] 30; *undivided Gifford*   II. iii. 2–3. description / I] *Gifford*; *undivided* 30

Carazie. O women, women!
What are you? a great Lady dote vpon
A Haberdasher of small wares!
  Manto.   Pish, thou hast none.   5
  Carazie. No, if I had I might haue seru'd the turne:
This tis to want munition when a man
Should make a breach and enter.

       Enter VITELLI.

  Manto.   Sir, you are wellcome:
Thinke what tis to be happy and possesse it.
  Carazie. Perfume the Roomes there, and make way. Let Musique
With choyce notes entertaine the man, the *Princesse* 11
Now purposes to honour.
  Vitelli.   I am rauish'd!   *Exeunt.*

[II. iv]   *Actus Secundus, Scæna Quarta.*

A Table set forth, Iewels and Bagges vpon it: loude Musicque. Enter
  DONUSA, *takes a chaire, to her* CARAZIE, VITELLI, MANTO.

  Donusa. Sing ore the Dittie, that I last composde
Vpon my Loue-sicke passions, sute your Voice
To the Musique thats plac'de yonder, we shall heare you
With more delight and pleasure.
  Carazie.   I obey you.   *Song.*
  Vitelli. Is not this *Tempe*, or the blessed shades, 5
Where innocent Spirits reside? Or doe I dreame,
And this a heauenly vision? Howsoeuer
It is a sight too glorious to behold
For such a wretch as I am.   *Stands amazde.*
  Carazie.   He is daunted.
  Manto. Speake to him Madam, cheere him vp, or you 10
Destroy what you haue builded.
  Carazie.   Would I were furnishde [*Aside.*]
With his artillerie, and if I stood

---

10. way. Let] *30³*; way. / Let *30¹,²* 10–11. Musique / With] *30³*; Musique with *30¹,²* 11–12. man, the *Princesse* / Now] *30³*; man, / The *Princesse* now *30¹,²*
II. iv. 2. passions, sute] *Massinger MS*; passions sute, *30* 11 SD. *Aside.*] *editor; not in 30*

II. iv. 13–46 — *The Renegado* — 37

Gaping as he does, hang me.
    Vitelli. That I might euer dreame thus.   *Kneeles.*
    Donusa.   Banish amazement,
You wake; your debtor tells you so, your debtor,   15
And to assure you that I am a substance
And no aæriall figure, thus I raise you.
Why doe you shake? My soft touch brings no Ague,
No biting frost is in this palme: Nor are
My lookes like to the Gorgons head, that turne   20
Men into Statues, rather they haue power
(Or I haue been abusde) where they bestow
Their influence (let me prooue it truth in you)
To giue to dead men motion.
    Vitelli.   Can this be?
May I beleeue my sences? Dare I thinke   25
I haue a memory? Or that you are
That excellent creature, that of late disdain'de not
To looke on my poore trifles?
    Donusa.   I am shee.
    Vitelli. The owner of that blessed name *Donusa*,
Which like a potent charme, although pronounc'de   30
By my prophane, but much vnworthyer tongue,
Hath brought me safe to this forbidden place,
Where Christian yet ne're trode.
    Donusa.   I am the same.
    Vitelli. And to what end, great Lady pardon me,
That I presume to aske, did your command   35
Command me hither? or what am I? to whom
You should vouchsafe your fauours; nay, your angers?
If any wilde or vncollected speech
Offensiuely deliuer'd, or my doubt
Of your vnknowne perfections, haue displeasde you,   40
You wrong your indignation, to pronounce
Your selfe my sentence: to haue seene you onely,
And to haue touchde that fortune-making hand,
Will with delight waigh downe all tortures, that
A flinty hangmans rage could execute,   45
Or rigide tyranny command with pleasure.

15. You wake] *Coxeter*; You, wake *30*   20. turne] *30*; turns *Mason*; turnd *conj. editor*   46. command] *30*; ~, *McIlwraith*

Donusa. How the aboundance of good flowing to thee,
Is wrongde in this simplicitie: and these bounties
Which all our Easterne Kings haue kneeld in vaine for,
Doe by thy ignorance, or wilfull feare,   50
Meete with a false construction. *Christian*, know
(For till thou art mine by a neerer name,
That title though abhord here, takes not from
Thy entertainement) that tis not the fashion
Among the greatest and the fairest Dames   55
This Turkish Empire gladly owes, and bowes to,
To punish where theres no offence, or nourish
Displeasures against those, without whose mercie
They part with all felicity. Prethee be wise,
And gently vnderstand mee; Doe not force her   60
That ne're knew ought but to command, nor ere read
The elements of affection, but from such
As gladly sude to her, in the infancie
Of her new borne desires, to be at once
Importunate, and immodest.
    Vitelli.   Did I know   65
Great Lady your commands, or to what purpose
This personated passion tends, (since twere
A crime in mee deseruing death, to thinke
It is your owne) I should to make you sport
Take any shape you please to impose vpon me: 70
And with ioy striue to serue you.
    Donusa.   Sport? thou art cruell,
If that thou canst interpret my descent,
From my high byrth and greatnesse, but to be
A part in which I truely acte my selfe!
And I must hold thee for a dull spectator   75
If it stirre not affection, and inuite
Compassion for my sufferings. Be thou taught
By my example, to make satisfaction
For wrongs vniustly offer'd. Willingly
I doe confesse my fault; I iniurd thee   80
In some poore pettie trifles; Thus I pay for
The trespasse I did to thee. Here receiue

    61. nor] *Coxeter*; not *30*   69. owne)] *Massinger MS*; ~: *30*   73. greatnesse,] *Massinger MS*, *30³*; ~? *30¹,²*   74. selfe!] *Massinger MS* (~?); ~. *30*

II. iv. 83–114 *The Renegado* 39

These baggs stuft full of our imperiall coyne,
Or if this payment be too light, take heere
These Iems for which the slauish *Indian* diues 85
To the bottome of the Maine. Or if thou scorne
These as base drosse (which take but common minds)
But fancie any honour in my guift
(Which is vnbounded as the *Sultans* Power)
And bee possest of't.
   Vitelli.   I am ouerwhelm'd 90
With the weight of happinesse you throwe vpon me.
Nor can it fall in my imagination,
What wrong I ere haue done you: and much lesse
How like a Royall Marchant to returne
Your great magnificence.
   Donusa.   They are degrees, 95
Not ends of my intended fauors to thee.
These seeds of bountie I yet scatter on
A glebe I haue not tride, but be thou thankefull,
The haruest is to come.
   Vitelli.   What can be added
To that which I already haue recieu'd, 100
I cannot comprehend.
   Donusa.   The tender of
My selfe. Why dost thou start? and in that guift,
Full restitution of that Virgin freedome
Which thou hast rob'd mee of. Yet I professe
I so farre prize the louely theefe that stole it, 105
That were it possible thou couldest restore
What thou vnwittingly hast rauisht from me,
I should refuse the present.
   Vitelli.   How I shake
In my constant resolution! and my flesh
Rebellious to my better part now tells me, 110
As if it were a strong defence of frailtie,
A *Hermit* in a desert trenchd with prayers
Could not resist this batterie.
   Donusa.   Thou an *Italian*?
Nay more I know't, a naturall *Venetian*,

---

93. I ... you] *30*; you ... me *Gifford*   98. thankefull,] *Coxeter*; ∼∧ *30*

Such as are Courtiers borne to please fayre Ladies, 115
Yet come thus slowely on?
    Vitelli.   Excuse me Madame,
What imputation so ere the world
Is pleasde to lay vpon vs: in my selfe
I am so innocent that I know not what tis
That I should offer.
    Donusa.   By instinct I'le teach thee, 120
And with such ease as loue makes me to aske it.
When a young Lady wrings you by the hand thus,
Or with an amorous touch presses your foote,
Lookes babies in your eyes, playes with your locks,
Doe not you find without a tutors helpe 125
What tis she lookes for?
    Vitelli.   I am growne already
Skilfull in the mysterie.
    Donusa.   Or if thus she kisse you,
Then tast's your lips againe.
    Vitelli.   That latter blow
Has beate all chaste thoughts from me.
    Donusa.   Say she poynts to
Some priuate roome, the Sunne beames neuer enters, 130
Prouoking dishes, passing by to heighten
Declined appetite, actiue Musicque vshering
Your faynting steps, the wayters too as borne dumbe,
Not daring to looke on you.   *Exit, inuiting him to follow.*
    Vitelli.   Though the Diuell
Stood by, and rorde, I follow: now I finde 135
That Vertue's but a word, and no sure garde
If set vpon by beauty, and reward.   *Exeunt.*

[II. v]   *Actus Secundus, Scæna Quinta.*

    Enter AGA, CAPIAGA, GRIMALDI, MASTER, BOTESWAINE, *etc.*

  Aga. The Diuels in him I thinke.
  Grimaldi.   Let him be damn'd too.
Ile looke on him though he stard as wild as hell,

        130. enters] *30*; enter *Gifford*

II. v. 3-32 *The Renegado*

Nay Ile goe neere to tell him to his teeth
If he mends not suddenly, and prooues more thankefull,
We doe him too much seruice. Were't not for shame now   5
I could turne honest and forsweare my trade,
Which next to being trust vp at the maine yard
By some low cuntrey butterbox, I hate
As deadly as I doe fasting, or long grace
When meate cooles on the table.
   Capiaga.   But take heede,   10
You know his violent nature.
   Grimaldi.   Let his Whores
And Catamites, know't; I vnderstand my selfe,
And how vnmanly tis to sit at home
And rayle at vs, that run abroad all hazards,
If euery weeke we bring not home new pillage,   15
For the fatting his Serraglio.

          Enter ASAMBEG, MUSTAPHA.

   Aga.   Heere he comes.
   Capiaga. How terrible he lookes!
   Grimaldi.   To such as feare him:
The viceroy *Asambeg*! were he the Sultans selfe
He will let vs know a reason for his fury,
Or we must take leaue without his allowance   20
To be merry with our ignorance.
   Asambeg.   *Mahomets* hell
Light on you all, you crouch, and cringe now; where
Was the terrour of my iust frownes, when you suffered
Those theeues of Malta, almost in our harbor
To board a ship, and beare her safely off,   25
While you stood idle lookers on?
   Aga.   The ods
In the men and shipping, and the suddainnesse
Of their departure yeelding vs no leasure
To send forth others to relieue our owne,
Deterd vs mighty Sir.
   Asambeg.   Deterde you cowards?   30
How durst you only entertaine the knowledge
Of what feare was, but in the not performance

       II. v. 18. *Asambeg*!] *Massinger MS*; ~ ∧ 30

Of our command? in me great *Amurah* spake,
My voyce did eccho to your eares his thunder,
And wild you like so many Seaborne-Tritons, 35
Arm'd onely with the Trumpets of your courage,
To swimme vp to her, and like Remoras,
Hanging vpon her keele, to stay her flight
Till rescue sent from vs, had fetcht you off.
You thinke you are safe now; who durst but dispute it 40
Or make it questionable, if this moment
I charg'd you from yon hanging cliffe, that glasses
His rugged forhead in the neighbour lake,
To throw your selues downe headlong? or like fagots
To fill the ditches of defended Forts, 45
While on your backs we march'd vp to the breache?
 Grimaldi. That would not I.
 Asambeg.   Ha?
 Grimaldi.   Yet I dare as much
As any of the Sultans boldest sonnes,
(Whose heauen, and hell, hang on his frowne, or smile,)
His warlike Ianisaries.
 Asambeg.   Adde one syllable more 50
Thou doest pronounce vpon thy selfe a sentence
That earthquake-like will swallow thee.
 Grimaldi.   Let it open,
Ile stand the hazard; those contemned theeues
Your fellow *Pirats* Sir, the bold Malteze
Whom with your lookes you thinke to quell, at Rhodes 55
Laugh'de at great *Solymans* anger: and if treason
Had not deliuerde them into his power,
Hee had growne olde in glory as in yeeres
At that so fatall siege, or risne with shame,
His hopes, and threates deluded.
 Asambeg.   Our great Prophet, 60
How haue I lost my anger, and my Power!
 Grimaldi. Find it and vse it on thy flatterers:
And not vpon thy friends that dare speake truth.
These Knights of Malta, but a handfull to
Your armies that drinke riuers vp, haue stood 65

46. breache?] *Massinger MS* (breache); breac *30*   47. *rearranged by Coxeter*;
30 reads That ... Ha? / Yet ... much   52. thee] *30*$^{1-4}$; the *30*^{5}

Your furie at the height, and with their crosses
Strooke pale your horned moones; These men of Malta
Since I tooke pay from you, I haue met and fought with
Vpon aduantage too. Yet to speake truth
By the soule of honor, I haue euer found them
As prouident to direct, and bold to doe
As any traynde vp in your discipline:
Rauishde from other nations.
   Mustapha.   I perceiue
The lightning in his fierie lookes, the cloude
Is broke already.
   Grimaldi.   Thinke not therefore sir,
That you alone are Giants, and such *Pigmies*
You war vpon.
   Asambeg.   Villaine, Ile make thee know
Thou hast blasphemde the *Ottoman* power, and safer
At noone day might haue giuen fire to St *Markes*
Your proud *Venetian* Temple. Ceize vpon him;
I am not so neere reconcild to him
To bid him die: that were a benefit
The dog's vnworthy of. To our vse confiscate
All that he stands possesde of: Let him tast
The miserie of want, and his vaine riots
Like to so many walking Ghosts affright him
Where ere he sets his desperate foote. Who is't
That does command you?
   Grimaldi.   Is this the reward
For all my seruice, and the rape I made
On fayre *Paulina*?
   Asambeg.   Drag him hence, he dies
That dallies but a minute.
   Boteswaine.   What's become
Of our shares now Master?
                         GRIMALDI *dragde off, his head couered.*
   Master.   Would he had been borne dumbe:
The beggers cure, patience is all that's left vs.
                        Exeunt MASTER *and* BOTESWAINE.
   Mustapha. Twas but intemperance of speech, excuse him;
Let me preuaile so far. Fame giues him out

92. *Master.*] *Coxeter*; *Must.* 30

For a deseruing fellow.
    Asambeg.   At Aleppo
I durst not presse you so far, giue me leaue
To vse my owne will and command in Tunis,
And if you please, my priuacie.
    Mustapha.   I will see you
When this high wind's blowne ore.
    Asambeg.   So shall you find me   100
Ready to doe you seruice. Rage now leaue me,   *Exit* MUSTAPHA.
Sterne lookes, and all the ceremonious formes
Attending on dread Maiestie, flie from
Transformed *Asambeg*. Why should I hug   *Plucks out a guilt key.*
So neere my hart, what leades me to my prison?   105
Where she that is inthrald commands her keeper,
And robs me of the fiercenesse I was borne with.
Stout men quake at my frownes, and in returne
I tremble at her softnesse. Base *Grimaldi*
But only nam'd *Paulina*, and the charme   110
Had almost chok'd my fury ere I could
Pronounce his sentence. Would when first I saw her
Mine eyes had met with lightning, and in place
Of hearing her inchanting tongue, the shrikes
Of Mandrakes had made musicke to my slumbers,   115
For now I only walke a louing dreame
And but to my dishonour neuer wake,
And yet am blind, but when I see the obiect,
And madly dote on it. Appeare bright sparke   *Opens a doore,*
Of all perfection: any simile   PAULINA *discouerd comes forth.*
Borow'd from Diamonds, or the fayrest stars   121
To helpe me to expresse, how deere I prize
Thy vnmatcht graces, will rise vp and chide me
For poore detraction.
    Paulina.   I despise thy flatteries,
Thus spit at 'em, and scorne 'em, and being arm'd   125
In the assurance of my innocent vertue
I stampe vpon all doubts, all feares, all tortures
Thy barbarous cruelty, or what's worse, thy dotage
(The worthy parent of thy iealousie)

---

    101 SD. *Exit* MUSTAPHA.] *editor*; *follows* ore (l. 100) 30   123. Thy] *Coxeter*; The 30

II. v. 130–59 *The Renegado* 45

    Can showre vpon me.
     Asambeg.   If these bitter taunts   130
Rauish me from my selfe, and make me thinke
My greedy eares receiue Angelicall sounds,
How would this tongue tunde to a louing note
Inuade, and take possession of my soule
Which then I durst not call mine owne.
    Paulina.   Thou art false,   135
Falser then thy religion. Doe but thinke me
Something aboue a beast; nay more, a monster,
Would fright the Sun to looke on, and then tell me
If this base vsage can inuite affection?
If to be mewde vp, and excluded from   140
Humane society; the vse of pleasures;
The necessary, not superfluous duties
Of seruants to discharge those offices,
I blush to name—
    Asambeg.   Of seruants? can you thinke
That I, that dare not trust the eie of Heauen   145
To looke vpon your beauties, that denie
My selfe the happinesse to touch your purenesse
Will ere consent an Eunuch, or bought handmaid
Shall once approch you? there is something in you
That can worke Miracles, or I am cousende,   150
Dispose and alter sexes. To my wrong,
In spite of nature, I will be your nurse,
Your woman, your physitian, and your foole,
Till with your free consent, which I haue vowde
Neuer to force, you grace me with a name   155
That shall supplie all these.
    Paulina.   What is't?
    Asambeg.   Your husband.
    Paulina. My hangman when thou pleasest.
    Asambeg.   Thus I garde me,
Against your further angers.   *Puts to the doore*
    Paulina.   Which shall reach thee   *and lockes it.*
Though I were in the Center.
    Asambeg.   Such a spirit

    150. cousende,] *30*; ~; Mason   151. sexes.] *30*; ~, Mason

In such a small proportion I nere reade of 160
Which time must alter. Rauish her I dare not;
The magique that she weares about her necke,
I thinke defends her. This deuotion payde
To this sweete Saint, mistresse of my sower payne,
Tis fit I take mine owne rough shape againe.   *Exit* ASAMBEG.

[II. vi]   *Actus Secundus, Scæna Sexta.*

Enter FRANCISO, GAZET.

Francisco. I thinke hee's lost.
Gazet.   Tis ten to one of that,
I nere knew Cittizen turne Courtier yet,
But he lost his credit, though he sau'd himselfe.
Why, looke you sir, there are so many lobbies,
Out offices, and disputations heere   5
Behind these Turkish hangings, that a Christian
Hardly gets off but circumcised.
Francisco.   I am troublde,

Enter VITELLI, CARAZIE, MANTO.

Troublde exceedingly. Ha! what are these?
Gazet. One by his rich sute should bee some french Embassador;
For his trayne I thinke they are Turkes.
Francisco.   Peace, be not seene.   10
Carazie. You are now past all the gards, and vndiscouerd
You may returne.
Vitelli.   There's for your paynes, forget not
My humblest seruice to the best of Ladies.
Manto. Deserue her fauour sir, in making haste
For a second entertainement.
Vitelli.   Doe not doubt me,   15
I shall not liue till then.   *Exeunt* CARAZIE, MANTO.
Gazet.   The trayne is vanish'd.
They haue done him some good office hee's so free

II. vi. 2. I nere] 30²⁻⁵; I neuer 30¹   5. disputations] 30²⁻⁵; dispute actions 30¹;
dispartations *conj.* Davies   6. hangings] 30²⁻⁵; hanging 30¹   Christian] 30³⁻⁵;
Cristian 30¹; Christians 30²   8. Troublde] 30²⁻⁵; Trouble 30¹

And liberall of his gold. Ha, doe I dreame,
Or is this mine owne naturall Master?
 Francisco.   Tis he,
But strangely metamorphosde. You haue made sir,
A prosperous voyage, heauen grant it be honest,
I shall reioyce then too.
 Gazet.   You make him blush
To talke of honesty; you were but now
In the giuing vaine, and may thinke of *Gazet*
Your worships prentice.
 Vitelli.   There's gold, be thou free too
And Master of my shop, and all the wares
Wee brought from Venice.
 Gazet.   Riuo then.
 Vitelli.   Deere sir
This place affords not priuacie for discourse
But I can tell you wonders. My rich habit
Deserues least admiration; thers nothing
That can fall in the compasse of your wishes
Though it were to redeeme a thousand slaues
From the Turkish gallies, or at home to erect
Some pious worke, to shame all Hospitalls,
But I am master of the meanes.
 Francisco.   Tis strange.
 Vitelli. As I walke Ile tell you more.
 Gazet.   Pray you a word Sir,
And then I will put on. I haue one boone more.
 Vitelli. What is't? speake freely.
 Gazet.   Thus then, as I am Master
Of your Shop, and wares, pray you help me to some trucking
With your last shee customer; though shee cracke my best peece
I will indure it with patience.
 Vitelli.   Leaue your prating.
 Gazet. I may; you haue beene doing, we will doe too.
 Francisco. I am amazde, yet will nor blame, nor chide you,
Till you informe me further. Yet must say
They steere not the right course, nor trafficke well,
That seeke a passage to reach Heauen, through Hell. *Exeunt.*

Actus Tertius. Scæna prima.

Enter DONUSA, MANTO.

Donusa. WHEN said he, he would come againe?
Manto. He swore,
Short Minutes should be tedious Ages to him,
Vntill the tender of his second seruice,
So much he seemde transported with the first.
 Donusa. I am sure I was. I charge thee *Manto* tell me 5
By all my fauors, and my bounties truely
Whether thou art a Virgin, or like me
Hast forfeited that name.
 Manto. A Virgine Madame?
At my yeeres being a wayting-woman, and in Court to?
That were miraculous. I so long since lost 10
That barren burthen, I almost forget
That euer I was one.
 Donusa. And could thy friends
Reade in thy face, thy maidenhead gone, that thou
Hadst parted with it?
 Manto. Noe indeed. I past
For currant many yeeres after, till by fortune, 15
Long and continewed practise in the sport
Blew vp my decke. A husband then was found out
By my indulgent father, and to the world
All was made whole againe. What neede you feare then
That at your pleasure may repayre your honour 20
Durst any enuious, or malitious tongue,
Presume to taint it?
 Donusa. How now?

Enter CARAZIE.

 Carazie. Madam, the Basha
Humbly desires accesse.
 Donusa. If it had beene
My neate Italian, thou hadst met my wishes.
Tell him we would be priuate.
 Carazie. So I did, 25
But he is much importunate.

Manto.   Best dispatch him,
His lingring heere else will deter the other,
From making his approch.
   Donusa.   His entertainement
Shall not inuite a second visit, goe
Say we are pleasde.

Enter MUSTAPHA.

   Mustapha.   All happinesse.
   Donusa.   Bee suddaine.   30
T'was sawcie rudenesse in you sir to presse
On my retirements, but ridiculous folly
To wast the time that might be better spent
In complementall wishes.
   Carazie.   There's a coolling   [*Aside.*]
For his hot encounter.
   Donusa.   Come you heere to stare?   35
If you haue lost your tongue, and vse of speech,
Resigne your gouernment, there's a mutes place voyde
In my vncles Court I heare, and you may worke me
To write for your preferment.
   Mustapha.   This is strange!
I know not Madam, what neglect of mine   40
Has calde this scorne vpon me.
   Donusa.   To the purpose:
My will's a reason, and we stand not bound
To yeeld account to you.
   Mustapha.   Not of your angers,
But with erected eares I should heare from you
The story of your good opinion of me   45
Confirmde by loue, and fauours.
   Donusa.   How deseru'd?
I haue consider'd you from head to foote,
And can find nothing in that waynscote face,
That can teach me to dote, nor am I taken
With your grimme aspect, or toadepoole-like complexion   50
Those scarres you glorie in, I feare to looke on;
And had much rather heare a merrie tale
Then all your battayles wonne with blood and sweate,

III. i. 34 SD. *Aside.*] *editor; not in* 30

Though you belch forth the stincke too, in the seruice,
And sweare by your Mustachios all is true. 55
You are yet too rough for me, purge and take physicke,
Purchase perfumers, get me some French taylor,
To new create you; the first shape you were made with
Is quite worne out. Let your barbar wash your face too,
You looke yet like a bugbeare to fright children, 60
Till when I take my leaue; wayte me *Carazie.*
                              Exeunt DONUSA, CARAZIE.

   Mustapha. Stay you, my Ladies Cabinet key.
   Manto.   How's this sir?
   Mustapha. Stay and stand quietly, or you shall fall else,
Not to firke your belly vp flounder-like, but neuer
To rise again. Offer but to vnlocke 65
These dores that stop your fugitiue tongue (obserue me)
And by my fury, I'll fixe there this bolte
To barre thy speech for euer. So, be safe now
And but resolue me, not of what I doubt
But bring assurance to a thing beleeu'd, 70
Thou mak'st thy selfe a fortune, not depending
On the vncertaine fauours of a Mistresse,
But art thy selfe one. I'll not so far question
My iudgement, and obseruance, as to aske
Why I am slighted, and contemnde, but in 75
Whose fauour it is done. I that haue read
The copious volumes of all womens falsehood,
Commented on by the heart breaking groanes
Of abusde louers, all the doubts washde off
With fruitlesse teares, the Spiders cobweb vayle 80
Of arguments, alleadgde in their defence,
Blowne off with sighs of desperate men, and they
Appearing in their full deformitie,
Know that some other hath displanted me,
With her dishonor. Has she giuen it vp? 85
Confirme it in two sillables.
   Manto.   She has.
   Mustapha. I cherish thy confession thus, and thus, *Giues her*
Bee mine, againe I court thee thus, and thus.   *iewels.*
Now prooue but constant to my ends.

        81. alleadgde] *Coxeter*; alleadge *30*

Manto.   By all—
  Mustapha. Enough, I dare not doubt thee. O land Crocodiles 90
Made of Ægyptian slime, accursed women!
But tis no time to rayle: come my best *Manto*.   *Exeunt.*

Actus tertius, Scæna Secunda.

Enter VITELLI, FRANCISCO.

  Vitelli. Sir, as you are my confessor, you stand bound
Not to reueale what euer I discouer
In that Religious way: nor dare I doubt you.
Let it suffice, you haue made me see my follies,
And wrought perhaps compunction; for I would not   5
Appeare an Hyppocrite. But when you impose
A penance on me, beyond flesh, and blood
To vndergoe, you must instructe me how
To put off the condition of a man:
Or if not pardon, at the least, excuse   10
My disobedience. Yet despayre not sir,
For though I take mine owne way, I shall doe
Something that may hereafter to my glory,
Speake me your Scholler.
  Francisco.   I inioyne you not
To goe, but send.
  Vitelli.   That were a pettie triall   15
Not worth one so long taught, and exercisde
Vnder so graue a master. Reuerende *Francisco*
My friend, my father, in that word, my all;
Rest confident, you shall heare something of mee
That will redeeme me in your good opinion,   20
Or iudge me lost for euer. Send *Gazet*
(Shee shall giue order that hee may haue enterance)
To acquaint you with my fortunes.   *Exit* VITELLI.
  Francisco.   Goe and prosper,
Holy Saints guide and strengthen thee. Howsoeuer
As my endeauours are, so may they find   25
Gracious acceptance.

Enter GAZET, GRIMALDI, *in raggs.*

Gazet. Now you doe not rore sir,
You speake not tempests, nor take eare-rent from
A poore shopkeeper. Doe you remember that sir?
I weare your marks heere still.
 Francisco. Can this be possible?
All wonders are not ceas'd then.
 Grimaldi. Doe, abuse me,
Spit on me, spurne me, pull me by the nose,
Thrust out these fiery eies, that yesterday
Would haue lookde thee dead.
 Gazet. O saue me sir.
 Grimaldi. Feare nothing,
I am tame, and quiet, there's noe wrong can force me
To remember what I was. I haue forgot,
I ere had irefull fiercenesse, a steelde heart,
Insensible of compassion to others,
Nor is it fit that I should thinke my selfe
Worth mine owne pittie, Oh.
 Francisco. Growes this deiection,
From his disgrace doe you say?
 Gazet. Why hees casherde sir,
His ships, his goods, his liuery-puncks confiscate,
And there is such a punishment laid vpon him,
The miserable rogue must steale no more,
Nor drinke, nor drab.
 Francisco. Does that torment him?
 Gazet. O Sir!
Should the State take order to bar men of acres,
From those two laudable recreations,
Drinking, and whoring, how should Panders purchase,
Or thrifty Whores build Hospitals? slid if I
That since I am made free, may write my selfe,
A Citty gallant, should forfeit two such charters
I should be ston'd to death, and nere be pittied,
By the liueries of those companies.
 Francisco. You'll be whip'd sir,
If you bridle not your tongue. Haste to the Palace,

III. ii. 33. *Gazet.*] *Coxeter*; *Graz.* 30

Your Master lookes for you.
 Gazet.   My quondam Master.
Rich sonnes forget they euer had poore fathers,
In seruants tis more pardonable; as a companion,
Or so, I may consent, but is there hope sir,
He has got me a good chapwoman? pray you write
A word or two in my behalfe.
 Francisco.   Out rascall.
 Gazet. I feele some insurrections.
 Francisco.   Hence.
 Gazet.   I vanish. *Exit* GAZET.
 Grimaldi. Why should I study a defence, or comfort?
In whom blacke guilt, and misery if ballanc'd,
I know not which would turne the scale. Looke vpward
I dare not, for should it but be beleeu'd,
That I (dide deepe in hells most horrid colours,)
Should dare to hope for mercy, it would leaue
No checke or feeling, in men innocent
To catch at sinnes the diuell nere taught mankind yet.
No, I must downeward, downeward: though repentance
Could borrow all the glorious wings of grace,
My mountainous waight of sins, would cracke their pinions,
And sincke them to hell with me.
 Francisco.   Dreadfull! heare me,
Thou miserable man.
 Grimaldi. Good sir deny not,
But that there is no punishment beyond
Damnation.
    Enter MASTER, BOTESWAINE.
 Master. Yonder he is, I pitty him.
 Boteswaine. Take comfort Captaine, we liue still to serue you.
 Grimaldi. Serue me? I am a diuell already, leaue me,
Stand further off, you are blasted else. I haue heard
Schoolemen affirme mans body is compos'd
Of the foure elements, and as in league together
They nourish life, so each of them affords
Liberty to the soule, when it growes wearie
Of this fleshie prison. Which shall I make choice of?
The fire? no (I shall feele that heereafter.)
The earth will not receiue me. Should some whirlewind

Snatch me into the ayre, and I hang there,
Perpetuall plagues would dwell vpon the earth,
And those superior bodies that powre downe
Their cheerefull influence denie to passe it,
Through those vast regions I haue infected.   90
The Sea? I that is iustice, there. I ploude vp
Mischiefe as deepe as Hell there: there I'le hide
This cursed lumpe of clay, may it turne Rocks
Where plummets weight could neuer reach the sands,
And grinde the ribs of all such barkes as presse   95
The *Oceans* breast in my vnlawfull course.
I haste then to thee, let thy rauenous wombe
Whom all things else denie, be now my tombe.   *Exit* GRIMALDI.
  Master. Follow him and restraine him.
  Francisco.   Let this stand
For an example to you. I'le prouide   100
A lodging for him, and apply such cures
To his wounded conscience, as heauen hath lent mee.
Hee's now my second care: and my profession
Bindes me to teach the desperate to repent   104
As farre as to confirme the innocent.   *Exeunt.*

[III. iii]   *Actus tertius, Scæna tertia.*

Enter ASAMBEG, MUSTAPHA, AGA, CAPIAGA.

  Asambeg. Your pleasure,
  Mustapha.   T'will exact your priuate eare,
And when you haue receiude it, you will thinke
Too many know it.
  Asambeg.   Leaue the roome, but bee
Within our call.   *Exeunt* AGA, CAPIAGA.
             Now sir, what burning secret
Brings you (with which it seemes you are turnde Cynders)   5
To quench in my aduise, or power?

---

91. iustice, there] *editor*; iustice there, *30*; iustice; there *Coxeter*   92. Hell there:] *30*; Hell: there, *Coxeter*   III. iii. 1. T'will] *Massinger MS* (t'will); T'will *30 (defective* T)   4 SD. *Exeunt* ... CAPIAGA.] *Gifford; follows* it (l. 3) *30*   4–5. secret / Brings you (with ... Cynders)] *McIlwraith*; secret brings you / (With ... Cynders) *30*; secret / (With ... cinders) bring you *Gifford*   5. Brings] *30* (brings); bring *Mason*

  Mustapha.   The fire
Will rather reach you.
 Asambeg.   Mee?
  Mustapha.   And consume both,
For tis impossible to be put out
But with the blood of those that kindle it:
And yet one viall of it is so pretious,   10
It being borrow'd from the *Ottoman* spring,
That better tis I thinke, both we should perish
Then proue the desperate meanes that must restraine it,
From spreading further.
  Asambeg.   To the poynte, and quickely.
These winding circumstances in relations   15
Seldome enuiron truth.
  Mustapha.   Truth *Asambeg?*
  Asambeg. Truth *Mustapha.* I sayd it, and adde more,
You touch vpon a string that to my eare,
Do's sound *Donusa.*
  Mustapha.   You then vnderstand
Who tis I aime at.
  Asambeg.   Take heed *Mustapha*,   20
Remember what she is, and whose we are.
Tis her neglect perhaps, that you complaine of,
And should you practise to reuenge her scorne,
With any plot to taynt her in her honor,
  Mustapha. Heare mee.
  Asambeg.   I will be heard first, there's no tongue 25
A subiect owes, that shall out thunder mine.
  Mustapha. Well take your way.
  Asambeg.   I then againe repeate it.
If *Mustapha* dares with malitious breath
(On iealous suppositions) presume
To blast the blossome of *Donusas* Fame   30
Because he is denide a happinesse
Which men of equall, nay of more desert,
Haue su'd in vaine for—
  Mustapha.   More?
  Asambeg.   More. Twas I spake it.
The Basha of *Natolia* and my selfe

   11. It] *30*; In *Mason* 21. are.] *Massinger MS*; ~; *30*

G1ᵛ Were Riualls for her; either of vs brought
More Victories, more Trophies, to pleade for vs
To our great Master, then you dare lay claime to,
Yet still by his allowance she was left
To her election. Each of vs ow'd nature
As much for outward forme, and inward worth
To make way for vs to her grace and fauour,
As you brought with you. We were heard, repuls'd,
Yet thought it no dishonour to sit downe,
With the disgrace; if not to force affection,
May merit such a name.
    Mustapha. Haue you done yet?
    Asambeg. Be therfore more then sure the ground on which
You rayse your accusation, may admit
No vndermining of defence in her,
For if with pregnant and apparent proofes
Such as may force a iudge, more then inclin'd
Or partiall in her cause to sweare her guilty,
You win not me to bee of your beleefe;
Neither our ancient friendship, nor the rites
Of sacred hospitality (to which
I would not offer violence) shall protect you:
Now when you please.
    Mustapha. I will not dwell vpon
Much circumstance, yet cannot but professe,
With the assurance of a loyalty,
Equall to yours, the reuerence I owe
The Sultan, and all such his blood makes sacred;
That there is not a veyne of mine which yet is
Vnemptied in his seruice, but this moment
Should freely open, so it might wash off
The staynes of her dishonor. Could you thinke?
Or though you saw it credit your owne eyes?
That she, the wonder and amazement of
Her sex, the pride, and glory of the empire,
That hath disdain'd you, sleighted me, and boasted
A frozen coldnesse which no appetite,
G2ʳ Or height of blood could thaw, should now so far
Be hurried with the violence of her lust,

    52. bee of] *McIlwraith*; set off *30*

As in it burying her high birth and fame,
Basely descend to fill a Christians armes
And to him yeeld her Virgin honour vp,
Nay sue to him to take't?
   Asambeg.   A Christian?
   Mustapha.   Temper   75
Your admiration: and what Christian thinke you?
No Prince disguis'd; no man of marke, nor honour,
No daring vndertaker in our seruice,
But one whose lips her foote should scorne to touch,
A poore Mechanicke-Pedler.
   Asambeg.   Hee?
   Mustapha.   Nay more,   80
Whom doe you thinke she made her scout, nay baude,
To finde him out but me? What place makes choyce of
To wallow in her foule and lothsome pleasures,
But in the pallace? Who the instruments
Of close conueyance, but the captaine of   85
Your gard the *Aga*, and that man of trust
The warden of the inmost port? I'll proue this,
And though I fayle to shew her in the act,
Glew'd like a neighing mare to her prowd Stallion,
Your incredulity shall be conuinc'd   90
With proofes I blush to thinke on.
   Asambeg.   Neuer yet
This flesh felt such a feuer, by the life
And fortune of great *Amurah*, should our prophet
(Whose name I bow to) in a vision speake this,
T'would make me doubtfull of my faith: leade on,   95
And when my eies, and eares, are like yours, guilty,
My rage shall then appeare, for I will doe
Something; but what, I am not yet determin'd.   *Exeunt.*

Actus Tertius, Scæna Quarta.

Enter CARAZIE, MANTO, GAZET.

   Carazie. They are priuate, to their wishes.
   Manto.   Doubt it not.
   Gazet. A prettie structure this! a court doe you call it?

     89. mare to her prowd] *Massinger MS*; Gennet to her *30*

58   *The Renegado*   III. iv. 3–31

Valted and arch'd: O heere has beene old iumbling
Behind this arras.
    Carazie.   Prethee let's haue some sport,
With this fresh Codshead.
    Manto.   I am out of tune,   5
But doe as you please.—My conscience! tush, the hope   [*Aside.*]
Of liberty throwes that burthen off, I must
Goe watch, and make discouery.   *Exit.*
    Carazie.   He's musing,
And will talke to himselfe, he cannot hold,
The poore foole's rauish'd.
    Gazet.   I am in my masters clothes,   10
They fit me to a hayre too; let but any
Indifferent gamester measure vs inch, by inch,
Or waigh vs by the standard, I may passe.
I haue beene prou'd, and prou'd againe, true mettall.
    Carazie. How he suruayes himselfe.
    Gazet.   I haue heard that some   15
Haue fool'd themselues at Court into good fortunes,
That neuer hop'd to thriue by wit in the City,
Or honesty in the Countrey. If I doe not
Make the best laugh at me Ile weepe for my selfe,
If they giue me hearing. Tis resolu'd I'll trie   20
What may be done. By your fauour sir, I pray you
Were you borne a Courtier?
    Carazie.   No sir, why doe you aske?
    Gazet. Because I thought that none could be preferd,
But such as were begot there.
    Carazie.   O sir! many,
And howsoere you are a Citizen borne,   25
Yet if your mother were a handsome woman,
And euer long'd to see a Maske at Court,
It is an euen lay but that you had
A Courtier to your Father; and I thinke so;
You beare you selfe so sprightly.
    Gazet.   It may be,   30
But pray you sir, had I such an itch vpon me

    III. iv. 6 SD. *Aside.*] *editor*; *not in* 30   7-8. off, I must / Goe] *Gifford*; off, / I must goe 30   13. passe.] *Massinger MS*; ~ ⌃ 30   24-5. many, / And] *Coxeter*; undivided 30

To change my coppy, is there hope a place
May be had heere for money?
   Carazie.   Not without it
That I dare warrant you.
   Gazet.   I haue a pretty stocke,
And would not haue my good parts vndiscouer'd.   35
What places of credit are there?
   Carazie.   There's your Beglerbeg.
   Gazet. By no meanes that, it comes to neere the begger
And most prooue so that come there.
   Carazie.   Or your Sanzacke.
   Gazet. Sans-iacke, fie none of that.
   Carazie.   Your Chiaus.
   Gazet.   Nor that.
   Carazie. Chiefe Gardiner.
   Gazet.   Out vpon't,   40
Twill put me in mind my Mother was an herb-woman,
What is your place I pray you?
   Carazie.   Sir an Euenuch.
   Gazet. An Euenuch! very fine, I faith, an Euenuch!
And what are your employments? neate and easie?
   Carazie. In the day I waite on my Lady when she eates,   45
Carry her pantophles, beare vp her trayne,
Sing her asleepe at night, and when she pleases
I am her bedfellow.
   Gazet.   How? her bedfellow,
And lye with her?
   Carazie.   Yes, and lye with her.
   Gazet.   O rare!
Ile be an Eunuch, though I sell my shop for't   50
And all my wares.
   Carazie.   It is but parting with
A precious stone or two. I know the price on't.
   Gazet. Ile part with all my stones, and when I am
An Eunuch, Ile so tosse and towse the Ladies;
Pray you helpe me to a chapman.
   Carazie.   The court Surgion   55

---

   39. Sans-iacke] *McIlwraith*; Saus-iacke *30*; Sauce-iacke *Gifford*   41. in mind] *Coxeter*; mind *30*   44. neate and easie?] *Massinger MS*; neate and easie. *30*; Car. Neate and easie. *Gifford*

Shall doe you that fauour.
Gazet. I am made! an Eunuch!

Enter MANTO.

Manto. Carazie, quit the roome.
Carazie. Come sir, wee'll treat of
Your businesse further.
Gazet. Excellent! an Eunuch! *Exeunt.*

Actus Tertius. Scæna Quinta.

Enter DONUSA, VITELLI.

Vitelli. Leaue me, or I am lost againe, no prayers,
No penitence, can redeeme me.
   Donusa. Am I growne
Olde, or deform'd since yesterday?
   Vitelli. You are still,
Although the sating of your lust hath sullied
The immaculate whitenesse of your Virgin beauties,   5
Too fayre for me to looke on. And though purenesse,
The sword with which you euer fought, and conquer'd,
Is rauish'd from you by vnchaste desires,
You are too strong for flesh and blood to treat with,
Though iron grates were interpos'd betweene vs,   10
To warrant me from treason.
   Donusa. Whom doe you feare?
   Vitelli. That humane frailety I tooke from my mother,
That, as my youth increas'd, grew stronger on me,
That still pursues me, and though once recouer'd,
In scorne of reason, and what's more, religion,   15
Againe seekes to betray me.
   Donusa. If you meane sir,
To my embraces, you turne rebell to
The lawes of nature, the great Queene, and Mother
Of all productions, and denie alleageance,
Where you stand bound to pay it.
   Vitelli. I will stoppe   20
Mine eares against these charmes, which if *Vlysses*

III. v. 5. immaculate] *Massinger MS* (im̅aculate); imaculate *30*

Could liue againe, and heare this second Siren,
Though bound with Cables to his Mast, his Ship too
Fasten'd with all her Anchors, this inchantment
Would force him in despite of all resistance,
To leape into the Sea, and follow her,
Although destruction with outstretch'd armes,
Stood ready to receaue him.
  Donusa.   Gentle sir,
Though you deny to heare me, yet vouchsafe
To looke vpon me. Though I vse no language
The griefe for this vnkind repulse will print
Such a dumbe eloquence vpon my face,
As will not onely pleade, but preuaile for me.
  Vitelli. I am a coward, I will see and heere you;
The triall else is nothing, nor the conquest,
My temperance shall crowne me with heereafter,
Worthy to be remembred. Vp my vertue,
And holy thoughts, and resolutions arme me,
Against this fierce temptation; giue me voyce
Tun'd to a zealous anger to expresse
At what an ouerualue I haue purchas'd
The wanton treasure of your Virgin bounties,
That in their false fruition heape vpon me
Despayre, and horror. That I could with that ease
Redeeme my forfeit innocence, or cast vp
The poyson I receiu'd into my entrayles,
From the alluring cup of your inticements
As now I doe deliuer backe the price,   *Returnes the Casket.*
And salarie of your lust: or thus vncloth me
Of sins gay trappings, (the proud liuery   *Throwes off his*
Of wicked pleasure) which but worn, and heated *cloke and doublet.*
With the fire of entertaynement, and consent,
Like to *Alcides* fatall shirt, teares off
Our flesh, and reputation both together,
Leauing our vlcerous follies bare, and open,
To all malicious censure.
  Donusa.   You must grant,
If you hold that a losse to you, mine equals,
If not transcends it. If you then first tasted
That poyson as you call it, I brought with me

A palat vnacquainted with the rellish
Of those delights which most (as I haue heard)
Greedily swallow; and then the offence
(If my opinion may be beleeu'd)
Is not so greate: how ere, the wrong's no more
Then if *Hippollitus* and the Virgin Huntresse,
Should meete and kisse together.
    Vitelli.   What defences
Can lust rayse to maintaine a precipice

           ASAMBEG *and* MUSTAPHA *aboue.*

To the Abisse of loosenes! but affords not
The least stayre, or the fastening of one foote,
To reascend that glorious height we fell from.
    Mustapha. By *Mahomet* she courts him.
    Asambeg.   Nay kneeles to him;
Obserue the scornefull villaine turnes away too,
As glorying in his conquest.
    Donusa.   Are you Marble?   *Kneeles.*
If Christians haue mothers, sure they share in
The tigresse fiercenesse, for if you were owner
Of humane pitty, you could not indure
A Princes to kneele to you, or looke on
These falling teares which hardest rocks would soften,
And yet remaine vnmou'd. Did you but giue me
A tast of happinesse in your embraces
That the remembrance of the sweetenesse of it
Might leaue perpetuall bitternes behind it?
Or shew'd me what it was to be a wife,
To liue a widow euer?
    Asambeg.   She has confest it;
Ceise on him villaines. O the furies.

     Enter CAPIAGA, AGA, *with others.* ASAMBEG *and* MUSTAPHA
                               descend.

    Donusa.   How!
Are we betray'd?
    Vitelli.   The better, I expected
A Turkish Faith.

           64. wrong's] *conj. McIlwraith*; wrong 30

Donusa. Who am I that you dare this?
Tis I that doe command you to forbeare
A touch of violence.
    Aga. We already Madam
Haue satisfied your pleasure further then   90
Wee know to answere it.
    Capiaga. Would we were well off,
We stand too far ingag'd I feare.
    Donusa. For vs?
We'll bring you safe off; who dares contradict
What is our pleasure?

        Enter ASAMBEG, MUSTAPHA.

    Asambeg. Spurne the dog to prison,
I'll answere you anon.
    Vitelli. What punishment   95
So ere I vndergoe, I am still a Christian. *Exit [Gard] with* VITELLI.
    Donusa. What bold presumption's this? vnder what law
Am I to fall that set my foote vpon
Your Statutes and decrees?
    Mustapha. The crime committed
Our Alcoran calls death.
    Donusa. Tush, who is heere   100
That is not *Amurahs* slaue, and so vnfit
To sit a iudge vpon his blood?
    Asambeg. You haue lost
And sham'd the priueledge of it, rob'd me to
Of my soule, my vnderstanding to behold
Your base vnworthy fall, from your high vertue.   105
    Donusa. I doe appeale to *Amurah*.
    Asambeg. We will offer
No violence to your person, till we know
His sacred pleasure, till when vnder gard
You shall continue heere.
    Donusa. Shall?
    Asambeg. I haue said it.
    Donusa. We shall remember this. *The Gard leades off* DONUSA.
    Asambeg. It ill becomes   110
Such as are guilty to deliuer threats

        96 SD. *Exit Gard*] *Gifford*; *Ex.* 30

Against the innocent. I could teare this flesh now,
But tis in vaine, nor must I talke but do:
Prouide a well man'd galley for Constantinople,
Such sad newes neuer came to our great Master;   115
As hee directs, we must proceed, and know
No will but his, to whom what's ours we owe.   *Exeunt.*

The end of the third Act.

Actus Quartus, Scæna Prima.

[IV. i]

Enter MASTER, BOTESWAINE.

Master. HE does begin to eate?
   Boteswaine.   A little, Master,
But our best hope for his recouery, is that
His rauing leaues him, and those dreadfull words,
Damnation, and despayre, with which he euer
Ended all his discourses are forgotten.   5
   Master. This stranger is a most religious man sure,
And I am doubtfull whether his charity,
In the relieuing of our wants, or care
To cure the wounded conscience of *Grimaldi*,
Deserues more admiration.
   Boteswaine.   Can you guesse   10
What the reason should be that we neuer mention
The Church, or the high Altar, but his melancholie
Growes, and increases on him?
   Master.   I haue heard him
(When he gloried to professe himselfe an Atheist,)
Talke often and with much delight and boasting,   15
Of a rude prancke he did ere he turn'd Pirat,
The memory of which, as it appeares,
Lies heauy on him.
   Boteswaine.   Pray you let me vnderstand it.
   Master. Vpon a solemne day when the whole City
Ioyn'd in deuotion, and with barefoote steps   20
Pass'd to S. *Markes*, the Duke and the whole Signiory,
Helping to perfit the Religious pompe,

114. man'd] *Massinger MS* (mam'd); made *30¹*; mande *30²*

With which they were receaued; when all men else
Were full of teares, and gron'd beneath the waight
Of past offences (of whose heauy burden
They came to be absolu'd and freed,) our Captaine,
Whether in scorne of those so pious rites
He had no feeling of, or else drawne to it
Out of a wanton irreligious madnesse,
(I know not which) ranne to the holy man,
As he was doing of the worke of grace,
And snatching from his hands the sanctifide meanes
Dash'd it vpon the pauement.
 Boteswaine.   How escaped he?
It being a deede deseruing death with torture.
 Master. The generall amazement of the people
Gaue him leaue to quit the Temple, and a Gundelo,
(Prepar'd it seemes before) brought him aboard,
Since which he nere saw Venice. The remembrance
Of this, it seemes, torments him; aggrauated
With a strong beleefe he cannot receaue pardon
For this fowle fact, but from his hands against whom
It was committed.
 Boteswaine. And what course intendes
His heauenly Physitian, reuerend *Francisco*,
To beate downe this opinion?
 Master.   He promis'd
To vse some holy and religious finenesse,
To this good end, and in the meane time charg'd me
To keepe him darke, and to admit no visitants
But on no termes to crosse him. Heere he comes.

    Enter GRIMALDI, *with a Booke.*

 Grimaldi. For theft! he that restores trebble the value,
Makes satisfaction, and for want of meanes
To doe so, as a slaue must serue it out
Till he hath made full payment. Ther's hope left heere.
O with what willingnesse would I giue vp
My liberty to those that I haue pillag'd,
And wish the numbers of my yeeres though wasted
In the most sordid slauery might equall

   IV. i. 31. doing of] *Coxeter*; of doing 30

The rapines I haue made, till with one voyce
My patient sufferings, might exact from my
Most cruell creditors, a full remission,
An eies losse with an eie, limbs with a limb, 60
A sad accompt! yet to finde peace within heere,
Though all such as I haue maim'd, and dismembred
In drunken quarrells, or orecome with rage
When they were giu'n vp to my power, stood heere now
And cride for restitution; to appease 'em, 65
I would doe a bloody iustice on my selfe;
Pull out these eies that guided me to rauish
Their sight from others; lop these legs that bore me
To barbarous violence; with this hand cut off
This instrument of wrong, till nought were left me 70
But this poore bleeding limblesse truncke, which gladly
I would diuide among them.

   Enter FRANCISCO *in a Cope like a Bishop.*

        Ha! what thinke I
Of petty forfeiturcs, in this reuerend habit,
(All that I am turnd into eies) I looke on
A deede of mine so fiendlike, that repentance, 75
Though with my teares I taught the sea new tides,
Can neuer wash off; all my thefts, my rapes
Are veniall trespasses compar'd to what
I offer'd to that shape, and in a place too
Where I stood bound to kneele to't.   *Kneeles.*
  Francisco.   Tis forgiuen, 80
I with his tongue (whom in these sacred vestments
With impure hands thou didst offend) pronounce it,
I bring peace to thee, see that thou deserue it
In thy fayre life heereafter.
  Grimaldi.   Can it bee!
Dare I beleeue this vision, or hope 85
A pardon ere may finde me?
  Francisco.   Purchase it
By zealous vndertakings, and no more
T'will be remembred.

---

  69. violence;] *Massinger MS*; ~, *30* 72 SD. *Enter . . . Bishop.*] *Coxeter*; *at l. 80 in 30*

Grimaldi.   What celestiall balme
I feele now pour'd into my wounded conscience!
What penance is there Ile not vndergoe
Though nere so sharpe and rugged, with more pleasure
Then flesh and blood ere tasted; shew me true sorrow,
Arm'd with an iron whip, and I will meete
The stripes she brings along with her, as if
They were the gentle touches of a hand,
That comes to cure me. Can good deeds redeeme me?
I will rise vp a wonder to the world,
When I haue giuen strong proofes how I am altred,
I that haue sold such as profest the Faith,
That I was borne in, to captiuity,
Will make their number equall, that I shall
Deliuer from the oare; and winne as many
By the cleerenesse of my actions, to looke on
Their misbeleefe, and loth it. I will be
A conuoy for all Marchants: and thought worthy
To be reported to the world heereafter,
The child of your deuotion, nurs'd vp
And made strong by your charity, to breake through
All dangers Hell can bring foorth to oppose me;
Nor am I though my fortunes were thought desperate,
Now you haue reconcil'd me to my selfe,
So voyd of worldly meanes, but in despight
Of the proud Viceroyes wrongs I can doe something
To witnesse my good change; when you please trye me,
And I will perfit what you shall inioyne me,
Or fall a ioyfull Martyr.
    Francisco.   You will reape
The comfort of it. Liue yet vndiscouer'd,
And with your holy meditations strengthen
Your Christian resolution; ere long
You shall heare further from me.
    Grimaldi.   I'll attend   *Exit* FRANCISCO.
All your commands with patience; come my Mates,
I hitherto haue liu'd an ill example,
And as your Captaine lead you on to mischiefe,

---

113. Viceroyes] *Coxeter*; ~, *30*   114. witnesse my good change] *Massinger MS*; witnesse of my change *30¹*; prooue that I haue power *30²*

But now will truely labour, that good men
May say hereafter of me to my glory,   125
Let but my power and meanes, hande with my will,
His good endeuours, did waigh downe his ill.
                  Exeunt GRIMALDI, MASTER, BOTESWAINE.

            Enter FRANCISCO.

  Francisco. This penitence is not counterfeit, howsoeuer
Good actions are in themselues rewarded.
My trauailes to meete with a double crowne,   130
If that *Vitelli* come off safe, and prooue
Himselfe the Master of his wilde affections.

            Enter GAZET.

O I shall haue intelligence, how now *Gazet*,
Why these sad lookes and teares?
  Gazet.   Teares sir? I haue lost
My worthy Master! Your rich heyre seemes to mourne for   135
A miserable father, your young widow
Following a bedrid husband to his graue,
Would haue her neighbours thinke she cries, and rores,
That she must part with such a goodman doe nothing,
When t'is because he stayes so long aboue ground,   140
And hinders a rich suitor: all is come out sir,
We are smok'd for being cunnicatchers, my master
Is put in prison, his she customer
Is vnder garde to, these are things to weepe for;
But mine owne losse considerd, and what a fortune   145
I haue, as they say, had snatch'd out of my chops,
Would make a man runne mad.
  Francisco.   I scarce haue leasure,
I am so wholy taken vp with sorrow,
For my lou'de pupill, to enquire thy fate,
Yet I will heare it.
  Gazet.   Why sir, I had bought a place,   150
A place of credit to, and had gone through with it;
I should haue beene made an Eunuch (there was honour,

---

126. meanes, hande] *30*; meanes stande *McIlwraith*   130. My trauailes to] *30*;
My travail's to *Coxeter*   146. haue ... had snatch'd] *McIlwraith*; haue ... snatch'd
30; have had ... snatch'd *Mason*

For a late poore prentice) when vpon the suddaine
There was such a hurleburley in the Court,
That I was glad to runne away and carry 155
The price of my office with me.
   Francisco.   Is that all?
You haue made a sauing voyage; we must thinke now,
Though not to free, to comfort sad *Vitelli*,
My greeu'd soule suffers for him.
   Gazet.   I am sad too; 159
But had I beene an Eunuch—
   Francisco.   Thinke not on it.   *Exeunt.*

Actus Quartus, Scæna Secunda.

Enter ASAMBEG. *Vnlocks the doore, leades forth* PAULINA.

Asambeg. Be your owne gard; obsequiousnesse, and seruice
Shall winne you to be mine. Of all restraint
For euer take your leaue, no threats shall awe you,
No iealous doubts of mine disturbe your freedome,
No fee'd spies, wayte vpon your steps; your vertue 5
And due consideration in your selfe,
Of what is Noble, are the faithfull helps
I leaue you as supporters to defend you,
From falling basely.
   Paulina.   This is wondrous strange.
Whence flowes this alteration?
   Asambeg.   From true iudgement, 10
And strong assurance, neither grates of iron,
Hemde in with walls of brasse, stricte gards, high birth,
The forfeiture of Honour, nor the feare
Of infamie, or punishment, can stay
A woman slaude to appetite from being 15
False, and vnworthy.
   Paulina.   You are growne Satyricall
Against our sex, why sir I durst produce
My selfe in our defence, and from you challenge
A testimony not to be deni'd,
All fall not vnder this vnequall censure. 20
I that haue stood your flatteries, your threats,

Bore vp against your fierce temptations; scorn'd
The cruell meanes you practis'd to supplant me,
Hauing no armes to helpe me, to hold out,
But loue of piety, and constant goodnesse. 25
If you are vnconfirm'd, dare againe bouldly
Enter into the lists and combat with
All opposites mans malice can bring forth
To shake me in my chastetie built vpon
The rocke of my religion.
 Asambeg.   I doe wish 30
I could beleeue you, but when I shall shew you
A most incredible example of
Your frayletie in a Princesse, su'de and sought to
By men of worth, of ranck, of eminence; courted
By happinesse it selfe, and her cold temper 35
Approou'd by many yeeres; yet she to fall,
Fall from her selfe, her glories, nay her safetie
Into a gulfe of shame, and blacke despayre,
I thinke you'll doubt your selfe, or in beholding
Her punishment for euer be deterde 40
From yeelding basely.
 Paulina.   I would see this wonder;
Tis sir my first petition.
 Asambeg.   And thus granted;
Aboue you shall obserue all.   PAULINA *steps aside.*

    Enter MUSTAPHA.

 Mustapha.   Sir I sought you
And must relate a wonder: since I studied
And knew what man was, I was neuer witnesse 45
Of such inuincible fortitude as this Christian
Showes in his sufferings; all the torments that
We could present him with to fright his constancy
Confirm'd, not shooke it; and those heauy chaines
That eate into his flesh, appear'd to him 50
Like bracelets made of some lou'd mistrisse hayres
We kisse in the remembrance of her fauours.
I am strangely taken with it, and haue lost
Much of my furie.

    IV. ii. 37. safetie] *Massinger MS*; safet, 30

IV. ii. 54-82　　　　　*The Renegado*　　　　　　71

　Asambeg.　　　　Had he suffer'd poorely
It had call'd on my contempt, but manly patience　　55
And all commanding vertue, wins vpon
An enemy. I shall thinke vpon him, ha!

　　　　　Enter AGA *with a black box.*

So soone return'd? this speede pleads in excuse
Of your late fault, which I no more remember.
What's the grand Signiors pleasure?
　Aga.　　　　　Tis inclos'd heere.　　　60
The box to, that contaynes it, may informe you
How he stands affected: I am trusted with
Nothing but this, on forfeit of your head
She must haue a speedy triall.
　Asambeg.　　　　Bring her in
In blacke as to her funerall, tis the colour　　　65
Her fault wils her to weare, and which, in iustice
I dare not pitty. Sit and take your place.
Howeuer in her life she has degenerated
May she die nobly, and in that confirme
Her greatnesse, and high blood.

A solemne musicque. A garde. The AGA, *and* CAPIAGA, *leading in* DONUSA *in blacke, her trayne borne vp by* CARAZIE, *and* MANTO.

　Mustapha.　　　　I now could melt;　　70
But soft compassion leaue me.
　Manto.　　　　I am affrighted
With this dismall preparation. Should the enioying
Of loose desires finde euer such conclusions,
All Women would be Vestalls.
　Donusa.　　　　That you cloth me
In this sad liuery of death, assures me　　　75
Your sentence is gone out before, and I
To late am cald for, in my guilty cause
To vse qualification, or excuse—
Yet must I not part so with mine owne strengths,
But borrow from my modesty boldnesse, to　　80
Enquire by whose authority you sit
My iudges, and whose warrant digs my graue

　　　71. *Manto.*] *Coxeter*; *Fran.* 30

In the frownes you dart against my life?
    Asambeg.   See heere
This fatall signe, and warrant: this brought to
A Generall fighting in the head of his   85
Victorious troopes, rauishes from his hand
His eu'n then conquering sword; this showne vnto
The Sultans brothers, or his sonnes, deliuers
His deadly anger, and all hopes lay'd by
Commands them to prepare themselues for heauen.   90
Which would stand with the quiet of your soule
To thinke vpon, and imitate.
    Donusa.   Giue me leaue
A little to complayne, first of the hard
Condition of my Fortune, which may moue you
Though not to rise vp intercessors for me,   95
Yet in remembrance of my former life,
(This being the first spot, tainting mine honor)
To be the meanes to bring me to his presence;
And then I doubt not, but I could alleage
Such reasons in mine owne defence, or pleade   100
So humbly (my teares helpinge) that it should
Awake his sleeping pitty.
    Asambeg.   Tis in vayne.
If you haue ought to say you shall haue hearing,
And in me thinke him present.
    Donusa.   I would thus then
First kneele, and kisse his feete, and after tell him   105
How long I had beene his darling, what delight
My infant yeeres afforded him; how deere
Hee prizde his sister, in both bloods, my mother;
That she like him had frailety, that to me
Descends as an inheritance; then coniure him   110
By her blest ashes, and his fathers soule,
The sword that rides vpon his thigh, his right hand
Holding the Scepter and the Ottoman fortune,
To haue compassion on me.
    Asambeg.   But suppose
(As I am sure) he would be deafe, what then   115
Could you inferre?
    Donusa.   I then would thus rise vp,

And to his teeth tell him he was a tyrant,
A most voluptuous, and insatiable Epicure
In his owne pleasures: which he hugs so deerely,
As proper, and peculiar to himselfe,
That he denies a moderate lawfull vse
Of all delight to others. And to thee
Vnequall iudge I speake as much, and charge thee
But with impartiall eies to looke into
Thy selfe, and then consider with what iustice
Thou canst pronounce my sentence. Vnkind nature,
To make weake women seruants, proud men Masters!
Indulgent *Mahomet*, doe thy bloudy lawes
Call my embraces with a Christian, death?
Hauing my heate and May of youth to pleade
In my excuse? and yet want power to punish
These that with scorne breake throgh thy Cobweb edicts
And laugh at thy decrees? to tame their lusts
There's no religious bit; let her be fayre
And pleasing to the eye, though Persian, Moore,
Idolatresse, Turke, or Christian, you are priueledg'd
And freely may enioy her. At this instant
I know, vniust man, thou hast in thy power
A louely Christian Virgin; thy offence
Equall, if not transcending mine, why then
We being both guilty doest thou not descend
From that vsurp'd Tribunall and with me
Walke hand in hand to death?
   Asambeg.   She raues, and we
Loose time to heare her: reade the Law.
   Donusa.   Doe, doe,
I stand resolu'd to suffer.
   Aga. If any Virgin of what degree or quality soeuer, borne a naturall Turke, shall bee conuicted of corporall loosenesse, and incontinence, with any Christian, she is by the decree of our great Prophet *Mahomet* to loose her head.
   Asambeg. Marke that, then taxe our iustice.
   Aga. Euer prouided that if shee, the sayd offender, by any reasons, arguments or perswasion, can win and preuaile with the sayd Christian offending with her, to alter his religion, and marry

146. *Aga.*] Coxeter; *Asa.* 30

her, that then the winning of a soule to the *Mahometan* sect, shall
acquit her from all shame, disgrace and punishment whatsoeuer.
 Donusa. I lay hold on that clause and challenge from you
The priueledge of the Law.
  Mustapha.   What will you doe?
 Donusa. Grant me accesse and meanes, I'll vndertake
To turne this Christian Turke, and marry him:
This triall you cannot denie.
  Mustapha.   O base!
Can feare to die make you descend so low
From your high birth, and brand the *Ottoman* line
With such a marke of infamy?
  Asambeg.   This is worse
Then the parting with your honour! better suffer
Ten thousand deaths, and without hope to haue
A place in our great Prophets Paradice,
Then haue an acte to after times remembred
So foule as this is.
  Mustapha. Cheere your spirits Madam,
To die is nothing, tis but parting with
A mountaine of vexations.
  Asambeg.   Thinke of your honour;
In dying nobly you make satisfaction
For your offence, and you shall liue a story
Of bould Heroicke courage.
  Donusa.   You shall not foole me
Out of my life, I claime the Law and sue for
A speedy triall; if I fayle, you may
Determine of me as you please.
  Asambeg.   Base woman!
But vse thy wayes, and see thou prosper in 'em
For if thou fall againe into my power
Thou shalt in vaine after a thousand tortures
Cry out for death, that death which now thou fliest from.
Vnloose the prisoners chaynes, goe leade her on
To try the Magique of her tongue; I follow:
I am on the racke, descend my best *Paulina*. [*Exeunt.*]

   183 SD. *Exeunt.*] Coxeter; *not in* 30

Actus Quartus. Scæna Tertia.

Enter FRANCISCO, IAYLOR.

Francisco. I come not empty handed, I will purchase
Your fauour at what rate you please. There's gold.
   Iaylor. Tis the best oratory. I will hazard
A checke for your content. Below there?
   Vitelli.   Welcome.
                          VITELLI *vnder the Stage.*
Art thou the happy messenger that brings me   5
Newes of my death?
   Iaylor.   Your hand.   VITELLI *pluck'd vp.*
   Francisco.   Now if you please,
A little priuacie.
   Iaylor.   You haue bought it sir,
Enioy it freely.   *Exit* IAYLOR.
   Francisco. O my deerest pupill,
Witnesse these teares of ioy, I neuer saw you
Till now looke louely; nor durst I ere glory   10
In the mind of any man I had built vp
With the hands of vertuous, and religious precepts,
Till this glad minute. Now you haue made good
My expectation of you. By my order,
All Roman *Cæsars*, that ledde kings in chaines   15
Fast bound to their triumphant chariots, if
Compar'd with that true glory, and full luster
You now appeare in, all their boasted honors
Purchas'd with blood, and wrong, would loose their names
And be no more remembred.
   Vitelli.   This applause   20
Confirm'd in your allowance ioyes me more,
Then if a thousand full cram'd Theaters
Should clap their eager hands to witnesse that
The Scene I act did please, and they admire it.
But these are (father) but beginnings, not   25
The ends of my high aimes. I grant to haue master'd
The rebell appetite of flesh and blood
Was far aboue my strength; and still owe for it

IV. iii. 4. content.] *Coxeter*; ~ ∧ *30*

To that great power that lent it. But when I
Shall make't apparant, the grimme lookes of death 30
Affright me not, and that I can put off
The fonde desire of life (that like a garment
Couers, and clothes our frailty) hastening to
My Martirdome, as to a heauenly banquet,
To which I was a choyce inuited guest; 35
Then you may boldly say, you did not plough
Or trust the barren, and vngratefull sands
With the fruitfull graine of your religious counsels.
    Francisco. You doe instruct your teacher. Let the Sun
Of your cleere life (that lends to good men light) 40
But set as gloriously, as it did rise,
(Though sometimes clouded) you may write *nil vltra*
To humane wishes.
    Vitelli.   I haue almost gain'd
The end of the race, and will not faynt, or tire now.

                Enter AGA *and* IAYLOR.

    Aga. Sir by your leaue (nay stay not)   [*Exit* IAYLOR.]
                            I bring comfort; 45
The Viceroy taken with the constant bearing
Of your afflictions, and presuming to
You will not change your temper, does command
Your irons should be tane off. Now arme your selfe
With your olde resolution, suddenly   *The chayne taken off.*
You shall be visited. You must leaue the roome to 51
And doe it without reply.
    Francisco.   There's no contending,
Bee still thy selfe my sonne.   *Exit* FRANCISCO.
    Vitelli.   Tis not in man

        Enter DONUSA, ASAMBEG, MUSTAPHA, PAULINA.

To change or alter me.
    Paulina.   Whom doe I looke on?   [*Aside.*]
My brother? tis he! but no more my tongue, 55
Thou wilt betray all.

---

45. stay] *30*; stare *Coxeter*; start *Gifford¹*   45 SD. Exit IAYLOR.] *after Gifford²*;
not in 30   54 SD. Aside.] *Coxeter*; *not in 30*

Asambeg.   Let vs heare this temptresse,
The fellow lookes as he would stop his eares
Against her powerfull spels.
    Paulina.   He is vndone else.
    Vitelli. I'll stand th' incounter, charge me home.
    Donusa.   I come sir,   *Bowes her selfe.*
A begger to you, and doubt not to finde
A good mans charity, which if you denie,
You are cruell to your selfe, a crime, a wiseman
(And such I hold you) would not willingly
Be guilty of; nor let it find lesse welcome
Though I (a creature you contemne) now shew you
The way to certaine happinesse, nor thinke it
Imaginarie, or phantasticall,
And so not worth th' acquiring, in respect
The passage to it is nor rough nor thornie;
No steepe hills in the way which you must climbe vp;
No monsters to be conquer'd; no inchantments
To be dissolu'd by counter charmes, before
You take possession of it.
    Vitelli.   What strong poyson
Is wrap'd vp in these sugred pills?
    Donusa.   My suite is
That you would quit your shoulders of a burthen
Vnder whose ponderous waight you wilfully
Haue too long groan'd, to cast those fetters off,
With which with your own hands you chaine your freedome.
Forsake a seuere, nay imperious mistresse,
Whose seruice does exact perpetuall cares,
Watchings, and troubles, and giue entertainement
To one that courts you, whose least fauours are
Variety, and choyce of all delights
Mankind is capable of.
    Vitelli.   You speake in riddles.
What burthen, or what mistrisse? or what fetters?
Are those you poynt at?
    Donusa.   Those which your religion,
The mistresse you too long haue seru'd, compells you
To beare with slaue-like patience.
    Vitelli.   Ha!

Paulina. How brauely [*Aside.*]
That vertuous anger showes!
　　Donusa. Be wise, and waigh
The prosperous successe of things: if blessings
Are donatiues from Heauen (which you must grant
Were blasphemy to question) and that
They are call'd downe, and powr'd on such as are
Most gracious with the great disposer of 'em,
Looke on our flourishing Empire; if the splendor,
The Maiestie, and glory of it dimme not
Your feeble sight; and then turne backe, and see
The narrow bounds of yours, yet that poore remnant
Rent in as many factions, and opinions,
As you haue petty kingdomes, and then if
You are not obstinate against truth and reason,
You must confesse the Deity you worship
Wants care, or power to helpe you.
　　Paulina. Hold out now [*Aside.*]
And then thou art victorious.
　　Asambeg. How he eies her!
　　Mustapha. As if he would looke through her.
　　Asambeg. His eyes flame too,
As threatning violence.
　　Vitelli. But that I know
The Diuell thy Tutor fills each part about thee,
And that I cannot play the exorcist
To dispossesse thee, vnlesse I should teare
Thy body limbe by limbe, and throw it to
The furies that expect it, I would now
Plucke out that wicked tongue, that hath blasphem'd
That great omnipotency at whose nod
The fabricke of the World shakes. Dare you bring
Your iugling Prophet in comparison with
That most inscrutable, and infinite essence
That made this all, and comprehends his worke?
The place is too prophane to mention him
Whose onely name is sacred. O *Donusa*!
How much in my compassion I suffer,
That thou, on whom this most excelling forme

88 SD. *Aside.*] *Coxeter; not in* 30　　103 SD. *Aside.*] *Gifford*[2]; *not in* 30

And faculties of discourse, beyond a woman,
Were by his liberall guift confer'd, should'st still
Remaine in ignorance of him that gaue it!
I will not foule my mouth to speake the Sorceries 125
Of your seducer, his base birth, his whoredomes,
His strange impostures; nor deliuer how
He taught a Pigeon to feede in his eare,
Then made his credulous followers beleeue
It was an Angell that instructed him 130
In the framing of his Alcoran. Pray you marke me.
   Asambeg. These words are death, were he in nought else guilty.
   Vitelli. Your intent to winne me
To be of your beleefe proceeded from
Your feare to die. Can there be strength in that 135
Religion, that suffers vs to tremble
At that which euery day, nay hower wee hast to?
   Donusa. This is vnanswerable and there's something tells mee
I erre in my opinion.
   Vitelli.   Cherish it,
It is a Heauenly prompter, entertaine 140
This holy motion, and weare on your forehead
The Sacred badge he armes His seruants with,
You shall, like mee, with scorne looke downe vpon
All engines tyranny can aduance to batter
Your constant resolution. Then you shall 145
Looke truely fayre, when your minds purenesse answers
Your outward beauties.
   Donusa.   I came heere to take you,
But I perceiue a yeelding in my selfe
To be your prisoner.
   Vitelli.   Tis an ouerthrow
That will outshine all victories. O *Donusa,* 150
Dye in my faith like me, and tis a marriage
At which celestiall Angels shall be waiters,
And such as haue beene Sainted welcome vs.
Are you confirm'd?
   Donusa.   I would bee; but the meanes
That may assure mee?
   Vitelli.   Heauen is mercifull, 155

      138. tells] *Massinger MS*; tells *30* (s *blurred*)

And will not suffer you to want a man,
To doe that sacred office, build vpon it.
  Donusa. Then thus I spit at *Mahomet.*
  Asambeg.   Stoppe her mouth:
In death to turne Apostata! I'll not heare
One sillable from any; wretched creature!   160
With the next rising Sunne prepare to die.
Yet Christian, in reward of thy braue courage,
Bee thy faith right, or wrong, receiue this fauour.
In person Ile attend thee to thy death,
And bouldly challenge all that I can giue   165
But what's not in my grant, which is to liue.   *Exeunt.*

        The end of the fourth Act.

             Actus Quintus, Scæna Prima.

           Enter VITELLI, FRANCISCO.
  Francisco. You are wondrous braue, and iocound.
  Vitelli.   Welcome Father.
Should I spare cost, or not weare cheerefull lookes
Vpon my wedding day, it were omenous
And shew'd I did repent it, which I dare not,
It being a marriage, howsoeuer sad   5
In the first ceremonies that confirme it,
That will for euer arme me against feares,
Repentance, doubts, or iealousies, and bring
Perpetuall comforts, peace of minde, and quiet
To the glad couple.
  Francisco.   I well vnderstand you;   10
And my full ioy to see you so resolu'd
Weake words cannot expresse. What is the howre
Design'd for this solemnity?
  Vitelli.   The sixth,
Something before the setting of the Sun
We take our last leaue of his fading light,   15
And with our soules eies seeke for beames eternall,
Yet there's one scruple with which I am much
Perplex'd, and troubl'd, which I know you can
Resolue me of.

Francisco. What is't?
Vitelli. This sir, my Bride
Whom I first courted, and then wonne (not with
Loose layes, poore flatteries, apish complements,
But Sacred, and Religious zeale) yet wants
The holy badge that should proclaime her fit
For these Celestiall Nuptialls; willing she is,
I know, to weare it, as the choicest iewell
On her fayre forehead; but to you, that well
Could doe that worke of Grace, I know the Viceroy
Will neuer grant accesse. Now in a case
Of this necessity, I would gladly learne,
Whether in me a layman, without orders,
It may not be religious, and lawfull
As we goe to our deaths to doe that office?
 Francisco. A question in it selfe, with much ease answer'd;
Midwiues vpon necessity performe it,
And Knights that in the Holy-Land fought for
The freedome of Hierusalem, when full
Of sweat, and enemies blood, haue made their Helmets
The fount, out of which with their holy hands
They drew that heauenly liquor: 't was approu'd then
By the Holy Church, nor must I thinke it now
In you a worke lesse pious.
 Vitelli. You confirme me,
I will find a way to doe it. In the meane time
Your holy vowes assist me.
 Francisco. They shall euer
Be present with you.
 Vitelli. You shall see me act
This last Scæne to the life.
 Francisco. And though now fall,
Rise a bles'd Martyr.
 Vitelli. That's my end, my all. *Exeunt.*

Actus Quintus, Scæna Secunda.

Enter GRIMALDI, MASTER, BOTESWAINE, *Saylors.*

 Boteswaine. Sir, if you slip this opportunity,
Neuer expect the like.

Master. With as much ease now
We may steal the ship out of the harbor, Captaine,
As euer Gallants in a wanton brauery
Haue set vpon a drunken Constable,
And bore him from a sleepy ruggown'd watch:
Be therefore wise.
    Grimaldi. I must be honest too
And you shall weare that shape, you shall obserue me,
If that you purpose to continue mine.
Thinke you ingratitude can be the parent
To our vnfayn'd repentance? doe I owe
A peace within heere, Kingdoms could not purchase,
To my religious creditor, to leaue him
Open to danger, the great benefit
Neuer remembred? no, though in her bottome
We could stow vp the tribute of the Turke,
Nay, grant the passage safe too: I will neuer
Consent to waigh an Anchor vp, till hee,
That onely must, commands it.
    Boteswaine. This Religion
Will keepe vs slaues and Beggars.
    Master. The Fiend prompts me
To change my coppy: Plague vpon't, we are Seamen,
What haue we to doe with't, but for a snatch, or so,
At the end of a long Lent?
    Boteswaine. Mum, see who is here?

        Enter FRANCISCO.

    Grimaldi. My Father!
    Francisco. My good conuert. I am full
Of serious businesse which denies me leaue
To holde long conference with you: Onely thus much
Briefely receiue; a day, or two, at the most
Shall make me fit to take my leaue of Tunis,
Or giue me lost for euer.
    Grimaldi. Dayes, nor yeares,
Prouided that my stay may doe you seruice,
But to me shall be minuits.
    Francisco. I much thanke you:
In this small scrole you may in priuate reade

What my intents are, and as they growe ripe
I will instruct you further. In the meane time
Borrow your late distracted lookes, and gesture;
The more deiected you appeare, the lesse
The Viceroy must suspect you.
  Grimaldi.   I am nothing,
But what you please to haue me be.
  Francisco.   Farewell sir,
Be cheerefull Master, something we will doe
That shall reward it selfe in the performance,
And that's true prize indeede.
  Master.   I am obedient.
  Boteswaine. And I, there's no contending.
  Francisco.   Peace to you all.
    Exeunt GRIMALDI, MASTER, BOTESWAINE, [*Saylors.*]
Prosper thou great Existence my endeauours,
As they religiously are vndertaken,
And distant equally from seruile gaine,

    Enter PAULINA, CARAZIE, *and* MANTO.

Or glorious ostentation. I am heard
In this blest opportunity, which in vaine
I long haue waited for. I must show my selfe.
O she has found me. Now if she prooue right
All hope will not forsake vs.
  Paulina.   Farther off,
And in that distance know your duties too.
You were bestowed on me as slaues to serue me
And not as spies to prie into my actions,
And after to betray me. You shall finde
If any looke of mine be vnobseru'd,
I am not ignorant of a mistresse power,
And from whom I receiue it.
  Carazie.   Note this, *Manto.*
The pride, and scorne, with which she entertaynes vs
Now we are made hers by the Viceroyes guift.
Our sweete condition'd princesse, fayre *Donusa,*
Rest in her death waite on her, neuer vs'd vs
With such contempt. I would he had sent me

    V. ii. 42 SD. *Saylors*] *Gifford; not in* 30

To the Gallies, or the Gallows, when he gaue me
To this proude little diuell.
   Manto.   I expect
All tyrannous vsage, but I must be patient;   65
And though ten times a day, she teares these locks,
Or makes this face her footstoole, tis but iustice.
   Paulina. Tis a true story of my fortunes, father,
My chastity preseru'd by miracle,
Or your deuotions for me; and beleeue it,   70
What outward pride so ere I counterfeite,
Or state to these appoynted to attend me,
I am not in my disposition alter'd,
But still your humble daughter, and share with you
In my poore brothers sufferings, all hels torments.   75
Reuenge it on accurs'd *Grimaldies* soule
That in his rape of me gaue a beginning
To all the miseries that since haue follow'd.
   Francisco. Be charitable, and forgiue him gentle daughter;
Hee's a chang'd man, and may redeeme his fault   80
In his faire life heereafter. You must beare too
Your forc'd captiuity (for tis no better,
Though you weare golden fetters) and of him,
Whom death affrights not, learne to hold out nobly.
   Paulina. You are still the same good counsellor.
   Francisco.   And who knowes
(Since what aboue is purpos'd, is inscrutable)   86
But that the Viceroyes extreme dotage on you
May be the parent of a happier birth
Then yet our hopes dare fashion. Longer conference
May prooue vnsafe for you, and me, howeuer   90
Perhaps for triall he allowes you freedome.
From this learne therefore what you must attempt, *Deliuers a paper.*
Though with the hazarde of your selfe. Heauen gard you,
And giue *Vitelli* patience, then I doubt not
But he will haue a glorious day since some   95
Hold truely, such as suffer, ouercome.   *Exeunt.*

   V. ii. 78. To] *underlined by Massinger (indicating end of speech)*   79. *Francisco.*
Be] *Massinger MS* (franci: Be); Be *30*

Actus Quintus, Scæna Tertia.

Enter ASAMBEG, MUSTAPHA, AGA, CAPIAGA.

Asambeg. What we commanded, see perform'd, and fayle not
In all things to be punctuall.
    Aga.   We shall sir. *Exeunt* AGA, CAPIAGA.
    Mustapha. Tis strange that you should vse such circumstance
To a delinquent of so meane condition.
    Asambeg. Had he appear'd in a more sordid shape   5
Then disguis'd greatenes euer dain'd to maske in,
The gallant bearing of his present fortune
Aloud proclaimes him noble.
    Mustapha.   If you doubt him
To be a man built vp for great imployments,
And as a cunning spie sent to explore   10
The Cities strength, or weakenesse, you by torture
May force him to discouer it.
    Asambeg.   That were base;
Nor dare I doe such iniury to Vertue
And bold assured courage, neither can I
Be wonne to thinke, but if I should attempt it,   15
I shoote against the Moone. He that hath stood
The roughest battery, that captiuity
Could euer bring to shake a constant temper;
Despis'd the fawnings of a future greatnesse,
By beauty in her full perfection tender'd;   20
That heares of death as of a quiet slumber,
And from the surplusage of his owne firmenesse
Can spare enough of fortitude, to assure
A feeble woman; will not, *Mustapha*,
Be alter'd in his soule for any torments   25
We can afflict his body with!
    Mustapha.   Doe your pleasure,
I only offer'd you a friends aduice,
But without gall, or enuy to the man
That is to suffer. But what doe you determine
Of poore *Grimaldi*? the disgrace cal'd on him   30
I heare has ran him madde.

V. iii. 24. not, *Mustapha*,] *Gifford*; now, *Mustapha* 30; now, *Mustapha*, never *Coxeter*

Asambeg. There waigh the difference
In the true temper of their minds. The one,
A Pirat sould to mischiefes, rapes, and all
That make a slaue relentlesse, and obdurate;
Yet of himselfe wanting the inward strengths   35
That should defend him, sinckes beneath compassion
Or pitty of a man; where as this marchant,
Acquainted only with a ciuill life,
Arm'd in himselfe; intrench'd, and fortifide
With his owne vertue, valewing life and death,   40
At the same price, poorely does not inuite
A fauour, but commands vs doe him right,
Which vnto him, and her (we both once honour'd)
As a iust debt I gladly pay. They enter,
Now sit wee equall hearers.

A dreadfull musicke; at one doore, the AGA, *Ianizaries*, VITELLI, FRANCISCO, GAZET: *at the other*, DONUSA, PAULINA, CARAZIE, MANTO.

Mustapha. I shall heare   45
And see, sir, without passion, my wrongs arme me.
Vitelli. A ioyfull preparation! To whose bountie
Owe wee our thankes for gracing thus our Himen?
The notes though dreadfull to the eare, sound heere
As our *Epithalamium* were sung   50
By a Cælestiall quire, and a full *Chorus*
Assurde vs future happinesse. These that leade me
Gaze not with wanton eyes vpon my bride,
Nor for their seruice are repayde by me
With iealousies, or feares; nor doe they enuy   55
My passage to those pleasures from which death
Cannot deterre me. Great sir pardon me;
Imagination of the ioyes I haste to,
Made me forget my duty, but the forme
And ceremony past, I will attend you,   60
And with our constant resolution feast you,
Not with course cates, forgot as soone as tasted,
But such as shall, while you haue memory,
Be pleasing to the palate.

44. pay] *Gifford*; pay'm *30*; pay 'em *Coxeter*

Francisco.   Bee not lost
In what you purpose.   *Exit* FRANCISCO.
　Gazet.   Call you this a marriage?
It differs little from hanging, I cry at it.
　Vitelli. See where my bride appeares! in what full luster!
As if the Virgins that beare vp her trayne,
Had long contended to receiue an honor
Aboue their births, in doing her this seruice.
Nor comes she fearefull to meete those delights,
Which once past ore, immortall pleasures follow.
I need not therefore comfort, or encourage
Her forwarde steps, and I should offer wrong
To her minds fortitude, should I but aske
How she can brooke the rough high going Sea,
Ouer whose foamie backe our shippe well rig'd
With hope and strong assurance must transport vs.
Nor will I tell her when we reach the Hauen
(Which tempests shall not hinder) what loud welcoms
Shall entertaine vs; nor commend the place,
To tell whose least perfection would strike dumbe
The eloquence of all boasted in story,
Though ioynd together.
　Donusa.   Tis enough my deerest;
I dare not doubt you, as your humble shadow,
Leade where you please, I follow.
　Vitelli.   One suite sir,
And willingly I cease to be a begger,
And that you may with more security heare it,
Know tis not life Ile aske, nor to deferre
Our deaths, but a few minutes.
　Asambeg.   Speake, tis granted.
　Vitelli. We being now to take our latest leaue
And growne of one beleefe, I doe desire
I may haue your allowance to performe it
But in the fashion which we Christians vse
Vpon the like occasions.
　Asambeg.   Tis allow'd of.
　Vitelli. My seruice; haste *Gazet* to the next spring,
And bring me of it.
　Gazet.   Would I could as well

Fetch you a pardon, I would not run but flie,
And be heere in a moment.
    Mustapha.   What's the mystery
Of this? discouer it.
    Vitelli.   Great sir, I'll tell you.   100
Each countrey hath it's owne peculiar rites:
Some when they are to die drinke store of wine,
Which powr'd in liberally does oft beget
A bastarde valour, with which armde, they beare
The not to bee declined charge of death   105
With lesse feare, and astonishment; Others take
Drugs to procure a heauie sleepe, that so
They may insensibly receiue the meanes
That casts them in an euerlasting slumber;
Others—

                Enter GAZET *with water.*

           O welcome.
    Asambeg.   Now the vse of yours?   110
    Vitelli. The cleerenesse of this is a perfit signe
Of innocence, and as this washes off
Staines, and pollutions from the things we weare,
Throwne thus vpon the forehead, it hath power
To purge those spots that cleaue vpon the mind,   *Throwes it*
If thankfully receiu'd.   *on her face.*
    Asambeg.   Tis a strange custome!   116
    Vitelli. How doe you entertaine it my *Donusa*?
Feele you no alteration? No new motiues?
No vnexpected ayds that may confirme you
In that to which you were inclinde before?   120
    Donusa. I am an other woman; till this minute
I neuer liu'de, nor durst thinke how to dye.
How long haue I beene blinde? Yet on the suddaine,
By this blest meanes I feele the filmes of error
Tane from my soules eyes. O diuine *Physitian*,   125
That hast bestowde a sight on mee, which death,
Though readie to embrace me in his armes,
Cannot take from me. Let me kisse the hand

    110. *Asambeg.*] 30[1,2] (*Asam.*) *underlined by Massinger (indicating end of speech);*
Vitelli. 30[3,4]   111. *Vitelli.* The] *Massinger MS* (Vitelli: The); The *30*

V. iii. 129–57   *The Renegado*   89

 That did this miracle, and seale my thanks
Vpon those Lips from whence these sweet words vanishde   130
That freede me from the cruellest of prisons,
Blinde ignorance, and misbeliefe: false Prophet,
Impostor *Mahomet*.
 Asambeg.   I'll heare no more;
You doe abuse my fauors, seuer 'em:
Wretch if thou hadst another life to loose,   135
This Blasphemie deseru'de it, instantly
Carry them to their deaths.
 Vitelli.   Wee part now, blest one,
To meet hereafter in a Kingdome, where
Hells malice shall not reach vs.
 Paulina.   Ha, ha, ha.
 Asambeg. What meanes my Mistres?
 Paulina.   Who can hold her spleene,
When such ridiculous follies are presented,   141
The Scene too made religion? O my Lord,
How from one cause two contrary effects
Spring vp vpon the suddaine.
 Asambeg.   This is strange.
 Paulina. That which hath foolde her in her death, winnes me,   145
That hitherto haue barde my selfe from pleasure,
To liue in all delight.
 Asambeg. There's Musicke in this.
 Paulina. I now will runn as fiercely to your armes
As euer longing woman did, borne high
On the swift wings of appetite.
 Vitelli.   O Diuell!   150
 Paulina. Nay more, for there shall be no ods betwixt vs,
I will turne Turke.
 Gazet. Most of your tribe doe so
When they beginne in whore.   *Aside.*
 Asambeg.   You are serious Ladie?
 Paulina. Serious? but satisfie me in a suite
That to the world may witnesse that I haue   155
Some power vpon you, and to morrow challenge
What euer's in my guift, for I will bee

145–6. death, winnes me, / That] *Coxeter*; death, / Winns mee, / That *30¹*; death, / Winnes me, That *30²⁻⁴* 154. Serious?] *30²⁻⁴*; ~: *30¹*

At your dispose.
    Gazet. That's euer the subscription
To a damn'd whores false Epistle.   *Aside.*
    Asambeg. Aske this hand,
Or if thou wilt, the heads of these. I am rapt   160
Beyond my selfe with ioy, speake, speake, what is it?
    Paulina. But twelue short houres repriue for this base couple.
    Asambeg. The reason, since you hate them?
    Paulina. That I may
Haue time to triumph ore this wretched woman:
I'll be my selfe her guardian. I will feast,   165
Adorned in her choice and richest Iewells.
Commit him to what gards you please. Grant this,
I am no more mine owne, but yours.
    Asambeg. Enioy it;
Repine at it who dares: beare him safe off
To the blacke Tower, but giue him all things vsefull;   170
The contrary was not in your request.
    Paulina. I doe contemne him.
    Donusa. Peace in death deny'd me?
    Paulina. Thou shalt not goe in liberty to thy graue,
For one night a Sultana is my slaue.
    Mustapha. A terrible little tyrannesse.
    Asambeg. No more;   175
Her will shall be a law. Till now nere happy.   *Exeunt.*

Actus Quintus, Scæna quarta.

Enter FRANCISCO, GRIMALDI, MASTER, BOTESWAINE, *and Saylors.*

    Grimaldi. Sir, all things are in readinesse, the Turkes
That seas'd vpon my Ship stow'd vnder hatches,
My men resolu'd, and cheerefull. Vse but meanes
To get out of the Ports, we will be ready
To bring you aboard, and then (heauen be but pleas'd)   5
This for the Viceroyes fleete.
    Francisco. Discharge your parts,

164. woman:] 30²; wo 30¹   167. Grant this,] 30²; Gra 30¹

In mine I'll not be wanting; feare not *Master*,
Something will come along to fraught your Barke,
That you will haue iust cause to say you neuer
Made such a Voyage.
    Master.   We will stand the hazard.
    Francisco. What's the best hower?
    Boteswaine.   After the second watch.
    Francisco. Enough; each to his charge.
    Grimaldi.   We will be carefull.   *Exeunt.*

Actus Quintus, Scæna quinta.

Enter PAULINA, DONUSA, CARAZIE, MANTO.

    Paulina. Sit Madam, it is fit that I attend you;
And pardon, I beseech you, my rude language,
To which the sooner you will be inuited,
When you shall vnderstand, no way was left me
To free you from a present execution,
But by my personating that, which neuer
My nature was acquainted with.
    Donusa.   I beleeue you.
    Paulina. You will when you shall vnderstand, I may
Receiue the honour to be knowen vnto you
By a neerer name. And not to wracke you further,
The man you please to fauour is my brother,
No Marchant, Madam, but a Gentleman
Of the best ranke in Venice.
    Donusa.   I reioyce in't
But what's this to his freedome? for my selfe,
Were he well off, I were secure.
    Paulina.   I haue
A present meanes, not plotted by my selfe,
But a religious man, my confessor,
That may preserue all, if we had a seruant
Whose faith we might relie on.
    Donusa.   She that's now
Your slaue was once mine; had I twenty liues
I durst commit them to her trust.

   Manto.   O Madam,
I haue beene false, forgiue me. I'll redeeme it
By any thing howeuer desperate
You please to impose vpon me.
   Paulina.   Troth these teares
I thinke cannot be counterfeit, I beleeue her,   25
And if you please will try her.
   Donusa.   At your perill;
There is no further danger can looke towards me.
   Paulina. This only then, canst thou vse meanes to carry
This bakemeate to *Vitelli*?
   Manto.   With much ease,
I am familiar with the gard; beside,   30
It being knowne it was I that betrayde him,
My entrance hardly will of them be question'd!
   Paulina. About it then, say that it was sent to him
From his *Donusa*, bid him search the midst of't,
He there shall finde a cordiall.
   Manto.   What I doe   35
Shall speake my care and faith.   *Exit* MANTO.
   Donusa.   Good fortune with thee.
   Paulina. You cannot eate.
   Donusa.   The time we thus abuse
We might imploy much better.
   Paulina.   I am glad
To heare this from you. As for you *Carazie*,
If our intents do prosper, make choyce whether   40
You'l steale away with your two Mistresses
Or take your fortune.
   Carazie.   I'll be gelded twice first;
Hang him that stayes behind.
   Paulina.   I waite you Madame.
Were but my brother off, by the command
Of the doting Viceroy there's no garde dare stay me.   45
And I will safely bring you to the place
Where we must expect him.
   Donusa.   Heauen be gracious to vs.   *Exeunt.*

  V. v. 31. It being] *30³, ⁴*; Being *30¹, ²* betrayde him,] *30¹, ²*; betrayde, *30³, ⁴*
40. our] *Mason*; your *30* whether] *30⁴*; whither *30¹⁻³*

Actus Quintus, Scæna Sexta.

Enter VITELLI, AGA, *and a* GARDE.

Vitelli. Paulina to fall off thus? tis to mee
More terrible then death, and like an earthquake
Totters this walking building (such I am)
And in my suddaine ruine would preuent,
By choaking vp at once my vitall spirits, 5
This pompous preparation for my death.
But I am lost; that good man, good *Francisco*
Deliuered me a paper which till now
I wanted leasure to peruse. *Reads the paper.*
 Aga. This Christian
Feares not, it seemes, the neere approching Sun 10
Whose second rise he neuer must salute.

Enter MANTO, *with the Bak't-meat.*

 1. *Garde.* Who's that?
 2. *Garde.* Stand.
 Aga. Manto.
 Manto. Heere's the Viceroyes ring
Giues warrant to my entrance, yet you may
Partake of any thing I shall deliuer;
Tis but a present to a dying man 15
Sent from the princesse that must suffer with him.
 Aga. Vse your owne freedome.
 Manto. I would not disturbe
This his last contemplation.
 Vitelli. O tis well!
He has restor'd all, and I at peace againe
With my *Paulina.*
 Manto. Sir, the sad *Donusa* 20
Grieued for your sufferings, more then for her owne,
Knowing the long and tedious pilgrimage
You are to take, presents you with this cordiall,
Which priuately she wishes you should taste of,
And search the middle part, where you shall find 25
Something that hath the operation, to
Make death looke louely.

Vitelli. I will not dispute
What she commands but serue it. *Exit* VITELLI.
　　Aga.　　　　　　　　Prethee *Manto*
How hath the vnfortunate Princes spent this night
Vnder her proud new mistresse?
　　Manto.　　　　　　With such patience
As it orecomes the others insolence,
Nay triumphs ore her pride. My much hast now
Commands me hence, but the sad Tragedy past,
Ile giue you satisfaction to the full
Of all hath pass'd, and a true character
Of the proud Christians nature. *Exit* MANTO.
　　Aga.　　　　　　Breake the watch vp,
What should we feare in the midst of our owne strengths?
Tis but the Bashas iealousie. Farewell souldiers. *Exeunt.*

Actus Quintus. Scæna Septima.

Enter VITELLI, *with the bak't-meates, aboue.*

Vitelli. There's something more in this then meanes to cloy
A hungry appetite, which I must discouer.
Shee will'd me search the midst. Thus, thus I pierce it:
Ha! what is this? a scrole bound vp in packthread?
What may the misterie be?

The Scrole.

Sonne, let downe this packethread, at the West window of the
Castle. By it you shall draw vp a Ladder of ropes, by which you may
descend. Your deerest *Donusa* with the rest of your friends, below
attend you. Heauen prosper you. *Francisco.*

O best of men! he that giues vp himselfe
To a true religious friend, leanes not vpon
A false deceiuing reede, but boldly builds
Vpon a rocke, which now with ioy I finde
In reuerend *Francisco*, whose good vowes,
Labors, and watchings in my hopd-for freedome
Appeare a pious miracle. I come,
I come, good man, with confidence; though the descent
Were steepe as hell, I know I cannot slide,
Beeing cal'd downe, by such a faithfull guide. *Exit* VITELLI.

Actus Quintus, Scæna Vltima.

ASAMBEG, MUSTAPHA, *Ianizaries.*

Asambeg. Excuse me *Mustapha*, though this night to me
Appeare as tedious as that treble one
Was to the world, when *Ioue* on faire *Alcmena*
Begot *Alcides*. Were you to encounter
Those rauishing pleasures, which the slow pac'd howres   5
(To me they are such) bar me from, you would
With your continued wishes striue to impe
New feathers to the broken wings of Time
And chide the amorous Sun, for too long dalliance
In *Thetis* watry bosome.
   Mustapha.   You are to violent   10
In your desires, of which you are yet vncertaine,
Hauing no more assurance to enioy 'em
Then a weake womans promise, on which wisemen
Faintely relye.
   Asambeg.   Tush, she is made of truth,
And what she says she will doe, holds as firme   15
As laws in brasse that know no change; what's this? *The chamber*
Some new prize broght in sure.   *shot off.*

Enter AGA.

                      Why are thy looks
So ghastly? Villaine speake.
   Aga.   Great sir heare me
Then after kill me: we are all betrayde,
The false *Grimaldi* suncke in your disgrace,   20
With his confederates, haue seas'd his ship
And those that garded it stow'd vnder hatches.
With him the condemn'd Princesse, and the Marchant
That with a ladder made of ropes descended
From the blacke Tower in which he was inclos'd,   25
And your fayre mistresse,
   Asambeg.   Ha!
   Aga.   With all their trayne
And choysest iewels are gone safe aboard,

V. viii. 16. what's this] *30²*; what' this *30¹*

Their sayles spread forth and with a fore-right gale
Leauing our cost. In scorne of all pursuite
As a farewell they shew'd a broad side to vs. 30
   Asambeg. No more.
   Mustapha.   Now note your confidence.
   Asambeg.   No more.
O my credulity! I am too full
Of griefe, and rage to speake. Dull, heauy foole
Worthy of all the tortures that the frowne
Of thy incensed Master can throw on thee! 35
Without one mans compassion, I will hide
This head among the desarts, or some caue
Fil'd with my shame and me, where I alone
May dye without a partner in my mone.   *Exeunt.*

FINIS.

28. fore-right gale] *Massinger MS*; fore-gale *30*

THE PARLIAMENT OF LOVE

INTRODUCTION

(a) *Date, Authorship and Text*

The Parliament of Love was licensed by Sir Henry Herbert on 3 November 1624. As recorded by G. Chalmers in his extracts from the office-book in his *Supplemental Apology*, 1799, the licence ran:

3 November. For the Cockpit Company; A new Play, called, The Parliament of Love: Written by Massinger.[1]

The play was not published in Massinger's lifetime. A manuscript of the play (the title is written on the back of the last leaf) almost certainly dating from the time of the first production, or intended production, and possibly the actual copy submitted to Herbert for licensing,[2] came into Malone's hands and in 1803 was lent by him to Gifford,[3] who transcribed it for the first publication of the play in the 1805 edition. This manuscript may have been the same as that which Moseley owned when he entered the play for publication on 29 June 1660 (Greg, *Bibliography*, i. 69); the ascription of the play in the Stationers' Register to William Rowley means little, for then as now the manuscript may have lacked any mention of the author's name.[4] Warburton's claim that *The Parliament of Love* was one of the manuscripts which he had owned and which had been destroyed is of uncertain value (see General Introduction, vol. i, p. xxvi).

---

[1] See Adams, *Herbert*, p. 30. A second and perhaps closer transcript of Herbert's entry is in J. O. Halliwell-Phillips's scrap-books in the Folger Library, Washington: 'For the Cock: comp: A new P. call: The Parlam^t. of Love writt: by Massinger 3^d Novr. 1624. l^{li}' (Bentley, iv. 806).

[2] A piece which is usually assumed to have contained Herbert's signature and licence has been cut out of folio 19 below the word '*finis*'.

[3] See the Malone Society reprint of the play, by K. M. Lea and W. W. Greg, 1928 (1929), for the full details of the transmission of the manuscript so far as they can now be ascertained.

[4] C. W. Stork believed that Rowley was responsible for the Leonora–Cleremond story; see his edition of Rowley's *All's Lost by Lust*, 1910, pp. 50–1.

The manuscript is now in the Dyce collection at the Victoria and Albert Museum, South Kensington. Part of the first act is missing and portions of the text throughout the play have been lost through the crumbling away of the lower part of the sheets, probably caused by damp at some stage. It was noted in the Malone Society reprint (pp. xi, xii)[1] that the handwriting was the same as that of the manuscript of Dekker's *The Welsh Ambassador*, which is also damaged at the foot of the leaves, and it was conjectured that both manuscripts were prepared by the same scribe for the same company, were stored together and suffered from the same damp conditions. There is good evidence for dating *The Welsh Ambassador* about 1623 (Bentley, iii. 267).

After copying *The Welsh Ambassador*, the scribe went through the play again, preparing it for stage use by adding warning notes for entries ('bee redy winchester') and directions for flourishes.[2] *The Parliament of Love* was not so treated, though a second person went through the latter part of the play making alterations in the interests of clarity, brevity, and modesty (see, e.g., notes to IV. ii. 4–11, V. i. 120–36, V. i. 293–5).

It is not clear how much of the first act of *The Parliament of Love* is missing. In a note at the beginning of the play as it now is, Gifford suggested that 'two or three scenes' had gone:

> One must have taken place between Chamont and Beaupré, in which the latter disclosed her history; another, perhaps, between Cleremond and Leonora; the assemblage of the 'guests' at Bellisant's house probably formed a third, and the present conference, in which she quits her guests, to attend on Chamont, may be the fourth.

Chelli adds that Montross's suit to Bellisant must have been introduced (*Le Drame de Massinger*, p. 129). McIlwraith (i. 287–8) observed that the extant text is approximately 2,122 lines, and that neighbouring plays, *The Renegado* and *A New Way to Pay Old Debts*, are 2,332 and 2,266 lines.

The damage at the foot of the pages presents many problems.[3] Gifford supplies much more in his text than is now legible; some of

---

[1] See also W. W. Greg, *Dramatic Documents from the Elizabethan Playhouses*, 1931, p. 282.

[2] See the Malone Society reprint of the play, by H. Littledale and W. W. Greg, 1920, and Dekker, *Works*, ed. Bowers, vol. iv.

[3] A conjectural reconstruction made by F. G. Waldron in 1805 of what is missing was reprinted 'as a curiosity' in the Malone Society reprint.

Introduction

what he gives may have been invented or indeed misread, but some of it may be genuine because the manuscript was undoubtedly in a better state in his day than it is now; the present text gives a certain amount of this material as conjectural readings within pointed brackets. At times it is very hard to decide how many lines have been lost at the foot of a page. In general, the present edition accepts McIlwraith's estimate, though folios 13 verso and 15 recto are problematic. McIlwraith appears to have made a mistake in supposing that 2½ lines were missing from the foot of folio 16 verso. There is space only for one extra line, and the sense (suggested by Gifford's reading) does not require more.

Because the manuscript of *The Parliament of Love* is not in Massinger's hand, and because there is in the Malone Society reprint a faithful transcription of the original, it has been decided to use in this edition the general lines of the editorial principles laid down and followed by F. T. Bowers for *The Welsh Ambassador* in his edition of Dekker. The play, that is to say, is printed in the way a seventeenth-century compositor might have printed it from the existing manuscript, and the general conventions of the present edition for printed texts have been followed.

No attempt is made to print or record the scribe's deletions since these are all false starts and errors and have no textual importance. Alterations made silently are as follows. Capital letters are supplied at the beginning of lines and speeches and for names. Names of persons and places are italicized whether or not they are differentiated in the manuscript. The scribe's capital forms of a, c, i, l, n, p, r, s, t, which are indiscriminately and arbitrarily used at the beginnings of words are all silently reduced. Abbreviations are expanded silently unless there is a possibility of error, when the original is recorded. Final ſ has been read as s. Speech-headings and stage directions are treated in the usual manner of this edition, except that editorial '[*Aside*.]' is added silently.

All other departures from the manuscript are recorded either in the textual notes or the table of running corections. Punctuation in the original manuscript is very light indeed, and ease of understanding demanded a liberal additional supply; all changes and additions are recorded, including those at the end of speeches.

The text which follows is based on the transcript which McIlwraith made in 1927. He checked his transcript twice: against the Malone Society reprint in 1929, and then against the manuscript in the same year. All discrepancies between McIlwraith and the Malone Society reprint have been checked against the manuscript, and a table of corrections to the Malone Society reprint is appended (p. 177). Pointed brackets are used where the manuscript is defective; the manuscript is now illegible to the left of ⟩ and to the right of ⟨ ; readings inside a pointed bracket are conjectural.

In the textual footnotes, the sigla '*MS*' refer to the original manuscript, 'Lea' to the Malone Society reprint.

(b) *Sources*

The Parliament of Love, wrote Gifford, was 'founded upon those celebrated Courts or Parliaments of Love, said to be holden in France during the twelfth, thirteenth, and fourteenth centuries, for the discussion of amorous questions, and the distribution of rewards and punishments among faithful and perfidious lovers' (1813 edition, ii. 237). Gifford recognized that the tradition was more literary than real. Debate and judgement in matters of love are spread wide through European literature, entering with the dawn of *amour courtois* but continuing long after its disappearance; generally the cases were questions of interpretation of the higher niceties of the code of courtly love; evidence that courts were ever really held is slight.[1]

A recent example of the tradition in English drama which Massinger may well have known was Marston's *Parasitaster, or The Fawn* (1604–6, published 1606); the similarity was first noted by Koeppel, p. 105. Like Massinger, Marston ended his play with a formal 'Cupid's parliament' in which those who had offended against the laws of Cupid (by being jealous, or deceitful, or impotent, or by boasting untruthfully of favours received, and so on) were arraigned and punished. While Marston does not go in for moral earnestness, the way in which each dramatist introduces his court of love with a speech on the abuse of love in degenerate times is worth comparing (*The Fawn*, V. i. 180–95; *Parliament of Love*, V. i. 42–68).

In planning *The Parliament of Love*, Massinger certainly used the popular *Les Arrêts d'amour* attributed to Martial d'Auvergne. Again, Koeppel was the first to note the indebtedness. Jean Rychner's

---

[1] See W. A. Neilson, *The Origins and Sources of the 'Court of Love'*, Harvard Studies in Philology and Literature, vol. vi, 1899.

Introduction

scholarly edition for the Société des Anciens Textes Français (1951) accepts Martial d'Auvergne's authorship of *Les Arrêts* and dates them between 1460 and 1466. Martial was not an original writer: he borrowed largely from the cycle of writings associated with *Belle dame sans merci* at Charles VI's court dating from about 1424 (among these is a *Parlement d'amour* by Baudet Herence). In these writings there was a full elaboration of the idea of a really judicial court of love where complainants and defendants argued their cases and where judgements were given and sentences meted out. Martial d'Auvergne borrowed the apparatus and wrote 51 *arrêts*, or descriptions of particular cases with the judgements (in the 35 editions between 1500 and 1734 there are many variations in the title and the number of cases). Massinger may not have read far into the book, but he certainly used the first case for his story of Clarindor's wooing of Bellisant. Martial's case was against a man who had got his mistress's favour by threatening to kill himself. He first pretended to be mortally ill and won a kiss, but his mistress extricated herself. He then came to her house in disguise, like Clarindor (III. iii. 10) and threatened to kill himself (*cf.* III. iii. 106). The lady 'fut contrainte de luy souffrir accomplir sa mauvaise voulenté' (*cf.* III. iii. 137–50). Following his victory, the defendant, like Clarindor (IV. v. 163–71) went off to brag to his acquaintance that by a trick he had managed to succeed where everyone else had failed. Massinger has added to Martial's story the 'substituted bride' element familiar from *All's Well that Ends Well* and *Measure for Measure*.[1]

A number of the names in the play come straight from *The Little French Lawyer*, written by Fletcher and Massinger at some date between May 1619 and May 1623: Dinant, Cleremond, Beaupré, Lamira. The borrowing was first commented on by Gifford (1805 edition, ii. 286). Massinger also repeated in the later play some of the duelling material from *The Little French Lawyer*, though the closeness of the relation between the two plays was exaggerated by E. E. Stoll (see below). Massinger had previously used the name Novall in *The Fatal Dowry*.

Gifford pointed out that the French court supposed to witness

---

[1] H. D. Sykes in *NQ*, 11th Series, vol. x, 8 Aug. 1914, argued that the wooing of Clarindor was borrowed from Chapman's *The Widow's Tears*; there *is* a boisterous wooer in *The Widow's Tears*, and he *is* thrown out once, but there is no real link between the plays.

the parliament of love was meant to be that of Charles VIII, because of the reference in I. b. 2–5 to the king's return from his campaigns in Italy, including his victories over Rome and Florence. Charles VIII came back from Italy (less unequivocally triumphant than Massinger's monarch) in late 1495. Though the play is completely unhistorical, Massinger had some slight justification for fathering the rituals of the play onto Charles VIII. Commines, for example, writes in his history (Book VIII, chapter 16; Tudor Translations, ii. 342):

> That happened from the Kings returne out of Italie (which was about 3 or 4 moneths before the end of the yeere 1495,) till the beginning of the yeere 1498, I have alreadie rehearsed ... The King rode about from Lyons to Moulins, and from Moulins to Tours, holding tourneies and justs in all places, and minding nothing else.

A further indebtedness of Massinger to Marston has been widely discussed. This time the play is *The Dutch Courtesan* (1603–4) and the relevant part of *The Parliament of Love* is the story of Leonora and Cleremond. The link between the two plays is complicated by the existence of a closely-related version of the story in *A Cure for a Cuckold*, by Webster and Rowley, date unknown. There are systematic studies of the relation between the three plays in E. E. Stoll's *John Webster*, 1905, pp. 162–71, Rupert Brooke's *John Webster and the Elizabethan Drama*, 1916, pp. 255–69, and F. L. Lucas, *Complete Works of John Webster*, iii. 3–9.

The kernel of the story as it is told by Marston and by his source, Montreulx's *Les Bergeries de Juliette*, and by Painter in the novella of the Countess of Celant,[1] which was formerly thought to be the source, is that a woman (A), angry at being cast off by her former lover (B), uses the infatuation of his friend (C) to encompass her revenge, getting C to promise to kill B. In *The Dutch Courtesan*, Freevill surrenders his courtesan to his friend Malheureux, who has fallen in love with her. She is furious at being discarded and tells Malheureux that she will grant him her love if he kills Freevill. Malheureux tells Freevill, and they resolve to trick the courtesan by pretending that the killing has been carried out. When she hears that Freevill is dead, the courtesan betrays Malheureux to the authorities. Finally, Freevill reveals himself.

A Cure for a Cuckold and *The Parliament of Love* are linked

---

[1] Painter, *Palace of Pleasure*, ii. 24, from Bandello, i. 4.

Introduction

together by an episode not in Marston. In both plays, the would-be lover does not confess his mission to his friend, but tries to get him to act as his second in a fictitious duel. The friend consents, showing the quality of his friendship by forgoing an important engagement with his bride/mistress. On arriving at the duelling ground, the friend wonders where their opponents are. The lover explains that he is going to kill him, but the combat does not take place.

The question is whether Massinger borrowed all this from Webster or *vice versa*. Stoll thought that Massinger must have come first, on the grounds that Webster did not have the power to originate this new material, and that in *The Little French Lawyer* Massinger tried out the moral design of the duel which, by inverting the details, he improved on in *The Parliament of Love*. Rupert Brooke was rightly unconvinced by Stoll's arguments, but, though he wondered about an intermediate source from which both Webster and Massinger independently drew, he accepted Stoll's conclusion that Massinger's was the earlier work, as did Lucas.

There is an important reason for arguing that in fact Massinger followed Webster, and took his story from both Webster and Marston.

If we take the essential paradigm as woman (A) inducing would-be lover (C) to kill former lover (B), we see that Webster's play has a very confused complication of this. Clare (A) says to Lessingham (C):

> Prove all thy friends, find out the best and nearest,
> Kill for my sake that Friend that loves thee dearest.

Lessingham goes to each of his friends to ask him to second him in the duel, but the only one to agree to help is Bonvile, whom we may call B though the relation between him and A is simply that Clare is silently and desperately in love with him. Clare is horrified to learn (it is not true, of course) that Bonvile is dead; by 'that Friend that loves thee dearest', she had meant (she says) ... herself! Rupert Brooke in his intelligent discussion points out that Clare must have intended this absurdity and could not have intended that Bonvile should die, because she could not have known that he would prove to be Lessingham's most trustworthy friend.

In Massinger, the relation between A and C is quite different, and there is no former lover, B. Leonora (A) rejects Cleremond (C) for having tried to seduce her, and she hates him. He still pleads for her love; he promises to do *anything* she asks. She laughs at him: 'Thou art caught!' (II. ii. 131) and rehearses the possible ways of punishing him. She finally tells him to 'kill the best deserver' among 'the number of thie trustie faithfull freinds' (II. ii. 154, 151). We do not see Cleremond soliciting his friends, he merely reports none too clearly (III. ii. 29–36) that of the many who profess to be his friends 'not one indures the test'. Then Montross, who stands in no relation to Leonora, agrees to forgo his all-important tryst with Bellisant in order to help Cleremond.

It seems a rational progression (i) that Webster bent the original triangle of A getting C to kill B by weakening the relation between A and B and introducing the delphic command to kill 'Friend', who turns into B; (ii) that Massinger collapsed the triangle altogether by seeing in this new element of Webster's, 'kill your best friend', a suitably prohibitive task for a malicious woman to impose, and by using it in a situation where there is no former lover at all. It is very hard to see the story developing in the reverse direction, to think that Webster could have taken Massinger's couple, and the unaimed order to kill, and then have partially restored the original triangle. To accept that the order is Marston–Webster–Massinger makes Massinger's omission of the testing of the friends more understandable; it is what the later dramatist is more likely to omit than to add. There are difficulties in this order, however, and we have to believe that Massinger went back independently to Marston for the conclusion in which the woman accuses the would-be lover of murder.

It is impossible in the end to be certain of more than that one of the two plays, *Cure for a Cuckold* and *Parliament of Love*, depends on the other; the similarity is too great for coincidence, and the likelihood of a lost intermediate version is small. Which ever way the dependence was, each dramatist has created what is essentially a new story by giving a different motivation to the woman who commands a killing. In Marston it is jealousy; in Webster it is despair; in Massinger it is sheer hate. In Massinger the command to murder becomes a punishment solely for the murderer without a thought for the victim; his alteration makes for a grim primitiveness not found in his colleagues, and illustrates once more the truth that the value of studying sources is to establish differences.

(c) *Stage history*

There is no record of *The Parliament of Love* having been acted, either in its own time or since. The fact that the manuscript, unlike that of *The Welsh Ambassador*, bears no sign of preparation for stage use may make one ask whether the play ever reached the stage of the Cockpit—but again, there is no evidence that the play, licensed for the stage, was not then performed.

THE
PARLIAMENT OF LOVE

[THE PERSONS PRESENTED

Charles, *king of France.*
Orleans } *dukes.*
Nemures }
Philamor } *councillors.*
Lafort }

Chamont, *a nobleman.*
Montross, *in love with* Bellisant.
Cleremond, *in love with* Leonora.
Clarindor }
Perigot } *philanderers.*
Novall }
Dinant, *court-physician.*

Bellisant, *a rich young noblewoman.*
Leonora.
Lamira, *wife to* Chamont.
Clarinda, *wife to* Dinant.
Beaupré, *wife to* Clarindor, *disguised as* Calista, *a Moor.*

Officer of the Court.
Servant *to* Bellisant.
Servant *to* Leonora.
2 Servants *to* Chamont.

Priest of Cupid, courtiers, servants.]

The Parliament of Love

[CHAMONT, BELLISANT.]

[*Chamont.*] . . . .
I did dischardge the trust imposd vppon mee
Beinge your guardian.
    Bellisant.   Tis with thancks acknowledgd.
    Chamont. The loue I then bore to you, and desire
To doe you all good offices of a freind,
Contynewes with mee, nay increases lady,   5
And out of this assurance I presume
What from a true hart I shall now deliuer
Will meet a gentle censure.
    Bellisant.   When you speake
Whatere the subiect bee I gladlie heare.
    Chamont. To tell you of the greatnes of your state   10
And from what noble stock you are derivd
Weare but impertinence and a comon theame,
Since you well know both. What I am to speake of
Touches you neerer; therefore giue mee leaue
To saie that how soeuer your greate bounties,   15
Continuall feastinge, princelike entertainements,
May gaine you the opinion of some few
Of a braue and generous sperrit (which is the best
Harvest you can hope for such costlie seede)
You cannot yett amonge the multitude   20
(Since next vnto the princes of the blood
The eyes of all are fixd on you) but giue
Some wound (which will not close without a scarr)
To your faire reputation and good name
In sufferinge such a crew of riotous gallants,   25
Not of the best repute, to bee so frequent
Both in your howse and presence; this tis rumerd
Little agrees with the curiousnes of honor

        I. a. 8. meet] *Gifford*; mee *MS*

Or modesty of a maid.
    Bellisant.   Not to dwell longe
Vppon my answer, I must thanck your goodnes
And provident care that haue instructed mee
What my revenues are, by which I measure
How farr I may expend, and yet I find not
That I begin to waste, nor would I ad
To what I now possesse; I am my self,
And for my fame, since I am inocent heere,
This for the worlds opinion.
    Chamont.   Take heede madam.
That opinion which you slight confirmes
This lady for imodest and proclaimes
Annother virtuous, where as the first
Nere knew what loose thoughts weare and the praisd second
Had never a could dreame.
    Bellisant.   I dare not argue,
But what meanes to prevent this?
    Chamont.   Noble marriage.
    Bellisant. Pardon mee sir, and doe not thinck I scorne
Your graue advise which I haue euer followd
Tho not pleasd int,
Would you haue mee match with wealth? I neede it not;
Or hunt for honor and increase of tytles?
In truth I rest ambitious of noe greater
Then what my father left; or doe you iudge
My blood to runne so high that tis not in
Phisick to coole mee? I yet feele noe such heate,
But when against my will it growes vppon mee,
Ile thinck vppon your counsell.
    Chamont.   Yf you resolue then
To liue a virgin you haue tw⟨
To which you may retire and ho⟨
Of s⟨   ⟩ke you⟨   ⟩liud to⟨
In sa⟨intel⟩ike contem⟨pl⟩ation⟨
And liue or ages w⟨
    Bellisant.   ⟨T⟩en ⟨ty⟩mes⟨

---

38. That] *MS*; That world's *Gifford*   40. virtuous] *conj. Lea*; for imodest *MS*; for a modest *Gifford*   55. tw⟨] *reading doubtful* (*McIlwraith*)   57. liud] *reading doubtful* (*McIlwraith*); loud *Lea*

⟨   ⟩   60
Should I giue of my continence if I liu'd
Not seene or seinge any? Spartan *Hellen*,
Corinthian *Lays*, or *Romes Messaline*,
So mu'de vpp might haue dy'd as they weare borne,
By lust vntempted; noe, it is the glory   65
Of chastety to bee tempted, tempted home to,
The honor else is nothinge. I would bee
The first example to convince for lyers
Those poets that with sharpe and bitter rymes
Proclaimes alowd that chastety has noe beinge   70
But in a cottage, and so confident
I am in this to conquer, that I will
Expose my self to all assaults, see maskes
And heare bewitchinge sonnetts, change discourse
With one that for experience could teach *Ouid*   75
To write a better waie his art of loue,
Feede high, and take and giue free entertainement,
Lend *Cupid* eyes and new artillery,
Denie his mother for a deitie,
Yet euery burninge shot hee made at mee,   80
Meetinge with my chaste thoughts, should loose theire ardor;
Which when I haue orecome, malitious men
Must to theire shame confesse tis possible
For a younge lady (some saie faire) at Court
To keepe her virgin honor.
 Chamont.   May you prosper   85
In this greate vndertakinge; Ile not vse
A sillable to divert you, but must bee
A suiter in annother kind.
 Bellisant.   What ere it bee,
Tis graunted.
 Chamont. Tis only to accept
A present from mee.
 Bellisant.   Call you this a suite?   90
 Chamont. Come in *Caliste.*

    Enter BEAUPRÉ *like a More.*

       This is one I would
Bestow vppon you.

The Parliament of Love

Bellisant.   Tis the hansomest
I ere saw of her cuntry; shee hath neither
Thick lips nor rough curld haire.
   Chamont.   Her manners lady
Vppon my honnor better her good shape;   95
Shee speakes our language to, for beinge surprisd
In *Barbarie*, shee was bestowd vppon
A pirat of *Marselles*, with whose wife
Shee liu'd five yeares and learnt it; there I bought her
As pittyinge her hard vsage; yf you please   100
To make her yours, you maie.
   Bellisant.   With many thancks.
Come heather pritty one; feare not, thou shalt finde mee
A gentle mistress.
   Beaupré.   With my care and service
Ile study to preserve you such.
   Bellisant.   Well answerd.
Come follow mee, wee'l instantlie to Court   105
And take my guests alonge.
   Chamont.   They waite you madam.   *Exeunt.*

[I. b]   *Enter* CHARLES, ORLEANS, PHILAMOR,
              [NEMURES] *and* LAFORT.

   Charles. What sollitude does dwell about our court!
Whie this dull entertainement? Haue I marchd
Victorious through *Italie*, enterd *Rome*
Like a trivmphant conquerer, sett my foote
Vppon the neck of *Florence*, tamd the pride   5
Of t⟨he⟩ V⟨e⟩net⟨ians,⟩ scourgd those petty Tyrants
           ⟩den of the world to bee
           ⟩me nay my howse neglected
           ⟩the courtiers would appeare
           ⟩fore they presumd   10
           ⟩the ladies sir
                ⟩had tyme
                ⟩ke choyce
⟨   ⟩

   106. guests] *Gifford*; guesse *MS*   I. b. SD. NEMURES] *Gifford* (NEMOURS);
not in *MS*

[*Enter* BELLISANT, LEONORA, LAMIRA, CLARINDA;
CHAMONT, MONTROSS, CLEREMOND, CLARINDOR,
PERIGOT, NOVALL *and other courtiers.*]

 Philamor. Heere they come.
 Ladies.   All happines to your Majestie!
 Courtiers. And victorie sitt euer on your sword!
 Charles. Our thancks to all.
But wherefore come you in devided troopes
As if the mistresses would not accept
Theire servants guardship, or the servants slighted
Refuse to offer it? You all weare sad lookes;
In *Perigot* appeares not that blunt mirth
Which his face vsd to promise, on *Montrosse*
There hanges a heavie dulnes, *Cleremond*
Droopes euen to death, and *Clarindore* hath lost
Much of his sharpnes; nay theis ladys to,
Whose sparklinge eyes did vse to fyer the Court
With various inventions of delight,
Part with theire splendor; whats the cause? from whence
Proceeds this alteration?
 Perigot.   I am trobled
With the tooth ach, or with loue, I know not whether;
There is a worme in both.
 Clarindor.   It is theire pride.
 Bellisant. Or your vnworthines.
 Cleremond.   The honor that
The French dames held for curtesie, aboue
All ladies of the earth, dwells not in theis
That glorie in theire cruelty.
 Leonora.   The desert
The chevaleers of *Fraunce* weare trulie lords of,
And which your grandsires really did possesse,
At noe part you inherritt.
 Bellisant.   Ere they durst
Presume to offer service to a lady,
In person they performd some gallant acts
The fame of which prepard them gratious hearinge,
Ere they made there approches; what coy shee then,

  14 SD. *Enter* BELLISANT ... *courtiers.*] *Gifford; not in MS*

Tho greate in birth, not to bee paralelld
For natures liberall bounties, both sett of 45
With fortunes trappings, wealth, but with delight
Gladly acknowledgd such a man her servant,
To whose heroicque courage and deepe wisdome
The florishinge Comon wealth, and thanckfull kinge
Confessd them selues for debtors? Whereas now, 50
Yf you haue travelld *Italie* and brought home
Some remnants of the language and can sett
Your faces in some strange, and nere seene posture,
Daunce a lavolto, and bee rude and sawcy,
Protest and sweare and dam, (for theis are arts 55
That most thinck grace them) and then view yourselues
In the deceavinge mirror of self loue,
You doe conclude theire hardlie is a woman
That can bee worthie of you.
  Montross.   Wee would graunt
Wee are not equall to our ancestors 60
In noble vndertakinges, yf wee thought
In vs a free confession would perswade you
Not to deny your owne most wilfull errors:
And where you tax vs for vnactiue lady,
I never knew a souldier yet that could 65
Arive into your favour; wee may suffer
The winters frost, and scorchinge summers heate,
When the hott lyons breath singeth the feilds,
To seeke out victorie, yet at our retorne,
Tho honord in our manly wounds well tak⟨en, 70
You saie they doe deforme vs, and the lo⟨sse
Of much blood that waie renders vs ⟨vnable
To please you in your chambers.
  Clarindor.   I must speake
A little in the generall cause yo⟨
Are charmes⟨ ⟩at doe inch⟨ 75
⟨ ⟩
But when that wee are fast and in your toyles,
In which to struggle or strive to breake out
Increases the captivitie, neuer *Circe*,
Sated with such shee purposd to transforme, 80
Or cuninge Siren, for whose fatall musique

Naught but the hearers death could satisfie,
Knew lesse of pitty; nay, I dare goe farther
And iustifie your majesty hath lost
More resolute and braue coragious sperrits
In this same dull and languishinge fight of loue
Then ere your warrs tooke from you.
    Charles.   Noe reply.
This is a cause wee will determyne of
And suddainely redresse: tam'd *Italie*
With feare confesses mee a war like kinge,
And *Fraunce* shall boaste I am a prince of loue.
Shall wee that keepe perpetuall parliaments
For petty suits, or the least iniury
Offerd the goods or bodies of our subiects,
Not studie a cure for the sicknes of the mynd,
Whose venemous contagion hath infected
Our brauest servants and the choycest bewties
Our court is proud of? Theis are wounds require
A kingelie surgion, and the honor worthie
By vs to bee accepted.
    Philamor.   It would ad
To the rest of your greate actions.
    Lafort.   But the meanes
Most difficult I feare.
    Chamont.   You shall doe more sir,
Yf you performe this, then I ere could reade
The sonnes of *Saturne*, that by lott devided
The gouernment of the ayre, the sea and hell,
Had sperit to vndertake.
    Charles.   Whie this more fires mee,
And now partake of my designe. With speede
Erect a place of iustice neere the court,
Which weel haue stild the parliament of loue:
Heere such whose humble service not considerd
By theire proud mistresses freely may complaine,
And shall haue hearinge and redresse.
    Novall.   Oh rare!
    Perigot. I like this well.
    Charles.   And ladies that are wrongd
By such as doe professe them selues theire servants,

May cite them heather and, theire cause deliuerd 115
Or by theire owne tongues or feed advocates,
Finde suddaine satisfaction.
   Novall.   What a rascall
Was I to leaue the law! I might haue had
Clyents and clyents; nere was such a tyme
For anie smoth chind advocate.
   Perigot.   They will gett the start 120
Of the ladies spruce phisitians, starue theire chaplaines,
Tho never so well tymberd.
   Charles.   Tis our will,
Nor shall it bee disputed. Of this court,
Or rather sanctuarie, of poore louers,
My lords of *Orleans* and *Nemures* assisted 125
By the messeures *Philamor* and *Lafort* are iudges.
You haue worne *Venus* cullers from your youth
And cannot therefore but bee sencible
Of all her misteries; what you shall determyne
In the waie of pennance, punishment or reward 130
Sha⟨ll be au⟩thenticall; a moneth wee graunt you
        yo⟩ur soft amors, which expird
          ⟩your complaints and bee assurd
          ⟩iall hearinge, this determynd
          ⟩affaires.   *Exeunt.*

⟨*Finis Actus*⟩ *Primi*

Actus Secundus

Enter CLARINDOR, MONTROSS, PERIGOT, *and* NOVALL.

   Perigot. I DOE not rellish the last parte of the kings speech
Tho I was much taken with the first.
   Novall.   Your reason tutor?
   Perigot. Whie looke you pupill, the decree that women
Should not neglect the service of theire louers
But paie them from th' exchequer they weare borne with, 5
Was good and laudable, they beinge created
To bee both tractable and tactable

      117-18. rascall / Was I to] *Gifford*; MS *reads* rascall was I / to

When they are vsefull; but to haue it orderd
All women that haue stombled in the darke
Or given by owlelight favors, should complaine,
Is most intollerable; I myself shall haue,
Of such as trade in the streetes, and scapd my pockets,
Of progresse landresses and market women,
When the kings pleasures knowne, a thowsand bills
Preferd against mee.
   Clarindor.   This is out of season,
Nothinge to madam *Bellisant* that in publique
Hath so enveighd against vs.
   Novall.   Shees a fury,
I dare noe more attempt her.
   Perigot.   Ile not venter
To change six words with her for half her state,
Or staie, till shee bee trymd, from wine and women
For anie new monopolie.
   Montross.   I will studie
How to forgett her, shunn the temptinge poyson
Her lookes and magicque of discourse still offer,
And bee my self againe; since theres noe hope,
Tweare madnes to pursue her.
   Perigot.   There are madams
Better brought vpp tis thought, and wiues that dare not
Complaine in parliament, theres safe tradinge pupill;
And when shee finds shee is of all forsaken,
Lett my lady Pride repent in vaine, and mumpe,
And envie others marketts.
   Clarindor.   May I nere prosper
But you are three of the most faintinge sperrits
That euer I conversd with; you doe well
To talke of lawndresses, progresse puncks and beggers,
The wife of some rich tradesman with three teeth
And twice so manie haires: truck with ould ladies
Whome nature hath given ore, that owe theire docters
For an artificiall life, that are so frozen
That a sound plague cannot thaw them, but dispaire,
I giue you ore, but never hope to take
A velvet petticoate vpp, or to comitt

      II. i. 39. but] *MS*; **omitted** *Gifford*

With an Italian cutwork smock, when torne too.
   Montross. And what hopes norish you?
   Clarindor.   Troath, myne are modest:
I am onlie confident to win the lady
You dare not looke on, and now in the hight
Of her contempt and scorne to humble her   45
And teach her at what game her mother plaid
When she was gott; and cloyd with those poore toyes,
As I finde her obedient and pleasinge,
I may perhaps descend to marry her.
Then with a kinde of state I take my chaire,   50
Comaund a suddaine muster of my servants,
And after two or three maiestick hums,
It beinge knowne all is myne per v⟨
Lett out this manner at an easie re⟨nt
To such a freind, lend this ten tho⟨usand crowns   55
For the redemption of his m⟨
Give to each by blow I know⟨
       ⟩e⟨

fol. 3ᵛ That pleasd mee in my youth, but now growne stale.
Theis things first orderd by mee, and confirmd   60
By *Bellisant* my wife, I care not much
Yf out of her owne lands I doe assigne her
Some petty ioynture.
   Perigot.   Talkest thou in thie sleepe?
   Novall. Or art thou mad?
   Clarindor.   A little ellevated
With the assurance of my future fortune.   65
Whie doe you stare and grin? I know this must bee
And I will lay three thowsand crownes, within
A moneth I will effect this.
   Montross.   How?
   Clarindor.   Giue proofe
I haue enioyd faire *Bellisant*, evident proofe
I haue pluckd her virgin rose so long preservd,   70
Not like a play trick with a chaine or ringe
Stolne by corruption, but against her will
Make her confesse so much.
   Montross.   Impossible!
   Clarindor. Then the disgrace bee myne, the proffit yours;

II. i. 75–ii. 11   *The Parliament of Love*   119

Yf that you thinck her chastety a rock   75
Not to bee mou'd or shaken, or hold mee
A flatterer of my self, or ouerweener,
Lett mee paie for my foolery.
    Perigot.   Ile ingage
My self for a thowsand.
    Novall.   Ile not out for a second.
    Montross. I would gladlie loose a third parte for assurance   80
Noe virgin can stand constant longe.
    Clarindor.   Leaue that
To the tryall, lett vs to a notarie,
Draw the conditions, see the crownes deposited,
And then I will not crye *St Denis for mee*
But *Loue, blynd archer, aide mee.*
    Perigot.   Looke thou thrive;   85
I would not bee so ieerd and hooted at
As thou wilt bee ells.
    Clarindor.   I will runne the hazzard.   *Exeunt.*

[II. ii]   *Enter* LEONORA, *and a* SERVANT.

    Servant. Hee will not bee denied.
    Leonora.   Slaue, beate him back.
I feede such whelpes—
    Servant.   Madam I rattled him,
Rattled him home.
    Leonora.   Rattle him hence you rascall
Or never see mee more.
                Enter CLEREMOND.
    Servant.   Hee comes, a sword!
What would you haue mee doe? Shall I cry murther?   5
Or raise the cunstable?
    Leonora.   Hence you shakinge coward.
    Servant. I am glad I am so gott off; heeres a round sum
For a few bitter words. Bee not shooke of sir,
Ile see none shall disturbe you.   *Exit* SERVANT.
    Cleremond.   You might spare
Theis frownes good Lady, on mee they are vselesse;   10
I am shot through and through with your disdaine,

        II. ii. 7. sum] *Gifford*; sonne *MS* (m *with 4 minims*)

And on my hart the darts of scorne so thick
That theres noe vacant place left to receaue
Annother wound; theire multitude is growne
My best defence, and doe confirme mee that
You cannot hurt mee further.
    Leonora.   We⟨re yo⟩u not
Made up⟩ of impudence and slau'd to follie,
Did any dr⟩op of noble blood remaine
In thy lustfu⟩ll vaynes, hadst thou or touch or rellish
Of modesty, civi⟩litie or manners,
Or but in thy defo⟩rmed outside onlie
Thou didst retain the⟩ essence of a m⟨an⟩
⟨   so many   ⟩
And loathinge to thie person, thou wouldst not
Force from a blushinge woman that rude language
Thie basenes first made mee acquainted with.
    Cleremond. Now saintlike patience guard mee!
    Leonora.   I haue heard
Of mountebancks that to vent theire druggs and oyles
Haue so invrd themselves to poyson that
They could digest a venomd tode or spider
Better then wholesome viands: in the list
Of such I hould thee, for that bitternes
Of speech, reproofe and scorne, by her deliuerd
Whome thou professest to adore and shake at
(Which would deter all mankind but thieself)
Doe nourish in thee sawcy hopes with pleasure.
    Cleremond. Heare but my iust defence.
    Leonora.   Yet since thou art
So spaniell like affected, and thie dotage
Increases from abuse and iniury,
That way I'le once more feast thee. Of all men
I euer saw yett, in my setled iudgment,
Spight of thie barber, tayler and perfumer
And theire adulterate and borrowed helps,
Thou art the vgliest creature, and when trymd vpp
To the hight as thou imaginst, in myne eyes
A leaper with a clapdish (to giue notice
Hee is infectious) in respect of thee
Appeares a younge *Adonis*.

Cleremond.   You looke on mee
In a falce glasse madam.
   Leonora.   Then thie dunghill mynd,
Sutable to the out side, never yet
Producd one gentle thought, knowinge her want
Of faculties to putt it into act:
Thie courtship as absurd as anie zanies
After a practizd master; thie discourse
Tho full of bumbast phrase never brought matter
Worthie the laughinge at, much lesse the hearinge.
But I grow wearie, for indeede to speake thee,
Thie ills I meane, and speake them to the full,
Would tyre a thowsand womens voluble tongues
And twice so manie lawyers; for a farwell,
Ile sooner claspe an Incubus, or hugg
A forckd tongud adder, then meete thie embraces
Which as the divell I flye from.
   Cleremond.   Now you haue spent
The vtmost of your spleene, I would not saie
Your mallice, sett of to the height with fixion,
Allow mee leaue, (a poore request, which iudges
Seldome denie vnto a man condemd)
A little to complaine, for, beinge censurd,
Or to extenuate or excuse my guilt
Weare but to wash an *Ethiop.* How oft with teares,
When the inhuman porter has forbid
My entrance by your more seveere comaund,
Haue theis eyes washd your threshold. Did there euer
Come noveltie to *Paris* rich or rare
Which but as soone as knowne was not presented,
How ere with scorne refusd? Haue I not brought
The braueries of *Fraunce* before your window
To fight at barriers, or to breake a launce,
Or in theire full careere to take the rin⟨g,   ⟩
To doe you honor? and then beinge refus⟨d
To speake my greefe, my arms, my ⟨impresses,
The cullers that I weare, in a du⟨mb sorrow
Expressd how much I sufferd ⟨in the rigour
Of your displeasure.

54. master] *editor;* m^r *MS*; manner *Gifford*   82. weare] *MS*; wore *Gifford*

Leonora. Twoe m⟨onth⟩es he⟨nc⟩e Ile⟨ ⟩
⟨   ⟩

Cleremond. Staie best madam,
I am growinge to a period.
  Leonora. Pray you doe;
I heere shall take a napp else, tis so pleasinge.
  Cleremond. Then onlie this; the voyce you now contem,
You once did sweare was musicall; you haue mett to
Theis lips in a soft encounter, and haue brought
An equall ardor with you; never liu'd
A happier paire of louers. I confesse,
After you promisd marriage, nothinge wantinge
But a few daies expird, to make mee happie,
My violent impatience of delay
Made mee presume, and with some amorous force,
To aske a full fruition of those pleasures
Which sacred *Hymen* to the world makes lawfull,
Before his torch was lighted; in this onlie
You iustly can accuse mee.
  Leonora. Darst thou thinck
That this offence can euer finde a pardon,
Vnworthie as thou art?
  Cleremond. But you most cruell
That in your studied purpose of revenge
Cast both devine and human lawes behinde you
And onlie see theire rigor, not theire mercy.
Offences of foule shap by holy writt
Are warranted remission, prouided
That the delinquent vndergoe the pennance
Imposd vppon him by his confessor,
But you that should bee myne, and onlie can
Or punish or absolue mee, are so farr
From doinge mee right that you disdaine to heare mee.
  Leonora. Now I may catch him in my longe wishd toyle; [*Aside.*]
My hate helpe mee to worke it.—To what purpose,
Poore and pale sperrited man, should I expect
From thee the satisfaction of a wronge
Compard to which the murther of a brother
Weare but a gentle iniury?
  Cleremond. Witnes heaven,

II. ii. 119–52 *The Parliament of Love* 123

All blessings by good men desir'd, all tortors
The wicked shake at, noe saint left vnsworne by, 120
That vncompelld I heere give vpp my self
Wholly to your devotion; if I faile
To doe what euer you please to comaund
To expiat my trespasse to your honor,
So that the taske performd you like wise sweare 125
First to forgiue and after marrie mee,
May I indure more sharpe and lingringe torments
Then euer tyrants found out, may my freinds
With scorne not pitty looke vppon my sufferings,
And at my last gaspe, in the place of hope 130
Horrid dispaire possesse mee.
   Leonora.   Thou art caught,
Most miserable foole, but fitt to bee so,
And tis but iustice that thou art deliuerd
Into her power thats sencible of a wronge
And glories to revenge it. Lett mee study 135
What dredfull punishment worthie my fury
I shall inflict vppon thee; all the mallice
Of iniurd women helpe mee! death? thats nothinge;
Tis to a conscious wretch a bennifitt
And not ⟨a⟩ pennance, ells on the next tree 140
For ⟨sport's s⟩ake I could make thee hange thie self.
   Cleremond. W⟨hat have⟩ I done?
   Leonora.   ⟨What cannot⟩ bee recalld.
To row for seven ye⟩ares in the Turkish gallies?
A flea-biting! To⟩ bee sould to a brothell,
Or a common bagnio?⟩ thats ⟨a t⟩r⟨i⟩f⟨le too. 145
⟨   Furies   ⟩
The lashes of theire whipps peirce through the mynde;
Ile imitate them, I haue it to.
   Cleremond.   Remember
You are a woman.
   Leonora.   I haue heard thee boast
That of all blessings in the earth next mee, 150
The number of thie trustie faithfull freinds
Made vpp thie happines; out of theis I chardge thee,

   119. desir'd, all] *McIlwraith*; are *MS*   131–2. caught, / Most] *Gifford*; *undivided MS*   147. mynde] *Gifford* (mind); mynds *MS*

And by thine owne repeated oathes coniure thee,
To kill the best deserver. Doe not start,
Ile haue noe other penance, then to practize   155
To find some meanes gainst him deserves thee best,
By vndertakinge some thinge others flie from;
This done, I am thine.
   Cleremond.   But heare mee—
   Leonora.   Not a sillable;
And till then never see mee.   *Exit.*
   Cleremond.   I am lost,
Foolishlie lost and sunck by myne owne basenes;   160
Ile say onlie,
With a hart breakinge patience, yet not raue,
Better the divells then a womans slaue.   *Exit.*

[II. iii]   *Enter* CLARINDOR *and* BEAUPRÉ.

   Clarindor. Nay prithee good *Caliste*—
   Beaupré.   As I liue sir,
Shee is determynd to bee privat, chardgd mee
Till of herself shee broke vpp her retyrements
Not to admit a visitant.
   Clarindor.   Thou art a foole
And I must haue thee learne to know thie strength;   5
There never was a sure path to the mistress
But by her ministers helpe, which I will pay for:
But yett this is but trash. Harke in thine eare:
By Loue, I like thie person and will make
Full payment that waie; bee thou wise.
   Beaupré.   Like mee sir?   10
One of my dark complexion?
   Clarindor.   I am serious;
The curtains drawne and envious light putt out,
The soft tuch hightens appetite, and takes more
Then culler, *Venus* dressinge in the daie tyme,
But neuer thought on in her midnight revells.   15
Come, I must haue thee myne.
   Beaupré.   But how to serve you?
   Clarindor. Bee speakinge still my praises to thie lady,

---

   156. gainst him] *editor;* that hee *MS*; he that *Gifford*   160-1. basenes; / Ile] *Gifford; undivided MS*

How much I loue and languish for her bounties;
You may remember to, how many madams
Are rivalls for mee, and in waie of caution   20
Saie you haue heard when I was wild how dreadfull
My name was to a professd curtesan,
Still askinge more then shee could giue.

      Enter BELLISANT.

 Beaupré.   My lady!
 Bellisant. Bee within call;—how now *Clarindore*,
Courtinge my servant? nay tis not my envie;   25
You now expresse your self a compleate louer,
That for varieties sake, if shee bee woman,
Can change discourse with anie.
 Clarindor.   All are foyles
I practize on, but when you make mee happie
In doinge mee that honor. I desird   30
To heare her speake in the morisco tongue;
Troath, tis a pritty language.
 Bellisant.   Yes, to daunce to:—
Looke to those sweetemeates.   *Exit* BEAUPRE.
 Clarindor.   How, by heauen? shee aymes
To speake with mee in privat.
 Bellisant.   Come sitt downe,
Letts haue some merry con⟨fere⟩nce.
 Clarindor.   ⟨In⟩ w⟨hich   35
⟨It   ⟩
That my whole life imployd to doe you service
At noe parte can deserve.
 Bellisant.   Yf you esteeme it
At such a rate, doe not abuse my bountie
Or coment on the graunted privacy farther   40
Then what the text may warrant; so you shall
Destroy what I haue built.
 Clarindor.   I like not this.   [*Aside.*]
 Bellisant. This new erected parliament of loue
It seemes has frighted hence my visitants;
How spend *Montrosse* and *Perigot* theire howers?   45
Novall and *Cleremond*, vanishd in a moment;

   II. iii. 33. heauen?] *editor*; ~. *MS*; ~, *Lea, Gifford*

I like your constancy yet.
   Clarindor.   Thats good againe,   [*Aside.*]
She hath restord all.—Pitty them good maddam;
The splendor of your howse and entertainement,
Inrichd with all perfections by yourself,
Is to to glorious for theire dim eyes;
You are aboue theire element, modest fooles
That onlie dare admire, and barr them from
Comparinge of theis eyes to the fairest starrs,
Givinge you *Iunos* maiesty, *Pallas* witt,
Dianas hand and *Thetis* pritty foote,
Or when you daunce to sweare that *Venus* leads
The graces so on the Idalian greene,
And such hiperboles stolne out of play bookes:
They would stand all daie mute and as you weare
Some curious picter onlie to bee lookd on,
Presume noe farther.
   Bellisant.   Pray you keepe your distance
And grow not rude.
   Clarindor.   Rude lady? manlie bouldnes
Cannot deserve that name. I haue studied you,
And Loue hath made an easie glosse vppon
The most abstruce and hidden misteries
Which you may keepe conceald; you well may praise
A bashfull suiter that is ravishd with
A feather of your fan, or if hee gaine
A ribbond from your shoe cryes out *Nil Vltra*.
   Bellisant. And what would satisfie you?
   Clarindor.   Noe such poore trifles
I can assure you lady; doe not I see
You are gamesome, younge and active? that you loue
A man that of himself comes bouldlie on,
That will not putt your modestie to troble
To teach him how to feede when meates before him,
That knowes that you are flesh and blood, a creature,
And borne with such affections, that like mee,
Now I haue oppertunitie and your favor,
Will not abuse my fortune? Should I stand now
Lickinge my fingers, cry *ay mee*—then kneele
And sweare you weare a goddesse, kisse the skirts

Of your proud garments, when I weare gon, I am sure
I should bee kindlie laughd at for a coxcombe,
The storie made the subiect of your mirth 85
At the next meetinge when you sitt in connsaile
Amonge the bewties.
   Bellisant.   Is this possible?
All due respect forgotten?
   Clarindor.   Hange respect!
Are wee not alone? See I dare touch this hand
And without adoration vngloue it; 90
A springe of youth is in this palme, heere *Cupid*,
The moysture turnd to diamonds, heads his arrowes;
The farr famd English *Bath*, or German *Spaw*,
One dropp of this will purchase. Shall this nectar
Runn⟨e⟩ vseless then to waste? or weare theis lips 95
     ⟩like the morne, breathinge perfumes
To such a⟩s dare approch them, bee vntouchd
     ⟩st (nay tis in vaine to make resistance)
     ⟩kist and tasted. You seeme angrie
     ⟩I haue ⟨displea⟩sd you.
   ⟨*Bellisant.*⟩   ⟩ 100
And come prepard as if some affrick monster
By force had broke into my howse.

Enter Seruants.

   Clarindor.   How's this?
   Bellisant. Circle him round with death, and if hee stirr
Or but presume to speake till I allow it,
His bodie bee the nauell to the wheele 105
In which your rapiers like so many spokes
Shall meete and fix them selues.
   Clarindor.   Weare I off with life, [*Aside.*]
This for my wager!
   Bellisant.   Villaine, shake and tremble
At my iust anger; which of all my actions,
Confind in vertuous lymitts, haue giuen life 110
And birth to this presumption? Hast thou euer
Observd in mee a wanton looke or gesture
Not suitinge with a virgin? Haue I been

83. gon, I] *Gifford;* gon, I gon I *MS*

Prodigall in my favors or giuen hopes
To nourish such attempts? Sweare, and sweare trulie, 115
What in thie soule thou thinckst of mee.
    Clarindor. As of one
Made vpp of chastety; and onlie tryed,
Which I repent, what this might woorke vppon you.
    Bellisant. Thie intent deserves not death; but sirra know
Tis in my power to looke thee dead.
    Clarindor. Tis graunted. 120
    Bellisant. I am not so cruell, yet for this insolence
Forbeare my howse foreuer; yf you are hott,
You ruffian like may force a partinge kisse
As from a comon gamster.
    Clarindor. I am coold.—
Heeres a virago. [*Aside.*]
    Bellisant. Or you may goe boast 125
How brauely you came on, to your companions;
I will not bribe thie silence. Noe reply?
Now thrust him headlonge out of dores and see
Hee neuer more passe my threshold. *Exit.*
    Clarindor. This comes of
My daringe, all hells plagues light on the proverb 130
That saies *Faint hart*—but it is stale.
    Servant. Pray you walke sir,
Wee must shew you the waie ells.
    Clarindor. Bee not to officious,
I am noe barr for you to try your strength on.
Sitt quiet by this disgrace I cannot;
Some other course I must bee forcd to take, 135
Not for my wager now, but honors sake. *Exeunt.*

              Finis Actus Secundi

[III. i]
Actus Tertius

Enter CHAMONT, PERIGOT, NOVALL, DINANT,
LAMIRA *and* CLARINDA.

    Perigot. Twas princelike entertainement.
    Chamont. You ore prize it.

    124-5. coold.— | Heeres] *McIlwraith*; *undivided MS*; cool: | She's *Gifford*
134. Sitt quiet] *MS*; Sit quietly *Gifford*

III. i. 2-32   *The Parliament of Love*

Dinant. Your cheerefull lookes made eu'ry dish a feast,
And tis that crownes a welcome.
    Lamira.   For my part,
I hold society and honest mirth
The greatest blessinge of a civell life.   5
    Clarinda. Without good companie indeede all dainties
Loose theire true rellish, and like painted grapes
Are onlie seene not tasted.
    Novall.   By this light   [*Aside.*]
Shee speakes well to; Ile haue a flinge at her;
Shee is noe fitt electuary for a docter,   10
A courser iulip may well coole his worship,
This cordiall is for gallants.
    Chamont.   Lett mee see,
The night growes old. Pray you often bee my guests;
Such as dare come vnto an empty table,
Altho not crackd with curious delicates,   15
Haue liberty to comaund it as theire owne;
I may doe the like with you when you are marri⟨ed.
    Perigot. Yes tis likely,
When theres noe forrage to bee had abro⟨ad,
Nor credulous husbands left to father ⟨children   20
Of batchellors begettinge, when cour⟨t ladies
Are won to graunt variety is not p⟨leasure
And that a ⟨friend at a p⟩inch is v⟨seless to them,
⟨I . . . . . . till then.⟩
    Chamont.   You haue a merry tyme of't,
But wee forgett our selves; gallants good night.   25
Good master docter, when your leisure serves,
Visitt my howse; when wee least neede theire art
Phisitians looke most louely.
    Dinant.   All thats in mee
Is at your Lordships service; mounsier *Perigot*,
Mounsier *Novall*, in what I may bee vsefull   30
Pray you comaund mee.
    Novall.   Weel waite on you home.
    Dinant. By no meanes sir; good night.
                      Exeunt, manet NOVALL *and* PERIGOT.

III. i. 14. an empty table] *MS* (take *crossed out before* table); a - - - table *Gifford*; a homely table *editor conj.*   22. won] *Gifford*; wone *MS*   24. of't] *Gifford*; oft *MS*

Novall.   The knaue is ielous.
Perigot. Tis a disease few docters cure them selues of.
Novall. I would hee weare my patient.
Perigot.   Doe but practize
To gett his wiues consent, the waie is easie.
  Novall. You may conclude so, for my self I graunt
I never was so taken with a woman
Nor euer had lesse hope.
  Perigot.   Bee not deiected:
Follow but my directions, shees thine owne;
I'le sett thee in a course that shall not faile.
I like thie choyce, but more of that hereafter;
Adultery is a safe and secure sin,
The purchase of a maiden head seldome quitts
The danger and the labour; build on this,
Hee that putts home shall find all women cominge
(The frozen *Bellisant* euer excepted).
Could you beleeue the faire wife of *Chamont*,
A lady never tainted in her honor,
Should at the first assault, for till this night
I never courted her, yeild vpp the fort
That shee hath kepd so longe?
  Novall.   Tis wondrous strange,
What wininge language vsd you?
  Perigot.   Thou art a child,
Tis action not fine speeches take a woman.
Pleasures theire heaven, and hee that giues assurance
That hee hath strength to tame theire hot desires
Is the prevalinge orrator; shee but saw mee
Iumpe ouer six ioynd stooles and after cutt
Some forty capers, (tricks that never misd
In a magnificent maske to draw the eyes
Of all the bewties in the court vppon mee)
But straite shee wrunge my hand, trod on my toe
And said my mistress could not but bee happie
In such an able servant; I replyd
Bluntlie I was ambitious to bee hers
And shee nor coy nor shie straite entertaind mee;
I vrgd a privat meetinge, it was graunted,

            39–40. owne; / I'le] *Gifford; undivided MS*

The tyme and place appoynted.
 Novall.   But remember
Chamont is your freind.
 Perigot.   Now out vppon thee puny;
As if a man so farr ere lou'd that tytle
But twas much more delight and ticklinge to him
To hugg him self and saie this is my cuckold.
 Novall. But did hee not observe you?
 Perigot.   Tho hee did
(As I am doubtfull) I will not desist,
The danger will indeere the sport.

     Enter CLARINDOR.

 Novall.   Forbeare,
Heeres *Clarindore.*
 Perigot. Wee wilbee merry with him,
I haue heard his entertainement; ioyne but with mee
And wee will ieere this self opiniond foole
Almost to madnes.
 Novall.   Hees already growne
Ex⟨ce⟩edinge mellanchollie and some saie
⟨That's⟩ the first step to phrensie.
 ⟨*Perigot.*   I'll upo⟩n ⟨h⟩im.
   ⟩mounsier! noe replie? growne prowd
   ⟩is not well.
   h⟩is ⟨b⟩ostings
⟨   ⟩
 Novall.   Wee gratulate
(Tho wee paie fort) your happie entrance to
The certaine favors, nay the sure possession
Of madam *Bellisant.*
 Clarindor. The yonge whelpe to:
Tis well, exceedinge well.
 Perigot.   Tis so with you sir,
But beare it modestlie, faith it will become you,
And beinge arivd at such a lardge revenew
As this your happie match instates you with,
Twoe thowsand crownes from mee, and from *Novall,*
Tho wee almost confesse our wager lost,
Wilbee a small addition.

Novall. You mistake him,
Nor doe I feare out of his noble nature
But that hee may bee won to lycence vs
To draw our venture.
   Clarindor. Spend your frothie witts,
Doe, doe, you snarle but hurt not.
   Novall. Oh giue leaue
To loosers ser to speake.
   Perigot. Tis a strange fate
Some men are borne to, and a happie starr
That raignd at your nativitie, it could not bee ells
A lady of a constancy like a rock
Not to bee moud, and held impregnable
Should yeild at the first assault.
   Novall. Tis the reward
Of a braue daringe sperrit.
   Perigot. Tush wee are dull,
Abuse our oppertunitie.
   Clarindor. Haue you done yet?
   Perigot. Whcn hee had privacie of discourse hee knew
How to vse th' advantage; did hee stand
Fauninge and crouchinge? noe, hee came vpp bouldlie,
Tould her what shee was borne to, ruffled her,
Kissd her and towsd her; all the passages
Are at court already, and tis said a pattent
Is graunted him if anie maid be harsh
For him to humble her, and a new name given him,
The scornefull virgin tamer.
   Clarindor. I may tame
Your buffon tongues if you proceede.
   Novall. Noe anger;
I haue heard that *Bellisant* was so taken with
Your manlie carriage that shee straight prepard you
A sumptuous banquet.
   Perigot. Yet his enimyes
Report it was a blancket.

    104–5. reward / Of] *Gifford*; *undivided MS*   105–6. dull, / Abuse] *Gifford*; *undivided MS*   106. Abuse] *Gifford*; abusd *MS*   114. given] *Gifford*; give *MS*   115–16. tame / Your] *Gifford*; *undivided MS*   116–19. *rearranged by Gifford*; *MS reads* noe . . . heard / that . . . Carriage / that . . . banquet   119–20. enimyes / Report] *Gifford*; *undivided MS*

Novall.   Mallice mallice.
Shee was shewinge him her chamber to and calld for
Perfumes and cambrick sheetes.
   Perigot.   When see the luck ont,
Against her will her most vnmannerlie groomes
(For so tis rumerd) tooke him by the shoulders
And thrust him out of dores.
   Novall.   Faith sir, resolue vs,
How was it? wee would gladlie know the truth
To stop the mouth of calumny.
   Clarindor.   Troth sir Ile tell you,
One tooke mee by the nose thus, and a second
Made bould with mee thus; but one word more, you shall
Feele new expressions, and so my gentle boobies
Farwell and bee hangd—   *Exit.*
   Novall.   Wee haue netled him.
   Perigot. Had wee stunge him to death it weare but iustice:
An ouer weeninge bragart.
   Novall.   This is nothinge
To the docters wife.
   Perigot.   Come weel consult of it,
And suddenlie.
   Novall.   I feele a womans longing
Till I am at it.
   Perigot.   Never feare, shees thine owne, boy.   *Exeunt.*

Enter CLEREMOND.

   Cleremond. What haue my sins been, heaven? yet th⟨y ⟩pleasure
Must not bee argued; was wretch eu⟨er
On such a black adventure, in which onl⟨y
To wish ⟨to⟩ prosper is ⟨a⟩ gre⟨ater crime
Then ⟨to
⟨   ⟩
Of reason, vnderstandinge and true iudgment.
T'weare a degree of comfort to mee, yf
I weare starke madd, or like a beast of pray
Prickd on by gripinge hunger, all my thoughts

133-4. nothinge / To] *Gifford*; *undivided MS*   134-5. it, / And] *Gifford*; *undivided MS*   135-6. longing / Till] *Gifford*; *undivided MS*

And faculties weare wholly taken vpp
To cloy my appetite and could looke noe further;
But I rise vpp a new example of
Calamity, transcendinge all before mee;
And I should guild my miseries with falce comforts   15
If I compard it to an Indian slaues
That with incessant labor to search out
Some vnknowne myne, diggs almost to the center,
And yf then found, not thanckd of his prowd master.
But this if putt into an equall scale   20
With my vnparraleld fortune will waigh nothinge,
For from a cabinet of the choycest iewells
That mankind ere was ritch in; (whose least iem
All treasure of the earth or what is hid
In *Neptunes* watrie boosome cannot purchase)   25
I must seeke out the richest fairest purest,
And when by proofe tis knowne it houlds the vallue,
As soone as found destroy it, oh most cruell.
And yet when I consider of the many
That haue professd themselues my freinds and vowd   30
Theire lives weare not theire owne when my engagments
Should summon them to bee at my devotion,
Not one indures the test; I almost grow
Of the worlds receaud opinion that houlds
Freindship but a meere name that bindes noe farther   35
Then to the alter, to retire with safety.

     Enter MONTROSS *and* BEAUPRÉ.

Heere comes *Montrosse*, what sudden ioy transports him?
I never saw man wrapd so.
 Montross.   Purse and all,
And tis to little tho it weare cramd full
With crownes of the sunne. Oh blessed blessed paper,   40
But made so by the touch of her faire hand.
What shall I answer? Say, I am her creature,
Or if thou canst find out a word that may
Expresse subiection in an humbler stile
Vse it I prithee; ad to, her comaunds   45
Shalbee with as much willingnes performd

    III. ii. 23. iem] *MS*; gem *Gifford*

As I in this fould, thus receaue her favors.
   Beaupré. I shall retorne so much.
   Montross.   And that two howers
Shall bring mee to attend her.
   Beaupré.   With all care
And circumstance of service from yourself,   50
I will deliuer it.
   Montross.   I am still thie debtor.   *Exit* BEAUPRÉ.
   Cleremond. I reade the cause now cleirely; Ile slip by,
For tho euen at this instant hee should proue
Him self (which others falcehood makes mee doubt)
That constant and best freind I goe in quest of,   55
It weare inhuman in theire birth to strangle
His promisinge hopes of comfort.
   Montross.   *Cleremond*
Passe by mee as a stranger? at a tyme to
When I am filld with such excesse of ioy,
So swolne and surfited with true delight,   60
That had I not found out a freind to whome
I might impart em and so giue em vent,
In theire aboundance they would force a passage
And lett out life togeither. Prithee beare
For freindships sake a parte of that sweete burthen   65
Which I shrinck vnder; and when thou hast read
Faire *Bellisant* subscribd so neere my name, to
Observe but that thou must with mee confesse
Th⟨er⟩e cannot bee roome in one lovers hart
C⟨apa⟩tious enough to entertaine   70
S⟨uch mu⟩ltitudes of pleasure.
   Cleremond. ⟨   I joy with yo⟩u,
⟨Let that suffice,⟩ and envie not your blessings;
⟨May they increase! Farewell, friend.⟩
   Montross.   How, noe more?
By the snow white hand that writt theis charracters,
It is a breach to curtesie and manners   75
So couldlie to take notice of his good
Whome you call freind. See further, heere shee writes
That shee is trulie sensible of my sufferings
And not alone voutsafes to call mee servant

---

47. thus] *editor*; this *MS, Gifford*   64. lett out life] *Gifford*; lett life *MS*

But to imploy mee in a cause that much 80
Concernes her in her honor, theres a favor.
Are yee yet stupid? and that two howers hence
Shee does expect mee in the privat walkes
Neighboringe the *Louvre*; cannot all this moue you?
I could bee angrie, a tenth of theis bounties 85
But promisd to you from *Leonora*,
To witnes my affection to my freind
In his behalf, had taught mee to forgett
All myne owne miseries.
   Cleremond.   Doe not misinterpret
This couldnes in mee, for alas *Montrosse* 90
I am a thinge so made vpp of affliction,
So euery waie contemd, that I conclude
My sorrowes are infectious, and my companie,
Like such as haue foule vlcers runinge on them,
To bee with care avoyded; may your happines 95
In the favor of the matchles *Bellisant*
Howerlie increase, and my best wishes guard you,
Tis all that I can giue.
   Montross.   You must not leaue mee.
   Cleremond. Indeede I must and will, myne owne ingagements
Call mee awaie.
   Montross.   What are they? I presume 100
There cannot bee a secret of that waight
You dare not trust mee with, and should you doubt mee
I iustly might complaine that my affection
Is placd vnfortunately.
   Cleremond.   I know you are honest,
But this is such a busines and requires 105
Such suddaine execution that it cannot
Fall in the compasse of your will or power
To doe mee a freinds office; in a word,
On termes that neere concerne mee in myne honor
I am to fight the quarrell, mortall to, 110
The tyme some two howers hence, the place ten myles
Distant from *Paris*, and when you shall know
I yet am vnprovided of a second,
You will excuse my soden partinge from you.
Farwell *Montrosse*.

Montross. Not so, I am the man
Will runne the danger with you, and muste tell you
That whilst I liue it was a wronge to seeke
Annothers arme to side you. Leade the waie,
My horse stands ready.
    Cleremond. I confesse tis noble
For you to offer this but it weare base
In mee to accept it.
    Montross. Doe not scorne mee freind.
    Cleremond. Noe but admire and honor you, and from that
Serious consideration must refuse
The tender of your aid. *Fraunce* knowes you valliant
And that you might in single opposition
Fight for a crowne, but millions of reasons
Forbid mee your assistance; you forgett
Your owne designes, beinge, the very minute
I am to encounter with myne enimy,
To meete your mistress, such a mistress to,
Whose favor you so manie yeares haue sought:
And will you then when shee voutsafes accesse,
Nay more invites you, check at her faire offer?
Or shall it bee reported to my shame
For my owne ends I robd you of a fortune
Princes might envie? Can you euer hope⟨
Sh⟨e   ⟩u ⟨
If you neglect her now? Bee wise deere freind
And in your prodigallitie of goodnes
Doe not vndoe yourself: live longe and happie
And leaue mee to my dangers.
    Montross.   *Cleremond*,
I haue with patience heard you and considerd
The strength of your best arguments, waid the dangers
I runne in my owne fortunes, but againe
When I oppose the sacred name of freind
Against those ioyes I haue so longe pursuide,
Neither the bewtie of faire *Bellisant*,
Her welth, her virtues can prevale so far
In such a desperate case as this to leaue you;
To haue it to posteritie recorded

        122. that] *Gifford*; what *MS*

138 *The Parliament of Love* III. ii. 151–iii. 12

At such a tyme as this I prou'd true gould
And currant in my freindship shalbee to mee
A thowsand mistresses and such embraces
As leaue noe stinge behinde them. Therefore on:
I am resolud vnles you beate mee off 155
I will not leaue you.
    Cleremond.   Oh heere is a iewell
Fitt for the cabinet of the greatest monarch,
But I of all men miserable.
    Montross.   Come bee cheerefull,
Good fortune will attend vs.
    Cleremond.   That to mee,
To haue the greatest blessinge, a true freind, 160
Should bee the greatest curse; bee yet advisd.
    Montross. It is in vaine.
    Cleremond.   That ere I should haue cause
To wish you had lou'd lesse.
    Montross.   The hower drawes on,
Weel talke more as wee ride.
    Cleremond.   Of men most wretched!   *Exeunt.*

[III. iii]   *Enter* BELLISANT *and* BEAUPRÉ.

    Bellisant. Nay praie you drye your eyes, or your sad storie
(Whose euery accent still methincks I heare,
Twas with such passion and true greefe deliuerd)
Will make myne beare yours companie. All my feare is,
The rigerous repulse this worst of men, 5
Falce periurd *Clarindor* (I am sick to name him)
Receaud at his last visitt will deter him
From cominge againe.
fol. 9ʳ   *Beaupré.*   Noe, hees resolud to venture
And has bribd mee, with hazzard of your anger,
To gett him access, but in annother shape; 10
The tyme prefixd drawes neere to.
    Bellisant.   Tis the better.   *Knock.*
One knocks.
    Beaupré. I am sure tis his.
    Bellisant.   Convey him in,

III. iii. 10. access, but] *Gifford*; acc but *MS*

III. iii. 13-40   *The Parliament of Love*   139

But doe it with a face of feare. I cannot   [*Exit* BEAUPRÉ.]
Resolue yet with what lookes to entertaine him,
Much lesse what prosperous course to take to worke him.   15
You powers that favor inocence, and revenge
Wrongs done by such as scornefully deride
Your awfull names, inspire mee!

Enter CLARINDOR [*disguised*] *and* BEAUPRÉ.

Beaupré.   Sir, I hazzard
My service in this action.
    Clarindor.   Thou shalt liue
To bee the mistress of thie self and others   20
If that my proiects hitt; alls at the stake now
And as the dye falls I am made most happie
Or past expression wretched.
    Bellisant.   Ha, whoes that?
What bould intruder vsher you? This rudenes—
From whence, what would hee?
    Beaupré.   Hee brings letters madam,   25
As hee saies, from lord *Chamont*.
    Clarindor.   How her frownes fright mee! [*Aside.*]
    Bellisant. From lord *Chamont*? Are they of such import
That you before my pleasure bee enquird
Dare bringe the bearer to my privat chamber?
Noe more of this, your packet sir.
    Clarindor.   The letters   30
Deliuerd to my trust and faith are writt
In such misterious and darke characters
As theile require the iudgment of your soule
More then your eye to reade and vnderstand them.
    Bellisant. What riddles this?   [*He takes off his disguise.*]
            Am I then contemd?   35
Dare you doe this presuminge on my soft
And gentle nature? (Feare not, I must shew   [*Aside to* BEAUPRÉ.]
A seeminge anger.) What new boystrous courtship
After your late loose language and forcd kisse
Come you to practize? I know none beyond yt.   40

    13 SD. *Exit* BEAUPRÉ.] *Gifford; not in MS*   18 SD. *disguised*] *Gifford; not
in MS*   35. Am I] *MS* (am I); Ha! am I *Gifford*   SD. *He . . . disguise.*]
editor; not in MS; Discovering Clarin. *Gifford.*

Yf you imagin that you may comitt
A rape in myne owne howse and that my servants
Will stand tame lookers on—
    Clarindor.   Yf I bringe with mee
One thought but of submission and sorrow,
Or norish anie hope but that your goodnes   45
May please to signe my pardon, may I perish
In your displeasure, which to mee is more
Then feare of hell hereafter. I confesse
The violence I offerd to your sweetenes
In my presumption, with lips impure   50
To force a touch from yours, a greater cryme
Then if I should haue mixd lacivious flames
With those chaste fires that burne at *Dians* alter,
That twas a plott of treason to your vertues
To thinck you could bee tempted, or beleeue   55
You weare not fashiond in a better mould
And made of purer clay then other women.
Since you are then the phenix of your tyme
And e'en now while you blesse the earth pertake
Of theire Angelicall essence, imitate   60
Heavens aptness to forgiue when mercyes sui'd fo⟨r,   ⟩
And once more take mee to your grace and favor. ⟨   ⟩
    Bellisant. What charmes are theis! what an inchantin⟨g tongue!⟩
fol. 9ᵛ What pitty tis one that can speake so well
Should in his actions bee so ill!
    Beaupré.   Take heede, [*Aside to* BELLISANT.]
Loose not your self.
    Bellisant.   So well sir you haue pleaded   66
And like an advocate in your owne cause,
That tho your guilt weare greater I acquit you,
The fault noe more rememberd; and for proofe
My hart speakes in my tongue, thus seale your pardon, [*Kisses him.*]
And with this willinge favor (which forcd from mee   71
Calld on my anger) make attonement with you.
    Clarindor. Yf I dreame now, oh may I never wake,
But slumber thus ten ages.
    Bellisant.   Till this minute
You nere to mee lookd louelie.

            70 SD. *Kisses him.*] *Gifford; not in MS*

Clarindor. How?
Bellisant. Nor haue I
Ere seene a man in my opinion worthie
The bounty I voutsafe you, therefore fix heere
And make mee vnderstand that you can beare
Your fortune modestly.
   Clarindor. I finde her cominge; [*Aside.*]
This kisse was but the prologue to the plaie
And not to seeke the rest weare cowardice.
Helpe mee dissemulation.—Pardon madam,
Tho now when I should putt on cheerefull lookes
In beinge blest with what I durst not hope for,
I change the comick sceane and doe present you
With a most tragick spectacle.
   Bellisant. Heaven avert
This prodegie, what meane you?
   Clarindor. To confirme
In death how trulie I haue lou'd. I graunt
Your favors done mee yeild this benifitt,
As to make waie for mee to passe in pease
To my longe rest; what I haue tasted from you
Informes mee onlie of the much I want:
For in your pardon, and the kisse voutsafd mee,
You did but poynt mee out a fore right waie
To leade to certaine happines, and then willd mee
To moue noe further. Pray you excuse mee therefore
Tho I desire to end a lingringe torment,
And if you please with your faire hands to make mee
A sacrifice to your chastety I will meete
The instrument you make choyce of with more fervor
Then euer *Cesar* did to hugg the mistress
Hee doted on, plumd victorie: but if that
You doe abhor the office as to full
Of crueltie and horror, yet giue leaue
That in your presence I myself may bee
Both preist and offeringe. *Offers to kill himself.*
   Bellisant. Hold hold frantick man,
The shrine of loue shall not bee bathd in blood!

76. in my] *Gifford*; my *MS*   106. Both] *Gifford*; bost *MS*   107. blood] *Gifford*; loue *MS*

Women tho faire weare made to bringe forth men
And not destroy 'em, therefore hold I saie!
I had a mother and shee lookd vppon mee   110
As on a true epitomie of her youth,
Nor can I thinck I am forbid the comfort
To bringe forth little modells of myself
Yf heaven bee pleasd, (my nuptiall ioyes performd)
To make mee fruitefull.
    Clarindor.   Such celestiall musique   115
Nere blest theis eares, oh you haue argued better
For mee then I could for my self.
    Bellisant.   For you?
Whe⟩re did I giue you hope to bee my husband?
    Clarindor. ⟨Fallen⟩ of againe!
    Bellisant.   ⟨Yet since y⟩ou haue giuen such proofe
Of loue and constancie, Ile vnmaske those thoughts   120
That longe haue been conceald; I am yours, but how?
In an honorable waie.
    Clarindor.   I weare more then base
Should I desire you otherwise.
    Bellisant.   True affection
Needs not a contract, and it weare to doubt mee
To engage mee further, yet my vow expird,   125
Which is to liue a virgin for a yeare,
Challenge my promise.
    Clarindor.   How, a yeare? Oh madam
Plaie not the tyranesse, doe not giue mee hopes
And in a moment change them to dispaire!
A yeare? alas this bodie thats all fyer,   130
Yf you refuse to quench it with your favor,
Will ere three daies bee cinders, and your mercy
Will come to late thenn; deerest ladie, marriage
Is but a ceremony, and a hurtfull vow
Is in the breach of it better comended   135
Then in the keepinge. Oh I burne I burne
And if you take noe pitty I must flie
To my last refuge.
    Bellisant.   Hold, saie I should yeild
This night to satisfie you to the full,
And you should sweare vntill the weddinge daie   140

To keepe the favors I now graunt conceald,
You would bee talkinge.
 Clarindor.   May my tongue rott out then!
 Bellisant. Or boast to your companions of your conquest
And of my easines.
 Clarindor.   Ile indure the rack first.
 Bellisant. And havinge what you longe for cast mee of,   145
As you did madam *Beaupré.*
 Clarindor.   May the earth
First gape and swallow mee!
 Bellisant.   Ile presse you noe further.
Goe in, your chambers ready; yf you haue
A bedfellow, so; but silence I enioyne you
And libertie to leaue you when I please.   150
I blush if you replie.
 Clarindor.   Till now nere happie!   *Exit.*
 Beaupré. What meanes your ladiship?
 Bellisant.   Doe not aske, but doe
As I direct you. Tho as yet wee tread
A rough and thorny waie, faint not, the ends
I hope to reach shall make a lardge amends.   *Exeunt.*

Finis Actus Tertij

Actus Quartus

Enter NOVALL *and* DINANT.

 Dinant. YOU are welcome first sir, and that spoke, receaue
A faithfull promise all that art, or longe
Experience hath taught mee shall enlarge
Them selues for your recouery.
 Novall.   Sir I thanck you,
As far as a weake, sick and an vnable man   5
Has power to expresse, but what wants in my tongue,
My hand (for yet my fingers feele noe gowte)
Shall speake in this dumbe language.   [*Gives money.*]
 Dinant.   You are to munificent.

IV. i. 8 SD. *Gives money.*] editor; *not in MS*; *Gives him his purse.* Gifford

Novall. Fie noe sir, health is such a pretious iewell
Wee cannot buy it to deere.
 Dinant.   Take comfort sir,
I find not by your vrin or your pulse
Or anie outward simptom that you are
In anie certen danger.
 Novall.   Oh the more my feare:
Infirmities that ⟨are⟩ kn⟨o⟩w⟨ne   ⟩
⟨   ⟩
But when the causes of them are conceald
(As theis of myne are, docter) they proue mortall.
How e're, Ile not forgett you while I liue,
Doe but your parts.
 Dinant.   Sir they are at your service.
Ile giue you some preparatiues to instruct mee
Of your inward temper, then as I find cause,
Some gentle purge.
 Novall.   Yes I must purge, I die ells,
(But where deere docter you shall not find out.)
This is a happie entrance, maie it end well!
Ile mount your night cap, dodipoll.   [*Aside.*]
 Dinant.   In what parte
(Wee are sworne to secresie, and you must bee free)
Doe you finde your greatest agonie?
 Novall.   Oh I haue
Strange motions on the sudden, villanous tumers
Which rise then fall, then rise againe, oh docter
Not to bee shewne or namd.
 Dinant.   Then in my iudgment
You had best leaue *Paris,* choose some fresher ayre;
That does helpe much in phisique.
 Novall.   By noe meanes:
Heere in your howse or noe where you must cure mee;
The eye of the master fatts the horse, and when
His docters by, the patient may drinck wine
In a fitt of a burninge feaver, for your presence
Workes more then what you minister; take phisique
Attended on by ignorant groomes, meere strangers
To your directions, I must hazzard life
And you your reputation; whereas sir,

IV. i. 41-69   *The Parliament of Love*   145

I hold your howse a colledge of your art
And euery boy you keepe, by you instructed,
A pritty peice of a gallenist; then the females,
From your most faire wife to your kitchen drudge,
Are so famillier with your learned courses   45
That to an herbe they know to make thin broath
Or when occasion serves to cheere the hart,
(And such ingredients I shall haue most neede of)
How manie cocks of the game make a stronge cullice
Or pheasants eggs a cawdle.
   Dinant.   I am glad   50
To heare you argue with such strength.
               Enter CLARINDA.
   Novall.   A flash sir,
But now I feele my fitt againe.—Shee is   [*Aside.*]
Made vpp of all perfection, anie danger
That leads to the enioyinge so much sweetnes
Is pleasure at the height, I am ravisht with   55
The meere imagination, oh happines!
   Dinant. Howes this, one from the duke *Nemures?*
   Clarinda.   Yes sir.
   Dinant.   Tis ranck
The sight of my wife hath forcd him to forget
To counterfeit, I now guesse at your sicknes
And if I fitt you not—
   Clarinda.   The gentleman staies you.   60
   Dinant. I come to him presentlie; in the meane tyme wife,
Bee carefull of this mounsier, naie noe coynes,
You may salute him bouldlie, his pale lips
Inchant not in the touch.
   Novall.   Hers doe I'me sure.
   Dinant. Kisse him againe.
   Clarinda.   Sir this is more then modest.   65
   Dinant. Modest? whie foole, desire is dead in him;
Call it a charitable pious woorke
If it refresh his sperrits.
   Novall.⟩   Yes indeede sir,
I finde greate ease int.

   43. gallenist] *Gifford* (Galenist); gallinest *MS*   50–1. glad / To] *Gifford*; un-
divided *MS*   68–9. sir, / I] *Gifford*; undivided *MS*

   Dinant.   Mark⟩ that, and would you
Deny⟩ a sick man comfort, meates against   70
                    ⟩must bee graunted to
  ⟨   ⟩
In person waite on him, nay nere hange off,
I saie you shall, this night with your owne hands
Ile haue you aire his bed, and when he eates   75
Of what you haue prepard, you shall sitt by him
And with some merry chat helpe to repaire
Decayed appetite, watch by him when hee slumbers,
Nay play his pages part; more, I durst trust you,
Weare this our weddinge daie, you yet a virgin,   80
To bee his bedfellow, for well I know
Old *Priams* impotence, or *Nestors* hernias
Herculian activenes, yf but compard
To his debility: putt him to his oath,
Heel sweare hee can doe nothinge.
   Novall.   Doe? oh noe Sir,   85
I am past the thought of't.
   Dinant.   But how doe you like
The method I prescribe?
   Novall.   Beyond expression;
Vppon the meere report I doe conceaue
Hope of recouery.
   Clarinda.   Are you mad?
   Dinant.   Peace foole.
This night you shall take a cordiall to strengthen   90
Your feeble limbes, twill cost ten crownes a draught.
   Novall. Noe matter sir.
   Dinant.   To morrow you shall walke
To see my garden, then my wife shall shew you
The choyce roomes of my howse, when you are weary
Ease yourself on her couch.
   Novall.   Oh devine docter,   95
What man in health would not bee sick on purpose
To bee your patient?
   Dinant.   Come sir to your chamber,
And now I vnderstand where your disease lyes
(Nay leade him by the hand) doubt not Ile cure you.   *Exeunt.*

    75. Ile] *Gifford* (I'll); I *MS*   99 SD. *Exeunt.*] *Gifford*; *Exit MS*

Enter CLEREMOND *and* MONTROSS.

Cleremond. This is the place.
Montross. An euen peice of ground
Without advantage, but bee iocond freind,
The honor to haue enterd first the feild,
How euer wee come of, is ours.
Cleremond. I neede not,
So well I am acquainted with your vallor
To dare in a good cause as much as man,
Lend you encouragment, and should I ad
Your power to doe, which Fortune, howere blind,
Hath euer seconded, I cannot doubt
But victorie still sitts vppon your sword
And must not now forsake you.
Montross. You shall see mee
Come bouldlie vpp, nor will I shame your cause
By partinge with an inch of ground not bought
With blood on my parte.
Cleremond. Tis not to bee questiond.
That which I would intreate (and pray you graunt it)
Is that you would forget your vsuall softnes,
Your foe beinge at your mercy. It hath been
A custome in you, which I dare not praise,
Havinge disarmd your enimy of his sword,
To tempt your fate by yeildinge it againe,
Then runne a second hazzard.
Montross. When wee encounter
A noble foe wee cannot bee to noble.
Cleremond. That I confesse, but hee thats now to oppose you
I know for an archvillaine, one that hath lost⟨
All feelinge of humanitie, one that hates⟨
Goodnes in others ⟨cau⟩se hees il⟨l himself,⟩
A most ingratefull wretch (the names to gentle,
All attributes of wickednes cannot reach him)
Of whome to haue deservd beyond example
Or president of freindship is a wronge
Which onlie death can satisfie.
Montross. You describe
A monster to mee.

Cleremond. True *Montrosse*, hee is so.
Affrick, tho firtill of strange prodegies,
Never producd his equall; bee wise therefore
And if hee fall into your hands dispatch him,
Pitty to him is cruelty; the sad father
That sees his sonne stunge by a snake to death
May with more iustice staie his vengfull hand
And lett the worme escape, then you voutsafe him
A minute to repent, for tis a slaue
So sould to hell and mischeif, that a traytor
To his most lawfull prince, a church robber,
A parracid whoe, when his garners are
Cramd with the purest graine, suffers his parents,
Beinge old and weake, to starue for want of bread,
Compard to him are inocent.
   Montross.   I nere heard
Of such a cursed nature, if longe lyvd
Hee would infect man kind, rest you assurd
Hee finds from mee small curtesie.
   Cleremond.   And expect
As little from him; blood is that hee thirsts for,
Not honorable wounds.
   Montross.   I would I had him
Within my swords length.
   Cleremond.   Haue thie wish, thou hast.
Nay draw thie sword and sodenlie; I am   *They draw.*
That monster, temple robber, parracide,
Ingratefull wretch, freind hater, or what ells
Makes vpp the perfect figure of the divell,
Should hee appeare like man. Banish amazement
And call thie ablest sperrits vpp to guard thee
From him thats turnd a furie. I am made
Her minister, whose crueltie but nam'd
Would with more horror strike the pale cheekd hearers
Then all those dreadfull words which coniurers vse
To fright theire dam'd familliers; looke not on mee
As I am *Cleremond*, I haue parted with
The essence that was his and entertaind
The soule of some feirce tigresse, or a woolfes,

        IV. ii. 53 SD. *They draw*] *editor; at line 52 in MS*

New hangd for human slaughter, and tis fitt:
I could not ells bee an apt instrument
To bloody *Leonora*.
    Montross.   To my knowledge
I never wrongd her.
    Cleremond.   Yes in beinge a freind 70
To mee, shee hated my best freind, her mallice
Would looke noe lower, and for beinge such,
By her comaund *Montrosse*, I am to kill thee.
Oh that thou hadst like others been all words
And noe performance, or that thou hadst made 75
Some little stopp in thie careere of kindnes.
Whie wouldst thou to confirme the name of freind
Despise the favors of faire *Bellisant*
And all those certaine ioyes that waited for thee,
Snatch at this fatall office of a second 80
Which others fled from? Tis in vaine to mourne now
When theres noe helpe, and therefore good *Montrosse*
Rowse thie most manlie parts, and thinck thou standst now
A champion for more then kinge or cuntry
Since⟩ in thie fall goodnes it self must suffer. 85
Remem⟩ber to the basenes of the wronge
        fre⟩indship, lett it edge thie sword
And kill compassion in thee, and forgett not
I will take all advantages, and so
Without replie haue at thee—
                Fight: CLEREMOND *vnder* MONTROSS.
    Montross.   See how weake 90
An ill cause is, you are already falne;
What can you looke for now?
    Cleremond.   Foole, vse thie fortune,
And so hee counsailes thee that if wee had
Changd places instantlie would haue cutt thie throate
Or diggd thie hart out.
    Montross.   In requitall of 95
That savage purpose I much pittie you;
Witnes theis teares, not teares of ioy for conquest
But of true sorrow for your misery.

   76. Some] *Gifford*; so *MS*   80. Snatch] *Gifford*; snatchd *MS*   97. not teares] *Gifford* (tears); not teare *MS*

Liue, oh liue *Cleremond*, and like a man
Make vse of reason as an exorcist   100
To cast this divell out that does abuse you,
This feind of falce affection.
  Cleremond.   Will you not kill mee?
You are then more tyranous then *Leonora*:
An easie thrust will doe it, you had euer
A charitable hand, doe not denie mee   105
For our ould freindships sake. Noe, wilt not bee?
There are a thowsand dores to lett out life,
You keepe not guard of all, and I shall finde
By fallinge headlinge from some rockie cliff,
Poyson or fyre, that longe rest which your sword   110
Discurteously denies mee.   *Exit.*
  Montross.   I will follow,
And somethinge I must fancy to disswade him
From doinge suddaine violence on himself;
Thats now my onlie ayme, and that to mee,
Succeedinge well, is a true victorie.   *Exit.*

[IV. iii]   *Enter* CHAMONT *and* DINANT.

  Dinant. Your lady tempted to?
  Chamont.   And tempted home,
Sumond to parlie, the fort almost yeilded,
Had not I stepd in to remoue the seige;
But I haue countermynd his workes and yf
You second mee will blow the letcher vpp   5
And laugh to see him caper.
  Dinant.   Anie thinge,
Comaund mee as your servant to ioyne with you,
All waies are honest wee take to revenge vs
On theis lascivious monkies of the court
That make it theire profession to dishonor   10
Graue citizeins wiues, nay those of higher ranck
As tis in yours apparant. My yonge rambler
That thought to cheate mee with a faind disease,
I haue in the toyle already; I haue giuen him,
Vnder pretence to make him high and active,   15

---

109. headlinge] *MS*; headlong *Gifford*   IV. iii. 4–5. yf / You second] *Gifford*; *MS reads* yf you / second

A cooler I dare warrant; it will yeild
Rare sport to see it woorke, I would your Lordshipp
Could bee a spectator.
  Chamont.   Tis that I ayme at,
And might I but perswade you to dispence
A little with your candor, and consent   20
To make your howse the stage on which weel act
Our comick sceane, in the pride of all theire hopes
Weel shew theis shallow fooles sunck eyd dispaire
And trivmph in theire punishment.
  Dinant.   My howse
Or what soeuer ells is myne shall serve   25
As properties to grace it.
  Chamont.   In this shape then
Leaue mee to worke the rest.
  Dinant.   Doubt not my lord
You shall find all things ready.   [*Exit.*]

      Enter PERIGOT.

  Chamont.   This sorts well
With my other purposes. *Perigot*, to my w⟨ish!
Aid mee invention!
  Perigot.   Is the queane falne of,   30
I heare not from her? Tis the hower and place
That shee appoynted. Whoe haue wee heere? This fellow
Has a pimpes face and lookes as if he weare
Her call, her fetch. With mee?
  Chamont.   Sir from the partie,
The ladie you should truck with, the lords wife 35
Your worshipe is to dubb or to make free
Of the companie of the horners—
  Perigot. Faire *Lamira.*
  Chamont.   The same sir.
  Perigot. And how, my honest squire of the dames? I see
Thou art of her privie counsell.
  Chamont.   Her graunt holds sir. 40
  Perigot. Oh rare, but when?
  Chamont.   Marry instantlie.

28. SD. *Exit.*] *Gifford*; not in MS 31–4. *rearranged by McIlwraith*; MS reads I
... appoynted / whoe ... face / & ... mee

Perigot. But where?
Chamont. Shee has out gon the cuninge of a woman
In the orderinge it both privatlie and securely;
You know *Dinant* the docter?
Perigot. Good.
Chamont. His howse
And him shee has made at her devotion sir:
Nay wonder not, most of theis empricques
Thrive better by conivence in such cases
Then theire lame practize: framinge some distemper,
The foole her lord—
Perigot. Lords may bee what they please,
I question not theire pattent.
Chamont. —hath consented
That this night privatlie shee shall take a clister,
Which hee beleeues the docter ministers
And never thincks of you.
Perigot. A good wench still.
Chamont. And there without suspition—
Perigot. Excellent,
I make this lord my cuckold.
Chamont. True, and write
The reverend drudginge docter my copartener
And fellow bawd; next year wee will haue him warden
Of our societie.
Perigot. There, there, I shall burst,
I am so swolne with pleasure: noe more talkinge,
Deere keeper of the vaultinge dore, lead on.
Chamont. Chardge you as bouldlie.
Perigot. Doe not feare, I haue
A staff to taint and brauelie.
Chamont. Saue the splinters
If it break in the incounter.
Perigot. Witty rascall! *Exeunt.*

[IV. iv]   *Enter* CLARINDOR, BELLISANT, *and* BEAUPRÉ.

Clarindor. Boast of your favors madam!
Bellisant. Pardon sir
My feares, since it is growne a generall custome
In our hott youth to keepe a cattalogue

IV. iv. 4–38　　　*The Parliament of Love*　　　153

Of conquests this waie gott, nor doe they thinck
Theire victorie compleate vnlesse they publish,　　　5
To theire disgrace that are made captive to em,
How farr they haue prevaild.
　　Clarindor.　　　　　　I would haue such rascalls
First gelded and then hangd.
　　Bellisant.　　　　　　Remember to sir
To what extremities your loue had brought you,
And since I saud your life, I may with iustice　　　10
By silence chardge you to preserve myne honor,
Which howsoeuer to my conscious self
I am tainted, foulely tainted, to the world
I am free from all suspition.
　　Clarindor.　　　　　　Can you thinck
Il)e doe myself that wronge? Altho I had　　　15
A lawye)rs mercynarie tongue still mouinge
　　　)this pretious carkanet, theis iewells
　　　of your magnif)icence ⟨sho⟩uld keepe mee
13ʳ A *Pithagorean*, and euer silent.
Noe rest secure sweete Lady, and excuse　　　20
My suddaine and abrupt departure from you,
And if the fault makes forfeit of your grace,
A quick retorne shall ransome and redeeme it.
　　Bellisant. Bee myndfull of your oathes.　　　[*Walks aside.*]
　　Clarindor.　　　　　　I am gott off,
And leaue the memorie of them behind mee.　　　25
Now if I can find out my scoffinge gulls,
Novall and *Perigot*, besides my wage
Which is already sure, I shall retorne
Theire bitter iests and wound them with my tongue
Much deeper then my sword: oh but the oathes　　　30
I haue made to the contrary, and her creditt
Of which I should bee tender,—tush, both hould
With mee an equall vallue; the wise say
That the whole fabrique of a womans lighter
Then winde or feathers; what is then her fame?　　　35
A kind of nothinge, not to bee preservd
With the losse of so much money: tis sound doctrine
And I will follow it.　　　　　　　　　　*Exit.*

　　　IV. iv. 24 SD. *Walks aside.*] *after Gifford; not in MS*

    Bellisant.   Prithee bee not doubtfull,
Lett the wild coult runne his course.
    Beaupré.   I must confesse
I cannot sound the depth of what you purpose,   40
But I much feare—
    Bellisant.   That hee will blab; I know it,
And that a secret scalds him, that hee suffers
Till hee hath vented what I seeme to wish
Hee should conceale; but lett him, I am armd fort.   *Exeunt.*

[IV. v]   *Enter* CHAMONT, DINANT, LAMIRA, CLARINDA *and* SERVANTS.

    Chamont. For *Perigot*, hees in the toyle, nere doubt it.
Oh had you seene how his veynes sweld with lust
When I brought him to the chamber, how he gloried
And stretchd his limbs preparinge them for action,
And takinge mee to bee a pander, plainely tould mee   5
Twas more delight to haue a lord his cuckold
Then to enioy my lady; there I left him
In contemplation, greedilie expectinge
Lamiras presence, but in sted of her
I haue prepard him other visitants.   10
You know what you haue to doe?
    1 *Servant.*   Feare not my lord,
Hee shall curvet I warrant him in a blancket.
    2 *Servant.* Weel disciple him with dogg whips, and take off
His rampant edge.
    Chamont.   His life saud, that remember,
You cannot bee to cruell.
    Dinant.   For his pupill,   15
My wifes inamorato, if could weeds,
Remoud but one degree from deadlie poyson,
Haue not forgott theire certaine opperation,
You shall see his courage coold; and in that temper,
Till hee haue howld himself into my pardon,   20
I vow to keepe him.
    Within, Novall.   Ho docter, master docter!
    Dinant. The games afoote; wee will lett slipp; conceale
Your selues a little.
                Enter NOVALL.
    Novall.   Oh a thowsand agues

IV. v. 24-52   *The Parliament of Love*   155

Play at barlie breake in my bones, my bloods a poole
On the soden frozen and the isicles   25
Cutt euery veyne, tis heere, heere, euery where,
Oh deere deere master docter!
    Dinant.   I must seeme
Not to vnderstand him, twill increase his torture.—
How doe you sir, has the potion wrought? Doe you feele
An alteration? haue your swellings left you?   30
Is your blood still rebellious?
    Novall.   Oh good docter,
I am a ghost, I haue nor fle⟨sh nor blood
Nor heate nor warmth about mee.⟨
    Dinant.   Doe not desemble,
I know you ar⟨e⟩ high an⟨d jovial.
    Novall.   Iouiall docter?
Noe I am all amort, as if I had laine   35
Three daies in my graue alreadie.
    Dinant.   I will raise you,
For looke you sir you are a liberall patient,
Nor must I, while you can bee such, parte with you,
Tis against the lawes of our colledge. Pray you marke mee,
I haue with curiosity considerd   40
Your constitution to bee hot and moyst
And that at your nativitie *Iupiter*
And *Venus* weare in coniunction, whence followes
By necessarie consiquence you must bee
A most insatiat letcher.
    Novall.   Oh I haue beene,   45
I haue been I confesse, but now I cannot
Thinck of a woman.
    Dinant.   For your health you must sir
Both thinck, and see, and touch, you are but a dead man ells.
    Novall. That waie I am already.
    Dinant.   You must take
And sodenlie, tis a concealed receipt,   50
A buxsome iucy wench.
    Novall.   Oh twill not downe sir,
I haue noe swallow fort.

IV. v. 31-2. docter, / I] *Gifford*; undivided *MS*   49-50. take / And] *Gifford*;
undivided *MS*   51-2. sir, / I] *Gifford*; undivided *MS*

Dinant.   Now since I would
Haue the disease as priuat as the cure
(For tis a secret), I haue wrought my wife
To bee both phisique and phisitian
To giue you ease; will you walke to her?
    Novall.   Oh docter,
I cannot stand, in euerie part aboute mee
I haue the palsie but my tongue.
    Dinant.   Nay then
You are obstinate and refuse my gentle offer,
Or ells tis foolish modestie. Come heither,
Come my *Clarinda*, tis noe comon curtesie,
Comfort the gentleman.
    Novall.   This is ten tymes worse.
    Chamont. He does torment him rarely.
    Dinant.   Shee is not coy sir;
What thinck you, is not this a pritty foote
And a cleane instep? I will leaue the calf
For you to finde and iudge of; heeres a hand to,
Try it, the palme is moyst; her youthfull blood
Runnes stronge in euery azure veyne, the face to
Nere knew the helpe of art, and altogeither
May serue the turne after a longe sea voyage
For the captaine himself.
    Novall.   I am a swabber docter,
A bloodlesse swabber, haue not strength enough
To clense her poope.
    Dinant.   Fie, you shame yourself
And the profession of your ruttinge gallants,
That hold theire docters wiues as free for them
As some of vs our apothecaries.
    Novall. Good sir, noe more.
    Dinant.   Take her aside, cornute mee,
I giue you leaue, what should a quacksalver,
A fellow that does deale with druggs as I doe,
(That has not meanes to giue her choyce of gownes,
Iewells, and rich imbrotherd petticoates)
Doe with so faire a bedfellow, shee beinge fashiond

56–7. docter, / I] *Gifford*; *undivided MS*   58–9. then / You] *Gifford*; *undivided MS*

IV. v. 83-108   *The Parliament of Love*   157

To purge a rich heires raynes, to bee the mistress
Of a court gallant, did you not tell her so?
    Novall. I haue betrayd myself, I did, I did.   85
    Dinant. And that rich marchants, advocates and docters,
How ere deservinge from the comon wealth,
On forfeit of the citties charter weare
Predestind cuckolds.
    Novall.   Have s⟩ome pitty docter,
I was an herritique but now converted   90
    ⟩little, little respitt.
    Dinant.   tow⟩ne bull
        reveng⟩e all good mens wrongs
⟨   ⟩
And now will play the tyrant. To dissect thee,
14ʳ Eate thie flesh of with burninge corosiues,   95
Or write with Aqua fortis in thie forhead
Thie base intent to wronge my bed, weare iustice,
And to doe lesse weare foolish pitty in mee:
I speake it, ribald.
    Novall.   *Perigot, Perigot,*
Woe to thie cursed counsaile!
    Chamont.   *Perigot?*   100
Did hee advise you to this course?
    Novall.   Hee did.
    Chamont. And hee has his reward fort.
    Within, Perigot.   Will you murther mee?
    Servants. Once more aloft with him.
    Perigot.   Murther, murther, murther, murther!

    Enter SERVANTS *with* PERIGOT.

    Chamont. What conceald bakd meate haue you there? a present?
Is it goates flesh? It smells ranck.
    1 *Servant.*   Wee haue had   105
Sweete woorke ont my lord.
    2 *Servant.*   I warrant you tis tender,
It wants noe cookinge, yet if you thinck fitt
Weel bruise it againe.

    89. pitty] *Gifford*; tty *MS*   89–90. docter, / I] *Gifford*; *undivided MS*
99–100. *Perigot,* / Woe] *Gifford*; *undivided MS*   100–1. *Perigot?* / Did] *Gifford*;
undivided MS   105–6. had / Sweete] *Gifford*; *undivided MS*

Perigot.   As you are Christians spare mee,
I am ielly within already, and without
Imbrothered all ore with statute lace.
What would you more?
 Novall.   My tutor in the gynne to?
This is some comfort, hee is as good as drenchd
And now weel both bee chast.
 Chamont.   What, wast a catt
You haue encounterd mounsier, you are scratchd so?
My Ladie sure forgott to pare her nayles
Before your soft embraces.
 Dinant.   Hee has tooke greate paines,
What a sweate hees in.
 Chamont.   Oh hees a master dancer,
Knowes how to caper into a ladies favor.
One lofty trick more deere mounsier.
 Novall.   That I had
But strength to laugh at him, blancketted like a dogg
And like a cutpurse whipd: I am sure that now
Hee cannot ieere mee.
 Perigot.   May not a man haue leaue
To hange himself?
 Chamont.   Noe that weare too much mercy;
Live to bee wretched, live to bee the talke
Of the conduit and the bakehowse; I will haue thee
Picterd as thou art now, and thie whole story
Sunge to some villanous tune in a lewd ballet,
And make thee so notorious to the world
That boyes in the streetes shall hoot at the; come *Lamira*
And triumph ore him; dost thou see this lady
My wife, whose honor foolishlie thou thoughts
To vndermyne and make a servant to
Thie bruitish lust, laughinge at thie affliction?
And as a signe shee scornes thee sett her foote
Vppon thie head? doe so: sdeath, but resist
Once more, you caper.
 Perigot.   I am at the stake
And must indure it.

  122–3. leaue / To] *Gifford*; *undivided MS*   132–3. *rearranged by Gifford*; *MS reads*
  to ... lust / laughinge ... affliction   136–7. stake / And] *Gifford*; *undivided MS*

IV. v. 137–64   *The Parliament of Love*   159

 Chamont.   Spurne him to.
 Lamira.   Troth sir,
I doe him to much grace.
 Chamont.   Now as a schole boy
Does kisse the rod that gaue him chastizment,
To proue thou art a slaue, meete with thie lips 140
The instrument that corrects thee.
 Perigot.   Haue you done yet?
 Dinant. How like a paire of crest falne iades they looke now!
 Clarinda. They are not worth our scorne.
 Perigot.   Oh pupill, pupill!
 Novall. Tutor, I am drenchd; lett vs condole togeith⟨er.
 Chamont. And wheres the ticklinge itch now, my deere m⟨ounsier,
To saie this lords my cuckold? Im tyrd, ⟨ 146
That wee had fresh doggs to bait e⟨m.

     Enter CLARINDOR.

 Clarindor. I am acquainted with the storie,
The docters man has tould mee all.
 Dinant.   Vppon em!
 Perigot. Clarindore? worst of all; for him to know this 150
Is a second blancketinge.
 Novall.   I againe am drenchd
To looke vppon him.
 Clarindor.   How ist man? beare vpp;
You that comend adultery, I am glad
To see it thrive so well. Fie *Perrigot*,
Deiected? happilie thou wouldst haue vs thinck 155
This is the first tyme that thou didst curvet
And come aloft in a blancket, by *St Dennis*
Heere are shrewd scratches to, but nothinge to
A man of resolution whose shoulders
Are of them selues armor of proofe against 160
A bastinado, and will tyre ten beadles.
 Perigot. Mock on, know noe mercy.
 Clarindor.   Thrifty younge men!
What a chardge is sau'd in wenchinge, and tis tymely,
A certaine wager of three thowsand crownes

  137–8. sir, / I] *Gifford; undivided MS* 146. Im] *MS* (m *added by another hand*)
151–2. drenchd/ To *McIlwraith; undivided MS*

Is lost and must bee paid, my paire of puppies; 165
The coy dame *Bellisant* hath stoopd: beare witnes
This chaine and iewells you haue seene her weare;
The fellow that her groomes kickd downe the staires
Has crepd into her bed, and to assure you
Theres noe deceipt shee shall confesse so much: 170
I haue inioyd her.
    Chamont.   Are you serious?
    Clarindor.   Yes sir,
And glorie in it.
    Chamont.   Nay then giue ouer foolinge:
Thou lyest and art a villaine, a base villaine,
To slander her.
    Clarindor.   You are a lord, my Lord, and that
Bids mee forbeare you, but I will make good 175
What euer I haue said.
    Chamont.   Ile not loose tyme
To change words with the; the kinge hath ordaind
A parliament of loue to right her wrongs,
To which I summon thee.   *Exit.*
    Clarindor.   Your worst, I care not;
Farwell Babions.   *Exit.*
    Dinant.   Heere was a suddaine change. 180
Nay you must quitt my howse; shogge on kind patient,
And as you like my phisick, when you are
Rampant againe you know I haue that can coole you.
Nay mounsier *Perigot*, helpe your pupill of to;
Your counsaile brought him on; ha, noe replie? 185
Are you struck dumbe? Yf you are wrongd, complaine.
    Perigot. Wee shall find freinds to right vs.
    Dinant.   And I iustice;
The cause beinge heard I aske noe more. Hence, vanish!
                                                        Exeunt.

Finis Actus Quarti

171–2. sir, / And] *McIlwraith*; *undivided MS*

Actus Quintus

Enter CHAMONT, PHILAMOR, *and* LAFORT.

Philamor. Montrosse slaine, and by *Cleremond*!
Chamont.   Tis to true.
  Lafort. But wondrous strange that anie difference,
Espetially of such a deadlie nature,
Should ere devide so eminent a freindship.
  Philamor. The miracle is greater that a lady,
His most devoted mistress *Leonora*,
Against the vsuall softnes of her sex,
Should with such violence and hate pursue
Her amorous servant, since I am informd
That⟩ hee was apprehended by her practize;
And⟩ when hee comes to tryall for his life
She'll rise u⟩p his accuser.
  Chamont.   So tis rumerd,
And thats the motiue that younge *Cleremond*
Makes it his humble suite to haue his cause
Decided in the Parliament of loue,
For hee pretends the bloody quarrell grew
From grounds that clayme a reference to that place;
Nor feares hee, so you graunte him equall hearinge,
But with vnanswerable proofe to render
The cruell *Leonora* tainted with
A guilt beyond his.
  Lafort.   The kinge is acquainted
Alreadie with the accident; besides,
Hee hath voutsafd to read divers petitions
Preferd on seuerall causes, one against
Mounsier *Dinant* his docter by *Novall*,
A second in which madam *Bellisant*
Complaines against *Clarindore*; there is a bill to
Brought in by *Perigot* against your Lordshipp;
All which in person hee resolues to heare,
Then as a iudge to censure.
  Philamor.   See the forme,
Choyce musique vshers him.

Chamont. Lett vs meete the troope
And mixe with 'em.
　Philamor.　　　Twill poyse your expectation.

Enter CHARLES. *The Lords ioyne with the troopes. A preist with the image of Cupid. A barr sett forth.*

Then enter CLEREMOND, CLARINDOR, BELLISANT, LEONORA, BEAUPRÉ, PERIGOT, NOVALL, [DINANT,] *and* OFFICER. MONTROSS *on a beere before the barr.*

Charles. Lett it not seeme a wonder, nor begett
An ill opinion in this faire assembly,
That heere I place this statue; tis not done,
Vppon the forfeit of our grace, that you
Should with a superstitious reverence
Fall downe and worship it, nor can it bee
Presumd wee hope younge *Charles*, that iustlie holds
The honord tytle of most Christian kinge,
Should euer nourish such idolotrous thoughts.
Tis rather to instruct deceaud mankind
How much pure Loue, that had his birth in heaven
And scornes to bee receaud a guest but in
A noble hart prepard to entertaine him,
Is by the grosse misprition of weake men
Abusd and iniurd. That celestiall fyer
Which herogliphically is discribd
In this his bow, his quiuer, and his torch,
First warmd theire bloods and after gaue a name
To the old heroicque sperrits, such as *Orpheus*,
That drew men differinge little then from beasts
To civell gouerment, or famd *Alcides*
The tirant queller, that refusd the plaine
And easie path leadinge to vitious pleasures
And ending in a precipice deepe as hell,
To scale the ragged cliff on whose firme top
Virtue and honnor crownd with wreathes of starrs
Did sitt trivmphant. But it wilbee answerd,
The world decayinge in her strength, that now
Wee are not equall to those antient tymes

V. i. 46. Is] *Gifford*; as *MS*　　56. ending] *Gifford*; ended *MS*

V. i. 62–91   *The Parliament of Love*   163

And therefor tweare impertinent and tedious
To cite more presidents of that reverend age,
But rather to endevor as wee purposd
To giue encouragement by reward to such   65
As with theire best nerves imitate that old goodnes,
And with seveere correction to reforme
The moderne vices. Begin, reade the bills.
   Cleremond. Lett myne bee first my lord, twas first preferd.
   Bellisant. But till my cause bee heard our whole sex s⟨uffers. 70
   Officer. Back, keepe back there!
   Novall.   Prithee gentle officer,
Handle mee gingerlie or I fall t⟨o pieces
Before I can ple⟨ad⟩ myne⟨.
   Perigot.   I am br⟨uised
⟨   ⟩
   Omnes.   Iustice, iustice!
   Charles. Forbeare theis clamors! You shall all bee heard;   75
And to confirme I am noe partiall iudge,
By lottery decide it; heeres noe favor.
Whose bill is first, *Lafort*?
   Lafort.   Tis *Cleremonds*.
   Charles. The second?
   Lafort.   *Perigots*, the third *Novalls*.
   Novall. Our cases are both lamentable tutor.   80
   Perigot. And I am glad they shalbee heard togeither;
Wee cannot stand asunder.
   Charles.   Whats the last?
   Lafort. The iniurd ladie *Bellisants*.
   Charles.   To the first then,
And so proceede in order.
   Philamor.   Stand to the barr.
   Leonora. Speake *Cleremond* thie greefe, as I will myne.   85
   Perigot. A confident little pleader, weare I in case
I would giue her a doble fee.
   Novall.   So would I tutor.
   Officer. Silence, silence.
   Cleremond. Should I rise vpp to plead my innocence,
Tho with the favor of the court I stood   90
Acquitted to the world, yea tho the wounds

                91. yea] *Gifford*; ye MS

Of my dead freind (which like so manie mouthes
With bloody tongues cry out alowd against mee)
By your aucthoritie weare closd, yet heere
A not to bee corrupted iudge, my conscience,
Would not alone condem mee, but inflict
Such lingringe tortures on mee, as the hangman,
Tho witty in his crueltie, could not equall.
I therefore doe confesse a guilty cause
Touchinge the fact, and vncompelld acknowledge
My self the instrument of a cryme the sunne,
Hidinge his face in a thick maske of clowds
As frighted with the horror, durst not looke on.
But if your lawes with greater rigor punish
Such as invent a mischeif then the organs
By whome tis putt in act (they trulie beinge
The first greate wheeles by which the lesser moue)
Then stand forth *Leonora*, and Ile proue
The white robe of my inocence tainted with
But one black spott of guilt, and euen that one
By thie hand cast on mee, but thine dyed ore
Ten tymes in graine in hells most vglie cullors.
   Leonora. The fellow is distracted, see how hee raues;
Now as I liue yf detestation of
His basenes would but giue mee leaue I should
Begin to pitty him.
   Cleremond.   Frontless ympudence
And not to bee replide to. Sir to you
And theis subordinate ministers of yourself
I turne my speech, to her I doe repent
I ere voutsafd a sillable. My birth
Was noble as tis knowne, nor lett it rellish
Of arrogance to saie my fathers care
With curiousnes and cost did traine mee vpp
In all those liberall quallities that comend
A gentleman, and when the tender downe
Vppon my chin tould mee I was a man,
I came to court; there youth, ease and example
First made mee feele the pleasinge paines of loue,
And there I saw this woman, saw and lou'd her
With more then comon ardor, for that deitie

(Such our affection makes him) whose dread power
Tooke forth the choycest arrow headed with
Not loose but loyall flames, which aymed at mee,
I c⟩ame with greedie haste to meete the shaft
    ⟩ge that my captiue hart was made 135
      ⟩his devine artillery
          ⟩s⟨⟩rv⟨   ⟩d, ⟨ ⟩noe relation
⟨   ⟩
But the shott made at her was not like myne
Of gold, nor of pale lead that breeds disdaine, 140
Cupid himself disclaymes it; I thinck rather
(As by the sequell t'will appeare) some fury
From burninge *Acharon* snatch'd a sulpher brand
That smoakd with hate, the parent of red murther,
And threw it in her boosome. Pardon mee 145
Tho I dwell longe vppon the cause that did
Produce such dire effects; and to omitt
For your much patience sake the cuninge trap
In which shee caught mee, and with horrid oathes
Imbarqued mee on a sea of human blood, 150
I come to the last sceane.
  Leonora.   Tis tyme, for this
Growes stale and tedious.
  Cleremond.   When I saie shee had,
To satisfie her fell rage, as a pennance
Forcd mee to this black deede, her vow to given
That I should marrie her, and shee conceale mee: 155
When to her view I brought the slaughterd bodie
Of my deere freind, and labord with my teares
To stirr compunction in her, ayded to
By the sad obiect which might witnes for mee
At what an ouer rate I haue made purchase 160
Of her longe wishd embraces, then greate sir,
But that I had a mother and there may bee
Some two or three of her sex lesse faulty,
I should affirme shee was the perfect image
Of the divell her tutor that had left hell emptie 165
To dwell in wicked woman.
  Leonora.   Doe, rayle on.

       132. Tooke forth the] *conj. Lea*; tooke for the *MS*

Cleremond. For not alone shee gloried in my sufferings,
Forswore what shee had vowd, refusd to touch mee,
Much lesse to confort mee or giue mee harbor,
But instantlie, ere I could recollect 170
My scatterd scence, betrayd mee to your iustice
Which I submitt to hopinge in your wisdome
That as in mee you lopp a limbe of murder,
You will in her grubb vpp the roote. I haue said sir.
   Leonora. Much I confesse, but much to little purpose 175
And tho with gay rhetoricall florishes
You strive to guild a rotten cause, the touch
Of reason, fortified by truth, deliuerd
From my vnletterd tongue, shall shew it dust
And so to bee contemd. You haue trymd vpp 180
All your deservings (should I graunte them such)
With more care then a waiter of threescore
Does hide her wrinckles, which if shee encounter
The rayne, the winde, or sunne, the paint washd of
And to dim eyes discouerd,—I forbeare 185
The application and in a plaine stile
Come roundlie to the matter. Tis confessd
This pritty handsome gentleman (for theeues
Led to the gallowes are held proper men
And so I now will call him) would needs make mee 190
The mistress of his thoughts, nor did I scorne,
For truth is truth, to grace him as a servant.
Nay hee tooke pritty waies to win mee too,
For a court novice; euery yeare I was
His vallentine and in an anagram 195
My name worne in his hatt; hee made mee banquets
As if hee thought that ladies like to flyes
Weare to bee caught with sweete meates, quarrelld with
My taylor yf my gowne weare not the first
Of that edition, beate my shoemaker 200
If the least wrinckle on my foote appeard
As wronginge the proportion, and in t⟨y⟩me
Grew boulder, vsherd mee to m⟨asques
Or ells paid him that⟨

   186. plaine] *Gifford*; paine *MS*   191. scorne] *MS reviser*; scorne him *MS*
192. for truth is truth] *Gifford*; for truth is truth is truth *MS* (*deleted by the reviser*)

With such ⟨ ⟩ d⟨   205
And of good ranck are taken with such gambolls;
In a word I was so; and a sollem contract
Did passe betwixt vs, and the daie appoynted
That should make our embraces warrantable
And lawfull to the world, all things so carried   210
As hee ment naught but honorable loue.
    Charles. A pritty method.
    Philamor.   Quaintly to deliuerd.
    Leonora. But when hee thought mee sure, hee then gaue profe
That foule lust lurkd in the faire shape of loue;
For valuinge neither lawes devine nor human,   215
His credit nor my fame, with violence borne
On black saild wings of loose and base desires,
As yf his naturall parts had quite forsooke him,
And that the pleasures of the marriage bed
Weare to bee reapd with noe more ceremony   220
Then bruite beasts cupple, (I yet blush to speake it)
Hee tempted mee to yeild my honor vpp
To his libidinous twines, and like an athest
Scofd at the forme and orders of the church;
Nor ended so, but beinge by mee reproud,   225
Hee offerd violence but was prevented.
    Charles. Note a suddaine change.
    Lafort.   Twas foule in *Cleremond*.
    Leonora. I burninge then with a most virtuous anger
Raisd from my hart the memory of his name,
Revild and spitt at him, and knew twas iustice   230
That I should take those deities hee scornd,
Himen and *Cupid*, into my protection
And bee the instrument of theire revenge
And so I cast him off, scornd his submission,
His poore and childish whininges, willd my servants   235
To shutt my gates against him, but when neither
Disdaine, hate, nor contempt could free mee from
His loathsome importunities, and fyerd to
To wreake myne iniurd honor, I tooke gladlie
Advantage of his execrable oathes   240
To vndergoe what pennance I enioynd him;

           226. was] *inserted in MS by reviser*

Then to the terror of all future ribalds
That make noe difference betwene loue and lust
Imposd this taske vppon him. I haue said to;
Now when you please a censure.
  Chamont.   Shee has putt
The iudges to theire whisper.
  Novall.   What doe you thinck
Of theis proceedings tutor?
  Perigot.   The truth is
I like not the severytie of the court.
Would I weare quitt and in an hospitall;
I could lett fall my suite.
  Novall.   Tis still your counsaile.
  Charles. Wee are resolud, and with an equall hand
Will hold the scale of iustice, pitty shall not
Robb vs of strength and will to draw her sword
Nor passion transport vs. Lett a preist
And headsman bee in readines, doe you start
To heare them namd? Some little pawse wee graunt you
To take examination of yourselves,
What either of you haue deservd and whie
Theis instruments of our power are now thought vsefull:
You shall heare more anon—
  Cleremond.   I like not this.
  Leonora. A dredfull preperation, I confesse
It shakes my confidence.
  Clarindor.   I presumd this court
Had been in sport erected, but now I find
With horror to the strongest hopes I built on,
  ⟩tis not safe to bee subiect of
    ⟩kings
. . . To the second ca⟩use.
    . . . *Perigot's*⟩
  Novall.   Nay take mee alonge to,
And since that our complaints differ not much,
Dispatch vs both togeither: I accuse
This divilish docter.
  Perigot.   I this wicked lord.

245-6. putt / The] *Gifford*; undivided MS 246-7. thinck / Of] *McIlwraith*; undivided MS 247-8. is / I] *Gifford*; undivided MS

Novall. Tis knowne I was an able lustie man,
Fitt to gett souldiers to serve my kinge
And cuntry in the warrs, and how soeuer
Tis said I am not valliant of my self,
I was a striker, one that could strike home to,
And never did beget a girle tho drunk;
To make this good I could produce braue boyes
That others father, twiggs of myne owne graftinge
That lou'd a drume at four and ere full ten
Fought battailes for the parish they weare borne in;
And such by blowes, old stories saie, still prou'd
Fortunate captaines. Now where as in iustice
I should haue had a pention from the state
For my good service, this ingratefull docter,
Havinge noe child and never like to haue one,
Because in pitty of his barrennesse
I plotted how to help him to an heire,
Has with a drench so far disabled mee
That the greate Turke may trust mee with his virgins
And never vse a surgion; now consider
If this bee not hard measure and a wronge
To little don *Cupid*, if hee bee the god
Of cuplinge as tis said, and will vndoe,
Yf you giue way to this, all younger brothers
That carrie theire revenews in theire breeches.
Haue I not nickd it tutor?
  Perigot.   To a haire boy,
Our bills shall passe, nere feare it. For my case
It is the same sir, my intent as noble
As was my pupills.
  Chamont.   Plead it not ore againe then,
It takes much from the dignitie of the court
But to giue audience to such things as theis,
That doe in theire defence condem them selues
And neede not an accuser. To bee short sir,
And in a language as far from obsceanesse
As the foule cause will giue mee leaue, bee pleasd
To know thus much: theis hungrie paire of flesh flyes
And most inseperable brace of coxcombs,
Tho borne of divers mothers twins in basenes,

  Weare frequent at my table, had free welcome
And entertainement fitt for better men,
In the retorne of which this thanckfull mounsier
Tempted my wife, seducd her, at the least
To him shee did appeare so, which discouerd
And with what treachery hee did abuse
My bounties, treadinge vnderneath his feete
All due respect of hospitable rights
Or the honor of my familie, tho th' intent
Deservd a stabb e'ene at the holy alter,
I borrowed so much of your power to right mee
As to make him caper.
  Dinant.   For this gallant,
I doe confesse I coold him, spoyld his ramblinge;
Would all such as delight in it weare servd so,
And since you are acquainted with the motiues
That did induce mee to it I forbeare
A needlesse repetition.
  Chamont.   Tis not worth it.
The creminall iudge is ⟨fitter to take . . .
Of pleas of this ⟨base nature . . .
An ⟨in⟩iurd ladie ⟨for whose wrong . . .
I see the statue of the god of loue
Dropp downe teares of compassion, his sad mother
And faire cheekd graces that attend on her
Weepinge for companie, as if that all
The ornaments vppon the Paphian shrine
Weare with one gripe by sacrilidgious hands
Torne from the holy alter; tis a cause sir
That iustlie may exact your best attention
Which if you trulie vnderstand and censure
You not alone shall right the present tymes
But bind posterity to bee your debtor.
Stand forth deere madam. Looke vppon this face,
Examine euery feature and proportion
And you with mee must graunt this rare peice finishd,
Nature disparinge ere to make the like,
Brake sodenlie the mould in which twas fashiond;
Yet to increase your pitty and call on

    329. god] *Gifford*; good *MS*

Your iustice with seueritie, this faire outside
Was but the couer of a fairer mynd.
Thinck then what punishment hee must deserve
And iustlie suffer, that could arme his hart
With such impenitrable flinty hardnes   350
To iniure so much sweetenes.
    Clarindor.   I must stand
The furie of this tempest, which alreadie
Sings in my eares.
    Bellisant.   Greate sir, the too much praise
This lord (my guardian once) has showerd vppon mee
Could not but spring vpp blushes in my cheekes   355
Yf greefe had left mee blood enough to speake
My humble modestie; and so far I am
From beinge litigious, that though I weare robd
Of my whole estate, provided my faire name
Had been vnwounded, I had now been silent;   360
But since the wronge I vndergoe, if smotherd,
Would iniure our whole sex, I must laie by
My native bashfullnes and putt on bouldnes
Fitt to incounter with the impudence
Of this bad man; that from his birth hath been   365
So farr from nourishinge an honest thought
That the abuse of virgins was his studie
And dailie practize. His forsakinge of
His wife, distressed *Beaupré*, his lewd wager
With theis companions like himself to whore mee,   370
His desperate resolution in my presence
To bee his owne assassinate, to prevent which,
Foolish compassion forcd mee to surrender
The life of life, my honor, I passe ouer.
Ile onlie toutch his foule ingratitude,   375
To scourge which monster, yf your lawes prouide not
A punishment with rigor they are vselesse,
Or if the sword, the gallowes or the wheele
Bee due to such as spoyle vs of our goods,
Pirillus brazen bull, the English rack,   380
The German pincers, or the Scotch oyld boote,
Tho ioynd togeither, yet come short of tortore

    360. I had] *Gifford*; had *MS*   362. iniure] *Gifford*; inure *MS*

To theire full merrit those accursed wretches
That steale our reputations and good names,
As this base villaine has done myne. Forgiue mee 385
If rage provoke mee to vnciuell language;
The cause requires it. Was it not enough
That⟩ to preserve thie life, I lost myne honor,
But in reco⟩mpence of such a guift
      publi⟩sh it to my disgrace? 390
      u⟩nfortunate I:

fol. 18r Whome but of late the citty, nay all *Fraunce*
Durst bringe in opposition for chaste lyfe
With anie woman in the Christian world,
Am now become a by word and a scorne 395
In myne owne cuntry.
  Charles.   As I liue shee moues mee.
Is this true, *Clarindore*?
  Novall.   Oh tis very true sir,
Hee bragd of it to mee.
  Perigot.   And mee, nay since
Wee must bee censurd, weel giue evidence:
Tis comfort to haue fellowes in affliction; 400
You shall not scape fine mounsir.
  Clarindor.   Peace you dogboults.
Sir I adresse my self to you and hope
You haue reservd one eare for my defence,
The other freely given to my accuser.
This ladie that complaines of iniury, 405
If shee haue anie, was her self the cause
That brought it to her, for beinge younge and rich,
And faire to as you see, and from that prowd,
Shee bosted of her strength as if it weare not
In the power of loue to vndermyne the fort 410
On which her chastety was stronglie raizd.
I that was bred a courtier and servd
Almost my whole life vnder *Cupids* ensignes,
Could not in iustice but interpret this
As an affront to the greate god of loue 415
And all his followers, if shee weare not brought

398–9. since / Wee] *McIlwraith; undivided MS*   399. weel] *Gifford* (we'll); wee *MS*

To due obedience: theis stronge reasons sir
Made mee to vndertake her. How I woed
Or what I swore it skills not (since tis said
And trulie *Iupiter* and *Venus* smile   420
At louers periuries); to bee breefe, shee yeilded
And I enioyd her. If this bee a cryme
And all such as offend this plesant waie
Are to bee punishd, I am sure you would haue
Few followers in the court; you are younge your self sir,   425
And what would you in such a cause—?
　　Lafort.　　　　　　　　Forbeare!
　　Philamor. You are rude and insolent.
　　Clarindor.　　　　　　Good words gentle iudges,
I haue noe oyld tongue, and I hope my bluntnes
Will not offend.
　　Charles.　　But did you boast your conquest
Got on this lady?
　　Clarindor.　　After victory,   430
A little glorie in a souldiers mouth
Is not vncomly, loue beinge a kind of warr to,
And what I did atchiue was full of labor
As his that winnes stronge townes and merrits trivmphes.
I thought it could not but take from myne honor,   435
Besides the wager of three thowsand crownes
Made sure by her confession of my service,
If it had been conceald.
　　Charles.　　　　Whoe would haue thought
That such an impudence could ere haue harbord
In the brest of anie gentleman? In this   440
Thou dost degrade thie self of all the honors
Thie ancestors left thee, and in thie base natu⟨re
Tis to apparant that thou art a peasan⟨t.
Boast of a ladies favors? this ⟨confirms
Thou art the captain ⟨of that . . .   445
That glorie in th⟨eir sins . . .
With name of courtship, such as dare belye
Greate womens bounties and repulsd and scornd
Comitt adultery with theire good names,

438. conceald] *Gifford*; reueald *MS*

And never touch theire persons. I am sorry 450
For your sake madam that I cannot make
Such reparations for you in your honor
As I desire, for yf I should compell him
To marry you it weare to him a blessinge,
To you a punishment, hee beinge so vnworthie; 455
I therefore doe resigne my place to you:
Bee your owne iudge, what ere you shall determine,
By my crowne Ile see performd.
 Clarindor.   I am in a fine case
To stand at a womans mercy.
 Bellisant.   Then thus sir:
I am not bloody nor bent to revenge, 460
And studie his amendment not his ruin;
Yet since you haue given vpp your power to mee
For punishment I doe enioyne him to
Marry this More.
 Clarindor. A divell, hange mee rather!
 Charles. Tis not to bee alterd.
 Clarindor.   This is cruelty 465
Beyond expression; Sir I haue a wife.
 Chamont. I to good for thee. View her well
And then, this varnish from her face washd of,
Thou shalt find *Beaupré.*
 Clarindor.   *Beaupré!*
 Bellisant.   Yes, his wife sir,
Longe by him with violence cast of, 470
And in this shape shee servd mee; all my studies
Ayminge to make a faire attonement for her
To which your maiesty may now constraine him.
 Clarindor. It needs not, I receaue her and aske pardon
Of her and you.
 Bellisant. On both our parts tis graunted. 475
This was your bedfellow and filld your armes
When you thought you imbracd mee; I am yet
A virgin, nor had euer given consent
In my chast howse to such a wanton passage
But that I knew that her desires weare lawfull. 480
But now noe more personated passion:
This is the man I lou'd, that I lou'd trulie,

How euer I desembled; and with him
Dyes all affection in mee. So, greate sir,
Resume your seate.
    Charles. An vnexpected yssue
Which I reioyce in. Would tweare in our power
To give a period to the rest like this
And spare our heavie censure, but the death
Of good *Montrosse* forbids it. *Cleremond*
Thou instantlie shalt marry *Leonora*,
Which done, as sodenly thie head cutt off
And corpes interd, vppon thie graue Ile build
A roome of eight foote square, in which this lady
For punishment of her cruelty shall dye
An anchoresse.
    Leonora. I doe repent and rather
Will marry him and forgiue him.
    Cleremond. Bind her to
Her word greate sir, *Montrosse* liues, this a plott
      ⟩this obstinate lady
  [*Leonora.*] ⟩ b⟨e⟩ so cheated
⟨ ⟩
  [*Montross.*] ⟩ repent
Your good opinion of mee when thought dead,
Nor lett not my neglect to wait vppon you
(Consideringe what a busines of import
Diverted mee) bee thought vnpardonable.
    Bellisant. For my part tis forgiuen, and thus I seale
. . . . . .
    Charles. Nor are wee averse
To your desires, may you liue longe and happie.
    Novall. Mercy to vs greate sir!
    Perigot. Wee will become
Chast and reformed men.
    Chamont and Dinant. Wee both are suiters
On this submission for your pardon sir.
    Charles. Which wee in part will graunt, but to deter
Others by theire example from pursuinge
Vnlawfull lusts, that thinck adultery
A sport to bee oft practizd, fix on them

    483. and with] *Gifford*; w^th *MS*   511. but] *Gifford*; w^ch *MS*

Twoe Satirs heads, and so, in capitall letters 515
Theire foule intents written on theire brests, weel haue them
Led thrice through *Paris*, then at the court gate
To stand three howers, where *Clarindor* shall make
His recantation for the iniury
Done to the lady *Bellisant* and read 520
A sharp invective endinge with a curse
Against all such as boast of ladies favors;
Which done, both trulie penitent, my docter
Shall vse his best art to restore your strength
And render *Perigot* a perfect man. 525

So breake wee vpp loues parliament which wee hope,
Beinge for mirth intended, shall not meete with
An ill construction, and if then faire ladies and gratious spectators,
You please to approue it, wee hope youl invite
Your freinds to see it often with delight. 530

Finis

APPENDIX

CORRECTIONS TO THE MALONE SOCIETY REPRINT

[The first reading is the correct one of A. K. McIlwraith; the reading following the bracket is that of *MSR*. The figure in round brackets is the line number in *MSR*.]

I. a

2 gaardian] guardian (2)
3 yo^u,] yo^u (4)
46 int] wit (52)
64 dy'd] dyd (71)
70 chastety] chastity (77)
101 thancks] thanks (115)
106 madam] madam. (123)

I. b

4 Conquerer] Conqueror (128)
17 thancks] thanks (141)
22 appeares] appears (146)
24 dulnes] dulness (148)
   Cleremond] Claremond (148)
32 theire] their (158)
33 vnworthines] unworthines (159)
39 inherritt] inheritt (167)
49 thanckfull] thankfull (178)
56 thinck] think (185)
61 wee] we (191)
62 vs] us (192)
64 vnactiue] vnactive (194)
88 determyne] deterrmyne (220)
89 redresse,] redresse (221)
95 mynd] mind (227)
117 finde] find (255)
130 pennance,] pennance (271)

II. i

3 pupill,] pupill (282)
8 haue] have (287)
12 streetes] streets (291)
32 doe] do (317)
33 lawndresses,] lawndresses (318)
60 mee,] mee (347)

II. ii

1 back,] back (386)
4 SD. *Cleremond*] *Clerimond* (392)
17 slaud] slavd (409)
27 haue] have (421)
39 inreases] increases (434)
50 out side,] outside (447)
54 m^r,] m^r (451)
67 Condemd] Condemnd (465)
91 liu'd] liv'd (492)
109 vppon] vpon (512)
111 absolue] absolve (514)
118 iniury] iniury. (521)
    witnes] witness (522)
132 foole,] foole (536)
159 never] neuer (568)
    mee] me (568)

II. iii

14 tyme,] tyme (591)
25 servant] servant, (604)

178   *The Parliament of Love*

33 heauen.] heauen, (615)
46 Cleremond,] Cleremond (632)
65 Loue] loue (654)
81 mee;] mee, (671)
84 laughd] laught (674)
103 death,] death (697)
104 till] til (698)
121 Cruell,] Cruell (719)

III. i

7   theire] their (749)
51 longe] long (800)
52 vsd] usd (802)
54 hee] hell (805)
72 did hee] did he (825)
76 entertainem^t,]   entertainem^t (832)
83 ⟨b⟩ostings] ⟩oslings (841)
106 oppertunitie]   opportunitie (871)
109 noe,] noe (875)
111 towsd] tousd (877)
115 scornefull] scorneful (881)
125 dores] doo^{r}es (893)
128 and] & (897)
130 new] newe (900)
135 womans longing] Womans Longinge (907)

III. ii

3   adventure,] adventure (912)
8   mee,] mee (916)
30 freinds] frends (938)
35 bindes] binds (943)
    noe] no (943)
66 shrinck] shrink (979)
77 heere] heer (992)
84 moue] move (999)
85 angrie,] angrie (1000)
116 muste] must (1036)
124 aid,] aid (1046)
128 designes.] designes (1050)
162 haue] have (1089)

III. iii

2   methincks] me thinks (1096)
3   deliuerd] delivered (1097)
5   repulse] repulse, (1099)
17 scornefully] scornfully (1115)
18 names,] names (1116)
33 Iudgm^t] Iudgem^t (1137)
34 vnderstand] understand (1138)
85 yo^u] yo (1196)
106 bost] both (1219)
109 'em] em (1223)
142 would] woulde (1263)

IV. i

54 enioyinge] enjoyinge (1348)
84 hee] he (1385)

IV. ii

29 deservd] deserved (1442)
33 prodegies] prodigies (1448)
64 Cleremond] Clerimond (1483)

IV. iv

17 ⟩this] th⟩is (1650)
29 iests] jests (1663)

IV. v

2   seeme] seene (1684)
4   stretchd] stretched (1686)
21 ho docter] ho docter, (1707)
27 deere deere] deere, deere (1714)
67 noyst] moyst (1763)
72 swabber] swabber. (1769)
86 marchants,] marchants (1785)
110 imbrothered] imbrotherd (1814)
132 vndermyne] undermyne (1842)
137 to.] to (1848)
151 drenchd] drenched (1867)
170 noe] no (1887)

V. i

13 younge] young (1928)

Appendix

23 peticons] petitions (1939)
38 downe] down (1958)
53 gouerm^t] gouernm^t (1973)
59 wilbee] willbee (1979)
107 wheeles] wheele (2035)
115 mee] me (2043)
143 snatch'd] snatched (2071)
172 submitt] submitte (2103)
179 shew] show (2110)
230 knew] know (2163)

243 betwene] betweene (2176)
251 wee] we (2185)
254 trassport] transsport (2188)
307 inseperable] inseparable (2248)
335 Alter,] Alter (2278)
412 and] & (2360)
464 divell,] divell (2420)
466 expression;] expression. (2423)
472 attonement] atonement (2431)
483 desembled] disembled (2443)

THE UNNATURAL COMBAT

INTRODUCTION

(a) *Date*

From a note on the fly-leaf of his copy of *The Unnatural Combat* (Bodleian Mal. 237) it appears that Malone was unable to find any trace of a licence for performance in Sir Henry Herbert's Office Book. However, the manuscript was damaged when Malone saw it, and its record incomplete,[1] so that it is impossible to accept his confident conclusion, 'This play ought to have been placed as Massingers first play, now extant; for it was acted before the year 1622.'

Massinger's own reference to the play as '*this old Tragedie, without Prologue, or Epilogue, it being composed in a time (and that too, peradventure, as knowing as this) when such by ornaments, were not advanced above the fabricque of the whole worke*' (A2ᵛ) is less helpful than it appears. There have been vain attempts to date the tragedy by discovering a particular time at which Prologues and Epilogues fell out of use,[2] but contemporary remarks by other dramatists such as Shirley and Suckling (see the commentary on the Dedication, ll. 24–7) make it clear that Massinger only intended to apologize for not supplying a Prologue and Epilogue with his play, at a time when such 'by ornaments' were enjoying a vogue of which he thoroughly disapproved.[3]

A very clear echo in *The Unnatural Combat* of the famous line from *The Changeling*, 'Oh come not near me, sir, I shall defile

---

[1] See G. E. Bentley, 'Authenticity and Attribution in the Jacobean and Caroline Drama', *English Institute Essays 1942*, 1943, 101–18.

[2] 'The evidence does not indicate, nor indeed does Massinger suggest, that there was a period during which the prologue was abandoned', Baldwin Maxwell, *Studies in Beaumont, Fletcher, and Massinger*, 1939, p. 223. Within the text itself (IV. ii. 23–4) there is mention of a comedy and its prologue.

[3] A. N. Wiley, *Rare Prologues and Epilogues 1642–1700*, 1940, p. xxix, points out that towards 1640 the Prologue and Epilogue were developing an independent existence; in 1637 Heywood published thirty-five of them as *Sundry Fancies writ upon Several Occasions*. Massinger's resentment of the customary demand for a prologue is plainly expressed in the Blackfriars prologue to *The Emperor of the East*.

you',[1] establishes that Massinger's tragedy was written no earlier than May 1622, and Telfer (pp. 41-2) pointed out that in Belgarde's description of the poor soldier's privilege 'To be often drunke, and sweare, yet pay no forfeit / To the poore' (IV. ii. 74-5) there is an equally certain reference to the statutes against swearing and drunkenness passed between 19 February and 29 May 1624.[2] In his review of Telfer's edition of the play, A. K. McIlwraith observed that since these acts were before the two houses of parliament from March to May 1621, that year rather than 1624 was the *terminus a quo* for the play.[3] However, it was not until the enactment of the statutes in 1624 that popular support or criticism was widely expressed in ballads, broadsides, sermons, and plays.[4]

It is more difficult to establish a *terminus ad quem* for *The Unnatural Combat*, but there are sufficient correspondences between details in the play and contemporary events to strongly suggest that the tragedy was written late in 1624, or early in 1625.

There is a striking correspondence between the opening scenes of *The Unnatural Combat*, in which a great admiral is accused of dealings with 'the pirates of Argers and Tunis' who are raiding Marseilles, and the situation brought about by contemporary Turkish pirate raids on the English coast:

> Had he discharg'd the trust committed to him,
> With that experience and fidelitie
> He practis'd heretofore, it could not be
> Our Navie should be block'd up, and in our sight
> Our goods made prize, our Sailors sold for slaves.
>   (I. i. 188-92)

[1] *The Changeling*, V. iii. 149 (Revels edition); cf. *The Unnatural Combat*, V. ii. 198. Middleton and Rowley's play was licensed for performance on 7 May 1622; there is a record of a production at Court on 4 Jan. 1624.

[2] 21 James I, c. 8 and c. 20. The latter provided for a fine of one shilling for profanity, to be used for the relief of the poor. If the fine was not paid, an offender over the age of twelve was to be set in the stocks for three hours, while a child was to be given a whipping.

[3] *RES*, ix (1933), 484-5.

[4] A ballad of 1624 called 'A Statute for Swearers and Drunkards, or Forsake now your follies, your booke cannot save you, For if you sweare and be drunke, the Stockes will haue you' is reprinted in *A Pepysian Garland*, ed. H. E. Rollins, 1922, pp. 189-95. The broadside *Sundry Lawes against sweareing cursing and blaspheming the holy name of GOD* was entered in the Stationers' Register on June 24, and sermons titled *Drunkerds Cup*, and *NOAHS drunkenness*, were entered there on 3 May and 1 June 1624 (Arber, iv. 117-19). Jonson's *Masque of Owls*, which was performed on 19 Aug. 1624, presents a knight, 'a passionate wight, / Who, since the Act against swearing . . . Hath at twelve pence an oath / (For that (I take it) is the rate) / Sworne himselfe out of his estate' (ll. 158-65).

Introduction

A newsletter from John Chamberlain to Carleton, dated 4 September 1624, mentions both such piratical incursions and a number of sensational trials for 'unnaturall and inhuman facts':

> We may well thincke we live in a very wicked age, when so many unnaturall and inhuman facts are in triall at one sessions, the sonne for murthering the mother, the mother for drowning her own daughter of nine yeares old, and one brother for killing another. We heare out of the west countrie of 11 Turkish pirates on the Severnside, that have taken divers prises and caried away many prisoners from the land. Our East Indian marchants have presented many petitions and sent divers of their companie this progresse after the King to remonstrate that they cannot subsist, but must give over the trade yf they be no better protected. What aunswer soever they have, they seeme not satisfied, and thincke Secretarie Conway somwhat partiall and leaning to the other side.[1]

Malefort's otherwise gratuitous reference to 'a forraigne Queene' (III. iii. 9) may reflect contemporary public interest in a foreign bride and future queen of England. On the collapse of the Spanish Match in 1623, James and his advisers had turned in 1624 to France, and Sir Simons D'Ewes recorded that 'On Sunday, November the 21st, many bonfires were made in London, at night, by public command, because the match between Prince Charles and the Princess Henrietta Maria, the French King's sister, was concluded upon.'[2]

That part of Massinger's play which deals with the 'cast Captaine' Belgarde, left famished and penniless until he moves Beaufort Senior to pay and employ him, becomes highly topical seen against the background of military activity in 1624-5, a background also reflected in *A New Way to Pay Old Debts*.[3]

Count von Mansfeld arrived in London on 16 March to lead James's belated expedition to the Palatinate, and on 5 June Chamberlain reported to Carleton that there was 'much canvassing about the making of captains and colonells for these new forces that are to be raised to assist the Low-countries'. But the troops that were levied were shamefully neglected, being left unpaid, unfed, and 'discontented / For want of means' (III. iii. 112-13). Jonson, in *The Masque of Owls* (performed in August 1624), has 'A true Owle of

---

[1] *Letters*, ii. 579-80.
[2] *Autobiography*, ed. J. O. Halliwell, 1845, i. 257.
[3] See the discussion of the date of Massinger's comedy, below, pp. 273-5, for fuller details.

London / That gives out he is undone, / Being a Cheese-monger, / By trusting two of the younger / Captaines, for the hunger / Of their halfe-staru'd number; / Whom since they haue shipt away: / And left him God to pay' (ll. 106–13).

Within such a context, Massinger's Belgarde becomes a figure in whom the dramatist exploits patriotic enthusiasm for the expedition to the Palatinate, and widespread criticism of its totally inadequate means of support.[1]

(b) *Sources*

In 1932, R. S. Telfer demonstrated that the material first thought to be Massinger's source for the play, the events and persons associated with the Cenci trial (1598–9), bore only the most general resemblance to the plot of *The Unnatural Combat*. At the same time, he suggested new sources among earlier Jacobean plays, particularly *A King and No King*, *The Laws of Candy*, and *The Tragedy of Sir John Van Olden Barnavelt*.[2]

However, the main sources of Massinger's tragedy have now been discovered, in Jonson and in the *Minor Declamations* attributed to Quintilian.

Massinger found the model for Malefort and his crimes in the description of Catiline's life in Jonson's *Catiline* (1611), I. i. 30–6:

> Be still thy incests, murders, rapes before
> Thy sense; thy forcing first a *Vestall* nunne;
> Thy parricide, late, on thine owne onely sonne,
> After his mother; to make emptie way
> For thy last wicked nuptialls; worse, then they,
> That blaze that act of thy incestuous life,
> Which got thee, at once, a daughter, and a wife.

Sallust may have helped to complete the tragic conception of a man guilty of the most terrible acts and tormented in conscience, with his description of Catiline's inner torment: 'a Conscience accused of murder, hatefull to Gods and men, can neither take rest by day, nor by night, but is alwaies tormented with the appeal of its owne

---

[1] Three other topical allusions, with some bearing on the dating of the play, are discussed in the Commentary on I. i. 402, III. iii. 35–6, and IV. ii. 35.

[2] *The Unnatural Combat*, edited by R. S. Telfer (Princeton Studies in English, 7), Princeton, 1932, pp. 1–39. The earlier view was developed by Koeppel, *Quellen-Studien*, pp. 85–9, and C. Stratton, 'The Cenci Story in Literature and in Fact', *Studies in English Drama*, edited by A. Gaw, Baltimore, 1917, pp. 130–60.

Introduction

guiltinesse. And thereupon his complexion changed, his eye grewe dull, his pace variable, sometimes quick, sometimes slow; surely his face bewrayed his troubled conscience.'[1]

To fill in the outline provided by Jonson, Massinger fashioned a narrative from elements in several of the story sketches found in the *Declamations* attributed to Quintilian in his time, but now thought to be a later compilation.[2] There were ten editions printed before 1624, the latest being the Geneva and Paris editions of 1618. The particular text used by Massinger has not yet been determined.

In Declamation cccxvii, 'Imperator provocatus a filio', Massinger found the story of a general's son who fled to the enemy, and later sent out a challenge to his father. The general declined a duel, but killed his son in battle, whereupon he was charged with refusing to accept an enemy's challenge to single combat. From this the dramatist developed the trial of Malefort (I. i), and the 'unnatural combat' between the Admiral and his renegade son (II. i); supplying a motive for the son's hatred of his father in the Catiline-like murder of Malefort's first wife, and adding Theocrine's courtship by Beaufort, by way of preparation for the second action of the play.

Declamation cclxxxix, 'Amator filiae', supplied Massinger with the incest story which forms the basis of Acts III–V. 'A certain man handed his beautiful daughter over to the keeping of a friend, confessing to him that he had fallen in love with her, and asking him not to return her to him, even if he asked for her back. After some time he did ask for the girl's return, but was refused. The father hanged himself. The friend was accused of being the cause of his death.' As Massinger handles this story, the friend becomes a pitiless revenger who, given the opportunity, carries off Theocrine and rapes her—a change prompted both by Catiline's rape of a Vestal Virgin, and by another part of the same Declamation: 'Suppose the father had not left his daughter in my home; had given no instructions: nevertheless, as a close friend, I wanted to protect the girl, who was the object of her father's uncontrollable passion (for it was not parental love that drove him on). Suppose I carried her off; I kept her shut away . . . suppose that I didn't return her, and he took the matter to law.'

---

[1] Sallust, *Catiline*, xv. 4–5; translated by Thomas Heywood (1608).
[2] For an account of the *Declamations*, see *A Literary History of Rome in the Silver Age: From Tiberius to Hadrian*, J. Wight Duff (rev. ed. A. M. Duff, 1960), pp. 331–7. The Teubner text, edited by C. Ritter in 1884, has been used for translations.

Malefort's spectacular death by lightning (rather than by suicide, as in the original story), and the final attack on Montrevile's 'fort' came respectively from Declamation cclxxiv, which deals with the case of a tyrant struck down in the forum by a bolt of lightning, and from Declamation cclxxxii, which relates how, when a tyrant ordered that the sister of a certain man should be brought into his citadel, her brother, wearing his sister's clothes, made his way into the stronghold and killed the tyrant. The propriety of the assassin's disguise is debated in the second Declamation, and this suggested to Massinger the series of episodes in which Belgarde appears in different uniforms, from a soldier's buff jerkin to a gallant's impractical finery.

There are references to pirates in the *Declamations*, but it is probable that contemporary raids on the English coast by Barbary corsairs prompted the change from a military to a naval setting for the play. The specific French locale came from *The Theater of Honour and Knight-hood, or, A Compendious Chronicle and Historie of the whole Christian World* (1623), a translation by 'I. W.' of a French text by André Favyn, published at Paris in 1620. There Massinger found a description of Marseilles as 'one of the very goodliest Portes of Christendom', connected with a famous father and son, an English pirate, and 'the first Admirall of France' (pp. 358-9). Favyn also supplied useful information on French practice in a chapter on 'Duelloes, Fights *and Single* Combates, *perfourmed at the Sharpe, and to the extremitie of Life*' (Book 10, chapter 2).

As Telfer has shown in considerable detail (pp. 18-30), for his representation of an incestuous love, Massinger drew many ideas for behaviour and speech from Beaumont and Fletcher's *A King and No King* (1611). He also reworked material from some of his own earlier collaborated plays, occasionally repeating lines or short passages, but more often taking over the general framework of a dramatic episode, to fill it out with new material. C. L. Lockert noted that two of Theocrine's important scenes, the petition scene which opens the play, and Malefort's request for a marriage between his daughter and young Beaufort (II. iii), draw on the opening scene of *The Fatal Dowry*, and on the scene (II. ii) in which Beaumelle is bestowed on Charalois.[1] As in *The Fatal Dowry*, *The Unnatural Combat* moves from a petition for a hearing to a trial scene, and for

[1] Lockert's edition of *The Fatal Dowry*, Lancaster, Penn., 1918, pp. 4-5.

this Massinger went back to Barnavelt's trial before the Burgers, in *The Tragedy of Sir John Van Olden Barnavelt*, IV. iv. For the first climax of *The Unnatural Combat*, the duel between Malefort and his son (II. i), the dramatist drew on the confrontation of father and son in *The Laws of Candy*, I. ii. This is the method of a practical man of the theatre, returning to the formulae of two 'big' scenes, which, as Telfer suggests, had probably been very successful on the stage.[1]

(c) *Text*

The Unnatural Combat was entered in the Stationers' Register on February 14, 1639.

M^r. Waterson.   Entred for his Copy vnder the hands of m^r Wykes & m^r Mead warden a Tragedy called The vnnaturall Combatt by Phillip Massinger   vj^d.

(Register D 429; Greg, *Bibliography*, i. 50; Arber, iv. 455.)

Accordingly the tragedy was published in 1639, in quarto, for John Waterson, carrying the licence for printing on L2^v, '*Jmprimatur.* THO. WYKES. IAN. 21 1638 [i.e. 1639].'[2] The book was printed by 'E. G.' who, from his initials, was Edward Griffin junior.[3] This edition (the only seventeenth-century edition) is named in booksellers' lists and catalogues in 1640/1, 1656, 1661, 1663, 1671 and 1700.[4] The play described as 'Vnnaturall Brother by p. massing. Lond. 1639. Trag.' in a catalogue of Richard Sheldon's library drawn up between 1675 and 1680, must also be *The Unnatural Combat*.[5]

[1] Telfer, pp. 31–8.
[2] Thomas Wykes or Weekes was a Prebendary of St. Paul's, and chaplain to Bishop Juxon (1636–41). A later member of the panel of 'correctors of the press' set up by Archbishop Whitgift, he appears regularly as a licenser from 1634 onwards. His Imprimatur printed in *The Unnatural Combat* is the only one found among the Massinger quartos.
[3] The ornament on B1^r of *The Unnatural Combat* appears on A3^r and B1^r of Ford's *The Lady's Trial* (1639), and the ornament on A2^r of the quarto is found on A3^r of Suckling's *Brennoralt* (1648), both printed by Griffin. The four play quartos printed at his shop in 1639 (*The Unnatural Combat, The Lady's Trial, A King and No King, Philaster*) have the same style of speech heading, with the first speaker's name in each scene set above rather than at the side of the text, and a number of entries set in the right hand margin of the text.
[4] Greg, *Bibliography*, iii. 1189, 1317–18, 1326, 1351, and iv. 1661.
[5] See 'A Seventeenth Century Play-List', A. C. Baugh, *MLR*, xiii (1918), 401–11. The title occurs among a group of Massinger plays, and the catalogue was completed

The edition will be referred to from now on as *39*; the title-page is reproduced on page 195.

39 is in quarto, A², B–K⁴, L² (40 unnumbered leaves); see Greg, *Bibliography*, no. 559 (ii. 698). Signatures are in roman, except for E3, which is in italic; L2 is unsigned. The contents are: A1ʳ, *title*; A1ᵛ, 'The persons presented.'; A2ʳ, *dedication begins*, 'To my much Honoured Friend, ANTHONY SENTLIGER, Of Oukham in *Kent*, Esquire.'; A2ᵛ, *dedication ends, signed* 'PHILIP MASSINGER.'; B1ʳ, 'THE VNNATVRALL COMBAT.', *text begins*; L2ᵛ, *text ends*, '*FINIS.*', followed by the licence to print. The text is in roman, 20 lines measuring approximately 79 mm. There are usually 37 lines to the page (36 on B2ʳ, 32 on I3ʳ, and 29 on E3ʳ).

Two skeletons were used in the printing. The outer forme set of running titles made up for sheet B was transferred to the inner forme for sheets C–G, and I–L; conversely, the inner forme set of running titles was exchanged to the outer forme for those sheets. The running titles on I3ʳ and I4ʳ were reset.

It seems possible to distinguish the presence of four compositors working from cast-off copy, two of whom set up a comparatively small part of the play. The main shares in the work fell to compositor *A*, who set B1ʳ–B3ʳ, C (o), D (i), E (o), F (o), G (o), I, and K (i), and to compositor *B*, who set B3ᵛ–B4ᵛ, C (i), D (o), E (i), F (i), and G (i). The first man uses shorter speech headings (*Theo.*, *Ush.*, *Mon.*, as against *Theoc.*, *Usher.*, *Montr.*), and prefers *-y* to *-ie* endings, whereas the second man uses roughly the same number of both endings. Compositor *B* employs capitals much more frequently than his fellow, and prefers the *-'d* ending to *-d*, *-de*, or *-ed*, in the ratio 3 to 1, as against 5 to 3 for compositor *A*. In sheet B both men are easily distinguished; *A* by the anomalous speech heading *Iu. Beauf.*, and *B* by his failure to capitalize the initial letter of each line of verse, a practice which is continued on C1ᵛ and C2ʳ, and which almost certainly imitates the manuscript from which he was working.[1] The change from the speech heading *Mal. sen.* to

---

well before 1697, when Edward Filmer wrote his tragedy of the same name. Baugh notes that 'Brother' was written above the line of the entry, and it may be that it was filled in from memory. However, Antony á Wood, who drew up the catalogue, in his list of Massinger's plays in *Athenæ Oxonienses*, i (1691), gives 'Unnatural Brother/Combate' as alternative titles (column 536). There is no unnatural brother in Massinger's tragedy, and I am at a loss to explain such a title.

[1] Throughout the manuscript of *Believe As You List*, Massinger uses a capital at the beginning of a line of verse only where it would also be found in prose.

Mal. in the work of both compositors from D4ʳ through sheet G must reflect the author's practice (at that point, with the death of Malefort's son there is no longer any need to distinguish between father and son), but the appearance of a new speech heading *Malef.*, in sheets H and K, marks the introduction of a third compositor. In general he uses longer speech headings (*Theoc.*, *Usher.*, *Montr/e.*), and prefers *Ile* to the usual *I'll*. He strongly prefers *-y* to *ie*, but accepts variety in the forms of the past participle ending. Compositor *D* makes a brief appearance in sheet L. He alone uses roman as well as italic in stage directions, shows a strong preference for *-y* and *-'d* endings, and has a few distinctive speech headings (*Sold.*, as against *A*'s *Sould.*).

The quarto is insufficiently and at times wrongly punctuated, and has its share of misprints and turned letters, but on the whole is as carefully printed as the average Caroline quarto. Excluding shifts of type, seven of the twenty-two formes are variant. A (i), D (i), E (o), F (i), H (i) and L (o) exist in two states; I (o) in three states. McIlwraith found thirty-six press corrections in eighteen copies of the play, and their nature strongly suggests that Massinger was responsible for many of them. There are many spelling corrections which a press corrector would have been unlikely to bother with (e.g. II. iii. 100, IV. ii. 113, V. ii. 256), and a number of alterations to punctuation (brackets are added at II. iii. 75, 95–6, IV. i. 80, 94). In three instances (II. i. 217–19, IV. i. 241–2, IV. ii. 27–31), major changes are made which must be due to Massinger himself. In the last passage, for instance, the uncorrected text read,

> Doe you make an Owle of me? this day I will
> Receive no more Petitions,
> Here are bills of all sorts, and all sizes,
> If this be the pleasure of a rich suite, would I were
> Againe in my buffe jerkin, or my armour,

This must have been intended to read,

> Doe you make an Owle of me? this day I will
> Receive no more Petitions, here are bills
> Of all sorts, and all sizes, if this be
> The pleasure of a rich suite, would I were
> Againe in my buffe jerkin, or my armour,

but there is no attempt to recover this arrangement. (Perhaps

Massinger realized that the metrically irregular second and fourth lines pointed up the meaning more vigorously than the orthodox arrangement would have done.) Instead, the cliché 'all sorts, and all sizes' is removed by the substitution of 'occasions' for 'sorts', and the comma after 'sizes' is replaced by an appropriately stronger stop, an exclamation mark.

The printer's copy was very likely in the author's hand. The misreading 'their' for 'these' in two places (IV. i. 135, 156) suggests Massinger's spelling 'theis', and there are spellings characteristic of the author throughout the text (e.g. *ayre, carkase, counsaile, divell, ghesse, love-scæne, perfit*). Significantly 'which' never occurs for 'with' in *39*, though the reverse error appears twice (I. i. 72, III. iii. 47); this would follow if the copy-text had the abbreviation 'w^{c}h', but not 'wth', and in *Believe As You List* Massinger writes 'w^{c}h' commonly, but 'wth' only once. The number of passages in which verse is printed as prose, or wrongly divided, indicates a manuscript with several cramped or marginal additions and alterations, in the manner of the *Believe As You List* manuscript, and there are traces of Massinger's practice of massing names in a stage direction without prefixing 'Enter', and using stops rather than commas (e.g. II. i. 216, III. iii. 1, V. iii. 324).

The number of additions and alterations in the manuscript which have left their trace in the quarto might suggest a theatrical prompt copy with a long history, but there is little evidence of the prompter's hand in the positioning or wording of the stage directions, and ample evidence of the author's. There are several references to vaguely designated groups: '*wayting Women*'; '*Officers*'; '*Servants*'; '*Souldiers*'; '*others*'; '*the rest*'. At IV. ii. 89 there is an entry for '*a Bawd and two wenches, with two children*', but the children (non-speaking parts) are ignored in the exit direction, '*Exit Bawd and Whores*'. There are repeated calls for '*Loud Musicke*' or '*Sad musicke*', and for difficult stage effects—'*He's kill'd with a flash of lightning.*'—without any of the precise annotations expected of a book-keeper. Stage directions are frequently long and 'literary', describing gestures, appearance, actions, and dress: '*Enter Belgarde in a gallant habit*; *stayes at the door with his sword drawne*; *severall voyces within.*'; '*The souldiers thrust forth Theocrine, her garments loose, her haire disheveld.*'; '*Enter the Ghost of young* Malefort, *naked from the wast, full of wounds, leading in the shadow of a Ladie, her face leprous.*' Such directions are extremely interesting as

Introduction

indications of effects imagined by the author, but they are often inadequate or unnecessary as stage annotations.

There are copies of *39* in the following libraries and institutions: the University of Arizona; the Bodleian Library (2 copies); the Boston Public Library (2 copies); the British Museum (4 copies); Cambridge University Library; the Central Public Library, Cardiff; the Chapin Library; the University of Chicago; Columbia University; the Library of Congress; Cornell University; the Folger Shakespeare Library (3 copies); Harvard University; the Henry E. Huntington Library (2 copies); the University of Illinois; King's College, Cambridge; The University of Leeds; the University of Liverpool; the University of Manchester; Merton College, Oxford; the University of Michigan; the Pierpont Morgan Library; the Newberry Library; the College of the City of New York; the University of Pennsylvania (2 copies); the Carl H. Pforzheimer Library; Princeton University; Queen's College, Cambridge; the John Rylands Library; the National Library of Scotland (2 copies); the University of Sheffield; the Royal Library, Stockholm; the University of Texas; Trinity College, Cambridge; the Victoria and Albert Museum; Wadham College, Oxford; Worcester College, Oxford; and Yale University.

The present text has been prepared from the Bodleian Library copy, Malone 237.

The Unnatural Combat was printed in Dodsley's *A Select Collection of Old Plays*, viii (1744), and later in the collected editions of Coxeter, Mason, Gifford, Coleridge, and Cunningham. W. Harness, in the second volume of *The Plays of Philip Massinger adapted for Family Reading* (1830), printed most of the first three acts of the tragedy; an American edition of his bowdlerized text was published by Harper in 1831. A. K. McIlwraith prepared the first modern critical edition as part of his unpublished doctoral thesis, 'The Life and Works of Philip Massinger', Oxford, 1931; this was shortly followed by R. S. Telfer's critical edition of *The Unnatural Combat* (Princeton Studies in English, 7), Princeton, 1932. The work of these two editors has greatly eased the preparation of the present edition.

Because of its subject, the play has never been a popular one, but excerpts from the text were printed in *The British Muse*, edited by T. Hayward, 1738, *The Beauties of the English Drama*, printed for G. Robinson, 1777, Capell's *The School of Shakespeare*, 1779, and

Charles Lamb's *Specimens of English Dramatic Poets*, 1808. Maurice Chelli translated II. ii of the tragedy into French, in *Le Drame de Massinger*, Lyons, 1924.

(d) *Stage History*

Apart from the statement on the title-page of *39* that the play is published 'As it was presented by the Kings Majesties Servants at the GLOBE', little is known of the early stage history of *The Unnatural Combat*. It is possible that the first production of the play was followed by a revival in the late 1630s. At III. iii. 35-6, Belgarde calls for a song, 'the new one cald / The souldiers delight'. A ballad with this title was entered in the Stationers' Register on 16 March 1635,[1] which gives some ground for supposing that the particular song to which Belgarde refers was introduced into the text at some time between 1634 and 1639. However the 'new one' may just as well have been contemporary with the first performances of the tragedy, for the same title is mentioned in the anonymous manuscript play *The Partial Law*,[2] written perhaps as early as 1615, and the ballad seems to have undergone several transformations in its life span. *The Soldiers Delight in the North* was entered in the Stationers' Register on 24 April 1640, and there is a ballad called *The Soldiers Delight; or the She Voluntier* (1676) among the Roxburgh ballads (vii. 732-3).

There is good evidence that the play was never very popular. Performances seem to have been confined to the Globe,[3] the title-page is silent about audience reaction and the frequency of performance, and only one seventeenth-century edition was printed.

Although *The Unnatural Combat* is listed among the plays assigned to Thomas Killigrew, manager of the King's Majesty's Servants at

[1] Arber, iv. 334. T. W. Baldwin, in an unpublished note cited by Telfer (p. 44), identified this ballad with 'a new one, / The Souldiers Joy', mentioned in Glapthorne's *Revenge for Honour* (?1640), III. ii. 20-2.

[2] *The Partial Law*, ed. B. Dobell, 1908, II. iv: '*Man*: What daunce shall's have? An old man's bagge full of bones? *Woman*: I never lov'd to have to doe with old men's bones. Play me The souldier's delight' (p. 43). Bentley (v. 1388-9) supports Greg's view that the play is a Caroline one.

[3] It is unlikely that production at Blackfriars would have gone unmentioned on the title-page, yet the inclusion of 'The vnnaturall Cumbat' in a 1669 'Catalogue of part of His Ma[tes] Servants Playes as they were formerly acted at the Blackfryers' (Nicoll, i. 353-4) makes the evidence of the title-page less than conclusive. Bentley (iv. 824) notes that at this date it was unusual for a King's men's play to advertise performance at the Globe alone.

Introduction

the New Theatre, on 12 January 1669, there is nothing to show that Massinger's tragedy was ever revived on the Restoration stage. Writing in 1834, an anonymous dramatic critic implied that a mid-eighteenth century performance had taken place,[1] but this was probably no more than a vague recollection of the publication date of the 1639 quarto.

In 1782 Isaac Reed suggested that 'with very little alteration it might be rendered a valuable acquisition to the present stage',[2] but it was not until 1834 that *The Unnatural Combat* was adapted by Elton, and performed under the title *The Fatal Passion; or, The Unnatural Combat*, at the Royal Victoria Theatre on 8, 9, 10, 11, 13, and 17 May.[3] Massinger's tragedy was followed by the farce *Frank Fox Phipps, Esquire*, and the melodrama *The Heart of Midlothian*. Elton's text has not survived. He himself played the part of Malefort, Greene played Montrevile, and Mrs. Fisher played Theocrine. The cast also included Williams (Dupont), Debar (the Governor of Marseilles), and Forrester (Belgarde). A playbill in the Enthoven collection at the Victoria and Albert Museum for the performance on 17 May shows that some rearrangement of the cast took place during the season (Chippendale played Dupont, Debar Young Beaufort, and Doyne the Governor of Marseilles), and the tragedy was followed on that occasion by the pantomime *Don Juan*, and *The Gamester of Milan*. The original play was compressed into three acts, and to satisfy decorum, Malefort's incestuous love for his daughter was altered to the attempted seduction of a ward by her guardian. According to *The Times*,[4] 'Elton did his part very respectably. In face and figure he has some resemblance to Kean; but though he evidently intends it, the resemblance goes no further'. Another reviewer noted that 'The play has been got up with great attention to all the minor departments, if scenery and dress can now be called minor departments. The last scene, representing the burning of the town after *Malefort* has been struck dead by lightning, is very effective. The whole went off with great applause.'[5] The

---

[1] *The Morning Chronicle*, 10 May 1834: 'If we recollect rightly, it is more than a century since the original play was performed'.

[2] Quoted in M. J. Harley, 'The 18th century interest in English Drama before 1640 outside Shakespeare', unpublished thesis, University of Birmingham, 1963. In a review of the performance on 11 May 1834 (*British Museum Theatrical Cuttings*, iii (1832–4)), the play was said to be one 'which the late Mr Kean longed to bring upon the stage, yet dared not'.

[3] The dates are drawn from *The Times* and from Telfer, p. 46.

[4] *The Times*, 9 May 1834, p. 3.   [5] *The Morning Chronicle*, 10 May 1834.

Times also reported an opening-night disaster: 'the concluding scene was rendered much less effective than intended. The fortress was set on fire before its time, and then the lightning which should have killed Malefort, fell out of time and place and struck a post, and when it should have fallen, it appeared the scenic Jove had not another bolt left, so that Malefort fell and died quietly without any visible cause.'

Further performances of *The Unnatural Combat*; *or, The Admiral of Marseilles* were given at the Royal Pavilion, Whitechapel, on 22, 23, 24, and 27 September 1834. Elton himself again took the part of Malefort, and Miss Grove that of Theocrine. The tragedy was followed by a melodrama, *The Red Maid*, and a burletta called *Quarter Day*.[1]

No later performance of Massinger's tragedy is known.

[1] *The Times*, 22 Sept. 1834, p. 2. The Enthoven collection has two playbills relating to these performances.

THE VNNATVRALL COMBAT.

A Tragedie.

The Scæne *Marsellis*.

Written
BY
PHILIP MASSINGER.

As it was presented by the Kings Majesties Servants at the GLOBE.

LONDON,
Printed by E. G. for IOHN WATERSON, and are to be sold at his shop, at the signe of the Crowne, in S. *Pauls* Church-yard.
1639.

The persons presented.

Beaufort senior, Governour of *Marsellis*.
Beaufort junior, his sonne.
Malefort senior, Admirall of *Marsellis*.
Malefort junior, his sonne.
Chamont
Montaigne } Assistants to the Governour.
Lanour
Montrevile, a pretended friend to *Malefort senior*.
Belgarde, a poore Captaine.
Three Sea Captaines of the Navy of *Malefort junior*.
Servants.
Souldiers.
Theocrine, daughter to *Malefort senior*.
Two waiting women.
Usher.
Bawde.
Page.
Two Wenches.
[Officers.]
[Priest.]
[Two Children.]
[Ghost of *Malefort's* wife.]

20–3. Officers . . . wife.] *editor; not in 39*

To my much Honoured Friend,
ANTHONY SENTLIGER,
Of Oukham in *Kent*, Esquire.

SIR,

That the Patronage of trifles, in this kinde, hath long since rendred Dedications, and Inscriptions obsolete, and out of fashion, I perfectly understand, and cannot but ingenuously confesse, that I walking in the same path, may be truly argued by you of weaknesse, or wilfull errour: but the reasons and defences, for the tender of my service this way to you, are so just, that I cannot (in my thankefulnesse for so many favours received) but be ambitious to publish them. Your noble Father, Sir Warham Sentliger *(whose remarkeable vertues must be ever remembred) being, while hee lived, a master, for his pleasure, in Poetry, feared not to hold converse with divers, whose necessitous fortunes made it their profession, among which, by the clemency of his judgement, I was not in the last place admitted. You (the Heire of his honour and estate) inherited his good inclinations to men of my poore quality, of which I cannot give any ampler testimony, than by my free and glad profession of it to the world. Besides, (and it was not the least encouragement to mee) many of eminence, and the best of such, who disdained not to take notice of mee, have not thought themselves disparaged, I dare not say honoured, to be celebrated the Patrons of my humble studies. In the first file of which, I am confident, you shall have no cause to blush, to finde your Name written. I present you with this old Tragedie, without Prologue, or Epilogue, it being composed in a time (and that too, peradventure, as knowing as this) when such by ornaments, were not advanced above the fabricque of the whole worke. Accept it I beseech you, as it is, and continue your favour to the Author.*

Your Servant,
PHILIP MASSINGER.

28. *your*] *Coxeter; you* 39

The Unnaturall Combat

Actus primus, Scæna prima.

MONTREVILE, THEOCRINE, USHER, PAGE, WAITING WOMEN.

Montrevile. Now to bee modest Madam, when you are
A suitor for your father, would appeare
Courser then bouldnesse; you a while must part with
Soft silence, and the blushings of a virgin,
Though I must grant (did not this cause command it) 5
They are rich jewells you have ever worne
To all mens admiration. In this age,
If by our owne forc'd importunity,
Or others purchasd intercession, or
Corrupting bribes we can make our approches 10
To justice, guarded from us by sterne power,
We blesse the meanes, and industry.
    Usher.   Heres musicke
In this bagge shall wake her, though shee had drunke *Opium*,
Or eaten Mandrakes; let commanders talke
Of cannons to make breaches, give but fire 15
To this petarde, it shall blow open Madam
The iron doores of a judge, and make you entrance,
When they (let them doe what they can) with all
Their mines, their culverins, and Basiliscos
Shall coole their feete without, this being the pickelocke 20
That never failes.
    Montrevile.   Tis true, gold can doe much,
But beauty more. Were I the governour,
Though the Admirall your father stood convicted
Of what he's only doubted, halfe a dozen
Of sweet close kisses from these cherry lips, 25

    I. i. 1. you] *Dodsley*; your *39*   3–4. *rearranged by Gifford*; *39 reads* Courser...
part / with ... virgin,   5–6. *rearranged by Dodsley*; *39 reads* Though ... cõmand
/ it) ... worne   7. admiration.] *Mason*; ~, *39*

With some short active conference in private,
Should signe his generall pardon.
   Theocrine.   These light words sir
Doe ill become the weight of my sad fortune
And I much wonder you that doe professe
Your selfe to be my fathers bosome friend,   30
Can raise mirth from his misery.
   Montrevile.   You mistake me,
I share in his calamity, and only
Deliver my thoughts freely, what I should doe
For such a rare petitioner, and if
Youle follow the directions I prescribe,   35
With my best judgement I'll marke out the way
For his inlargement.
   Theocrine.   With all reall joy,
I shall put what you counsell into act,
Provided it be honest.
   Montrevile.   Honesty
In a faire she client (trust to my experience)   40
Seldome or never prospers, the world's wicked.
Wee are men, not saints sweet Lady; you must practice
The manners of the time, if you intend
To have favour from it; do not deceive your selfe
By building too much on the false foundations   45
Of chastity and vertue. Bid your wayters
Stand farther of, and i'll come neerer to you.
   1. *Woman.* Some wicked counsaile on my life.
   2. *Woman.*   Nere doubt it,
If it proceed from him.
   Page.   I wonder that
My Lord so much affects him.
   Usher.   Thou art a child   50
And dost not understand on what strong bases
This freindship's raisd between this *Mountrevile*
And our Lord Monsieur *Malefort*, but ile teach thee;
From thy yeares they have been joynt purchasers,
In fire, and water-works, and truckt together.   55

   35. directions I prescribe,] *Gifford*; ~, ~ ~ˌ *39*   48. *1. Woman*] *Dodsley*; *2. Wom. 39*   50–5. as verse *Gifford*; as prose *39*   53. thee;] *Dodsley*; ~ˌ *39*
55. fire] *Mason*; furs *39*

Page. In fire and waterworks?
Usher.   Commodities boy
Which you may know hereafter.
    Page.   And deale in 'em
When the trade has given you over, as appeares
By the increase of your high forehead.
    Usher.   Heare's a cracke,
I thinke they sucke this knowledge in their milke.   60
    Page. I had had an ignorant nurse else. I have tide sir
My Ladies garter, and can ghesse—
    Usher.   Peace infant,
Tales out a schoole! take heed, you will be britchd else.
                                   THEOCRINE *falls off.*
    1. *Woman.* My Ladies colour changes.
    2. *Woman.*   She falls off too.
    Theocrine. You are a naughty man, indeed you are,   65
And I will sooner perish with my father
Then at this price redeeme him.
    Montrevile.   Take your owne way,
Your modest legall way, tis not your vayle
Nor mourning habit, nor these creatures taught
To howle, and cry, when you beginne to whimper,   70
Nor following my Lords coach in the dirt,
Nor that which you relie upon, a bribe,
Will doe it when there's something he likes better.
These courses fit an old crone of threescore,
That had seaven yeares together tirde the court   75
With tedious petitions and clamors,
For the recovery of a straggling husband,
To pay forsooth the duties of one to her,
But for a Lady of your tempting beauties,
Your youth and ravishing features to hope only   80
In such a suite as this is, to gaine favor
Without exchange of courtesie, you conceive me,
Were madnes at the height.

    58–9. *rearranged by Coxeter*; 39 *reads* When . . . of / your . . . forehead.   63 SD.
THEOCRINE . . . *off.*] *Gifford*; *follows* infant, (l. 62) 39   72. which] *Dodsley*;
with 39   74. fit] *McIlwraith*; in 39   77. straggling] *Mason*;
strangling 39

Enter BEAUFORT JUNIOR *and* BELGARDE.

<blockquote>
Heres brave yong *Beaufort*
The meteor of *Marsellis*, one that houlds
The governour his fathers will and power 85
In more awe then his owne; come, come advance,
Present your bag cramm'd with crowns of the sunne,
Doe you thinke he cares for money? he loves pleasure,
Burne your petition, burne it, he dotes on you,
Upon my knowledge; to his cabinet, doe 90
And hee will point you out a certaine course,
Be the cause right or wrong, to have your father
Releasd with much facility.   *Exit* MONTREVILE.
    Theocrine.   Doe you heare?
Take a pander with you.
    Beaufort junior.   I tell thee there is neither
Imployment yet nor money.
    Belgarde.   I have commanded 95
And spent my owne meanes in my countries service,
In hope to raise a fortune.
    Beaufort junior.   Many have hop'd so,
But hopes prove seldome certainties with souldiers.
    Belgarde. If no preferment, let me but receive
My pay that is behinde, to set me up 100
A taverne, or a vaulting house; while men love
Or drunkennesse, or lechery, they'l nere fayle me:
Shall I have that?
    Beaufort junior. As our prises are brought in,
Till then you must be patient.
    Belgarde.   In the meane time,
How shall I doe for cloths?
    Beaufort junior.   As most captaines doe; 105
Philosopher like, carry all you have about you.
    Belgarde. But how shall I do to satisfie Colon Mounsieur,
There lies the doubt.
    Beaufort junior.   Thats easily decided,
My fathers tables free for any man
That hath borne armes.
</blockquote>

83 SD. BEAUFORT JUNIOR] *Coxeter*; *Beaufort 39*   107. Colon Mounsieur] *Mason*; Calon Mounsieur 39

Belgarde. And theres good store of meat? 110
Beaufort junior. Never feare that.
Belgarde. I'le seeke no other ordinarie then,
But be his daily ghest without invitement,
And if my stomacke hould, Ile feed so heartily
As he shall pay me suddainely to be quit of me. 115
Beaufort junior. Tis shee.
Belgarde. And further—
Beaufort junior. Away, you are troublesome,
Designes of more weight—
Belgarde. Ha faire *Theocrine,*
Nay if a velvet peticote move in the front
Buffe jerkins must to the rere, I know my manners;
This is indeed great businesse, mine a gugawe, 120
I may dance attendance, this must be dispatchd,
And suddainly, or all will goe to wracke.
Charge her home in the flank my Lord, nay I am gone sir.
  Exit BELGARDE.
Beaufort junior. Nay pray you Madam rise, or I'll kneele with you.
Page. I would bring you on your knees, were I a woman. 125
Beaufort junior. What is it can deserve so poore a name,
As a suite to me? this more then mortall forme
Was fashioned to command and not intreate,
Your will but knowne is served.
Theocrine. Great Sir, my father
My brave deserving father, but that sorrow 130
Forbids the use of speech—
Beaufort junior. I understand you,
Without the ayds of those interpreters
That fall from your faire eies, I know you labour
The libertie of your father, at the least
An equall hearing to acquit himselfe: 135
And 'tis not to endeere my service to you,
Though I must adde and pray you with patience heare it,
'Tis hard to be effected, in respect
The State's incens'd against him: all presuming
The world of outrages his impious sonne, 140
Turn'd worse than Pirat in his cruelties

134–224. *39 capitalizes the initial letter of a line only where it coincides with the beginning of a sentence*

Expres'd to this poore Countrey, could not be
With such ease put in execution, if
Your father (of late our great Admirall)
Held not or correspondencie, or conniv'd   145
At his proceedings.
    Theocrine.   And must he then suffer,
His cause unheard?
    Beaufort junior.   As yet it is resolv'd so,
In their determination. But suppose,
For I would nourish hope, not kill it in you,
I should divert the torrent of their purpose,   150
And render them that are implacable,
Impartiall Judges, and not sway'd with spleene:
Will you, I dare not say in recompence,
For that includes a debt you cannot owe me,
But in your liberall bountie, in my suit   155
To you be gracious?
    Theocrine.   You entreat of me, Sir,
What I should offer to you, with confession
That you much undervalue your owne worth,
Should you receive me, since there come with you
Not lustfull fires, but faire and lawfull flames.   160
But I must be excus'd, 'tis now no time
For me to thinke of Hymenæall joyes.
Can he (and pray you, Sir, consider it)
That gave me life, and faculties to love,
Be, as he is now, ready to be devour'd   165
By ravenous wolves, and at that instant, I
But entertaine a thought of those delights
In which perhaps my ardor meets with yours?
Dutie and pietie forbid it, Sir.
    Beaufort junior. But this effected, and your father free,   170
What is your answer?
    Theocrine.   Everie minute to me
Will be a tedious age till our embraces
Are warrantable to the world.
    Beaufort junior.   I urge no more,
Confirme it with a kisse.
    Theocrine.   I doubly seale it.

    173-4. more, / Confirme] *Coxeter*; *undivided 39*

Usher. This would doe better a bed, the businesse ended, [*Aside.*]
They are the lovingest Couple. 176

Enter BEAUFORT SENIOR, *the Governour,* MONTAIGNE, CHAMONT, LANOUR.

Beaufort junior. Here comes my father
With the Councell of war, deliver your petition,
And leave the rest to me.
 Beaufort senior. I am sorrie, Lady,
Your fathers guilt compels your innocence
To aske what I in justice must denie. 180
 Beaufort junior. For my sake, Sir, pray you receive, and read it.
 Beaufort senior. Thou foolish boy, I can deny thee nothing.
 Beaufort junior. Thus far we are happie. Madam quit the place,
You shall heare how we succeed.
 Theocrine. Goodnesse reward you.
 Exeunt THEOCRINE, USHER, PAGE, WOMEN.
 Montaigne. It is apparent, and we stay too long 185
To censure *Malefort* as he deserves.
 Chamont. There is no colour of reason that makes for him:
Had he discharg'd the trust committed to him,
With that experience and fidelitie
He practis'd heretofore, it could not be 190
Our Navie should be block'd up, and in our sight
Our goods made prize, our Sailors sold for slaves,
By his prodigious issue.
 Lanour. I much grieve,
After so many brave and high atchievements,
He should in one ill forfeit all the good 195
He ever did his Countrey.
 Beaufort senior. Well, 'tis granted.
 Beaufort junior. I humbly thanke you, Sir.
 Beaufort senior. He shall have hearing,
His irons too strucke off, bring him before us;
But seeke no further favour.
 Beaufort junior. Sir, I dare not. *Exit* BEAUFORT JUNIOR.
 Beaufort senior. Monsieur *Chamont, Montaigne, Lanour,* assistants
By a Commission from the most Christian King 201
In punishing, or freeing *Malefort*

175 SD. *Aside.*] editor; not in 39   176 SD. *Governour,*] Coxeter; ~∧ 39

Our late great Admirall: though I know you need not
Instructions from me, how to dispose of
Your selves in this mans triall (that exacts   205
Your cleerest judgements) give me leave with favour
To offer my opinion: we are to heare him,
A little looking backe on his faire actions,
Loyall, and true demeanour, not as now
By the generall voyce, already he's condemn'd.   210
But if we finde (as most beleeve) he hath held
Intelligence with his accursed sonne,
Falne off from all allegeance, and turn'd
(But for what cause we know not) the most bloudy
And fatall enemie, this Countrey ever   215
Repented to have brought forth, all compassion
Of what he was, or may be, if now pardon'd,
We sit ingag'd to censure him with all
Extremitie and rigour.
    Chamont.   Your Lordship shewes us
A path which we will tread in.
    Lanour.   He that leaves   220
To follow, as you lead, will lose himselfe.
    Montaigne. I'le not be singular.

    Enter BEAUFORT JUNIOR, MONTREVILE, MALEFORT
        SENIOR, BELGARDE, *Officers.*

    Beaufort senior.   He comes, but with
A strange distracted looke.
    Malefort senior.   Live I once more
To see these hands and armes free? these, that often
In the most dreadfull horror of a fight,   225
Have beene as sea-markes to teach such as were
Seconds in my attempts, to steere betweene
The rocks of too much daring, and pale feare,
To reach the Port of victory? when my sword,
Advancd thus, to my enemies appear'd   230
A hairy comet, threatenning death and ruine
To such as durst behold it. These the legs
That when our ships were grappl'd, carried me

    216. all compassion] *39*; no compassion *conj. Mason*; all compassion / Of his years pass'd over, all consideration *conj. Gifford*; sans compassion *conj. McIlwraith*
    233. ships] *Coxeter*; ship *39*

With such swift motion from decke to decke,
As they that saw it, with amazment cri'd;   235
He does not runne, but flies.
    Montrevile.   He still retaines
The greatnesse of his spirit.
    Malefort senior.   Now crampt with irons,
Hunger, and could, they hardly doe support me,
But I forget my selfe. O my good Lords
That sit there as my judges to determine   240
The life and death of *Malefort*, where are now
Those shoutes, those chearefull lookes, those loud applauses
With which when I return'd loaden with spoile
You entertain'd your Admirall? all's forgotten,
And I stand here to give accompt for that   245
Of which I am as free, and innocent
As he that never saw the eyes of him,
For whom I stand suspected.
    Beaufort senior.   Monsieur *Malefort*
Let not your passion so farre transport you
As to believe from any private malice,   250
Or envie to your person you are question'd,
Nor doe the suppositions want waight,
That doe invite us to a strong assurance,
Your sonne—
    Malefort senior. My shame.
    Beaufort senior.   Pray you heare with patience, never
Without assistance, or sure aids from you,   255
Could with the pirates of Argers and Tunis,
Ev'n those that you had almost twice defeated,
Acquire such credit, as with them to be
Made absolute commander! (pray you observe me)
If there had not some contract pass'd betweene you,   260
That when occasion serv'd you would joyne with 'em
To the ruine of *Marsellis*!
    Montrevile.   More, what urg'd
Your sonne to turne Apostata?
    Chamont.   Had he from
The State, or Governour, the least neglect

---

254. never] *Dodsley*; ever *39*   257–323. *39 capitalizes the initial letter of a line only where it coincides with the beginning of a sentence*

Which envie could interpret for a wrong? 265
    Lanour. Or if you slept not in your charge, how could
So many ships as doe infest our Coast
And have in our owne Harbor shut our Navie
Come in unfought with?
    Beaufort junior.   They put him hardly to it.
    Malefort senior. My Lords, with as much brevitie as I can, 270
I'll answer each particular objection
With which you charge me. The maine ground, on which
You raise the building of your accusation,
Hath reference to my sonne: should I now curse him,
Or wish in th'agonie of my troubled soule, 275
Lightning had found him in his mothers womb
You'll say 'tis from the purpose, and I therefore
Betake him to the Devill, and so leave him.
Did never loyall father but my selfe
Beget a treacherous issue? was't in me 280
With as much ease to fashion up his minde,
As in his generation to forme
The organs to his body? must it follow
Because that he is impious, I am false?
I would not boast my actions, yet tis lawfull 285
To upbraid my benefits to unthankfull men.
Who suncke the Turkish gallies in the Straights,
But *Malefort?* who rescu'd the French Merchants,
When they were boorded, and stowed under hatches
By the Pirats of Argiers, when everie minute 290
They did expect to be chain'd to the oare,
But your now doubted Admirall? then you fill'd
The aire with shouts of joy, and did proclaime
When hope had left them, and grim-look'd Despaire
Hover'd with saile-stretcht wings over their heads, 295
To me, as to the *Neptune* of the Sea,
They ow'd the restitution of their goods,
Their lives, their liberties. O can it then
Be probable, my Lords, that he that never
Became the master of a Pirats ship, 300
But at the maine yard hung the Captaine up,
And caus'd the rest to be throwne over boord,

        277. 'tis] *Coxeter*; is 39

Should after all these proofes of deadly hate,
So oft expres'd against 'em, entertaine
A thought of quarter with 'em? but much lesse   305
(To the perpetuall ruine of my glories)
To joyne with them to lift a wicked arme
Against my mother Countrey, this Marsellis,
Which with my prodigall expence of bloud
I have so oft protected.
   Beaufort senior.   What you have done   310
Is granted, and applauded, but yet know
This glorious relation of your actions
Must not so blinde our judgements, as to suffer
This most unnaturall crime you stand accus'd of,
To passe unquestion'd.
   Chamont.   No, you must produce   315
Reasons of more validitie, and weight,
To plead in your defence, or we shall hardly
Conclude you innocent.
   Montrevile.   The large volume of
Your former worthy deeds, with your experience,
Both what, and when to doe, but makes against you.   320
   Lanour. For had your care and courage beene the same
As heretofore, the dangers we are plung'd in
Had beene with ease prevented.
   Malefort senior.   What have I
Omitted in the power of flesh, and bloud,
Even in the birth to strangle the designes   325
Of this hell-bred wolfe my sonne? alas my Lords,
I am no god, nor like him could foresee
His cruell thoughts, and cursed purposes,
Nor would the sun at my command forbeare
To make his progresse to the other world,   330
Affording to us one continued light.
Nor could my breath dispresse those foggie mists
Coverde with which, and darkenesse of the night,
Their navie undiscernd, without resistance
Beset our harbor! make not that my fault,   335
Which you in justice must ascribe to fortune.
But if that nor my former acts, nor what

332. dispresse] *39*; disperse *Dodsley*

I have deliverd, can prevaile with you
To make good my integritie and truth:
Rip up this bosome, and plucke out the heart   340
That hath beene ever loyall.   *A trumpet within.*
 Beaufort senior.   How! a trumpet!
Enquire the cause.   MONTREVILE *goes off.*
 Malefort senior. Thou searcher of mens hearts,
And sure defender of the innocent,
(My other crying sinnes, a while not lookd on)
If I in this am guiltie strike me dead,   345
Or by some unexpected meanes confirme,
I am accusd unjustly.

   Enter MONTREVILE *and a* SEA CAPTAIN.

 Beaufort senior.   Speake the motives
That brings thee hither.
 Captain.   From our Admirall thus,
He does salute you fairely, and desires
It may be understood no publike hate,   350
Hath brought him to Marsellis, nor seekes he
The ruine of his countrie, but aimes only
To wreake a private wrong; and if from you
He may have leave, and liberty to decide it
In a single combate, he'll give up good pledges   355
If he fall in the triall of his right,
Wee shall waigh anchor and no more molest
This towne with hostile armes.
 Beaufort senior.   Speake to the man,
(If in this presence he appeare to you)
To whom you bring this challenge.
 Captain.   Tis to you;   360
 Beaufort senior. His father!
 Montrevile.   Can it be!
 Beaufort junior.   Strange and prodigious.
 Malefort senior. Thou seest I stand unmovd; were thy voice thunder
It should not shake mee, say what would the viper?
 Captain. The reverence a fathers name may challenge,
And duty of a sonne, no more remembred,   365
He does defie thee to the death.

Malefort senior. Goe on.
   Captain. And with his sword will prove it on thy head,
Thou art a murtherer, an Atheist,
And that all attributes of men turnd furies
Cannot expresse thee, this he will make good   370
If thou darst give him meeting.
   Malefort senior.   Dare I live,
Dare I when mountaines of my sins orewhelme me
At my last gaspe aske for mercie? how I blesse
Thy comming, Captaine, never man to me
Arriv'd so opportunely; and thy message,   375
However it may seeme to threaten death,
Does yield to mee a second life in curing
My wounded honour. Stand I yet suspected
As a confederate with this enemie,
Whom of all men, against all ties of nature   380
He markes out for destruction? you are just,
Immortall powers, and in this merciful,
And it takes from my sorrow, and my shame
For being the father to so bad a sonne,
In that you are pleasd to offer up the monster   385
To my correction. Blush and repent
As you are bound, my honourable Lords,
Your ill opinions of me; not great *Brutus*
The father of the Roman liberty
With more assured constancy beheld   390
His traytor sons, for labouring to call home
The banished Tarquins, scourgd with rods to death,
Then I will show when I take backe the life
This prodigie of mankinde receivd from me.
   Beaufort senior. We are sory Monsieur *Malefort* for our errour 395
And are much taken with your resolution
But the disparity of yeares, and strength
Between you, and your sonne, duely considerd,
We would not so expose you.
   Malefort senior.   Then you kill me
Under pretence to save me. O my Lords   400
As you love honour, and a wrongd mans fame
Denie me not this faire, and noble meanes

367. will] *Dodsley*; well *39*   383. my sorrow] *Dodsley*; any sorrow *39*

To make me right againe to all the world.
Should any other but my selfe be chosen
To punish this Apostata with death, 405
You rob a wretched father of a justice
That to all after times will be recorded.
I wish his strength were centuple, his skill equall
To my experience, that in his fall
He may not shame my victory; I feele 410
The powers, and spirits of twenty strong men in me.
Were hee with wild fire circl'd, I undaunted
Would make way to him; as you doe affect Sir
My daughter *Theocrine*, as you are
My true and ancient friend, as thou art valiant, 415
And as all love a souldier, second me
In this my just petition. In your lookes   *They all sue*
I see a grant my Lord.   *to the governour.*
   Beaufort senior.   You shall orebeare me,
And since you are so confident in your cause,
Prepare you for the combate.
   Malefort senior.   With more joy 420
Then yet I ever tasted; by the next sunne,
The disobedient rebell shall heare from me,
And so returne in safety. My good Lords,
To all my service, I will die or purchase
Rest to Marsellis, nor can I make doubt, 425
But his impietie is a potent charme,
To edge my sword and adde strength to my arme.   *Exeunt.*

Actus secundi, Scæna prima.

Enter three SEA CAPTAINS.

    2. *Captain.* HEE did accept the challenge then?
    1. *Captain.*   Nay more,
Was overjoyd in't; and as it had beene
A faire invitement to a solemne feast,
And not a combate to conclude with death,
He chearefully imbrac'd it.

422. me,] *Gifford*; ~ˬ 39   423. safety.] *Gifford*; ~, 39

| | II. i. 5–38 | *The Unnatural Combat* | 213 |

  3. *Captain.*   Are the articles   5
Sign'd to on both parts?
  1. *Captain.*   At the fathers suit,
With much unwillingnesse the governour
Consented to 'em.
  2. *Captain.* You are inward with
Our Admirall; could you yet never learne
What the nature of the quarrell is, that renders   10
The sonne, more then incensed, implacable
Against the father?
  1. *Captain.*   Never; yet I have
As far as manners would give warrant to it,
With my best curiousnesse of care observ'd him,
I have sate with him in his cabin, a day together,   15
Yet not a sillable exchang'd between us;
Sigh he did often, as if inward griefe,
And melancholy at that instant would
Choke up his vitall spirits, and now and then
A teare, or two, as in derision of   20
The toughnesse of his rugged temper would
Fall on his hallow cheekes, which but once felt,
A sudden flash of fury did dry up,
And laying then his hand upon his sword,
He would murmure, but yet so as I oft hard him,   25
We shall meete cruell father, yes we shall,
When i'll exact for every womanish drop
Of sorrow from these eies, a strict accompt
Of much more from thy heart.
  2. *Captain.*   Tis wondrous **strange.**
  3. *Captain.* And past my apprehension.
  1. *Captain.*   Yet what makes   30
The miracle greater, when from the maine top
A sayle's descride, all thoughts that doe concerne
Himselfe layd by, no Lyon pinchd with hunger,
Rowzes himselfe more fiercely from his den,
Then he comes on the decke, and there how wisely   35
He gives directions, and how stout he is
In his executions, we to admiration,
Have beene eye-witnesses, yet he never minds

     II. i. 22. hallow] *39*; hollow *Dodsley*

The bootie when tis made ours, but as if
The danger, in the purchase of the prey 40
Delighted him much more then the rewarde,
His will made knowne he does retire himselfe
To his private contemplation, no joy
Express'd by him for victory.
    Enter MALEFORT JUNIOR.
 2. *Captain.*   Heare he comes
But with more chearefull lookes then ever yet 45
I saw him weare.
 Malefort junior. It was long since resolv'd on
Nor must I stagger now. May the cause
That forces mee to this unnaturall act,
Be buried in everlasting silence,
And I finde rest in death, or my revenge, 50
To either I stand equall. Pray you Gentlemen
Be charitable in your censures of me,
And doe not entertaine a false beleefe
That I am mad, for undertaking that
Which must be, when effected, still repented. 55
It addes to my calamitie that I have
Discourse and reason, and but too well know
I can nor live, nor end a wretched life,
But both wayes I am impious. Doe not therefore
Ascribe the perturbation of my soule 60
To a servile feare of death: I oft have view'd
All kindes of his inevitable darts,
Nor are they terrible. Were I condemn'd to leape
From the cloud-covered browes of a steepe rocke
Into the deepe; or *Curtius*-like to fill up, 65
For my Countries safetie and an after name,
A bottomlesse Abysse, or charge through fire,
It could not so much shake me, as th'encounter
Of this dayes single enemie.
 1. *Captain.*   If you please, Sir,
You may shun it, or defer it.
 Malefort junior.   Not for the world: 70
Yet two things I entreat you. The first is,

   47. now.] *Dodsley*; now, *39*; now in't *Gifford*

You'll not enquire the difference betweene
My selfe and him, which as a father once
I honour'd, now my deadliest enemie;
The last is, if I fall, to beare my body 75
Far from this place, and where you please interre it.
I should say more, but by his sudden comming
I am cut off.

Enter BEAUFORT JUNIOR, *and* MONTREVILE *leading in* MALEFORT
SENIOR; BELGARDE *following with others.*

   Beaufort junior. Let me, Sir, have the honour
To be your second.
   Montrevile.   With your pardon, Sir,
I must put in for that, since our tried friendship 80
Hath lasted from our infancie.
   Belgarde.   I have serv'd
Under your command, and you have seen me fight,
And handsomely, though I say it, and if now
At this downeright game, I may but hold your cards,
I'll not pull downe the side.
   Malefort senior.   I rest much bound 85
To your so noble offers, and I hope
Shall finde your pardon, though I now refuse 'em,
For which I'll yeeld strong reasons, but as briefly
As the time will give me leave. For me to borrow
(That am suppos'd the weaker) any aid 90
From the assistance of my Seconds sword,
Might write me downe in the blacke list of those,
That have nor fire, nor spirit of their owne;
But dare, and doe, as they derive their courage
From his example, on whose help and valour 95
They wholly doe depend. Let this suffice
In my excuse for that. Now if you please
On both parts to retire to yonder mount,
Where you, as in a Roman Theater,
May see the bloudy difference determin'd, 100
Your favours meet my wishes.
   Malefort junior.   'Tis approv'd of
By me, and I command you lead the way,
And leave me to my fortune.

  Beaufort junior.   I would gladly
Be a spectator (since I am deni'd
To be an Actor) of each blow, and thrust,   105
And punctually observe 'em.
  Malefort junior.   You shall have
All you desire; for in a word or two
I must make bold to entertaine the time,
If he give suffrage to it.
  Malefort senior. Yes, I will,
I'll heare thee, and then kill thee: nay farewell.   110
  Malefort junior. Embrace with love on both sides, and with us
Leave deadly hate, and furie.
  Malefort senior.   From this place
You nere shall see both living.
  Belgarde.   What's past help, is
Beyond prevention.
      *They embrace on both sides, and take leave
       severally of the father and sonne.*
  Malefort senior. Now we are alone, Sir,
And thou hast libertie to unlode the burthen   115
Which thou groan'st under. Speake thy griefes.
  Malefort junior.   I shall, Sir;
But in a perplext forme and method, which
You onely can interpret; would you had not
A guiltie knowledge in your bosome of
The language which you force me to deliver,   120
So I were nothing. As you are my father
I bend my knee, and uncompell'd professe
My life, and all thats mine, to be your gift;
And that in a sonnes dutie I stand bound
To lay this head beneath your feet, and run   125
All desperate hazards for your ease and safetie.
But this confest on my part, I rise up,
And not as with a father, (all respect,
Love, feare, and reverence cast off,) but as
A wicked man I thus expostulate with you.   130
Why have you done that which I dare not speake?
And in the action chang'd the humble shape
Of my obedience, to rebellious rage
And insolent pride? and with shut eyes constrain'd me

To run my Barke of honour on a shelfe, 135
I must not see, nor if I saw it, shun it?
In my wrongs nature suffers, and lookes backward,
And mankinde trembles to see me pursue
What beasts would flie from. For when I advance
This sword, as I must doe against your head, 140
Pietie will weepe, and filiall dutie mourne,
To see their altars which you built up in me,
In a moment raz'd and ruin'd. That you could
(From my griev'd soule I wish it) but produce
To qualifie, not excuse your deed of horror, 145
One seeming reason that I might fix here,
And move no farther.
 Malefort senior. Have I so far lost
A fathers power, that I must give account
Of my actions to my sonne? or must I plead
As a fearefull prisoner at the bar, while he 150
That owes his being to me sits a Judge
To censure that, which onely by my selfe
Ought to be question'd? mountaines sooner fall
Beneath their vallies, and the loftie Pine
Pay homage to the Bramble, or what else is 155
Preposterous in nature, ere my tongue
In one short sillable yeelds satisfaction
To any doubt of thine, nay though it were
A certaintie disdaining argument.
Since though my deeds wore Hels blacke liverie, 160
To thee they should appeare triumphall robes,
Set off with glorious honour, thou being bound
To see with my eyes, and to hold that reason,
That takes or birth or fashion from my will.
 Malefort junior. This sword divides that slavish knot.
 Malefort senior.   It cannot,
It cannot wretch, and if thou but remember 166
From whom thou hadst this spirit, thou dar'st not hope it.
Who train'd thee up in armes but I? Who taught thee
Men were men onely when they durst looke downe
With scorne on death and danger, and contemn'd 170
All opposition, till plum'd victorie
Had made her constant stand upon their helmets?

Under my shield thou hast fought as securely
As the young Eglet, covered with the wings
Of her fierce Dam, learnes how and where to prey.   175
All that is manly in thee, I call mine;
But what is weake and womanish, thine owne.
And what I gave, since thou art proud, ungratefull,
Presuming to contend with him, to whom
Submission is due, I will take from thee.   180
Looke therefore for extremities, and expect not
I will correct thee as a sonne, but kill thee
As a Serpent swolne with poyson, who surviving
A little longer, with infectious breath,
Would render all things neere him, like it selfe   185
Contagious. Nay, now my anger's up,
Ten thousand virgins kneeling at my feet,
And with one generall crie howling for mercie,
Shall not redeeme thee.
   Malefort junior.   Thou incensed Power,
A while forbeare thy thunder, let me have   190
No aid in my revenge, if from the grave
My mother—
   Malefort senior. Thou shalt never name her more.

     Above BEAUFORT JUNIOR, MONTREVILE, BELGARDE,
         the three SEA CAPTAINS.

   Beaufort junior. They are at it.
   2. Captain.   That thrust was put strongly home.
   Montrevile. But with more strength avoyded.
   Belgarde.   Well come in,
He has drawne bloud of him yet, well done old Cocke.   195
   1. Captain. That was a strange misse.
   Beaufort junior.   That a certaine hit.
   Belgarde. Hee's falne, the day is ours. *Young* MALEFORT *slaine.*
   2. Captain.   The Admiral's slaine.
   Montrevile. The father is victorious!
   Belgarde.   Let us haste
To gratulate his conquest.
   1. Captain.   Wee to mourne
The fortune of the sonne.

        199. 1. *Captain*] Dodsley; *1. 39*

Beaufort junior.   With utmost speed
Acquaint the Governour with the good successe,
That he may entertaine to his full merit,
The father of his Countries peace and safetie.   *They descend.*
    Malefort senior. Were a new life hid in each mangled limbe,
I would search, and finde it. And howere to some
I may seeme cruell, thus to tyrannize
Upon this senslesse flesh, I glorie in it.
That I have power to be unnaturall,
Is my securitie. Die all my feares,
And waking jealousies, which have so long
Beene my tormentors, theres now no suspition;
A fact, which I alone am conscious of,
Can never be discover'd, or the cause
That call'd this Duell on, I being above
All perturbations, nor is it in
The power of Fate, againe to make me wretched.

   Enter BEAUFORT JUNIOR, MONTREVILE, BELGARDE,
     the three SEA CAPTAINS.

    Beaufort junior. All honour to the Conquerour. Who dares tax
My friend of treacherie now?
    Belgarde.   I am verie glad, Sir,
You have sped so well. But I must tell you thus much,
To put you in minde that a low ebbe must follow
Your high swolne tide of happinesse, you have purchast
This honour at a high price.
    Malefort senior.   'Tis *Belgarde*,
Above all estimation, and a little
To be exalted with it cannot savour
Of arrogance: that to this arme and sword,
Marsellis owes the freedome of her feares,
Or that my loyaltie not long since eclips'd,
Shines now more bright than ever, are not things
To be lamented. Though indeed they may
Appeare too dearely bought, my falling glories
Being made up againe, and cemented
With a sonnes bloud. 'Tis true, he was my sonne

217. Conquerour. Who] *39²*; Conquerour. / Who *39¹*; Conquerour. / *Montrevile.* Who *conj.* McIlwraith 221–2. purchast / This] *Coxeter; undivided 39*

While he was worthy, but when he shooke off
His dutie to me, (which my fond indulgence
Vpon submission might perhaps have pardon'd)   235
And grew his Countries enemie, I look'd on him
As a Stranger to my family, and a Traytor
Justly proscrib'd, and he to be rewarded
That could bring in his head. I know in this
That I am censur'd rugged, and austere,   240
That will vouchsafe not one sad sigh or teare
Vpon his slaughter'd body. But I rest
Well satisfi'd in my selfe, being assur'd
That extraordinarie vertues, when they soare
Too high a pitch for common sights to judge of, 245
Losing their proper splendour, are condemn'd
For most remarkable vices.
 Beaufort junior.   Tis too true, Sir,
In the opinion of the multitude:
But for my selfe that would be held your friend,
And hope to know you by a nearer name,   250
They are as they deserve, receiv'd.
 Malefort.   My daughter
Shall thanke you for the favour.
 Beaufort junior.   I can wish
No happinesse beyond it.
 1. *Captain.*   Shall we have leave
To beare the corps of our dead Admirall,
As he enjoyn'd us from this Coast?
 Malefort.   Provided   255
The articles agreed on, be observ'd,
And you depart hence with it, making oath
Never hereafter but as friends to touch
Vpon this shore.
 1. *Captain.* Wee'll faithfully performe it.
 Malefort. Then as you please dispose of it. 'Tis an object   260
That I could wish remov'd. His sins die with him,
So far he has my charitie.
 1. *Captain.*   He shall have
A Souldiers funerall.

   The SEA CAPTAINS *beare the body off with sad musicke.*
 Malefort.   Farewell.

Beaufort junior. These rites
Paid to the dead, the Conquerour that survives
Must reape the harvest of his bloudy labour.
Sound all loud instruments of joy and triumph,
And with all circumstance, and ceremonie
Wait on the Patron of our libertie,
Which he at all parts merits.
Malefort. I am honour'd
Beyond my hopes.
Beaufort junior. 'Tis short of your deserts.
Lead on: Oh Sir you must: you are too modest.
Exeunt with loud musicke.

Actus secundi, Scæna secunda.

THEOCRINE, PAGE, WOMEN.

Theocrine. Talke not of comfort, I am both wayes wretched,
And so distracted with my doubts and feares,
I know not where to fix my hopes. My losse
Is certaine in a father, or a brother,
Or both, such is the crueltie of my fate,
And not to be avoyded.
 1. *Woman.* You must beare it
With patience, Madam.
 2. *Woman.* And what's not in you
To be prevented, should not cause a sorrow
Which cannot help it.
Page. Feare not my brave Lord
Your noble father; fighting is to him
Familiar as eating. He can teach
Our moderne Duellists how to cleave a button,
And in a new way, never yet found out
By old *Caranza*.
 1. *Woman.* May he be victorious,
And punish disobedience in his sonne,
Whose death in reason should at no part move you,
He being but halfe your brother, and the neernesse,
Which that might challenge from you, forfeited
By his impious purpose to kill him, from whom

He receiv'd life.   *A shout within.*
2. *Woman.*   A generall shout.
1. *Woman.*   Of joy.
   Page. Looke up deare Lady, sad newes never came
Usherd with loud applause.

Enter USHER.

   Theocrine.   I stand prepard,
To indure the shocke of it.
   Usher.   I am out of breath
With running to deliver first.
   Theocrine.   What?
   Usher.   Wee are all made,
My Lord has won the day, your brother's slaine,
The pirats gone, and by the governour,
And states, and all the men of war he is
Brought home in triumph, nay no musing, pay me
For my good newes hereafter.
   Theocrine.   Heaven is just!
   Usher. Give thankes at leasure, make all hast to meete him:
I coulde wish I were a horse that I might beare you
To him upon my backe.
   Page.   Thou art an asse,
And this is a sweete burthen.
   Usher.   Peace, you crackrope.   *Exeunt.*

Actus secundi, Scæna tertia.

Loud musicke. MONTREVILE, BELGARDE, BEAUFORT JUNIOR,
BEAUFORT SENIOR, MALEFORT, *followed by*
MONTAIGNE, CHAMONT, LANOUR.

   Beaufort senior. All honours we can give you and rewards,
Though all that's rich, or pretious in Marsellis
Were layd downe at your feet, can hold no waight
With your deservings; let me glory in
Your action as if it were mine owne,
And have the honour with the armes of love,
To embrace the great performer of a deed,

II. ii. 25. won] *Dodsley*; wont 39

Transcending all this Countrey ere could boast of.
   Montaigne. Imagine, noble Sir, in what we may
Expresse our thankfulnesse, and rest assur'd
It shall be freely granted.
   Chamont.   Hee's an enemie
To goodnesse and to vertue, that dares thinke
There's any thing within our power to give,
Which you in justice may not boldly challenge.
   Lanour. And as your owne, for we will ever be
At your devotion.
   Malefort.   Much honour'd Sir,
And you my noble Lords, I can say onely,
The greatnesse of your favours overwhelme me,
And like too large a saile, for the small barke
Of my poore merits, sinks me. That I stand
Vpright in your opinions, is an honour
Exceeding my deserts, I having done
Nothing but what in dutie I stood bound to:
And to expect a recompence were base,
Good deeds being ever in themselves rewarded.
Yet since your liberall bounties tell me that
I may with your allowance be a Suitor,
To you my Lord I am an humble one,
And must aske that, which knowne, I feare you will
Censure me over-bold.
   Beaufort senior.   It must be something
Of a strange nature, if it finde from me
Deniall or delay.
   Malefort.   Thus then my Lord,
Since you encourage me: You are happie in
A worthy sonne, and all the comfort that
Fortune has left me is one daughter; now
If it may not appeare too much presumption,
To seeke to match my lownesse with your height,
I should desire (and if I may obtaine it,
I write *Nil ultra* to my largest hopes)
She may in your opinion be thought worthy
To be receiv'd into your family,
And married to your sonne: their yeares are equall,

   II. iii. 13. any] *Mason*; any other *39*   18. overwhelme] *39*; overwhelms *Mason*

And their desires I thinke too, she is not
Ignoble, nor my state contemptible,
And if you thinke me worthy your alliance, 45
'Tis all I doe aspire to.
   Beaufort junior.   You demand
That which with all the service of my life
I should have labour'd to obtaine from you.
O, Sir, why are you slow to meet so faire
And noble an offer? Can France shew a virgin 50
That may be parallel'd with her? Is she not
The Phœnix of the time? the fairest star
In the bright sphere of women?
   Beaufort senior.   Be not rap'd so:
Though I dislike not what is motion'd, yet
In what so neere concernes me, it is fit 55
I should proceed with judgement.

     Enter USHER, THEOCRINE, PAGE, WOMEN.

   Beaufort junior.   Here she comes,
Looke on her with impartiall eyes, and then
Let envie if it can, name one grac'd feature
In which she is defective.
   Malefort.   Welcome Girle:
My joy, my comfort, my delight, my all, 60
Why dost thou come to greet my victorie
In such a sable habit? this shew'd well
When thy father was a prisoner, and suspected;
But now his faith and loyaltie are admir'd,
Rather than doubted, in your outward garments 65
You are to expresse the joy you feele within;
Nor should you with more curiousnesse and care,
Pace to the Temple to be made a Bride,
Than now, when all mens eyes are fixt upon you,
You should appeare to entertaine the honour 70
From me descending to you, and in which
You have an equall share.
   Theocrine.   Heaven has my thankes
With all humility payd for your faire fortune,
And so farre duty bindes me, yet a little

         48. you] *Dodsley;* yon *39*

To mourn a brothers losse (however wicked) 75
The tendernesse familiar to our sex
May if you please excuse.
    Malefort.   Thou art deceiv'd.
Hee living was a blemish to thy beauties,
But in his death gives ornament, and lustre
To thy perfections, but that they are 80
So exquisitly rare, that they admit not
The least addition. Ha! heres yet a print
Of a sad teare on thy cheeke, how it takes from
Our present happinesse! with a fathers lips,
A loving fathers lips, i'll kisse it off, 85
The cause no more remembred.
    Theocrine.   You forget Sir
The presence we are in.
    Malefort.   Tis well considered,
And yet who is the owner of a treasure,
Above all valew, but without offence,
May glory in the glad possession of it? 90
Nor let it in your excellence beget wonder,
Or any here, that looking on the daughter,
I feast my selfe in the imagination
Of those sweet pleasures, and allowd delights,
I tasted from the mother (who still lives 95
In this her perfit modell) for she had
Such smooth and high archd brows, such sparkling eies,
Whose every glance stord *Cupids* emptied quiver;
Such ruby lips, and such a lovely browne,
Disdaining all adulterate aydes of art, 100
Kep'd a perpetuall spring upon her face,
As death himselfe lamented being forc'd
To blast it with his palenesse, and if now,
Her brightnes dimd with sorrow, take and please you,
Thinke think young Lord, when she appeares her selfe 105
(This vayle remov'd) in her owne naturall purenesse
How farre she will transport you.
    Beaufort junior.   Did she need it,
The praise which you (and well deservd) give to her
Must of necessity raise new desires

       91. your] *39²* you *39¹*   99. browne] *39*; bloome *Mason*

In one indebted more to yeares; to me 110
Your words are but as oyle powr'd on a fire,
That flames already at the height.
  Malefort.   No more;
I doe believe you, and let me from you
Finde so much credit, when I make her yours
I doe possesse you of a gift, which I 115
With much unwillingnesse part from. My good Lords
Forbeare your further trouble, give me leave,
For on the suddaine I am indisposd,
To retire to my own house, and rest. To morrow
As you command me I will be your ghest, 120
And having deckt my daughter like her selfe,
You shall have farther conference.
  Beaufort senior.   You are Master
Of your owne will; but fayle not, i'll expect you.
  Malefort. Nay I will be excusd; I must part with you.
          To young BEAUFORT *and the rest.*
My dearest *Theocrine* give me thy hand, 125
I will support thee.
  Theocrine.   You gripe it too hard Sir.
  Malefort. Indeed I doe, but have no farther end in it,
But love and tendernesse such as I may challenge
And you must grant. Thou art a sweet one, yes,
And to be cherished.
  Theocrine.   May I still deserve it. 130
        They goe off several wayes.

Actus tertii, Scæna prima.

Enter BEAUFORT SENIOR, SERVANT.

  Beaufort senior. HAVE you beene carefull?
  Servant.   With my best endevours,
Let them bring stomacks, theres no want of meat Sir:
Portly and curious viands are prepar'd,
To please all kindes of appetites.
  Beaufort senior.   Tis well.

117–19. *rearranged by Coxeter; 39 reads* Forbeare ... suddaine / I ... To morrow
118. suddaine I am] *Coxeter;* suddaine I / am 39¹; suddaine / I am 39²

I love a table furnisht with full plentie,
And store of friends to eat it, but with this caution,
I would not have my house a common Inne,
For some men that come rather to devoure me,
Than to present their service. At this time too
It being a serious and solemne meeting,
I must not haue my boord pester'd with shadowes,
That under other mens protection breake in
Without invitement.
    Servant.   With your favour then,
You must double your gard, my Lord, for on my knowledge
There are some so sharp set, not to be kept out
By a file of Musketiers. And 'tis lesse danger,
I'll undertake, to stand at push of pike
With an enemie in a breach, that undermin'd too,
And the Cannon playing on it, than to stop
One Harpie, your perpetuall ghest, from entrance,
When the dresser, the Cookes drum, thunders come on,
The service will be lost else.
    Beaufort senior.   What is hee?
    Servant. As tall a trencher-man, that is most certaine,
As ere demolisht Pie-fortification
As soone as batter'd; and if the rim of his belly
Were not made up of a much tougher stuffe
Than his Buffe jerkin, there were no defence
Against the charge of his guts: you needs must know him,
He's eminent for his eating.
    Beaufort senior.   O *Belgarde*!
    Servant. The same, one of the Admirals cast Captaines,
Who sweare, there being no war, nor hope of any,
The onely drilling is to eat devoutly,
And to be ever drinking, (that's allow'd of)
But they know not where to get it, there's the spite on't.
    Beaufort senior. The more their miserie, yet if you can
For this day put him off.
    Servant.   It is beyond
Th' invention of man.
    Beaufort senior. No: say this onely,   *Whispers to him.*
And as from me; you apprehend me?

    III. i. 36–7. *rearranged by Gifford*; 39 *reads* It ... man. / No ... onely,

Servant.   Yes Sir.
Beaufort senior. But it must be done gravely.
Servant.   Never doubt me Sir.
Beaufort senior. Wee'll dine in the great roome, but let the musick
And banquet be prepar'd here.   *Exit* BEAUFORT SENIOR.
    Servant.   This will make him   41
Lose his dinner at the least, and that will vex him.
As for the sweet meats, when they are trod under foot,
Let him take his share with the Pages and Lacqueyes,
Or scramble in the rushes.

                   Enter BELGARDE.

    Belgarde.   Tis neere twelve,   45
I keepe a watch within me never misses.
Save thee Master Steward.
    Servant.   You are most welcome, Sir.
    Belgarde. Has thy Lord slept well to night? I come to enquire.
I had a foolish dreame, that against my will
Carried me from my lodging, to learne onely   50
How he's dispos'd.
    Servant.   He's in most perfect health, Sir.
    Belgarde. Let me but see him feed heartily at dinner,
And I'll beleeve so too, for from that ever
I make a certaine iudgement.
    Servant.   It holds surely
In your owne constitution.
    Belgarde.   And in all mens   55
Tis the best symptome, let us loose no time,
Delay is dangerous.
    Servant.   Troth Sir, if I might
Without offence deliver what my Lord has
Committed to my trust, I shall receive it
As a speciall favour.
    Belgarde.   Weell see't, and discourse   60
As the proverbe sayes for health sake after dinner,
Or rather after supper, willingly then
I'll walke a mile to here thee.
    Servant.   Nay good Sir
I will be briefe and pithee.
    Belgarde.   Prethee be so.

III. i. 65–98   *The Unnatural Combat*   229

   Servant. Hee bid me say of all his ghests, that he   65
Stands most affected to you, for the freedome,
And plainnesse of your maners. He ne're observ'd you
To twirle a dish about, you did not like of,
All being pleasing to you; or to take
A say of venison, or stale fowle by your nose,   70
(Which is a solecisme at anothers table)
But by strong eating of 'em did confirme
They never were delitious to your palat,
But when they were mortifi'd, as the Hugonot sayes,
And so your part growes greater; nor doe you   75
Find fault with the sawce, keen hunger being the best,
Which ever to your much praise, you bring with you;
Nor will you with impertinent relations,
Which is a master-peece, when meates before you
Forget your teeth to use your nimble tongue   80
But doe the feate you come for.
   Belgarde.   Be advis'd
And end your jeering; for if you proceede
You'll feele, as I can eate I can be angrie,
And beating may insue.
   Servant.   I'll take your counsell,
And roundly come to the point; my Lord much wonders   85
That you, that are a courtier as a souldier,
In all things else, and every day can vary
Your actions and discourse, continue constant
To this one suite.
   Belgarde.   To one? tis well I have one,
Unpawnd; in these dayes, every cast commander   90
Is not blest with the fortune, I assure you,
But why this question? does this offend him?
   Servant. Not much: but he believes it is the reason
You nere presume to sit above the salt,
And therefore this day (our great Admirall   95
With other states being invited ghests)
He does intreate you to appeare among 'em,
In some fresh habit.
   Belgarde.   This staffe shall not serve   [*Aside.*]

70. A say] *39;* Assay *Dodsley*   90–2. *as verse* Coxeter; *as prose* 39   98 SD. Aside.] *editor; not in* 39

To beat the dogge off, these are souldiers garments,
And so by consequence grow contemptible.
    Servant.   It has stung him.   100
    Belgarde. I would I were aquainted with the players,   [*Aside.*]
In charity they might furnish me, but there is
No faith in Brokers, and for believing Taylors
They are only to be read of, but not seene,
And sure they are confinde to their owne hells,   105
And there they live invisible; well I must not
Be fubd off thus—pray you report my service
To the Lord governour. I will obey him
And though my wardrop's poore, rather then loose
His company at this feast, I will put on   110
The richest suite I have, and fill the chaire,
That makes me worthy of.   *Exit* BELGARDE.
    Servant.   We are shut of him,
He will be seene no more here, how my fellowes
Will blesse me for his absence, he had starv'd em
Had he stayd a little longer. Would he cood,   115
For his owne sake shift a shirt, and thats the utmost
Of his ambition, adew good Captaine.   *Exit.*

[III. ii]   *Enter* BEAUFORT SENIOR *and* BEAUFORT JUNIOR.

    Beaufort senior. Tis a strange fondnesse.
    Beaufort junior.   Tis beyond example.
His resolution to part with his estate,
To make her dower the waightier is nothing,
But to observe how curious he is
In his owne person to adde ornament   5
To his daughters ravishing features, is the wonder.
I sent a page of mine in the way of courtship,
This morning to her to present my service,
From whom I understand all: there he found him
Sollicitous in what shape she should appeare,   10
This gowne was rich, but the fashion stale, the other
Was quaint, and neate, but the stuffe not rich enough;
Then does he curse the Taylor, and in rage

---

    101 SD. *Aside.*] *conj. Telfer; not in* 39   112. of.] *Gifford*; of— 39
    112–13. him, / He] *Coxeter; undivided* 39   III. ii. *Scene division Gifford; un-*
    divided 39   0 SD. SENIOR] 39² (*Sen.*); *jun.* 39¹   JUNIOR] 39² (*jun.*); *sen.* 39¹

Falls on her Shoomaker, for wanting art
To expresse in every circumstance, the forme
Of her most delicate foote, then sits in counsell
With much deliberation to finde out
What tire would best adorne her; and one chosen,
Varying in his opinion, he teares off,
And stamps it under foot, then tries a second
A third and fourth, and satisfied at length
With much a doe in that, he growes agen
Perplexd and troubl'd where to place her Jewells
To be most mark'd, and whether she should weare
This diamond on her forehead, or betweene
Her milke-white paps, disputing on it both wayes,
Then taking in his hand, a rope of pearle,
(The best of France) he seriously considers
Whither she should dispose it on her arme
Or on her necke, with twenty other trifles,
Too tedious to deliver.
 Beaufort senior. I have knowne him
From his first youth, but never yet observ'd
In all the passages of his life, and fortunes,
Vertues so mix'd with vices. Valiant the world speakes him,
But with that bloody; liberall in his gifts too,
But to maintaine his prodigall expence,
A fierce extortioner; an impotent lover
Of women for a flash, but his fires quench'd,
Hating as deadly; the truth is I am not
Ambitious of this match: nor will I crosse you
In your affections.
 Beaufort junior. I have ever found you,
(And tis my happinesse) a loving father, *Loud musicke.*
And carefull of my good:—by the loud musicke,
As you gave order for his entertainment,
He's come into the house. Two long houres since,
The Colonels, commissioners and captaines,
To pay him all the rites his worth can challenge,
Went to wayt on him hither.

---

27. his] *Gifford;* this *39* 30–1. trifles, / Too] *Coxeter; undivided 39*
31–2. him / From his] *Gifford; undivided 39* 40–1. you / In] *Gifford;*
undivided 39 45. house.] *Coxeter;* ~∧ *39*

Enter MALEFORT, MONTAIGNE, CHAMONT, LANOUR, MONTREVILE, THEOCRINE, USHER, PAGE, WOMEN.

 Beaufort senior.   You are most welcome,
And what I speake to you, does from my heart
Disperse it selfe to all.
 Malefort.   You meet my Lord   50
Your trouble.
 Beaufort senior. Rather Sir, increase of honour,
When you are pleas'd to grace my house.
 Beaufort junior.   The Favour
Is doubl'd on my part, most worthy Sir,
Since your faire daughter, my incomparable Mistresse,
Daines us her presence.
 Malefort.   View her well brave *Beaufort*, 55
But yet at distance; you hereafter may
Make your approaches neerer, when the priest
Hath made it lawfull, and were not shee mine,
I durst alowd proclaime it, *Hymen* never
Put on his saffron coloured robe to change   60
A barren virgin name with more good omens,
Then at her nuptialls. Looke on her againe,
Then tell me if she now appeare the same
That she was yesterday.
 Beaufort junior. Being her selfe
She cannot but be excellent, these rich   65
And curious dressings, which in others might
Cover deformities, from her take lustre
Nor can adde to her.
 Malefort.   You conceive her right,
And in your admiration of her sweetnesse,
You only can deserve her; blush not girle,   70
Thou art above his praise, or mine, nor can
Obsequious flattery though she should use
Her thousand oyld tongues to advance thy worth,
Give ought (for thats impossible) but take from
Thy more then humane graces, and even then   75

  50–3. *rearranged by Gifford; 39 reads* disperse . . . trouble. / Rather . . . honour, /
When . . . house. / The . . . Sir, 59. it,] *Mason;* ~. *39* 64. *Beaufort junior*]
Mason; Beauf. sen. *39*

III. ii. 76–102 *The Unnatural Combat* 233

When shee hath spent her selfe with her best strength,
The wrong she has done thee shall be so apparent,
That loosing her owne servile shape and name,
She will be thought detraction, but I
Forget my selfe, and something whispers to me, 80
I have said too much.
    Montrevile.   I know not what to thinke on't,   [*Aside.*]
But there's some mystery in it, which I feare
Will be too soone discover'd.
    Malefort.   I much wrong
Your patience noble Sir, by too much hugging
My proper issue, and like the foolish crow 85
Believe my blacke brood swans.
    Beaufort senior.   There needes not Sir
The least excuse for this, nay I must have
Your arme, you being the master of the feast,
And this the mistris.
    Theocrine.   I am any thing
That you shall please to make mee.
    Beaufort junior.   Nay tis yours 90
Without more complement.
    Malefort.   Your will's a law sir.   *Loud musicke.*
        Exeunt BEAUFORT SENIOR, MALEFORT, THEOCRINE,
        BEAUFORT JUNIOR, MONTAIGNE, CHAMONT,
        LANOUR, MONTREVILE.
    Usher. Would I had beene borne a Lord.
    1. *Woman.*   Or I a Lady.
    Page. It may be you were both begot in court,
Though bred up in the Citie, for your mothers,
As I have heard lov'd the lobbie, and there nightly 95
Are seen strange apparitions, and who knowes
But that some noble fawne, heated with wine,
And cloyde with partridge, had a kinde of longing
To trade in sprats? this needs no exposition,
But can you yeeld a reason for your wishes? 100
    Usher. Why had I beene borne a Lord, I had beene no servant.
    1. *Woman.* And where as now necessity makes us wayters,

---

81 SD. *Aside.*] Coxeter; *not in* 39   91. *Malefort*] *conj.* Gifford; *Mont.* 39; *Mon-*
trevile Coxeter; *Montaigne conj.* Telfer   91 SD. *Loud* . . . MONTREVILE.] *follows*
sir. Coxeter; *follows* complement. 39

We had been attended on.
  2. *Woman.*   And might have slept then,
As long as we pleas'd, and fed when we had stomackes,
And worne new cloths, nor liv'd as now in hope   105
Of a cast gowne, or petticote.
  Page.   You are fooles,
And ignorant of your happinesse; ere I was
Sworne to the pantofle, I have heard my tutor
Prove it by logicke, that a servants life
Was better then his masters, and by that   110
I learnd from him, if that my memory faile not,
I'll make it good.
  Usher.   Proceed my little wit
In decimo sexto.
  Page.   Thus then from the king
To the beggar, by gradation all are servants,
And you must grant the slavery is lesse   115
To studie to please one, then many.
  Usher.   True.
  Page. Well then, and first to you Sir, you complaine
You serve one Lord, but your Lord serves a thousand,
Besides his passions (that are his worst masters.)
You must humor him, and he is bound to sooth   120
Every grimme Sir above him, if he frowne;
For the least neglect you feare to loose your place,
But if, and with all slavish observation,
From the mignions selfe, to the groome of his close stoole,
He hourly seekes not favour, he is sure   125
To be eas'd of his office, though perhaps he bought it.
Nay more, that high disposer of all such
That are subordinate to him, serves, and feares
The fury of the many-headed monster,
The giddy multitude. And as a horse   130
Is still a horse, for all his golden trappings,
So your men of purchas'd titles, at their best are
But serving-men in rich liveries.
  Usher.   Most rare infant,
Where learnd'st thou this morality?

---

  111. learnd] *Gifford*; learne *39*   121. grimme] *39*; trim *Dodsley*   him,] *39*;
~; *Dodsley*   frowne;] *editor*; ~, *39*

Page.   Why thou dull pate,
As I tould thee, of my tutor.
   2. Woman.   Now for us boy.
Page. I am cut of. The governour.

Enter BEAUFORT SENIOR, BEAUFORT JUNIOR, *Servants setting
           forth a banquet.*

   Beaufort senior.   Quicke, quicke sirs,
See all things perfit.
   Servant.   Let the blame be ours else.
   Beaufort senior. And as I said, when we are at the banquet,
And high in our cups, (for tis no feast without it,
Especially among souldiers) *Theocrine*   140
Being retir'd, as that's no place for her,
Take you occasion to rise from the table,
And lose no opportunity.
   Beaufort junior.   Tis my purpose,
And if I can winne her to give her heart,
I have a holy man in readinesse   145
To joyne our hands, for the Admirall her father
Repents him of his grant to me, and growes
So far transported with a strange opinion
Of her faire features, that should we deferre it,
I thinke ere long he will beleeve, and strongly,   150
The Daulphine is not worthy of her, I
Am much amazd with't.
   Beaufort senior.   Nay dispatch there fellowes.
   Servant. We are ready when you please.
              Exeunt BEAUFORT SENIOR, BEAUFORT JUNIOR.
                            Sweet formes your pardon,
It has beene such a busy time I could not
Tender that ceremonious respect   155
Which you deserve, but now the great worke ended,
I will attend the lesse, and with all care
Observe, and serve you.
   Page.   This is a pend speech,

---

   136. of.] *Coxeter;* ~∧ *39*   146–7. father / Repents] *Coxeter; undivided 39*
   147. growes] *conj. McIlwraith; not in 39; is* Mason; *seems* Gifford   153 SD. *Exeunt
   . . .* JUNIOR.] *after Dodsley; follows* with't (l. 152) *39*

And serves as a perpetuall preface to
A dinner made of fragments.
  Usher.   Wee wayt on you.   160
           Loud Musicke. [*Exeunt.*]

Actus tertii, Scæna tertia.

BEAUFORT SENIOR, MALEFORT, MONTAIGNE, CHAMONT,
LANOUR, BEAUFORT JUNIOR, MONTREVILE, *Servants.*

 Beaufort senior. You are not merry Sir.
 Malefort.   Yes my good Lord,
You have given us ample meanes to drowne all cares,
And yet I nourish strange thoughts, which I would *Aside.*
Most willingly destroy.
 Beaufort senior. Pray you take your place,
 Beaufort junior. And drink a health, and let it be if you please 5
To the worthiest of Women: now observe him.
 Malefort. Give mee the bowle, since you doe me the honour,
I will beginne it.
 Chamont. May wee know her name Sir?
 Malefort. You shall, I will not choose a forraigne Queenes,
Nor yet our owne, for that would relish of   10
Tame flattery; nor doe their height of title,
Or absolute power confirme their worth and goodnesse,
These being heavens gifts and frequently confer'd
On such as are beneath em; nor will I
Name the kings Mistresse howsoever shee   15
In his esteeme may carry it; but if I,
As wine gives liberty, may use my freedome,
Not swayd this way, or that with confidence,
(And I will make it good on any equall)
If it must be to her, whose outward forme   20
Is better'd by the beauty of her minde,
She lives not that with justice can pretend
An interest to this so sacred health,
But my faire daughter. He that only doubts it,
I doe pronounce a villain, this to her then. *Drinkes.*
 Montaigne. What may we thinke of this? *Loud musicke.*
    160 SD. *Exeunt.*] *Gifford; not in* 39

III. iii. 26–53   *The Unnatural Combat*   237

 Beaufort senior.   It matters not.   26
 Lanour. For my part I will sooth him rather then
Draw on a quarrell.
 Chamont.   Tis the safest course,
And one I mean to follow.
 Beaufort junior.   It has gone round Sir.
          Exit BEAUFORT JUNIOR.
 Malefort. Now you have done her right, if there be any   30
Worthy to second this, propose it bouldly,
I am your pledge.
 Beaufort senior. Lets pause here if you please,
And entertaine the time with something else.
Musicke there in some lofty straine, the song too
That I gave order for; the new one cald   35
The souldiers delight!

   The song ended: enter BELGARDE *in armor, a case of
      Carbines by his side.*

 Belgarde.   Who stops mee now?
Or who dares only say that I appeare not
In the most rich and glorious habit that
Renders a man compleate? what court so set off
With state and ceremonious pompe, but thus   40
Accoutred I may enter? or what feast
Though all the elements at once were ransack'd,
To store it with varietie transcending
The curiousnesse, and cost, on *Trajans* birth day,
(Where princes only, and confederat kings   45
Did sit as ghests, serv'd, and attended on
By the senators of Rome) at which a souldier
In this his naturall, and proper shape
Might not and bouldly fill a seat, and by
G1ʳ His presence make the great solemnity   50
More honour'd and remarkeable?
 Beaufort senior.   Tis acknowledg'd,
And this a grace done to me unexpected.
 Montaigne. But why in armor?

  III. iii. 28. quarrell.] *Gifford*; quarrell, *Chamont*. 39   28. *Chamont*] *Gifford*;
 Mont. 39   28–9. course, / And] *Gifford*; *undivided* 39   47. at which] *Mason*;
 sat with 39   50. presence] *Dodsley*; present 39

  Malefort.   What's the mysterie?
Pray you reveale that.
  Belgarde.   Souldiers out of action,
That very rare, but like unbidden ghests   55
Bring their stooles with em, for their owne defence,
At court should feed in gauntlets, they may have
Their fingers cut else; there your carpet knights,
That never charg'd beyond a mistresse lips,
Are still most keene, and valiant, but to you   60
Whom it does most concern, my Lord, I will
Addresse my speech, and with a souldiers freedome
In my reproofe returne the bitter scoffe,
You threw upon my poverty. You contemn'd
My courser outside, and from that concluded,   65
(As by your groome you made me understand)
I was unworthy to sit at your table,
Among these tissues, and imbroideries,
Unlesse I chang'd my habit. I have done it,
And show my selfe in that which I have worne   70
In the heate and fervor of a bloudy fight,
And then it was in fashion, not as now
Ridiculous, and despis'd: this hath past through
A wood of pikes, and every one aim'd at it,
Yet scornd to take impression from their fury;   75
With this, as still you see it fresh and new
I have charg'd through fire that would have sing'd your sables,
Blacke fox, and ermins, and chang'd the proud colour
Of Skarlet though of the right Tirian die;
But now as if the trappings made the man,   80
Such only are admir'd that come adorn'd
With what's no part of them. This is mine owne
My richest suit, a suite I must not part from,
But not regarded now, and yet remember
Tis we that bring you in the meanes of feasts,   85
Banquets, and revels, which when you possesse,
With barbarous ingratitude you deny us
To be made sharers in the harvest, which
Our sweat and industrie reap'd, and sow'd for you.
The silks you weare, we with our bloud spin for you;   90

 55. *See Commentary* 80–1. *rearranged by Coxeter;* 39 *reads* But ... are / Admir'd

This massie plate, that with the ponderous waight
Does make your cupboords crack, we (unaffrighted
With tempests, or the long and tedious way,
Or dreadfull monsters of the deepe, that wait
With open jawes still ready to devoure us)   95
Fetch from the other world. Let it not then
In after ages to your shame be spoken,
That you with no relenting eyes looke on
Our wants that feed your plentie; or consume
In prodigall, and wanton gifts on Drones   100
The Kingdomes treasure, yet detaine from us
The debt that with the hazard of our lives,
We have made you stand ingag'd for: or force us
Against all civill government in armour
To require that, which with all willingnesse   105
Should be tender'd, ere demanded.
   Beaufort senior.   I commend
This wholsome sharpnesse in you, and prefer it
Before obsequious tamenesse, it shewes lovely:
Nor shall the raine of your good counsell fall
Upon the barren sands, but spring up fruit   110
Such as you long have wisht for. And the rest
Of your profession like you discontented
For want of meanes, shall in their present payment
Be bound to praise your boldnesse: and hereafter
I will take order you shall have no cause   115
For want of change to put your armour on
But in the face of an enemie; not as now
Among your friends. To that which is due to you,
To furnish you like your selfe, of mine owne bountie
I'll adde five hundred crownes.
   Chamont.   I to my power   120
Will follow the example.
   Montaigne.   Take this, Captaine,
Tis all my present store, but when you please,
Command me further.
   Lanour.   I could wish it more.
   Belgarde. This is the luckiest jest ever came from me.   [*Aside.*]
Let a Souldier use no other Scribe to draw   125

    91. the] *39*; its *McIlwraith*   124 SD. *Aside.*] *Gifford*[2]; *not in 39*

The forme of his petition. This will speed
When your thrice humble supplications,
With prayers for encrease of health and honours
To their grave Lordships shall as soone as read
Be pocketted up, the cause no more remembred.   130
When this dumb Rhetorique.—Well, I have a life,
Which I in thankfulnesse for your great favours,
My noble Lords, when you please to command it,
Must never thinke mine owne. Broker, be happie,
These golden birds flie to thee.   *Exit* BELGARDE.
   Beaufort senior.   You are dull, Sir,   135
And seeme not to be taken with the passage
You saw presented.
   Malefort.   Passage? I observ'd none,
My thoughts were elsewhere busied. Ha! she is
In danger to be lost, to be lost for ever,
If speedily I come not to her rescue,   140
For so my *Genius* tels me.
   Montrevile.   What *Chimera's*
Worke on your phantasie?
   Malefort.   Phantasies? They are truths.
Where is my *Theocrine*? You have plotted
To rob me of my Daughter: bring me to her,
Or I'll call downe the Saints to witnesse for me: 145
You are inhospitable.
   Beaufort senior.   You amaze me,
Your Daughter's safe, and now exchanging courtship
With my sonne her servant. Why doe you heare this
With such distracted lookes? since to that end
You brought her hither?
   Malefort.   Tis confess'd I did,   150
But now pray you pardon me, and if you please
Ere she deliver up her virgin fort,
I would observe what is the art he uses
In planting his artillery against it;
She is my only care, nor must she yield   155
But upon noble termes.
   Beaufort senior.   Tis so determin'd.
   Malefort. Yet I am jealous.

       157. *Montrevile*] Coxeter; *Mont.* 39

III. iii. 157–iv. 19 *The Unnatural Combat*

Montrevile. Overmuch I feare.
What passions are these?
   Beaufort senior. Come I will bring you
Where you, with these if they so please, may see   159
The love-scæne acted.
   Montrevile. There is something more   [*Aside.*]
Then fatherly love in this.
   Montaigne. We wayt upon you.   *Exeunt omnes.*

Actus tertij, Scæna ultima.

BEAUFORT JUNIOR, THEOCRINE.

   Beaufort junior. Since then you meet my flames with equall ardor
As you professe, it is your bounty mistresse,
Nor must I call it debt, yet tis your glory,
That your excesse supplies my want, and makes mee
Strong in my weakenesse, which could never bee,   5
But in your good opinion.
   Theocrine. You teach me Sir,
What I should say, since from your sun of favour,
I like dimme *Phœbe*, in her selfe obscure,
Borrow that light I have.
   Beaufort junior. Which you returne
With large increase (since that you will orecome,   10
And I dare not contend) were you but pleas'd
To make what's yet divided one.
   Theocrine. I have
Already in my wishes, modesty
Forbids me to speake more.
   Beaufort junior. But what assurance,
(But still without offence) may I demand   15
That may secure me that your heart and tongue
Joyne to make up this harmonie?
   Theocrine. Choose any
Suiting your love distinguished from lust,
To aske and mine to grant.

160 SD. *Aside.*] *Gifford*[2]; *not in 39*   III. iv. 1. ardor] *Dodsley*; *order 39*

Enter (as unseene) BEAUFORT SENIOR, MALEFORT,
MONTREVILE, *and the rest.*

Beaufort senior.   Yonder they are.
Malefort. At distance too, tis yet well.
Beaufort junior.   I may take then
This hand, and with a thousand burning kisses,
Sweare tis the anchor to my hopes?
Theocrine.   You may Sir.
Malefort. This is somewhat too much.
Beaufort junior.   And this done, view my selfe
In these true mirrors.
Theocrine.   Ever trew to you Sir,
And may they loose th'abilitie of sight,
When they seeke other object.
Malefort.   This is more
Then I can give consent to.
Beaufort junior.   And a kisse,
Thus printed on your lips will not distast you?
Malefort. Her lips!
Montrevile.   Why where should he kisse? are you distracted?
Beaufort junior. Then when this holy man hath made it lawfull—
     Brings in a Priest.
Malefort. A priest so ready too! I must breake in.
Beaufort junior. And what's spoke here is registred above,
I must ingrosse those favours to my selfe
Which are not to be nam'd.
Theocrine.   All I can give,
But what they are I know not.
Beaufort junior.   I'll instruct you.
Malefort. O how my bloud boyles!
Montrevile.   Pray you containe your selfe,
Me thinkes his courtship's modest.
Beaufort junior.   Thee being mine,
And wholly mine, the river of your love
To kinsmen and allies, nay to your father,
(Howere out of his tendernesse he admires you)
Must in the Ocean of your affection
To me be swallow'd up, and want a name
Compar'd with what you owe me.

Theocrine.   Tis most fit, Sir,
The stronger bond that bindes me to you, must
Dissolve the weaker.
    Malefort.   I am ruin'd if   [*Aside.*]
I come not fairely off.
    Beaufort senior.   Theres nothing wanting   46
But your consent.
    Malefort.   Some strange invention aid me.   *Aside.*
This! yes, it must be so.
    Montrevile.   Why doe you stagger,
When what you seem'd so much to wish is offerd?
    Beaufort junior. Both parties being agreed to.
    Beaufort senior.   I'll not court   50
A grant from you, nor doe I wrong your Daughter,
Though I say my sonne deserves her.
    Malefort.   Tis far from
My humble thoughts to undervalue him
I cannot prize too high. For howsoever
From my owne fond indulgence I have sung   55
Her praises with too prodigall a tongue,
That tendernesse laid by, I stand confirmd
All that I fancied excellent in her
Ballanc'd, with what is really his owne,
Holds waight in no proportion.
    Montrevile.   New turnings!   60
    Beaufort senior. Whither tends this?
    Malefort.   Had you observ'd, my Lord,
With what a sweet gradation he wood,
As I did punctually, you cannot blame her,
Though she did listen with a greedie eare
To his faire modest offers: but so great   65
A good as then flow'd to her, should have beene
With more deliberation entertaind,
And not with such haste swallowd; she shall first
Consider seriously what the blessing is,
And in what ample manner to give thanks for't,   70
And then receive it. And though I shall thinke
Short minutes yeeres till it be perfitted,
I will defer that which I most desire,

  45 SD. *Aside.*] *editor; not in* 39   50. *Beaufort junior.* Both] 39; Both *Dodsley*

And so must she, till longing expectation,
That heightens pleasure, makes her truly know 75
Her happinesse, and with what out-streatcht armes
She must embrace it.
  Beaufort junior.   This is curiousnesse
Beyond example.
  Malefort.   Let it then begin
From me, in whats mine owne I'll use my will,
And yeeld no further reason. I lay claime to 80
The libertie of a subject. Fall not off,
But be obedient, or by the haire
I'll drag thee home. Censure me as you please,
I'll take my owne way, O the inward fires
That wanting vent consume me!   *Exit with* THEOCRINE.
  Montrevile.   'Tis most certaine 85
Hees mad, or worse.
  Beaufort senior.   How, worse?
  Montrevile.   Nay, there I leave you,
My thoughts are free.
  Beaufort junior.   This I foresaw.
  Beaufort senior.   Take comfort,
He shall walke in clouds, but I'll discover him:
And he shall finde, and feele, if he excuse not,
And with strong reasons this grosse injurie, 90
I can make use of my authoritie.   *Exeunt omnes.*

[IV. i]   *Actus quarti, Scena prima.*

MALEFORT *solus.*

  Malefort. WHAT flames are these my wild desires fan in me?
The torch that feeds them, was not lighted at
Thy altars, *Cupid*: vindicate thy selfe,
And doe not own it: and confirme it rather,
That this infernall brand that turnes me cyndars, 5
Was by the snake-hair'd Sisters throwne into
My guiltie bosome. O that I was ever
Accurs'd in having issue: my sonnes bloud,
(That like the poyson'd shirt of *Hercules*

86. *Beaufort senior.*] *Dodsley; Beauf.* 39

IV. i. 10-46   *The Unnatural Combat*   245

 Growes to each part about me) which my hate   10
Forc'd from him with much willingnesse, may admit
Some weake defence; but my most impious love
To my faire daughter *Theocrine*, none,
Since my affection (rather wicked lust)
That does pursue her, is a greater crime   15
Than any detestation, with which
I should afflict her innocence. With what cunning
I have betray'd my selfe, and did not feele
The scorching heat that now with furie rages.
Why was I tender of her? cover'd with   20
That fond disguise, this mischiefe stole upon me.
I thought it no offence to kisse her often,
Or twine mine armes about her softer neck,
And by false shadowes of a fathers kindnesse
I long deceiv'd my selfe: but now the effect   25
Is too apparent. How I strove to be
In her opinion held the worthiest man
In courtship, forme, and feature, envying him
H1ʳ That was preferd before me, and yet then
My wishes to my selfe were not discover'd.   30
But still my fires increas'd, and with delight
I would call her mistresse, wilfully forgetting
The name of daughter, choosing rather she
Should stile me servant, then with reverence father;
Yet waking I nere cherish'd obscene hopes,   35
But in my troubled slumbers often thought
Shee was too neere to me, and then sleeping blush'd
At my imagination, which pass'd,
My eyes being open, not condemning it,
I was ravish'd with the pleasure of the dreame.   40
Yet spight of these temptations I have reason
That pleades against 'em, and commands me to
Extinguish these abhominable fires,
And I will doe it, I will send her backe
To him that loves her lawfully. Within there!   45

     Enter THEOCRINE.

 Theocrine. Sir did you call?

    IV. i. 35. waking] *Gifford*; mocking *39*

Malefort.   I looke no sooner on her,   [*Aside.*]
But all my boasted power of reason leaves me,
And passion againe usurpes her Empire,—
Does none else wait me?
    Theocrine.   I am wretched sir,
Should any owe more duty.
    Malefort.   This is worse   50
Then disobedience, leave me.
    Theocrine.   On my knees sir,
As I have ever squard my will by yours,
And lik'd, and loath'd with your eyes: I beseech you
To teach me what the nature of my fault is,
That hath incensd you, (sure tis one of weakenesse   55
And not of malice) which your gentler temper
On my submission I hope will pardon,
Which granted by your piety, if that I
Out of the least neglect of mine hereafter,
Make you remember it, may I sinke ever   60
Under your dread command.
    Malefort.   O my stars!
Who can but dote on this humility
That sweetens, lovely in her teares! the fetters
That seem'd to lessen in their waight; but now
By this grow heavier on me.
    Theocrine.   Deare sir:
    Malefort.   Peace,   65
I must not heare thee.
    Theocrine.   Nor looke on me?
    Malefort.   No,
Thy lookes and words are charmes.
    Theocrine.   May they have power then
To calme the tempest of your wrath; alas sir,
Did I but know in what I give offence
In my repentance I would shew my sorrow,   70
For what is past, and in my care hereafter
Kill the occasion or cease to be

    46 SD. *Aside.*] *editor; not in 39*   48–52. *rearranged by Gifford; 39 reads* And ... me? / I ... duty. / This ... me / On ... yours.   61–2. stars! / Who] *Gifford; undivided 39*   63. sweetens] *39;* sweetnes *McIlwraith*   65–7. *rearranged by Gifford; 39 reads* Peace ... thee. / Nor ... me. / No ... charmes.   66. me?] *Dodsley;* ~. *39*

Since life without your favour is to me
A load I would cast off.
    Malefort.   O that my heart
Were rent in sunder, that I might expire,   75
The cause in my death buried: yet I know not,
With such prevailing Oratory 'tis beg'd from me
That to deny thee would convince me to
Have suck'd the milke of Tigers. Rise, and I
(But in a perplexd, and misterious method,)   80
Will make relation that which all the world
Admires and cries up in thee for perfections,
Are to unhappy me foule blemishes,
And mulcts in nature. If thou hadst beene borne
Deformd and crooked, in the features of   85
Thy body, as the manners of thy mind,
Moore lip'd, flat nos'd, dimme ey'd, and beetle brow'd,
With a dwarfes stature to a gyant waste,
Sower breath'd, with clawes for fingers on thy hands,
Splay footed, gouty leg'd, and over all   90
A loathsome leprosie had spread it selfe,
And made thee shun'd of humane fellowships:
I had beene blest.
    Theocrine.   Why would you wish a monster
(For such a one or worse you have describ'd)
To call you father?
    Malefort.   Rather then as now,   95
Though I had drownd thee for it in the sea,
Appearing as thou dost a new *Pandora*,
With *Junos* faire cow eyes, *Minerva's* brow,
Aurora's blushing cheekes, *Hebes* fresh youth,
Venus soft paps, with *Thetis* silver feet.   100
    Theocrine. Sir you have lik'd and lov'd them, and oft forc'd
(With your hyperboles of praise powrd on them)
My modesty to a defensive red,
Strowd ore that palenesse, which you then were pleasd
To stile the purest white.
    Malefort.   And in that cup   105
I drank the poison I now feele dispersd

    73–5. *rearranged by Coxeter*; *39 reads* Since . . . off. / O . . . expire,   95. you]
Dodsley; your *39*   105–6. cup / I] *Coxeter*; *undivided 39*

Through every vaine and artery. Wherefore art thou
So cruell to me? This thy outward shape
Brought a fierce warre against me, not to be
By flesh and blood resisted: but to leave me 110
No hope of freedome, from the Magazine
Of thy minds forces, treacherously thou drewst up
Auxiliary helpes to strengthen that
Which was already in it selfe too potent:
Thy beauty gave the first charge, but thy duty 115
Seconded with thy care, and watchfull studies
To please, and serve my will in all that might
Raise up content in me, like thunder brake through
All opposition, and my rankes of reason
Disbanded, my victorious passions fell 120
To bloody execution, and compeld me
With willing hands to tie on my owne chaines,
And with a kinde of flattering joy to glory
In my captivity.
 Theocrine.   I, in this you speake, sir,
Am ignorance it selfe.
 Malefort.   And so continue, 125
For knowledge of the armes thou bearst against me
Would make thee curse thy selfe, but yield no ayds
For thee to helpe me, and 'twere cruelty
In me to wounde that spotlesse innocency
How ere it make me guilty; in a word 130
The plurisie of goodnesse is thy ill,
Thy vertues vices, and thy humble lownesse
Far worse than stubborne sullennesse, and pride;
Thy lookes that ravish all beholders else
As killing as the Basiliskes, theis teares 135
Expressd in sorrow for the much I suffer,
A glorious insultation, and no signe
Of pitty in thee, and to heare thee speake
In thy defence, though but in silent action,
Would make the hurt already deepely festerd 140
Incurable, and therefore as thou wouldst not

---

  111. freedome,] *Mason;* ~∧ *39*   123–6. *rearranged by Coxeter; 39 reads* And . . .
captivity. / I . . . selfe. / And . . . me   131. The] *39;* Thy *Gifford*   135. theis]
McIlwraith; their *39;* thy *Dodsley*

By thy presence raise fresh furies to torment me
I doe conjure thee by a fathers power,
(And tis my curse I dare not thinke it lawfull
To sue unto thee in a neerer name) 145
Without reply to leave me.
   Theocrine.   My obedience
Never learnd yet to question your commands,
But willingly to serve 'em, yet I must
Since that your will forbids the knowledge of
My fault, lament my fortune.   *Exit.*
   Malefort.   O that I 150
Have reason to discerne the better way
And yet pursue the worse. When I looke on her
I burne with heat, and in her absence freeze
With the cold blasts of jelousie, that another
Should ere taste those delights that are denide me, 155
And which of theis afflictions bring lesse torture
I hardly can distinguish. Is there then
No meane? no, so my understanding tels me,
And that by my crosse fates it is determind
That I am both waies wretched.

           Enter USHER, *and* MONTREVILE.

   Usher.   Yonder he walkes sir, 160
In much vexation: he hath sent my Lady
His daughter weeping in, but what the cause is
Rests yet in supposition.
   Montrevile.   I guesse at it,
But must be further satisfied. I will sift him
In private therefore, quit the roome.
   Usher.   I am gon, sir.   *Exit.*
   Malefort. Ha! who disturbes me? *Montrevile?* your pardon. 166
   Montrevile. Would you could grant one to your selfe, (I speake it
With the assurance of a friend) and yet
Before it be too late, make reparation
Of the grosse wrong, your indiscretion offered 170
To the governour and his sonne, nay to your selfe,

146–7. obedience / Never] *Coxeter; undivided 39*
undivided 39   156. theis] *after Gifford;* their *39*
undivided 39

150–1. I / Have] *Gifford;*
163–4. it, / But] *Coxeter;*

For there begins my sorrow.
  Malefort.   Would I had
No greater cause to mourne then their displeasure,
For I dare justifie—
  Montrevile. We must not doe
All that we dare; we 'are private friend, I observd   175
Your alterations with a stricter eye
Perhaps then others, and to loose no time
In repetition, your strange demeanour
To your sweet daughter.
  Malefort.   Would you could finde out
Some other theame to treat of.
  Montrevile.   None but this;   180
And this Ile dwell on, how ridiculous
And subject to construction—
  Malefort.   No more.
  Montrevile. You made your selfe, amazes me, and if
The frequent trials enterchanged betweene us
Of love and friendship, be to their desert   185
Esteem'd by you, as they hold waight with me,
No inward trouble should be of a shape
So horrid to your selfe, but that to me
You stand bound to discover it, and unlocke
Your secretst thoughts: though the most innocent were   190
Lowd crying sinnes.
  Malefort. And so perhaps they are.
And therefore be not curious to learne that
Which knowne must make you hate me.
  Montrevile.   Thinke not so,
I am yours in right and wrong, nor shall you finde
A verball friendship in me, but an active,   195
And here I vow, I shall no sooner know
What the disease is, but if you give leave
I will apply a remedy. Is it madnesse?
I am familiarly acquainted with
A deepe read man that can with charmes and hearbs   200

  172–4. *rearranged by Coxeter*; *39 reads* Would . . . mourne / Then . . . justifie.
174–5. *rearranged by Gifford*; *39 reads* We . . . friend / I . . . eye   175. dare; we
'are] *McIlwraith*; dare *39*; dare. / We're *Dodsley*   179–81. *rearranged by Gifford*;
39 reads Would . . . Of. / None . . . ridiculous   193–4. so, / I] *Coxeter*; *undivided*
39   199–200. *rearranged by Mason*; *39 reads* I . . . man / That . . . hearbs

Restore you to your reason, or suppose
You are bewitch'd, he with more potent spels
And magicall rites shall cure you. Is't heavens anger?
With penitence and sacrifice appease it,
Beyond this, there is nothing that I can
Imagine dreadfull. In your fame and fortunes
You are secure, your impious sonne removd to
That rendred you suspected to the state,
And your faire daughter—
   Malefort.   Oh presse me no farther.
   Montrevile. Are you wrung there? why what of her? hath she
Made shipwracke of her honour, or conspird
Against your life? or seald a contract with
The divell of hell, for the recovery of
Her young Inamorato?
   Malefort.   None of these,
And yet, what must increase the wonder in you,
Being Innocent in her selfe, she hath wounded me,
But where enquire not. Yet I know not how,
I am perswaded from my confidence
Of your vowd love to me, to trust you with
My dearest secret, pray you chide me for it,
But with a kind of pity, not insulting
On my calamity.
   Montrevile.   Forward.
   Malefort.   This same daughter—
   Montrevile. What is her fault?
   Malefort.   She is too faire to me.
   Montrevile. Ha! how is this?
   Malefort.   And I have lookd upon her
More than a father should, and languish to
Enjoy her as a husband.
   Montrevile.   Heaven forbid it.
   Malefort. And this is all the comfort you can give me,
Where are your promisd ayds, your charmes, your herbs?
Your deepe read scholler, spels, and magicke rites?
Can all these disenchaunt me? no, I must be
My owne Physitian, and upon my selfe
Practice a desperate cure.

213–14. of / Her] *Coxeter; undivided* 39

  Montrevile.   Doe not contemne me,
Injoyne me what you please with any hazzard,
Ile undertake it. What meanes have you practisd
To quench this hellish fire?
  Malefort.   All I could thinke on,   235
But to no purpose, and yet sometimes absence
Does yeeld a kinde of intermission to
The fury of the fit.
  Montrevile.   See her no more then.
  Malefort. Tis my last refuge, and twas my intent
And still tis, to desire your helpe.
  Montrevile.   Command it.   240
  Malefort. Thus then, you have a fort of which you are
The absolute Lord, to which I pray you beare her:
And that the sight of her may not againe
Nourish those flames, which I feele something lessend,
By all the ties of friendship I conjure you   245
And by a solemne oath you must confirme it,
That though my now calmd passions should rage higher
Then ever heretofore, and so compell me
Once more to wish to see her; though I use
Perswasions mixd with threatnings; nay adde to it   250
That I, this fayling, should with hands held up thus
Kneele at your feet, and bathe them with my teares,
Prayers or curses, vowes or imprecations
Onely to looke upon her though at distance,
You still must be obdurate.
  Montrevile.   If it be   255
Your pleasure sir that I shall be unmov'd,
I will endeavour.
  Malefort.   You must sweare to be
Inexorable as you would prevent
The greatest mischiefe to your friend, that fate
Could throw upon him.
  Montrevile.   Well, I will obey you.   260
But how the governour will be answer'd, yet,
And tis materiall, is not considered.
  Malefort. Leave that to me. Ile presently give order

---

242. to which] *McIlwraith*; which *39²*; whither *39¹*   256–7. unmov'd, / I]
Coxeter; *undivided 39*

How you shall surprize her, be not frighted with
Her exclamations.
 Montrevile. Be you constant to
Your resolution, I will not faile
In what concernes my part.
 Malefort. Be ever blessed for't. *Exeunt.*

Actus quarti, Scæna secunda.

Enter BEAUFORT JUNIOR, CHAMONT, LANOUR.

 Chamont. Not to be spoke with, say you?
 Beaufort junior. No.
 Lanour.   Nor you
Admitted to have conference with her?
 Beaufort junior. Neither.
His doores are fast lockd up, and solitude
Dwels round about em, no accesse allow'd
To friend or enemy, but—
 Chamont. Nay be not mov'd sir,
Let his passion worke, and like a hot rein'd horse
'Twill quickly tire it selfe.
 Beaufort junior. Or in his death
Which for her sake till now I have forborne
I will revenge the injury he hath done
To my true and lawfull love.
 Lanour. How does your father
The Governour rellish it?
 Beaufort junior. Troth he never had
Affection to the match: yet in his pitty
To me, he's gone in person to his house,
Nor will he be denide, and if he finde not
Strong and faire reasons *Malefort* will heare from him
In a kinde he does not looke for.
 Chamont. In the meane time
Pray you put on cheerefull lookes.

Enter MONTAIGNE.

 Beaufort junior. Mine suite my fortune.
 Lanour. O heer's *Montaigne.*

Montaigne. I never could have met you
More opportunely. Ile not stale the jest
By my relation: but if you will looke on
The malecontent *Belgarde*, newly rigde up,
With the traine that followes him, 'twill be an object
Worthy of your noting.
    Beaufort junior. Looke you the Comedy
Make good the Prologue, or the scorne will dwell
Upon your selfe.
    Montaigne. I'll hazard that, observe now.

Enter BELGARDE *in a gallant habit; stayes at the doore with his sword drawne; severall voyces within.*

Wenches. Nay, Captaine, glorious Captaine:
    Belgarde. Fall backe Rascalls,
Doe you make an Owle of me? this day I will
Receive no more Petitions,
Here are bills of all occasions, and all sizes!
If this be the pleasure of a rich suite, would I were
Againe in my buffe jerkin, or my armour,
Then I walk'd securely by my creditors noses,
And not a dog mark'd me, every officer shund me,
And not one lowzie prison would receive me;
But now, as the Ballade sayes, I am turnd gallant:
There does not live that thing I ow a sowse to,
But does torment me. A faithfull Cobler told me
With his awle in his hand, I was behind hand with him
For setting me upright, and bad me looke to my selfe.
A Sempstresse too, that traded but in sockes,
Swore she would set a Serjeant on my backe
For a borrowed shirt: my pay and the benevolence
The Governour and the States bestow'd upon me,
The citie cormorants, my monie-mongers,
Have swallow'd downe already; they were summes,
I grant, but that I should be such a foole
Against my othe, being a cashir'd Captaine,
To pay debts, though growne up to one and twenty,

    IV. ii. 24–5. will dwell / Upon] *39²*; will / dwell upon *39¹, ²*   25 SD. *Enter* . . . *within.*] *Coxeter*; *follows* Captaine: (l. 26) *39*   26. *Wenches.* Nay] *39²*; Nay *39¹, ²*
29. occasions] *39²*; sorts *39¹, ²*   sizes!] *39²*; ~, *39¹, ²*   36. sowse] *39²*; soule *39¹, ²*

IV. ii. 49-82   *The Unnatural Combat*   255

Deserves more reprehension, in my judgement,
Then a shop-keeper, or a Lawyer that lends money,　　50
In a long dead vacation.
　　Montaigne.　　　　　How doe you like
His meditation?
　　Chamont.　　Peace, let him proceed.
　　Belgarde. I cannot now goe on the score for shame,
And where I shall begin to pawne, I marry,
That is consider'd timely. I paid for　　55
This traine of yours Dame *Estridge* foureteen crowns,
And yet it is so light, 'twill hardly passe
For a Taverne reckoning, unlesse it be
To save the charge of paynting, naild on a post
For the signe of the feathers; pox upon the fashion,　　60
That a Captaine cannot thinke himselfe a Captaine,
If he weare not this like a fore-horse; yet it is not
Staple commodity; these are perfum'd too,
Of the Roman wash, and yet a stale red herring
Would fill the belly better, and hurt the head lesse:　　65
And this is Venice gold, would I had it againe
In french crownes in my pocket. O you commanders
That like me have no dead paies, nor can couzen
The Commissary at a muster, let me stand
For an example to you, as you would　　70
Injoy your priviledges: *videlicet*,
To pay your debts, and take your lechery gratis,
To have your issue warm'd by others fires,
To be often drunke, and sweare, yet pay no forfeit
To the poore, but when you share with one another,　　75
With all your other choyce immunities;
Onely of this I seriously advise you:
Let Courtiers trip like Courtiers, and your Lords
Of dirt and dung hills mete their woods and acres,
In velvets, sattins, tissues, but keepe you　　80
Constant to cloth and shamois.
　　Montaigne.　　　　　　Have you heard
Of such a penitent homily?
　　Belgarde.　　　　　I am studying now

78-82. *rearranged by Gifford; 39 reads* Let . . . like Courtiers, / And . . . mete / Their . . . tissues, / But . . . shamois. / Have . . . homily,　　79. mete] *39*; melt *Mason*

Where I shall hide my selfe till the rumor of
My wealth and braverie vanish, let me see,
There is a kinde of a vaulting house not farre off, 85
Where I us'd to spend my afternoones, among
Suburb shee-gamesters; and yet now I thinke on't
I have crackd a ring or two there, which they made
Others to solder, no,

Enter a BAWD *and two* WENCHES, *with two Children.*

1. *Wench.*   O, have we spide you?
Bawd. Upon him without ceremonie, nows the time 90
While he is in the paying veine.
2. *Wench.*   Save you brave Captaine.
Beaufort junior. 'Slight, how he stares, they are worse then she-
   wolves to him.
Belgarde. Shame me not in the streets, I was comming to you.
1. *Wench.* O Sir, you may in publique pay for the fidling
You had in private.
2. *Wench.*   We heare you are full of crownes, Sir. 95
1. *Wench.* And therefore knowing you are open-handed,
Before all be destroyd, I'll put you in mind, Sir,
Of your young heire here.
2. *Wench.*   Here's a second, Sir,
That lookes for a childs portion.
Bawd.   There are reckonings
For Muskadine and Egs too, must be thought on. 100
1. *Wench.* We have not beene hasty, Sir.
Bawd.   But staid your leasure;
But now you are ripe, and loden with fruit.
2. *Wench.* Tis fit you should be puld; here's a boy, Sir,
Pray you kisse him, tis your owne, Sir,
1. *Wench.*   Nay, busse this first,
It hath just your eyes, and such a promising nose, 105
That if the signe deceive me not, in time
Twill prove a notable striker, like his father.
Belgarde. And yet you laid it to another.
1. *Wench.*   True,
While you were poore, and it was policy,
But she that has varietie of fathers, 110

92. he] *Dodsley*; she 39

And makes not choyce of him that can maintaine it,
Nere studied *Aristotles* Problemes.
　Lanour.　　　　　　　　A smart queane.
　Belgarde. Why braches, will you whurry me?
　2. Wench.　　　　　　　　　　No, but ease you
Of your golden burthen, the heavie carriage may
Bring you to a sweating sicknesse.
　Belgarde.　　　　　　Very likely,　　　　115
I foame all ore alreadie.
　1. Wench.　　　Will you come off, Sir?
　Belgarde. Would I had ne're come on: heare me with patience,
Or I will anger you. Goe to, you know me,
And doe not vexe me further: by my sins
And your diseases, which are certaine truthes,　　120
What ere you thinke, I am not master at
This instant, of a livre.
　2. Wench.　　　　What, and in
Such a glorious suite?
　Belgarde.　　　　The liker wretched things
To have no mony.
　Bawd.　　　　You may pawne your clothes, Sir.　　124
　1. Wench. Will you see your issue starve?
　2. Wench.　　　　　　　　　　Or the mothers beg?
　Belgarde. Why, you unconscionable strumpets, would you have me
Transforme my hat to double clouts and biggins?
My corselet to a cradle? or my belt
To swaddlebands? or turne my cloke to blankets?
Or to sell my sword and spurs for sope and candles?　　130
Have you no mercy? what a chargeable divell
We carry in our breeches!
　Beaufort junior.　　　Now tis time
To fetch him off.

　　　　　　Enter BEAUFORT SENIOR.

　Montaigne.　　Your father does it for us.
　Bawd. The Governour!
　Beaufort senior.　　　What are these?
　1. Wench.　　　　　　And it like your Lordship,
Very poore spinsters.

112. *Aristotles* Problemes.] *39*; Aristotle. *Gifford*　　122. livre] *39²*; livery *39¹, ²*

Bawd.   I am his Nurse and Landresse.   135
Belgarde. You have nurs'd and lander'd me, hell take you for it.
Vanish.
  Chamont. Doe, doe, and talke with him hereafter.
  1. *Wench.* Tis our best course.
  2. *Wench.*   We'll find a time to fit him.
      Exeunt BAWD *and* WHORES [*with Children*].
Beaufort senior. Why in this heat, *Belgarde*?
Belgarde.   You are the cause of't.
Beaufort senior. Who, I?
  Belgarde.   Yes, your pied liverie, and your gold   140
Draw these vexations on mee, pray you strip me
And let me be as I was: I will not lose
The pleasures and the fredome which I had
In my certaine povertie; for all the wealth
Faire France is proud of!
  Beaufort senior.   Wee at better leasure   145
Will learne the cause of this.
  Beaufort junior.   What answer, Sir,
From the Admirall?
  Beaufort senior.   None, his daughter is remov'd
To the fort of *Montrevile*, and he himselfe
In person fled, but where is not discover'd.
I could tell you wonders, but the time denies mee   150
Fit libertie. In a word, let it suffice
The power of our great master is contemn'd,
The sacred lawes of God and man prophan'd,
And if I sit downe with this injury,
I am unworthy of my place, and thou   155
Of my acknowledgement: draw up all the troopes,
As I goe, I will instruct you to what purpose.
Such as have power to punish, and yet spare
From feare, or from connivence, others ill,   159
Though not in act assist them in their will.   *Exeunt.*

    138 SD. *with Children*] editor; *not in 39*   160. act] *39³*; art *39¹, ²*

Actus quinti, Scena prima.

MONTREVILE, THEOCRINE, SERVANTS [, PAGE, WOMEN].

Montrevile. Binde them, and gag their mouthes sure, I alone
Will be your convoy.
   1. *Woman.* Madam,
   2. *Woman.* Dearest Lady,
   Page. Let me fight for my Mistresse.
   Servant. Tis in vaine,
Little Cockerell of the kinde.
   Montrevile. Away with them,
And doe as I command you. *Exeunt* SERVANTS, PAGE, WOMEN.
   Theocrine. Montrevile
You are my fathers friend, nay, more, a souldier,
And if a right one, as I hope to find you,
Though in a lawfull war you had surpriz'd
A Citie, that bowd humbly to your pleasure,
In honour you stand bound to guard a virgin
From violence; but in a free estate
Of which you are a limb, to doe a wrong
Which noble enemies never consent to
Is such an insolence—
   Montrevile. How her heart beats!
Much like a Partridge in a Sparhawkes foot,
That with a panting silence does lament
The fate she cannot flie from! sweet, take comfort,
You are safe, and nothing is intended to you
But love and service.
   Theocrine. They came never cloth'd
In force, and outrage; upon what assurance
(Remembring only that my father lives
Who will not tamely suffer the disgrace)
Have you presum'd to hurry mee from his house,
And as I were not worth the waiting on,
To snatch me from the duty, and attendance
Of my poore servants?
   Montrevile. Let not that afflict you,
You shall not want observance, I will be

V. i. SD. PAGE, WOMEN.] *Gifford; not in* 39   22. disgrace)] *Mason;* ~, 39

    Your Page, your Woman, Parasite or Foole,
Or any other property, provided
You answer my affection.
      Theocrine.   In what kind?
      Montrevile. As you had done young *Beauforts.*
      Theocrine.   How?
      Montrevile.   So Lady,
Or, if the name of wife appeare a yoke
Too heavie for your tender necke, so I
Enjoy you as a private friend, or mistresse,
Twil be sufficient.
      Theocrine.   Blessed Angels guard me,
What frontlesse impudence is this? What divell
Hath to thy certaine ruine tempted thee
To offer me this motion? by my hopes
Of after joyes, submission, nor repentance
Shall expiate this foule intent.
      Montrevile.   Intent?
Tis more, I'll make it act.
      Theocrine.   Ribald, thou darest not,
And if (and with a feaver to thy soule)
Thou but consider that I have a father
And such a father, as when this arrives at
His knowledge, as it shall, the terrour of
His vengeance, which as sure as fate must follow,
Will make thee curse the houre in which lust taught thee
To nourish these base hopes, and tis my wonder
Thou darest forget how tender he is of mee
And that each shadow of wrong done to me
Will raise in him a tempest not to be
But with thy heart-blood calm'd: this when I see him.
      Montrevile. As thou shalt never.
      Theocrine.   Wilt thou murther me?
      Montrevile. No, no, tis otherwise determin'd, foole,
The master which in passion kills his slave
That may be usefull to him, does himselfe
The injurie. Know thou most wretched creature,
That father thou presum'st upon, that father,
That when I sought thee in a noble way,
Deny'd thee to me, fancying in his hope

A higher match from his excesse of dotage,
Hath in his bowels kindled such a flame
Of impious and most unnaturall lust,
That now he feares his furious desires
May force him to doe that he shakes to thinke on. 65
   Theocrine. O me most wretched.
   Montrevile.   Never hope againe
To blast him with those eyes, their golden beames
Are unto him arrowes of death and hell,
But unto me divine artillery.
And therefore since what I so long in vaine 70
Pursu'd, is offerd to me, and by him
Given up to my possession: doe not flatter
Thy selfe with an imaginary hope,
But that I'll take occasion by the forelock,
And make use of my fortune; as we walke 75
I'll tell the more.
   Theocrine.   I will not stirre.
   Montrevile.   I'll force thee:
   Theocrine. Helpe, helpe,
   Montrevile.   In vaine,
   Theocrine.   In mee my brothers blood
Is punish'd at the height.
   Montrevile.   The Coach there.
   Theocrine.   Deare Sir,
   Montrevile. Teares, curses, prayers, are alike to me,
I can, and must enjoy my present pleasure, 80
And shall take time to mourne for it at leasure.   *Exeunt.*

Actus quinti, Scæna secunda.

Enter MALEFORT *solus.*

   Malefort. I have playd the foole, the grosse foole, to believe
The bosome of a friend will hold a secret
Mine owne could not containe, and my industry
In taking liberty from my innocent daughter,
Out of false hopes of freedome to my selfe, 5

---

63. and most] *Gifford*; and 39[1, 2]; most 39[3]   81 SD. *Exeunt.*] *Coxeter*; *Exit.* 39

Is in the little helpe it yeelds me, punish'd.
Shee's absent, but I have her figure here,
And every grace, and rarity about her,
Are by the pencill of my memory
In living colours paynted on my heart. 10
My fires too, a short interim closd up
Breake out with greater fury. Why was I
(Since 'twas my fate, and not to be declin'd)
In this so tender consciencd? say I had
Injoyd what I desir'd, what had it beene 15
But incest? and there's something here that tels me
I stand accomptable for greater sinnes,
I never checkd at: neither had the crime
Wanted a præsident. I have read in story
Those first great Heroes that for their brave deeds 20
Were in the worlds first infancie stil'd gods,
Freely enjoyd what I deny my selfe.
Old *Saturne* in the golden age embraced
His sister *Ops* and in the same degree
The thunderer *Juno*, *Neptune Thetis*, and 25
By their example after the first deluge
Deucalion Pirrhæ. Universall nature
As every day tis evident allowes it
To creatures of all kinds. The gallant horse
Covers the Mare to which he was the sire, 30
The bird with fertile seed gives new encrease
To her that hatchd him. Why should envious man then
Brand that close act which adds proximity
To whats most neere him, with the abhorred title
Of incest? or our later lawes forbid 35
What by the first was granted? let old men
That are not capeable of these delights,
And solemne superstitious fooles prescribe
Rules to themselves, I will not curbe my freedome
But constantly go on, with this assurance, 40
I but walke in a path which greater men
Have trod before me. Ha this is the fort,
Open the gate. Within there.

V. ii. 22. deny] *39*; deny'd *Dodsley*   25. *Neptune*] *Dodsley*; ~, *39*   38. superstitious] *Dodsley*; superstitions *39*

Enter two SOULDIERS *with Muskets.*

    1. *Souldier.*   With your pardon
We must forbid your entrance.
    Malefort.   Doe you know me?
    2. *Souldier.* Perfectly my Lord.
    Malefort.   I am thy Captaines friend.   45
    1. *Souldier.* It may be so, but till we know his pleasure
You must excuse us.
    2. *Souldier.*   Wee'l acquaint him with
Your waiting here.
    Malefort.   Waiting, slave? he was ever
By me commanded.
    1. *Souldier.*   As we are by him.
    Malefort. So punctuall? pray you then in my name intreat   50
His presence.
    2. *Souldier.* That we shall doe.   *Exeunt* SOULDIERS.
    Malefort.   I must use
Some strange perswasions to worke him to
Deliver her, and to forget those vowes,
And horrid oaths I in my madnesse made him
Take to the contrary, and may I get her   55
Once more in my possession, I will beare her
Into some close cave, or desert, where wee'l end
Our lusts and lives together.

Enter MONTREVILE *and Souldiers.*

    Montrevile.   Faile not, on
The forfeit of your lives to execute
What I commanded.   [*Exeunt Souldiers.*]
    Malefort.   *Montrevile*, how is't friend?   60
    Montrevile. I am glad to see you weare such chearefull lookes,
The worlds well altred.
    Malefort.   Yes I thanke my stars.
But me thinks thou art troubled.
    Montrevile.   Some light crosse,
But of no moment.

---

45. thy] *Mason;* this 39   48. *Malefort*] *Coxeter; Mont.* 39   50. *Malefort*] *Coxeter; Montr.* 39   53. those] *McIlwraith;* her 39; the *Dodsley*   54. him] *Mason;* ~. 39   55. her] *Dodsley;* those 39   60 SD. *Exeunt Souldiers.*] *Gifford;* not in 39

Malefort. So I hope, beware
Of sad and impious thoughts, you know how far
They wrought on me.
    Montrevile. No such come neere me sir.
I have like you no daughter, and much wish
You never had been curs'd with one.
    Malefort. Who I?
Thou art deceiv'd, I am most happy in her.
    Montrevile. I am glad to heare it.
    Malefort. My incestuous fires
Towards her are quite burnt out, I love her now
As a father, and no further.
    Montrevile. Fix there then
Your constant peace, and doe not try a second
Temptation from her.
    Malefort. Yes friend, though shee were
By millions of degrees more excellent
In her perfections, Nay though she could borrow
A forme Angelicall to take my fraylty
It would not doe, and therefore *Montrevile*
(My chiefe delight next her) I come to tell thee
The governour and I are reconcil'd,
And I confirm'd, and with all possible speed,
To make large satisfaction to young *Beaufort*,
And her whom I have so much wrong'd, and for
Thy trouble in her custody, of which
Ile now discharge thee, there is nothing in
My nerves or fortunes, but shall ever be
At thy devotion.
    Montrevile. You promise fairely,
Nor doubt I the performance, yet I would not
Hereafter be reported, to have beene
The principall occasion of your falling
Into a relaps; or but suppose out of
The easinesse of my nature, and assurance
You are firme, and can hold out, I could consent:
You needs must know there are so many lets
That make against it, that it is my wonder
You offer me the motion, having bound me

    87. fairely] *Dodsley*; faintly *39*

With oathes and imprecations on no termes,
Reasons, or arguments, you could propose,
I ever should admit you to her sight,
Much lesse restore her to you.
 Malefort.   Are we souldiers,
And stand on othes?
 Montrevile. Tis beyond my knowledge
In what we are more worthy, then in keeping
Our words, much more our vowes.
 Malefort.   Heaven pardon all,
How many thousands in our heate of wine,
Quarrels and play, and in our younger daies
(In private, I may say) betweene our selves
In points of love, have we to answer for,
Should we be scrupulous that way.
 Montrevile.   You say well,
And very aptly call to memory
Two oathes against all ties and rites of friendship
Broken by you to me.
 Malefort.   No more of that.
 Montrevile. Yes tis materiall, and to the purpose.
The first (and think upon't) was when I brought you
As a visitant to my mistresse then, the mother
Of this same daughter, whom with dreadfull words
Too hideous to remember, you swore deepely
For my sake never to attempt, yet then,
Then, when you had a sweet wife of your owne,
I know not with what arts, philtres, and charmes,
(Unlesse in wealth and fame you were above me)
You won her from me, and her grant obtain'd,
A marriage with the second wayted on
The buriall of the first (that to the world
Brought your dead son); this I sate tamely down by,
Wanting indeed occasion and power
To be at the height revenged.
 Malefort.   Yet this you seem'd
Freely to pardon.
 Montrevile. As perhaps I did.
Your daughter *Theocrine* growing ripe,

    100–1. souldiers, / And] *Gifford; undivided* 39

(Her mother too deceas'd) and fit for marriage
I was a suitor for her, had your word
Upon your honour, and our friendship made
Authenticall, and ratified with an oath,
Shee should be mine, but vowes with you being like
To your religion, a nose of wax
To be turn'd every way, that very day
The governours sonne but making his approaches
Of Courtship to her, the winde of your ambition
For her advancement scatter'd the thin sand
In which you wrot your full consent to me,
And drew you to his party. What hath pas'd since
You beare a register in your owne bosome
That can at large informe you.
    Malefort.   *Montrevile*
I doe confesse all that you charge me with
To be strong truth, and that I bring a cause
Most miserably guilty, and acknowledge
That though your goodnesse made me mine owne judge,
I should not shew the least compassion,
Or mercy to my selfe. O let not yet
My foulenesse taint your purenesse, or my falshood
Divert the torrent of your loyall faith.
My ills, if not return'd by you, will adde
Lustre to your much good, and to orecome
With noble sufferance will expresse your strength,
And triumph ore my weakenesse. If you please to,
My blacke deeds being onely knowne to you,
And in surrendring up my daughter buried:
You not alone make me your slave (for I
At no part doe deserve the name of friend)
But in your owne brest raise a monument
Of pitty to a wretch on whom with justice
You may expresse all cruelty.
    Montrevile.   You much move me.
    Malefort. O that I could but hope it; to revenge
An injurie is proper to the wishes
Of feeble women, that want strength to act it:
But to have power to punish, and yet pardon
Peculiar to Princes. See these knees,

That have beene ever stiffe to bend to heaven
To you are supple. Is there ought beyond this
That may speake my submission? or can pride
(Though I well know it is a stranger to you) 170
Desire a feast of more humility
To kill her growing appetite?
    Montrevile.   I requir'd not
To be sought to this poore way, yet tis so far
A kind of satisfaction that I will
Dispence a little with those serious oaths 175
You made me take; your daughter shall come to you,
I will not say as you deliverd her,
But as she is you may dispose of her
As you shall thinke most requisite.   *Exit* MONTREVILE.
    Malefort.   His last words
Are riddles to me. Here the lyons force 180
Would have prov'd uselesse and against my nature
Compeld me from the Crocodile to borrow
Her counterfeit teares. Ther's now no turning backward,
May I but quench these fires that rage within me,
And fall what can fall, I am arm'd to beare it. 185

The SOULDIERS *thrust forth* THEOCRINE, *her garments loose,
her haire disheveld.*

    1. *Souldier.* You must be packing.
    Theocrine.   Hath he rob'd me of
Mine honour, and denies me now a roome
To hide my shame?
    2. *Souldier.*   My Lord the Admirall
Attends your Ladiship.
    1. *Souldier.*   Close the port, and leave em.
                              Exeunt SOULDIERS.
    Malefort. Ha! who is this? how alter'd! how deform'd! 190
It cannot be. And yet this creature has
A kinde of a resemblance to my daughter,
My *Theocrine*! but as different
From that she was, as bodies dead are in
Their best perfections, from what they were 195

    179–80. *rearranged by Coxeter; 39 reads* His ... me. / Here ... force   186. 1.
Souldier] *McIlwraith;* 2 Sould 39

When they had life and motion.
  Theocrine.   Tis most true sir,
I am dead indeed to all but misery.
O come not neere me sir, I am infectious;
To looke on me at distance is as dangerous
As from a pinacles cloud-kissing spire,
With giddy eyes to view the steepe descent,
But to acknowledge me a certaine ruine.
O sir.
  Malefort. Speake *Theocrine*, force me not
To farther question, my feares already
Have chok'd my vitall spirits.
  Theocrine.   Pray you turne away
Your face and heare me, and with my last breath
Give me leave to accuse you. What offence
From my first infancie did I commit
That for a punishment you should give up
My Virgin chastity to the trecherous guard
Of Goatish *Montrevile*?
  Malefort.   What hath he done?
  Theocrine. Abus'd me sir by violence, and this told
I cannot live to speake more; may the cause
In you finde pardon, but the speeding curse
Of a ravish'd maid fall heavie, heavie on him.
Beaufort my lawfull love, farewell for ever.   *She dies.*
  Malefort. Take not thy flight so soone immaculate spirit.
Tis fled already, how the innocent
As in a gentle slumber passe away,
But to cut off the knotty thred of life
In guilty men, must force sterne *Atropos*
To use her sharpe knife often. I would helpe
The edge of hers with the sharpe point of mine
But that I dare not die, till I have rent
This dogs heart peecemeale. O that I had wings
To scale these walls, or that my hands were Canons
To bore their flinty sides, that I might bring
The villaine in the reach of my good sword,
The Turkish Empire offer'd for his ransome
Should not redeeme his life. O that my voice
Were loud as thunder and with horrid sounds

Might force a dreadfull passage to his eares,
And through them reach his soule; libidinous monster,
Foule ravisher, as thou durst doe a deed
Which forc'd the Sun to hide his glorious face   235
Behinde a sable Masque of clouds appeare,
And as a man defend it, or like me
Shew some compunction for it.

        MONTREVILE *above, the curtaine suddenly drawn.*

Montrevile.   Ha, ha, ha.
Malefort. Is this an object to raise mirth?
Montrevile.   Yes, yes.
Malefort. My daughter's dead.
Montrevile.   Thou hadst best follow her, 240
Or if thou art the thing thou art reported,
Thou shouldst have led the way. Doe teare thy haire
Like a village nurse, and mourn while I laugh at thee.
Be but a just examiner of thy selfe
And in an equall ballance poise the nothing   245
Or little mischiefe I have done compard
With the ponderous weight of thine, and how canst thou
Accuse or argue with me? mine was a rape
And she being in a kinde contracted to me,
The fact may challenge some qualification: 250
But thy intent made natures selfe run backward,
And done, had caus'd an earth-quake.

            A SOULDIER *above.*

1. *Souldier.*   Captaine.
Montrevile.   Ha?
1. *Souldier.* Our outworkes are surpriz'd, the centinell slaine,
The corps du garde defeated too.
Montrevile.   By whom?
1. *Souldier.* The sudden storme and darknesse of the night 255
Forbids the knowledge, make up speedily,
Or all is lost.
    Montrevile. In the divels name, whence comes this! *They descend.*
    Malefort. Doe, doe, rage on, rend open Æolus

238 SD. above,] *Dodsley;* ~∧ *39*   curtaine] *Dodsley;* ~, *39*   252 SD. *A*
SOULDIER] *39*; Soldiers *Coxeter*   253. 1. Souldier] *conj. Telfer;* 2. Sold. *39*

Thy brazen prison, and let loose at once *A storme.*
Thy stormy issue; blustring *Boreas*,
Aided with all the gales, the Pilot numbers
Upon his compasse, cannot raise a tempest
Through the vast region of the ayre, like that
I feele within me: for I am possess'd
With whirle-winds, and each guilty thought to me is
A dreadfull Hurricano; though this centre
Labour to bring forth earthquake, and hell open
Her wide stretch'd jawes, and let out all her furies,
They cannot adde an atome to the mountaine
Of feares and terrors that each minute threaten
To fall on my accursed head. Ha, is't fancie?

Enter the Ghost of young MALEFORT, *naked from the wast, full of wounds, leading in the shadow of a Ladie, her face leprous.*

Or hath hell heard me, and makes proofe if I
Dare stand the tryall? yes, I doe, and now
I view these apparitions, I feele
I once did know the substances. For what come you?
Are your aeriall formes depriv'd of language,
And so deni'd to tell me? that by signes
You bid me aske here of my selfe? tis so
                    The Ghosts use severall gestures.
And there is somthing here makes answer for you.
You come to launce my sear'd up conscience? Yes,
And to instruct me, that those thunderbolts,
That hurl'd me headlong from the height of glory,
Wealth, honours, worldly happinesse, were forg'd
Upon the anvile of my impious wrongs
And cruelty to you? I doe confesse it;
And that my lust compelling me to make way
For a second wife, I poison'd thee, and that
The cause (which to the world is undiscover'd)
That forc'd thee to shake off thy filiall duty
To mee thy father, had it's spring and sourse
From thy impatience to know thy mother,
That with all duty, and obedience serv'd me
(For now with horror I acknowledge it)

275. substances] *39²*; substance *39¹*

V. ii. 294-324   *The Unnatural Combat*

Remov'd unjustly: yet thou being my sonne,
Were't not a competent judge mark'd out by heaven
For her revenger, which thy falling by
My weaker hand confirm'd. Tis granted by thee.
                              Answer'd still by signes.
Can any penance expiate my guilt?
Or can repentance save me? they are vanish'd.   *Exeunt Ghosts.*
What's left to doe then? I'll accuse my fate
That did not fashion me for nobler uses:
Or if those starres crosse to me in my birth,
Had not deni'd their prosperous influence to it,
With peace of conscience like to innocent men,
I might have ceas'd to be, and not as now,
To curse my cause of being.   *He's kill'd with a flash of lightning.*

            Enter BELGARDE *with* SOULDIERS.
    Belgarde.   Here is a night
To season my silkes. Buffe-jerkin, now I misse thee,
Thou hast endur'd many foule nights, but never
One like to this; how fine my feather looks now!
Just like a Capons taile stolne out of the pen
And hid in the sinke, and yet 't had beene dishonour
To have charg'd me without it. Wilt thou never cease?
Is the petarde, as I gave directions, fasten'd
On the portcullis?
    Another Souldier. It hath beene attempted
By divers, but in vaine.
    Belgarde.   These are your gallants,
That at a feast take the first place, poore I,
Hardly allow'd to follow; marry in
These foolish businesses they are content
That I shall have precedence, I much thanke
Their manners, or their feare; second me Souldiers,
They have had no time to undermine, or if
They have, it is but blowing up, and fetching
A caper or two in the ayre, and I will doe it,
Rather then blow my nailes here.
    Souldier.   O brave Captaine!   *Exeunt.*
        An alarum, noise and cryes within, a flourish.

312. charg'd me] *39*; charg'd *Mason*   322. but blowing] *Dodsley*; blowing *39*

Enter BEAUFORT SENIOR, BEAUFORT JUNIOR, MONTAIGNE, CHAMONT, LANOUR, BELGARDE, MONTREVILE, *Souldiers.*

   Montrevile. Rackes cannot force more from me then I have
Already told you. I expect no favour,
I have cast up my accompt.
   Beaufort senior.   Take you the charge
Of the fort, *Belgarde,* your dangers have deserv'd it.
   Belgarde. I thanke your excellence, this will keepe me safe yet
From being pull'd by the sleeve, and bid remember
The thing I wot of.
   Beaufort junior. All that have eyes to weepe,
Spare one teare with mee. *Theocrine's* dead.
   Montrevile. Her father too lies breathlesse here, I thinke,
Strucke dead with thunder.
   Chamont.   'Tis apparent: how
His carkase smells.
   Lanour.   His face is alter'd to
Another colour.
   Beaufort junior. But here's one retaines
Her native innocence, that never yet
Call'd downe heavens anger.
   Beaufort senior.   Tis in vaine to mourne
For whats past helpe. We will refer, bad man,
Your sentence to the King: may we make use of
This great example, and learne from it, that
There cannot be a want of power above
To punish murther, and unlawfull love.   *Exeunt omnes.*

FINIS.

Imprimatur.
      THO. WYKES.
      IAN. 21. 1638.

A NEW WAY TO PAY OLD DEBTS

INTRODUCTION

(a) *Date*

No record of the licence for performance of *A New Way to Pay Old Debts* has been preserved, and the earliest mention of the play is the entry for publication in November 1632. The title-page of the first edition of 1633 says 'As it hath beene often acted at the Phœnix in Drury-Lane, by the Queenes Maiesties seruants.' Queen Henrietta Maria arrived in England in mid May 1625 and it may be that her company of actors was formed about the same time as the new patent for the King's company was issued (24 June; see Bentley, i. 219). But, as we know from the case of *The Renegado* (see pp. 7-8), a title-page does not necessarily record the name of the first company to produce a play, and on this evidence *A New Way* could have been an earlier Cockpit play which passed to Christopher Beeston's new company in 1625. A date much later than 1625 is unlikely because except for the problematic *Great Duke of Florence* (see vol. iii p. 95) Massinger seems to have severed his connexions with Beeston after 1625.

Internal evidence is strongly in favour of 1625 as the date of composition. The evidence is in allusions to the campaigns in the Low Countries, and English efforts (if efforts is not too strong a word) to give assistance to the forlorn Elector Palatine by engaging with the Dutch against the Spaniards. The most notable of these allusions is to the siege of Breda (I. ii. 25-8):

> And raise fortifications in the pastrie,
> Such as might serue for modells in the Low-Countries,
> Which if they had beene practis'd at *Breda*,
> *Spinola* might haue throwne his cap at it, and ne're tooke it—

Spinola, the Spanish commander, had laid siege to Breda in the summer of 1624 and the town fell ten months later, at the end of

May 1625 (see the Commentary). English interest in the siege was great. In 1624, it was agreed to levy 12,000 men to go to the Continent in the service of Count von Mansfeld, the mercenary who had been Elector Frederick's commander, and in the tortuous international discussions about the use of these troops it was often argued that they should be sent to help relieve the siege of Breda (Gardiner, v. 276). There was great concern about the fate of English volunteers who were actually in the city.

A further allusion is at V. i. 231–3:

> ... whole families, who ...
> ... but enrol'd for souldiers were able
> To take in *Dunkerke* [i.e. capture it].

A joint attack on Dunkirk by the French and English was a favourite plan of Buckingham's which he tried to find support for in both the spring and late autumn of 1625 (Gardiner, v. 325; vi. 35). A combined fleet sent to blockade Dunkirk while the Cadiz expedition was afoot was dispersed by a storm (Rushworth, *Historical Collections*, i (1659), 195).

At I. ii. 74–5, we are told that Lord Lovell is on his way to fight in 'the Low-Countreyes'. Alworth intends to go with him and Lady Alworth instructs him in the requirements of military honour (I. ii. 99–114). Lovell is evidently the colonel of a regiment (III. ii. 150), and the token of Welborne's reformation is that he asks Lovell for the command of a company in that regiment (V. i. 395–9):

> It is a time of Action, if your Lordship
> Will please to conferre a company vpon mee
> In your command, I doubt not in my seruice
> To my King, and Country, but I shall do something
> That may make me right agen.

These references to recruitment for the Low Countries, leading to the enthusiastic note in the closing lines of the play of 'It is a time of Action', and 'King, and Country', when taken with the reference to the fall of Breda, may give us a quite precise date for the writing of *A New Way to Pay Old Debts*. It is necessary to review briefly the story of the levying of troops in 1624 and 1625.

At the end of 1624, the troops raised for Mansfeld, a very sorry collection of pressed men, were moving towards Dover, committing 'great Spoils and Rapines in their passage through the Counties' (Rushworth, i. 153). Chamberlain gives a vivid account (*Letters*, ii.

593) of how the wretched recruits maimed themselves and even committed suicide rather than go on the dreadful campaign which lay ahead. Those who took ship were wasted with disease and hunger before they joined in any action. By the time of the fall of Breda there was only a pitiful remnant left. All this was well known in England through the complaints of the colonels against Mansfeld (Gardiner, v. 336). But on 1 May 1625 the Privy Council gave order for a new levy of troops, for both the Low Countries and the Palatinate. 10,000 soldiers were to assemble at Plymouth and Hull and it was firmly intended that there should be no repetition of the disorder of the Mansfeld levy. It was hoped to bring trained English soldiers back from service with Dutch regiments to mix with the new recruits. Rushworth writes as follows (*Historical Collections*, i. 168):

The remembrance of the late violence committed by Count *Mansfield's* Army in their passage to *Dover*, occasioned a Proclamation to repress and prevent the like attempts of Souldiers, as they now passed through the Counties to the places of the Rendezvous, threatning the Offenders with the strictest proceedings against them, for an example of terror; and straitly commanding the Officers, who have the charge of the Conduct, for the removing of all occasions and pretences of disorders, to see their Companies duly paid, and provided of all necessaries, and to be always present with them, and carefully to conduct them from place to place.

In spite of all this brave language, the troops as they gathered at Plymouth were unpaid, unfed, and disorderly. And they did not go to the Low Countries, nor, in spite of the entreaties of the Elector's emissary, to Germany. They went instead on the futile Cadiz expedition, which sailed at the end of October and accomplished nothing.

A likely date for the writing of *A New Way to Pay Old Debts* would therefore be the midsummer of 1625, when the fall of Breda was still news, when activities against Dunkirk were in the air, when troops were being assembled for the Low Countries with firm indications that in the new king's reign military manners and efficiency were to be on a new footing—and before the new hopes were shown to be vain.

In 1933, A. K. McIlwraith put forward the view that the most likely date for the play was 1621–2, when a caricature of Sir Giles Mompesson as Overreach (see below) would have been most effective, and that the reference to the siege of Breda was a later interpolation (*MLR*, xxviii, 431–8). This dating was unfortunately adopted by Bentley, and also by Harbage in *Annals of English Drama*. McIlwraith retracted his theory in his manuscript life of Massinger written in the late 1940s and suggested that Massinger was engaged on the play when the theatres were closed for the death of James on 27 March 1625 and completed it 'during the summer of 1625'.

The summer of 1625 saw London in the grip of one of the worst attacks of the plague it had ever known. In the middle of August, over 4,000 people a week were dying (F. P. Wilson, *The Plague in Shakespeare's London*, chap. v). Although no order to close the theatres is extant, it is certain that the usual prohibitions operated. Even as late as the beginning of December, when the deaths had fallen below forty a week, there was an order restraining the Phoenix from putting on plays because of the danger of continuing the infection. Other theatres followed the example of the Phoenix in reopening, and the Lord Mayor complained about them on 21 December. Bentley has argued that the theatres may never have reopened after closing for James's death on 27 March until the very end of the year (Bentley, ii. 654–7). There is no reason why Massinger should not have written his play while the theatres were closed; no one knew how long playing would be suspended. It is conceivable that the play was written for performance in the provinces in the summer of 1625.[1] Satirical comedies with a provincial setting are rare, and *A New Way to Pay Old Debts* is very markedly set in the Nottinghamshire countryside, with the routine of a country house, a village (Gotham) mentioned by name, a country ale-house, justice of the peace, and so on. The Lady Elizabeth's men were at Nottingham in 1623–4, and it is just possible that their successors were there in 1625, although F. P. Wilson argues that 'few of the companies travelled in the country during the summer, for few towns or villages would have admitted them' (*The Plague in Shakespeare's London*, 1963 ed., p. 170). The first London performance of the play cannot have been before the end of December, 1625.

(b) *Sources*

That Sir Giles Overreach was based upon the historical figure of Sir Giles Mompesson has been generally accepted since it was

---

[1] It has been noted that even among Phoenix plays (which generally make small scenic demands), *A New Way* is remarkable in the absence of large properties etc. T. J. King, *Theatre Notebook*, xix (1964–5), 146–66.

suggested by O. G. Gilchrist to Gifford and recorded by the latter in his second edition (1813) of Massinger's plays (iii. 517–18). Mompesson was a 'projector', out to make money by instituting new schemes supposedly beneficial to the Crown. His chief iniquities arose from his project for the licensing of inns. In 1616 he had suggested a commission; he himself was made a commissioner and knighted into the bargain. With the help of his associate, Sir Francis Michell, a justice of the peace (the supposed prototype of Justice Greedy Woodcock), he flagrantly misused his powers by extorting fines from innkeepers for supposed infringements of the law and by granting licences to landlords who were in fact owners of brothels and disorderly houses (see Commentary, I. i. 82). In 1619, the ruthless energy of Mompesson was recognized when he was made a commissioner to oversee the scandalous monopoly for making gold and silver thread. Another lucrative patent was for the discovery of Crown estates which had come into private hands (Gardiner, iv. 44). Retribution came in a parliamentary investigation of 1621. Though Michell was disgraced, Mompesson managed to evade sentence by jumping through a window and fleeing the country.

Public indignation over Mompesson's activities and satisfaction at his fall are well expressed in the prints reproduced in R. H. Ball's book, *The Amazing Career of Sir Giles Overreach* (1939). As Ball says, Mompesson 'had become a monster in the public eye' (p. 9). But just how much of Mompesson and his deeds appears in Sir Giles Overreach? Overreach is an utterly corrupt tyrant. His most legal activity is enclosing common land for his own use. His main business is acquiring other men's estates by dishonest means; to this end he has made a J.P. his creature, ready to pervert justice as his master nods, and in this activity he leaves a trail of broken and destitute victims. He is of low city birth and is supremely ambitious for the social advancement of his family even as he delights in impoverishing those who are better born than he. Mompesson was born a gentleman and he spent his life in the public service, making money and acquiring land in the very shady ways made possible by an unsavoury economic and administrative system. It is true that he was a great perverter of justice, throwing tradesmen into the Fleet for not agreeing to deal only with his agents, and exacting great sums of money from people, but the only point at which the paths of Mompesson and Michell cross those of Overreach and Justice Greedy is the abuse of licensing inns and alehouses (cf. I. i. 62–3, IV. ii. 68–80). In his 1926 edition of the play, A. H. Cruickshank wrote: 'The resemblances, then, consist in these facts—the name Giles is common to both Mompesson and Overreach and they are both in partnership with a justice of the peace... While, therefore, the play may have owed some of its original success to the allusions which it makes to a public scandal of the day, the conclusion seems to be that the poet has had in view the more general evils of unjust money-lending and rural oppression' (pp. xiii–xiv).

Writing four years after Mompesson's disgrace, Massinger probably had no thought of specific caricature. Sir Giles had become a generic name to cover all the abuses permitted in James's reign, as we see from the opening lines of some anonymous doggerel:

> You wilye proiectors, why hang you the head?
> Promooters! Informers! What—are you all dead?
> Or will you beyond sea go frolick and play
> With Giles Mompesson that lead you the way?[1]

The danger of making too close a connection between Overreach and Mompesson is that we may obscure the carefully-drawn lines of Massinger's social satire. Overreach is a city-born speculator who trespasses against the gentry by swindling the Welbornes out of the land they have held for twenty generations and who trespasses against the aristocracy in trying to buy his way into a marriage alliance with Lord Lovell. We have been reminded[2] of the similarity in social origins between Overreach and one whose fall and disgrace are much nearer in time to *A New Way* than Mompesson's; Lionel Cranfield, Earl of Middlesex. He was 'bred in the City', as Clarendon remarked,[3] and had married out of his social class. He owed his prodigious success to his outstanding abilities in commerce and finance, but his fall from office, engineered by Buckingham in 1624, was brought about because, in Gardiner's words (v. 230), 'in taking care of his master's fortunes he had not forgotten to think of his own.'

---

[1] Printed from a Folger Library manuscript by R. H. Bowers in *MLR*, liii (1958), 214–15.
[2] By Patricia Thomson, 'The Old Way and the New Way in Dekker and Massinger', *MLR*, li (1956), 168–78.
[3] *History of the Rebellion*, 1704, i. 19.

Introduction

There is no direct source for Massinger's plot, though the themes of thwarting a father's tyrannical marriage-scheme and outwitting a wealthy cormorant are hardly original. Barry's *Ram Alley* of 1608 contains a double deception which makes it at least an analogue of *A New Way*. Middleton's *A Trick to Catch the Old One* (1605) is often named as a source[1] and it seems almost certain that Massinger had Middleton's play in mind when he was working on the Welborne plot. Middleton's Witgood is a young gentleman reduced to penury through riotous living. He had first mortgaged then forfeited his estates to his usurious uncle, Lucre. He pretends he is to marry a rich widow (the woman is in fact a prostitute) and at the news the uncle completely changes his behaviour towards his nephew and lends him money, having it in mind to trick the widow out of her land as he has tricked his nephew. On the strength of his supposed new fortune, all Witgood's creditors rush to him and fawn on him. All of this is closely similar to Massinger's picture of the relations between Welborne and Overreach, though there is a radical difference in the status of the pretended bride. The plots of the two plays are worked out in very different ways, though Massinger may have picked up the suggestion for Overreach's urging Margaret to be wanton with Lovell in his own house (III. iii) from Lucre's encouragement to Witgood to use the bedroom of his house to make the widow sure (II. i).

(c) Text

A New Way to Pay Old Debts was entered in the Stationers' Register on 10 November 1632:

> M^r. Seile ... Entred for his Copy vnder the same hands [*sc.* Sir Henry Herbert and Mr Aspley, Warden] a Comedy called A new way to pay old Debts by Phill: Massinger vj^d.
> (Register D 262; Greg, *Bibliography*, i. 41, Arber, iv. 288)

The play was published by Henry Seyle in 1633, printed by 'E. P.' (Elizabeth Purslowe). This is the only early edition and will be referred to as *33*; the title-page is reproduced on p. 293.

33 is in quarto, A–L⁴, M² (46 leaves); see Greg, *Bibliography*,

---

[1] e.g. Koeppel, *Quellen-Studien*, pp. 138–9; Cruickshank, *Philip Massinger*, pp. 203–8; M. S. Balch, 'The Dramatic Legacy of Thomas Middleton', unpublished Harvard dissertation, 1930, chap. 2; M. C. Bradbrook, *The Growth and Structure of Elizabethan Comedy*, 1955, p. 157; R. Levin, *MLQ*, xxv (1964), 140–52.

no. 474 (ii. 624). The contents are: A1r, *title*; A1v, *blank*; A2r, *dedication begins*, 'TO THE RIGHT HONORABLE ROBERT EARLE OF CARNARVAN, *Master Falconer of England*.'; A2v, (*headed* '*The Epistle Dedicatory*.') *dedication ends, signed* '*Philip Massinger*.'; A3r, *first verse epistle begins*, 'TO THE INGENIOVS AVTHOR MASTER PHILIP MASSINGER, ON HIS COMŒDIE *Called, A new way to pay old Debts*.'; A3v, (*headed* 'To the Author.') *first verse epistle ends, signed* '*Henry Moody. miles.*', *second verse epistle begins*, '*To his friend the Author*.'; A4r, (*headed* 'To the Author.') *second verse epistle ends, signed* '*Thomas Iay. Miles.*'; A4v, 'Dramatis personæ.'; B1r, *text begins*, A NEW WAY TO PAY OLD DEBTS: A COMEDIE.'; M2r, *text ends*; M2v, 'THE EPILOGVE.'... 'FINIS.' The text is in roman, 20 lines measuring approximately 81 mm.

There is little to call attention to in the printing of the play. McIlwraith found press-corrections (nine) in only three out of the twenty-four formes.[1] *33* is on the whole carefully and accurately printed, with a few misreadings and a few misprints. Punctuation is erratic. Presswork and spelling are too consistent to enable us to distinguish the work of different compositors. The characteristic literary and explanatory stage-directions of Massinger are present in such plenty that one wonders if some were added for the benefit of the reader. Against the phrase 'this scepter' (I. i. 92) we have the note '*His Cudgell*'; other descriptive directions are: '*Walke by musing*' (II. iii. 59); '*Enter Ouer. listning*' (III. ii. 201); '*Louell conferring with Welborne.*' (III. ii. 278); '*This interim, Tapwell and Froth flattering & bribing iustice Greedy.*' (IV. ii. 43); '*Enter Ouer. with distracted lookes, driuing in Marrall before him.*' (V. i. 88); '*flattering him*' (V. i. 200).

The presence of Massinger's characteristic spellings makes it likely that the copy for *33* was in the author's own hand (e.g. 'sawce' 'flowt', 'ghest', 'woemen', and the occasional 'Hee'). The full stops between names of characters at the beginning of scenes also indicate an autograph manuscript. It is unlikely that the manuscript had been through the prompter's hands.

There are copies of *33* in the following libraries and institutions: University of Arizona; Bodleian Library (2 copies); Boston Public Library; British Museum (3 copies); Cambridge University

---

[1] Some extraordinary errors attributed to the Chew copy of *33* by Brander Matthews in Gayley's *Representative English Comedies* are certainly ghost-readings provided by the graduate student who transcribed the quarto for him.

Library; Chapin Library, Williamstown; University of Chicago; Library of Congress; Folger Shakespeare Library; University of Glasgow, Hunterian Collection; Harvard College Library; Huntington Library; University of Illinois; King's College, Cambridge; Lehigh University, Honeyman Collection; University of Michigan; Pierpont Morgan Library; Newberry Library; Princeton University; John Rylands Library, Manchester; University of Texas (2 copies); Trinity College, Cambridge; Alexander Turnbull Collection, Wellington, New Zealand; Victoria and Albert Museum (2 copies); Wadham College, Oxford; Worcester College, Oxford; Yale University.

The present edition has been prepared from the Bodleian copy, Malone 184 (1).

Later Editions (excluding the collected editions of Massinger)

1748	. . . As it is now Acting at the Theatre-Royal in Drury-Lane . . . Dublin . . . S. Powell, for G. and A. Ewing . . . and G. Faulkner . . . MDCCXLVIII.
1775	. . . As it is Acted at the Theatre-Royal, in Smock-Alley . . . Dublin . . . for Thomas Wilkinson . . . M.DCC.LXXV.
?1801–4	. . . With the Variations in the Manager's Book. At the Theatres Royal. London: Printed by Barker and Son . . . [*n.d.*]
1804	The British Drama . . . London, published by William Miller . . . 1804. Vol. II, pp. 60–86.
1805	Sharpe's British Theatre, Vol. XV . . . London . . . 1805.
1808	The British Theatre . . . with . . . Remarks by Mrs Inchbald . . . London . . . 1808. . . . As performed at Covent Garden, printed under the authority of the Managers from the Prompt book . . . [*A copy in the Bodleian Library, not bound up as part of* The British Theatre, *has an engraved frontispiece dated 1807.*]
?1810	[*As above, but printed at Edinburgh, dated by water-mark on title-page.*]
1810	Massinger's New Way to Pay Old Debts . . . Adapted to the stage by J. P. Kemble; and now first published as it is acted at The Theatre Royal in Covent Garden. London: Printed for the Theatre. 1810.
1810	. . . As performed at the Theatres Covent Garden and New York . . . New York. D. Longworth . . . 1810.

1810	The Mirror of Taste, and Dramatic Censor. Philadelphia, 1810. Vol. I, no. 4 ... Printed for Bradford and Inskeep, Philadelphia ... Inskeep and Bradford, New-York ... William M'Ilhenny, Boston ... 1810.
1811	The Modern British Drama ... London ... for William Miller ... 1811. Vol. III, pp. 157–85.
1814	... Adapted to the stage by J. P. Kemble; and now published as it is performed at The Theatres Royal ... London ... 1814.
1816	... With the variations in the manager's book at the Theatre royal Drury-Lane ... London ... W. Lowndes ... 1816.
1816	The London Theatre ... correctly given, from the copies used in the Theatres, by Thomas Dibdin ... London ... 1816. Vol. XVIII.
?1816	The British Theatre ... with ... Remarks by Mrs Inchbald ... Vol. VI. ... As performed at the Theatres Royal, Covent-Garden and Drury-Lane. Printed under the authority of the Managers from the prompt-book ... [*n.d.*, *but engraved frontispiece dated 1816. Printed by Ballantyne.*]
?1816	... As performed at the Theatres Royal Drury-Lane and Covent-Garden. Printed, Under the authority of the managers, from the Prompt-Book ... London ... for John Fairburn ... [*n.d.*]
1818	Oxberry's edition ... faithfully marked with the stage business and stage directions. As it is performed at the Theatres Royal. London ... 1818.
1821	The English Theatre. Comedies. Vol. I. London ... for John Bumpus. 1821. ... Correctly Given, as performed at the Theatres Royal. With Remarks. Printed ... by D. S. Maurice. [*Appears with variant title-pages giving names of different booksellers on title-page, T. Hughes among others.*]
1824	The British Drama. Vol. I. London ... 1824. Pp. 441–61.
?1824	The London Stage ... London: G. Balne ... [*n.d.*] Vol. II.
1824	Dolby's British Theatre ... Vol. VII. ... Printed from the Acting Edition, with Remarks ... As now performed at the Theatres-Royal, London ... London ... 1824.
?1825	Duncombe's edition. ... The only edition correctly marked,

Introduction

by permission, from the prompter's book ... with a portrait of Mr. C. Kean ... London ... J. Duncombe & Co. [*n.d.*]

?1829   Cumberland's British Theatre. Vol. VII. .... Printed from the Acting Copy, with Remarks, Biographical and Critical, by D—— G. London. [*n.d.*]

?1830   The Penny National Library ... The Penny Acting Drama ... London. [*n.d.*] Pp. 271–90.

1834   The Acting Drama ... London ... 1834. Pp. 271–90.

1836   Ben Jonson und seine Schule ... übersetzt und erlautert durch Wolf Grafen von Baudissin. Leipzig. 1836. Band 2. Eine neue Weise alte Schulden zu zahlen.

1848   Modern Standard Drama. no. 33. Edited by Epes Sargent. New York. Douglas. 1848. [*Ball, p. 411.*]

?1850   [Lacy's Acting Edition] ... Thomas Hailes Lacy ... London [*n.d.*]

1864   The British Drama. Illustrated ... London ... 1864. Vol. II, pp. 321–41.

1870   The Works of the British Dramatists. ... by John S. Keltie ... Edinburgh: William P. Nimmo. 1870. Pp. 435–59.

1874   Neues Recept, alte Schulden zu zahlen ... zum erstenmal bühnengerecht für das deutsche Theater bearbeitet von S. Gatschenberger. ... Wohlbauer. 1874.

?1883   Dick's Standard Plays ... London. [*n.d.*]

1890   Famous Elizabethan Plays expurgated and adapted for modern readers by H. Macaulay Fitzgibbon ... London ... 1890. Pp. 273–364.

1893   ... With Introduction and Notes by K. Deighton ... London ... 1893. (Bell's English Classics.)

1904   ... Edited with a Preface, Notes and Glossary by George Stronach ... Dent ... London 1904. (The Temple Dramatists.)

1910   Elizabethan Drama. Edited by Charles W. Eliot ... The Harvard Classics ... 1910. Vol. II. Pp. 819–99.

1911   The Chief Elizabethan Dramatists ... edited ... by William Allan Neilson ... London ... [1911]. Pp. 741–69.

1912   Philip Massinger edited by Lucius A. Sherman ... New

	York . . . [1912]. (Masterpieces of the English Drama.) Pp. 209–303.
1914 **Matthews**	Representative English Comedies . . . [general editor C. M. Gayley] . . . New York . . . 1914. Vol. III, pp. 301–413. . . . edited . . . by Brander Matthews.
1915	Six Plays by Contemporaries of Shakespeare edited by C. B. Wheeler . . . [London, 1915]. (The World's Classics.) Pp. 503–95.
1926	. . . Edited by A. H. Cruickshank. Oxford . . . M CM XXVI.
1926	Typical Elizabethan Plays . . . edited . . . by Felix E. Schelling . . . New York and London MCMXXVI. Pp. 627–70.
1928	Great English Plays . . . edited . . . by H. F. Rubinstein . . . London . . . 1928. Pp. 560–607.
1929	Three Elizabethan Plays . . . edited for schools by J. D. Andrews and A. R. W. Smith . . . London . . . [1929].
[1931	A. K. McIlwraith, unpublished Oxford dissertation.]
1933 **Brooke**	English Drama 1580–1642. Selected and Edited by C. F. Tucker Brooke . . . and Nathaniel Burton Paradise . . . Boston [etc.] [1933]. Pp. 875–910.
1933	Elizabethan Plays, Written by Shakespeare's Friends, Colleagues, Rivals, and Successors . . . Edited . . . by Hazelton Spencer . . . London . . . M.CM.XXXIV. Pp. 1051–91.
1934	Elizabethan and Stuart Plays. Edited by Charles Read Baskervill, Virgil B. Heltzel, Arthur H. Nethercot . . . New York, 1934. Pp. 1355–1400.
1935	The English Drama . . . 900–1642. Edited by E. Winfield Parks and Richmond Croom Beatty. New York, 1935. Pp. 1231–99.
1949 **Byrne**	. . . Edited with an Introduction and Notes by M. St. Clare Byrne. [1949; *reissued* 1956.]
1963	Early Seventeenth Century Drama. Edited by Robert G. Lawrence . . . Everyman's Library. 1963. Pp. 301–88.
1964 **Craik**	. . . Edited by T. W. Craik . . . London [1964]. (The New Mermaids.)

(d) *Stage History*

The stage-history of *A New Way to Pay Old Debts* was the subject of a very full study by R. H. Ball in his book, *The Amazing Career of Sir Giles Overreach* (Princeton and London, 1939); even this, though it records several hundred productions, does not and could not provide a full index of all revivals of the play. It seems best to give here the 'story' of *A New Way to Pay Old Debts* in summary, and to refer those who wish for greater detail, especially about American productions, to R. H. Ball's book, to which this account is deeply indebted.

The original production of the play, it was suggested above, took place at the very end of 1625 (if it was not mounted earlier in the year in the provinces), being shown at the Phoenix (or Cockpit) in Drury Lane by the new Queen Henrietta's company. Beeston seems to have kept it in the Cockpit repertory, for it is one of the plays protected for performance by the King and Queen's young company by the Lord Chamberlain in 1639 (Bentley, i. 330–1). There was a performance at Skipton Castle in Yorkshire in 1635; the Cliffords' account-book records the payment of one pound 'to a certeyne company of Roguish players who represented A new way to pay old debtes'.[1] In 1662 two young Dutchmen recorded in their diary seeing the comedy 'De Nieuwe Wegh, om oude Schult te betaalen' in London.[2] This was very likely played by George Jolly, who was trying to establish his company in London at this time, playing at both the Cockpit and Salisbury Court in 1662.[3] Dr. Edward Browne (son of Sir Thomas) saw the play at the King's Arms in Norwich in 1663,[4] and once again this is thought to be Jolly's company, on tour.[5]

The play then seems to have disappeared from the stage for over eighty years, until Garrick revived it at Drury Lane in 1748 (four years after Dodsley had revived it in print); Garrick did not act in the play himself. The revival was not a great success and was given only four performances, but the play was now available as a stage possibility. It was acted at Norwich in 1749 and Richmond in 1752. Garrick revived it again in 1759, for one performance only. It was played in Dublin in 1760 and in Birmingham in 1762.[6]

[1] Malone Society Collections, v (1960), 26.
[2] E. Seaton, *Literary Relations of England and Scandinavia in the Seventeenth Century*, 1935, pp. 333–7.
[3] L. Hotson, *Commonwealth and Restoration Stage*, pp. 178–9.
[4] Greg, *Collected Papers*, p. 46.
[5] B. M. Wagner, *RES*, vi (1930), 450–1.
[6] Cruickshank noted the Birmingham production, but Ball said he could not confirm it. It was at the New Theatre in King Street, with Mr. Walker as Sir Giles; singing and dancing were apparently a part of the performance. (From a photocopy of the

Garrick revived it for a third time in October 1769, but once again it was not particularly successful, and had only three performances. It is not clear why Garrick never chose to act in the play himself.

After a gap of eleven years, the play was revived again, at Covent Garden in 1781 with John Henderson as Overreach. For the first time in the eighteenth century, the play was a stage success. Ball records sixteen performances in London, 1781–3, and a performance in Edinburgh (1784). Immediately after Henderson's London success, John Philip Kemble appeared as Sir Giles in Edinburgh and Dublin in the summer of 1781 and at Cork in 1782. He brought his production to London (Drury Lane) in September 1783, acted Sir Giles seven times in the 1783–4 season and repeated it every year until 1788 (Ball, pp. 44–5).

It is not certain who was responsible for the major changes in the action of Massinger's play which must have become established at this time, though no acting-version was printed before the first decade of the nineteenth century.[1] The first important alteration is that at the end of Act I, Welborne's plot with Lady Alworth that she should pretend to be attracted to him is not kept concealed from the audience. Welborne is given a speech of some eighteen lines telling Lady Alworth what he wants her to do, and at the end of the act he has a soliloquy explaining to the audience how he hopes this ruse will (literally) pay off:

—If this plot succeed,
'Tis a New way to pay old debts, indeed.

The second major alteration is that at the very end of the play, Overreach is not allowed to go off-stage in fury (V. i. 317) to return mad after the lull in which Marrall explains the trick with the invisible ink and is kicked out for his pains. Instead, Overreach remains on stage. His speech challenging Lovell and Welborne is run on (from V. i. 308) into the insane general challenge (at V. i. 357) which is arrested by his collapse. Then follows Marrall's explanation; instead of being kicked out, he is forgiven.

This is the version published in 1810, 'Adapted to the stage by J. P. Kemble; and now first published as it is acted at The Theatre Royal in Covent Garden.' Ball believes that this is basically Kemble's

advertisement in *Aris's Birmingham Gazette*, 16 Aug., 1762, kindly sent by Birmingham Public Library.)

[1] Ball's book includes an excellent study of the printed acting-versions, pp. 391–416, though he is not able to solve all the problems of authenticity and priority.

1780 version (pp. 393-4). But he describes another version, undated, printed by Barker, which the British Museum had dated '?1780' but which Ball convincingly argues was probably put out between 1801 and 1804. In this version, which is verbally much closer to Massinger's text in general, the whispering between Welborne and Lady Alworth is retained, though Welborne's soliloquy explaining his device to the audience is again inserted at the end of the first act. The action at the end of the play is basically the same as in the Kemble version, but Marrall is not forgiven. Kemble's version had not been published when the Barker edition came out; Ball suggests that the Barker version 'represents a partially independent alteration of the standard text by someone who plainly has had some kind of access to Kemble's version' (p. 408), that is, has heard it at the theatre, or has read it in manuscript. The innumerable acting-versions of the nineteenth century derive from either the Kemble or the 'Barker' version.

Ball attributes the Kemble version to Kemble himself (pp. 393-4, 404-6). However, on p. 320 of his *Irish Stage in the County Towns*, 1965, W. S. Clark listed under James Love an alteration of *A New Way to Pay Old Debts* at Smock Alley, Dublin, in 1781 and in Cork in 1782 and 1785. These performances can be no other than Kemble's performances. James Love (born James Dance, but being a gentleman he changed his name when he took to the stage) had died in 1774. He was responsible for alterations of *The City Madam* (q.v., vol. iv, p. 12), Brome's *The Jovial Crew* and Beaumont and Fletcher's *Rule a Wife and Have a Wife*. After spending a good deal of time in Ireland, Love had joined Garrick at Drury Lane in 1762, and had acted the part of Greedy in Garrick's 1769 revival of *A New Way* (Genest, v. 257). If Clark was correct in attributing the version which Kemble acted in 1781 to Love, then it is highly probable (a) that this acting-version dates back to the 1769 Drury Lane revival in which Love acted, and (b) that Love's alteration (perhaps slightly changed?) was what came to be known as Kemble's version, and is in fact the archetype of all the nineteenth-century versions. Unfortunately, it has not proved possible to find documentary evidence to corroborate Clark's attribution (he died in 1969).[1]

[1] Allardyce Nicoll suggests to me that Clark got his information from the notes of W. J. Lawrence, the use of which he acknowledges in the preface of both his books on the Irish drama. Much of this material was bought by the University of Cincinnati, but a search kindly undertaken by the Reference Librarian, Mr F. A. Marcotte, proved unsuccessful.

Two other actors playing Overreach before the end of the eighteenth century were Charles Murray (Bath, 1785) and Alexander Pope (Drury Lane, 1796). The play was given for the first time in America in 1795, with the English actor James Chalmers as Overreach. G. F. Cooke gave the first of his many performances in 1801 at Covent Garden. A contemporary said of Kemble that 'his appearance and manners were too gentlemanly for the part. Overreach is a parvenu—an ill-bred, ferocious man: the coarse violence of Cooke was exactly suited to its delineation.'[1] Scott also preferred Cooke to Kemble, admiring particularly the scene (IV. i) in which Overreach boasts of his malpractices to Lovell. 'Cooke contrived somehow to impress upon the audience the idea of such a monster of enormity as had learned to pique himself upon his own atrocious character.'[2] Cooke went to America in 1810 and played Overreach off and on until 1813. Kemble resumed his performances in 1810 and played from time to time until 1814.

It was on 12 January 1816 that Edmund Kean made his historic first appearance in *A New Way to Pay Old Debts* at Drury Lane. Critics agreed that this was his best part. The emotional impact of the final scenes, when, under the stress of the double betrayal by his daughter and Marrall, Overreach rages and goes mad, seems without parallel. Years afterwards Byron remembered this night; writing in 1819 he said the ending of Alfieri's *Mirra* threw him into convulsions: 'the agony of reluctant tears, and the choking shudder, which I do not often undergo for fiction. This is but the second time for anything under reality; the first was on seeing Kean's Sir Giles Overreach' (*Letters and Journals*, iv. 130). Mrs. Glover, acting Lady Alworth, was overcome on stage and sank into a chair. Hazlitt said, 'The conclusion was quite overwhelming' and, writing again a week later, he said, 'It would perhaps be as well, if in the concluding scene he would contrive not to frighten the ladies into hysterics.'[3] Proctor's life of Kean records or invents Kean's triumphant delight, 'The *pit* ROSE at me!' (Ball, p. 65). Kean's performance did not depend upon his power to rage: his interpretation of his part was thoughtful, subtle, and individual. Observers were struck by his treatment of Overreach's adulation of the aristocracy as a mask for his contempt and scorn for it. *The Times*' reviewer

---

[1] *Memoirs of Munden by his Son*, 1846, p. 190, quoted by Ball, p. 46.
[2] Letter of 1813 quoted by Ball, p. 57.
[3] *Works*, ed. Howe, v. 272–4, 277.

wrote, 'The tone of severe though almost involuntary sarcasm, with which he never failed to utter the title of "Lord", and epithet of "Right Honourable", had something in it strikingly characteristic of a spirit that mocked the puerility of its own ambition' (Ball, p. 66). Hazlitt, in his second notice of the production, speaking of Kean's 'mixture of fawning servility and sarcastic contempt', said, 'We think Mr. Kean never shewed more genius than in pronouncing this single word, *Lord* . . . Sir Giles . . . makes use of Lord Lovell merely as the stalking-horse of his ambition. In other respects, he has the greatest contempt for him, and the necessity he is under of paying court to him for his own purposes, infuses a double portion of gall and bitterness into the expression of his self-conscious superiority.'[1] Kean played Overreach 26 times that season, and everyone went to see him. In honour of his success, the Drury Lane Committee, including Byron, presented him with a silver cup, 'to commemorate his first representation of the character of Sir Giles Overreach', on 25 June 1816 (Ball, pp. 73-4).

Kean's success unfortunately moved Kemble to try his version out again; Hazlitt found it very tame—'Sir Giles in his dotage', he described it in an unkind comparison with Kean (*Examiner*, 5 May 1816). Kean went on to act Overreach everywhere: Sheffield, Belfast, Liverpool, Croydon, Dublin, Brighton, Southampton, Edinburgh, Dundee, Birmingham, Bath, Exeter, Plymouth, Penzance, Glasgow, Manchester.[2] He played it on his two visits to the United States in 1820-1 and 1825-6. His last performance in the part was on 26 February 1833 in Brighton (he died on 15 May).

It was because of Kean that *A New Way to Pay Old Debts* became a play for every theatre to stage, and Overreach a part for every ambitious actor to attempt. J. M. Vandenhoff started in November 1816; a reviewer in 1821 wrote, 'He displayed great judgement in many passages; but pitched the whole character in too low a key for the public taste, which, we cannot help thinking, the tragic harlequinade of Mr. Kean in the last scene has a little perverted.'[3] D. W. Osbaldiston played the part from 1819 to 1831; Charles Freer from 1829 to 1839; Charles Kean from 1829 to 1842; Samuel Phelps from 1836 to 1860; G. F. Brooke, in England and Australia, from 1843 to 1865. Ball notes the production of a German translation at the

---

[1] *Works*, ed. Howe, v. 277.
[2] A selection of the productions noted by Ball.
[3] *New Monthly Magazine*, 1 Feb. 1821; Ball, pp. 108-9.

Hoftheater in Berlin on 19 January 1821. J. B. Booth began in 1816, and seems to have deliberately set himself up as a rival to Kean. He went to America in 1821 and Sir Giles Overreach became one of his famous parts in an acting career lasting until 1852. There are several close accounts of his interpretation and delivery of different passages, the most interesting of which are recorded in the Commentary. An account of 1824 in *The New York Mirror* of Booth's action at the very end of the play shows how the ending (so radically altered from Massinger in the first place) had become an open field for bravura experiments:

... his exhausted strength gives way, and he faints; he is raised up, and as he revives, the death-sweat stands in drops upon his pale face—the colour came and went, and left it of an ashy and death-like paleness; one would have supposed repentance and returning affection, was the cause of his stretching forth his arms towards his trembling daughter—she accordingly approached to embrace him in his dying moments—but, as she drew near, with a hellish intent to cool his burning vengeance in her blood, he clutches at her throat; there was something so fiend-like—so diabolical in the motion, and Mr. Booth grasped at her with a spring so like some hungry tiger springing on his prey, that approbation lost its speech—[1]

The popularity of *A New Way to Pay Old Debts* seems to have lasted longer in the United States than in Britain, and Ball gives full details about the last two star performers of the part of Sir Giles Overreach: E. L. Davenport (who took the part from 1855 to 1874) and Edwin Booth, son of J. B. Booth, (from 1853 to 1887). Edwin Booth's interpretation was very different from the traditional:

His *Sir Giles Overreach* is a red-blooded, strong bodied Englishman, rosy in face, full in habit, abounding in physical life and in the joy of physical energy, with a voice like a trumpet, an eye like a hawk, a hand like a pugilist. The vast vitality of the man as Mr. Booth represents him is such as to stir the spectator with a certain strange but keen joy in his presence, even when he is busied with the worst of his schemes.[2]

Edwin Booth played Sir Giles when he visited England in 1861, and Ball notes that in Manchester, the Welborne was Henry Irving. Irving never acted Overreach, but Ball quotes a passage of reminiscences showing that the part fascinated Irving and that 'he had

---

[1] Ball, pp. 200–1. This business was developed even further by Davenport in the U.S. See Ball, pp. 288–9.
[2] Ball, p. 334.

Introduction

read and re-read everything he could lay his hands on concerning Edmund Kean's Overreach' (Ball, pp. 156–7).

With Hamlet and Richard III, Sir Giles Overreach had been one of the star-parts of the early and middle nineteenth century. *A New Way to Pay Old Debts* was part of the staple diet of the commercial theatre. The bust of Massinger flanked that of Shakespeare on the gateposts of Kean's house on the Isle of Bute. As the theatre changed, the play dropped quite out of fashion, to be revived more as an antiquarian curiosity than anything else. It has been popular with university and college dramatic societies. The first academic production noted by Ball is at Princeton in 1908. The Cambridge Marlowe Society produced the play in 1912, and there was a rather ambitious revival by Merton College, Oxford, in December, 1930. Produced by Sir Nigel Playfair and Wilfred Fletcher, it had a prologue by A. P. Herbert, and a printed commentary by George Saintsbury. Of Massinger, A. P. Herbert said, 'this ancient College is proud to own him as her son' (St. Alban Hall having been absorbed by Merton). Giles Playfair acted Overreach, and Hermione Baddeley Margaret. Since the Second World War, university revivals include productions at Corpus Christi College, Cambridge (1957), St. John's College, Oxford (1964), and King's College, Newcastle-upon-Tyne (1963). The play is frequently performed by amateur companies. It was one of the earliest productions by Nugent Monck at the Maddermarket Theatre in Norwich, 1921, and has been repeated there from time to time, the last production being in May 1969. (Sir Giles was played as a rather loveable rogue—perhaps in the Edwin Booth tradition.) It was played at the Glasgow Citizen's Theatre during the war and by the Merseyside Unity Theatre at Calderstones Park open-air theatre in July 1947 (claimed to be the first performance in Liverpool since 1851). Recent amateur productions have been by the Tavistock Repertory Company at Canonbury Tower Theatre, May 1968, and by Playcraft Productions of Canterbury in the University's Gulbenkian Theatre, July 1970. (This last production confirms that in amateur productions Marrall tends to carry away the acting honours; it also proved that if played cleverly Lovell (Mr. Alan Pope) can be far more sympathetic a figure than a reading suggests.)

Notable among professional productions this century are John Drinkwater's production by the Birmingham Repertory Theatre in October 1914, in modern dress, the 1922 production at the Old

Vic with Robert Atkins as Sir Giles,[1] and Donald Wolfit's revival in 1950. The latter opened at the Richmond Theatre and was reviewed by *The Times* on 10 May: 'Mr. Wolfit plays [Overreach] much as he would play one of Shakespeare's villains, Iachimo, say . . . Only in the final scene . . . does Mr Wolfit try to thrill the nerves in the old grand style. It is admirably done; yet we are not drawn cheering to our feet.' The reviewer concluded that an accomplished romantic actor was playing to an audience that vanished from the theatre a century ago. Wolfit brought his production back to London in November 1953 at the King's Theatre, Hammersmith (*The Times*, 3 November 1953).

A New Way to Pay Old Debts has been broadcast a number of times by the BBC: on 18 October 1948 (in 'World Theatre'), on 6 May 1960 (in 'British Drama 1600–1642'), on 5 February 1961, 8 October 1962, and 19 May 1968.

[1] See H. Child, *RES*, ii (1926), 184.

A NEW WAY TO PAY OLD DEBTS

A COMOEDIE

As it hath beene often acted at the Phœnix in Drury-Lane, by the Queenes Maiesties seruants.

The Author.

PHILIP MASSINGER.

LONDON,
Printed by *E. P.* for *Henry Seyle*, dwelling in S.
Pauls Church-yard, at the signe of the
Tygers head. Anno. M. DC.
XXXIII.

TO THE
RIGHT HONORABLE
ROBERT
EARLE OF CARNARVAN,
Master Falconer of England.

My Good Lord, Pardon I beseech you my boldnesse, in presuming to shelter this Comœdie vnder the wings of your Lordships fauour, and protection. I am not ignorant (hauing neuer yet deseru'd you in my seruice) that it cannot but meete with a seuere construction, if in the clemencie of your noble disposition, you fashion not a better defence for mee, than I can fancie for my selfe. All I can alleage is, that diuers *Italian* Princes, and Lords of eminent rancke in *England*, haue not disdain'd to receaue, and read Poems of this Nature, nor am I wholy lost in my hopes, but that your Honor (who haue euer exprest your selfe a fauourer, and friend to the Muses) may vouchsafe, in your gratious acceptance of this trifle, to giue me encouragement, to present you with some labour'd worke, and of a higher straine hereafter. I was borne a deuoted seruant, to the thrice noble Family of your incomparable Lady, and am most ambitious, but with a becomming distance, to be knowne to your Lordship, which if you please to admit, I shall embrace it as a bounty, that while I liue shall oblige me to acknowledge you for my noble Patron, and professe my selfe to be

Your Honours true seruant
Philip Massinger.

TO THE INGENIOVS
AVTHOR MASTER
PHILIP MASSINGER,
ON HIS COMŒDIE

Called, *A new way to pay*
old Debts.

Tis a rare charity, and thou couldst not
So proper to the time haue found a plot:
Yet whilst you teach to pay, you lend; the age
We wretches liue in, that to come, the stage,
The thronged audience that was thither brought   5
Inuited by your fame, and to be taught
This lesson, all are growne indebted more,
And when they look'd for freedome ran in score.
It was a cruell courtesie to call
In hope of liberty, and then, enthrall.   10
The nobles are your bond-men, Gentry, and
All besides those that did not vnderstand.
They were no men of credit, Banckroupts borne
Fit to be trusted with no stocke, but scorne.
You haue more wisely credited to such,   15
That though they cannot pay, can value much.
I am your debtor too, but to my shame
Repay you nothing backe, but your owne fame.

        Henry Moody. miles.

 3. lend;] *Gifford;* ~, 33   7. lesson, all] *after Gifford;* ~. *All* 33   8. look'd]
McIlwraith; looke 33

To his friend the Author.

You may remember how you chid me when
I ranckt you equall with those glorious men;
Beaumont, and Fletcher: *if you loue not praise*
You must forbeare the publishing of playes.
The craftie Mazes *of the cunning plot;* 5
The polish'd phrase; the sweet expressions; got
Neither by theft, nor violence; the conceipt
Fresh, and vnsullied; All is of weight,
Able to make the captiue Reader know
I did but iustice when I plac't you so. 10
A shamefast Blushing would become the brow
Of some weake Virgin writer; we allow
To you a kind of pride; and there where most
Should blush at commendations, you should boast.
If any thinke I flatter, let him looke 15
Of from my idle trifles on thy Booke.

Thomas Iay. Miles.

Dramatis Personæ.

Louell.   An English Lord.
Sir Giles Ouerreach.   A cruell extortioner.
Welborne.   A prodigall.
Alworth.   A young gentleman, page to Lord Louell.
Greedy.   A hungry Iustice of peace.
Marrall.   A Tearme-driuer. A creature of Sir Giles Ouerreach.
Order.
Amble.
Furnace. } *Seruants to the Lady Alworth.*
Watchall.
Will-doe.   A parson.
Tapwell.   An alehouse keeper.
Three Creditors.
The Ladie Alworth.   A Rich Widdowe.
Margaret.   Ouerreach his daughter.
Waiting Woman.
Chambermaide.
Froth.   Tapwells wife.

A New Way to Pay Old Debts
A Comedie

Actus primus, Scena prima.

WELBORNE. TAPWELL. FROTH.

Welborne. No bouze? nor no Tobacco?
Tapwell.   Not a sucke Sir,
Nor the remainder of a single canne
Left by a drunken porter, all night palde too.
  Froth. Not the dropping of the tappe for your mornings draught,
    Sir,
'Tis veritie I assure you.
  Welborne.   Verity, you brach!   5
The Diuell turn'd precisian? Rogue what am I?
  Tapwell. Troth durst I trust you with a looking glasse,
To let you see your trimme shape, you would quit me,
And take the name your selfe.
  Welborne.   How! dogge?
  Tapwell.   Euen so, Sir.
And I must tell you if you but aduance   10
Your plimworth cloke, you shall be soone instructed
There dwells, and within call, if it please your worship,
A potent monarch, call'd the Constable,
That does command a Citadell, call'd the Stockes;
Whose guards are certaine files of rusty Billmen,   15
Such as with great dexterity will hale
Your tatter'd, louzie—
  Welborne.   Rascall, slaue!
  Froth.   No rage, Sir.
  Tapwell. At his owne perill, doe not put your selfe
In too much heate, there being no water neare
To quench your thirst, and sure for other liquor,   20

I. i. 15. rusty] *33*; lusty *Coxeter*; trusty *Matthews*

As mighty Ale, or Beere, they are things I take it
You must no more remember, not in a dreame Sir.
  Welborne. Why thou vnthankefull villaine, dar'st thou talke thus?
Is not thy house, and all thou hast my gift?
  Tapwell. I find it not in chalke, and *Timothie Tapwell*   25
Does keepe no other register.
  Welborne.   Am not I Hee
Whose riots fed, and cloth'd thee? wert thou not
Borne on my fathers land, and proud to bee
A drudge in his house?
  Tapwell.   What I was Sir, it skills not,
What you are is apparent. Now for a farewell;   30
Since you talke of father, in my hope it will torment you,
I'le briefly tell your story. Your dead father,
My *quondam* master, was a man of worship,
Old Sir *John Wellborne*, Iustice of peace, and *quorum*,
And stood faire to bee *Custos rotulorum*;   35
Bare the whole sway of the shire; kep't a great house;
Relieu'd the poore, and so forth; but Hee dying,
And the twelue hundred a yeare comming to you,
Late Master *Francis*, but now forlorne *Welborne*—
  Welborne. Slaue, stoppe, or I shall lose my selfe.
  Froth.   Very hardly;   40
You cannot out of your way.
  Tapwell.   But to my story.
You were then a Lord of Akers; the prime gallant;
And I your vnder-butler; note the change now.
You had a merry time of't. Hawkes, and Hounds,
With choice of running horses; Mistrisses   45
Of all sorts, and all sizes; yet so hot
As their embraces made your Lordships melt;
Which your Vncle Sir *Giles Ouerreach* obseruing,
Resoluing not to lose a droppe of 'em,
On foolish mortgages, statutes, and bonds,   50
For a while suppli'd your loosenesse, and then left you.
  Welborne. Some Curate hath penn'd this inuectiue, mongrell,
And you haue studied it.
  Tapwell.   I haue not done yet:
Your land gone, and your credit not worth a token,
You grew the common borrower, no man scap'd   55

Your paper-pelletts, from the Gentleman
To the beggers on high wayes, that sold you switches
In your gallantry.
    Welborne.   I shall switch your braines out.
    Tapwell. Where poore *Tim Tapwell* with a little stocke,
Some forty pounds or so, bought a small cottage,
Humbled my selfe to marriage with my *Froth* here;
Gaue entertainment.
    Welborne.   Yes, to whores, and canters,
Clubbers by night.
    Tapwell.   True, but they brought in profit,
And had a gift to pay for what they call'd for,
And stucke not like your mastership. The poore Income
I glean'd from them, hath made mee in my parish,
Thought worthy to bee *Scauinger*, and in time
May rise to be *Ouerseer* of the poore;
Which if I doe, on your petition *Welborne*,
I may allow you thirteene pence a quarter,
And you shall thanke my worship.
    Welborne.   Thus you doggebolt,
And thus.   *Beates, and kicks him.*
    Tapwell. Cry out for helpe.
    Welborne.   Stirre and thou diest:
Your potent Prince the Constable shall not saue you.
Heare me vngratefull hell-hound; did not I
Make purses for you? Then you lick'd my bootes,
And thought your holy day cloke too course to cleane 'em.
'Twas I that when I heard thee sweare, if euer
Thou could'st arriue at forty pounds, thou would'st
Liue like an Emperour: 'twas I that gaue it,
In ready gold. Denie this, wretch.
    Tapwell.   I must Sir,
For from the tauerne to the taphouse, all
On forfeiture of their licences stand bound,
Neuer to remember who their best guests were,
If they grew poore like you.
    Welborne.   They are well rewarded
That begger themselues to make such cuckolds rich.
Thou viper, thanklesse viper; impudent bawde!

    84. grew] *33*; grow *conj. McIlwraith*

But since you are grow'n forgetfull, I will helpe
Your memory, and tread thee into mortar:
Not leaue one bone vnbroken.
 Tapwell.   Oh.
 Froth.   Aske mercie.

      Enter ALWORTH.

 Welborne. 'Twill not be granted.
 Alworth.   Hold, for my sake hold.   90
Deny mee, *Franke*? they are not worth your anger.
 Welborne. For once thou hast redeem'd them from this scepter:
              His Cudgell.
But let 'em vanish, creeping on their knees,
And if they grumble, I reuoke my pardon.
 Froth. This comes of your prating, husband, you presum'd   95
On your ambling wit, and must vse your glib tongue
Though you are beaten lame for't.
 Tapwell.   Patience *Froth.*
There's law to cure our bruizes.
       They goe off on their hands, and knees.
 Welborne.   Sent to your mother?
 Alworth. My Lady, *Franke*, my patronesse! my all!
Shee's such a mourner for my fathers death,   100
And in her loue to him, so fauours mee,
That I cannot pay too much obseruance to her.
There are few such stepdames.
 Welborne.   'Tis a noble widdow,
And keepes her reputation pure, and cleere
From the least taint of infamie; her life   105
With the splendour of her actions leaues no tongue
To Enuy, or Detraction. Prethee tell mee;
Has shee no suitors?
 Alworth.   Euen the best of the shire, *Franke*,
My Lord excepted. Such as sue, and send,
And send, and sue againe, but to no purpose.   110
Their frequent visits haue not gain'd her presence;
Yet shee's so far from sullennesse, and pride,
That I dare vndertake you shall meete from her
A liberall entertainment. I can giue you

      95. prating,] *Dodsley*; ~∧ 33

A catalogue of her suitors names.
  Welborne.   Forbeare it,   115
While I giue you good counsaile. I am bound to it;
Thy father was my friend, and that affection
I bore to him, in right descends to thee;
Thou art a handsome, and a hopefull youth,
Nor will I haue the least affront sticke on thee,   120
If I with any danger can preuent it.
  Alworth. I thanke your noble care, but pray you in what
Doe I run the hazard?
  Welborne.   Art thou not in loue?
Put it not off with wonder.
  Alworth.   In loue at my yeares?
  Welborne. You thinke you walke in clouds, but are transparent, 125
I haue heard all, and the choice that you haue made;
And with my finger can point out the North starre,
By which the loadstone of your follie's guided.
And to confirme this true, what thinke you of
Faire *Margaret* the only child, and heyre   130
Of *Cormorant Ouerreach*? does it blush? and start,
To heare her only nam'd? blush at your want
Of wit, and reason.
  Alworth.   You are too bitter Sir.
  Welborne. Wounds of this nature are not to bee cur'd
With balmes, but corrosiues. I must bee plaine: 135
Art thou scarce manumiz'd from the porters lodge,
And yet sworne seruant to the pantophle,
And dar'st thou dreame of marriage? I feare
'Twill bee concluded for impossible,
That there is now, nor ere shall bee hereafter,   140
A handsome page, or players boy of fourteene,
But either loues a Wench, or drabs loue him;
Court-waiters not exempted.
  Alworth.   This is madnesse.
How ere you haue discouer'd my intents,
You know my aimes are lawfull, and if euer   145
The Queene of flowers, the glory of the spring,
The sweetest comfort to our smell, the rose
Sprang from an enuious brier, I may inferre

  122. what] *Dodsley*; ~? *33*   125. transparent] *Dodsley*; trans- / rent *33*

There's such disparitie in their conditions,
Betweene the goddesse of my soule, the daughter, 150
And the base churle her father.
 Welborne.   Grant this true,
As I beleeue it; canst thou euer hope
To enioy a quiet bed with her, whose father
Ruin'd thy state?
 Alworth.   And yours too.
 Welborne.   I confesse it.
Tom I must tell you as a friend, and freely, 155
That where impossibilities are apparent,
'Tis indiscretion to nourish hopes.
Canst thou imagine, (let not selfe-loue blind thee)
That Sir *Giles Ouerreach*, that to make her great
In swelling titles, without touch of conscience, 160
Will cut his neighbours throate, and I hope his owne too,
Will ere consent to make her thine? Giue or'e
And thinke of some course sutable to thy rancke,
And prosper in it.
 Alworth.   You haue well aduis'd me.
But in the meane time, you that are so studious 165
Of my affaires, wholly neglect your owne.
Remember your selfe, and in what plight you are.
 Welborne. No matter, no matter.
 Alworth.   Yes, 'tis much materiall:
You know my fortune, and my meanes, yet something,
I can spare from my selfe, to helpe your wants. 170
 Welborne. How's this?
 Alworth.   Nay bee not angry. There's eight peeces
To put you in better fashion.
 Welborne.   Money from thee?
From a boy? a stipendary? one that liues
At the deuotion of a stepmother,
And the vncertaine fauour of a Lord? 175
Ile eate my armes first. Howsoe're blind fortune
Hath spent the vtmost of her malice on mee;
Though I am vomited out of an Alehouse,
And thus accoutred; know not where to eate,
Or drinke, or sleepe, but vnderneath this Canopie; 180

  155. *Tom*] *conj. Craik*; True 33

Although I thanke thee, I despise thy offer.
And as I in my madnesse broke my state,
Without th'assistance of anothers braine,
In my right wits Ile peece it; at the worst 184
Dye thus, and bee forgotten.
 Alworth.   A strange humor.   *Exeunt.*

Actus primi, Scena secunda.

ORDER. AMBLE. FURNACE. WATCHALL.

 Order. Set all things right, or as my name is *Order*,
And by this staffe of office that commands you,
This chaine, and dubble ruffe, Symboles of power;
Who euer misses in his function,
For one whole weeke makes forfeiture of his breakefast, 5
And priuilege in the wine-seller.
 Amble.   You are merrie
Good Master Steward.
 Furnace.   Let him; Ile bee angry.
 Amble. Why fellow *Furnace*, 'tis not twelue a clocke yet,
Nor dinner taking vp, then 'tis allow'd
Cookes by their places may bee cholericke. 10
 Furnace. You thinke you haue spoke wisely goodman *Amble*,
My Ladie's goe-before.
 Order.   Nay, nay; no wrangling.
 Furnace. Twit me with the Authority of the kitchin?
At all houres, and all places Ile be angrie;
And thus prouok'd, when I am at my prayers, 15
I will bee angry.
 Amble. There was no hurt meant.
 Furnace. I am friends with thee, and yet I will be angry.
 Order. With whom?
 Furnace.   No matter whom; yet now I thinke on't
I am angrie with my Lady.
 Watchall. Heauen forbid, man.
 Order. What cause has she giuen thee?
 Furnace.   Cause enough Master Steward.

I was entertain'd by her to please her palat,
And till she forswore eating I perform'd it.
Now since our master, noble *Alworth* died,
Though I cracke my braines to find out tempting sawces,
And raise fortifications in the pastrie,
Such as might serue for modells in the Low-Countries,
Which if they had beene practis'd at *Breda*,
Spinola might haue throwne his cap at it, and ne're tooke it—
   Amble. But you had wanted matter there to worke on.
   Furnace. Matter? with six egges, and a strike of rie-meale
I had kep't the Towne, till doomesday, perhaps longer.
   Order. But, what's this to your pet against my Lady?
   Furnace. What's this? Marrie this, when I am three parts rosted,
And the fourth part parboyld, to prepare her viands,
Shee keepes her chamber, dines with a panada,
Or water-gruell; my sweat neuer thought on.
   Order. But your art is seene in the dining-roome.
   Furnace.   By whom?
By such as pretend loue to her, but come,
To feed vpon her. Yet of all the Harpies,
That doe deuoure her, I am out of charity
With none so much, as the thinne-gutted Squire
That's stolne into commission.
   Order.   *Iustice Greedy?*
   Furnace. The same, the same. Meate's cast away vpon him,
It neuer thriues. He holds this Paradoxe,
Who eates not well, can ner'e doe iustice well:
His stomacke's as insatiate as the graue,
Or strumpetts rauenous appetites.
   Watchall.   One knockes.

ALWORTH *knockes, and enters.*

   Order. Our late young master.
   Amble.   Welcome, Sir.
   Furnace.   Your hand,
If you haue a stomake, a cold bake-meate's ready.
   Order. His fathers picture in little.
   Furnace.   We are all your seruants.
   Amble. In you he liues.

      I. ii. 28. it—] *after Coxeter;* ~. *33*   42. Greedy?] *Dodsley;* ~: *33*

Alworth. At once, my thankes to all;
This is yet some comfort. Is my Lady stirring?

Enter the LADY ALWORTH, WAITING WOMAN, CHAMBERMAID.

Order. Her presence answer for vs.
Lady. Sort those silkes well;
Ile take the ayre alone.
     Exeunt WAITING WOMAN, *and* CHAMBERMAID.
Furnace. You aire, and aire,
But will you neuer tast but spoonemeate more?   55
To what vse serue I?
Lady. Prethee be not angry,
I shall er'e long: I'the meane time, there is gold
To buy thee aprons, and a sommer suite.
Furnace. I am appeas'd, and *Furnace* now growes coole.
Lady. And as I gaue directions, if this morning   60
I am visited by any, entertaine 'em
As heretofore: but say in my excuse
I am indispos'd.
Order. I shall, Madam.
Lady. Doe, and leaue me.
Nay stay you *Alworth*.
    Exeunt ORDER, AMBLE, FURNACE, WATCHALL.
Alworth. I shall gladly grow here,
To waite on your commands.
Lady. So soone turn'd Courtier.   65
Alworth. Stile not that Courtship Madam, which is duty,
Purchas'd on your part.
Lady. Well, you shall or'ecome;
Ile not contend in words. How is it with
Your noble master?
Alworth. Euer like himselfe;
No scruple lessend in the full weight of honour;   70
He did command me (pardon my presumption)
As his vnworthy deputy to kisse
Your Ladyships faire hands.
Lady. I am honour'd in

<small>51. all;] *Dodsley*; ~ ^ 33 53. answer] *33*; answers *Dodsley* well;] *Dodsley* (well.); ~? *33* 59. coole] *Coxeter* (Cool); *Cooke 33*; cold *Dodsley* 70. honour;] *Dodsley* (honour:); ~, *33*</small>

His fauour to mee. Does he hold his purpose
For the Low-Countreyes?
  Alworth.   Constantly good Madam,   75
But he will in person first present his seruice.
  Lady. And how approue you of his course? you are yet
Like virgin parchement capable of any
Inscription, vitious, or honorable.
I will not force your will, but leaue you free   80
To your owne election.
  Alworth.   Any forme, you please,
I will put on: but might I make my choice,
With humble Emulation I would follow
The path my Lord markes to me.
  Lady.   'Tis well answer'd,
And I commend your spirit: you had a father   85
(Bless'd bee his memory) that some few houres
Before the will of heauen tooke him from me,
Who did commend you, by the dearest tyes
Of perfect loue betweene vs, to my charge:
And therefore what I speake, you are bound to heare   90
With such respect, as if he liu'd in me;
He was my husband, and how ere you are not
Sonne of my wombe, you may be of my loue,
Prouided you deserue it.
  Alworth.   I haue found you
(Most honor'd Madam) the best mother to me,   95
And with my vtmost strengths of care, and seruice,
Will labour that you neuer may repent
Your bounties showr'd vpon me.
  Lady.   I much hope it.
These were your fathers words. If ere my Sonne
Follow the warre, tell him it is a schoole   100
Where all the principles tending to honour
Are taught if truly followed: But for such
As repaire thither, as a place, in which
They doe presume they may with licence practise
Their lusts, and riots, they shall neuer merit   105
The noble name of souldiers. To dare boldly
In a faire cause, and for the Countries safety

    107. the] *33*; their *Coxeter*

> To runne vpon the cannons mouth vndaunted;
> To obey their leaders, and shunne mutenies;
> To beare, with patience, the winters cold,
> And sommers scorching heate, and not to faint,
> When plenty of prouision failes, with hunger,
> Are the essentiall parts make vp a souldier,
> Not swearing, dice, or drinking.
>   *Alworth.*   There's no syllable
> You speake, but is to me an Oracle,
> Which but to doubt, were impious.
>   *Lady.*   To conclude;
> Beware ill company, for often men
> Are like to those with whom they do conuerse,
> And from one man I warne you, and that's *Welborne*:
> Not cause Hee's poore, that rather claimes your pitty,
> But that hee's in his manners so debauch'd,
> And hath to vitious courses sold himselfe.
> 'Tis true your father lou'd him, while he was
> Worthy the louing, but if he had liu'd
> To haue seene him as he is, he had cast him off
> As you must doe.
>   *Alworth.*   I shall obey in all things.
>   *Lady.* Go, follow me to my chamber, you shall haue gold
> To furnish you like my sonne, and still supplied,
> As I heare from you.
>   *Alworth.*   I am still your creature.   *Exeunt.*

Actus primi, Scena tertia.

OVERREACH. GREEDY. ORDER. AMBLE. FURNACE.
WATCHALL. MARRALL.

> *Greedy.* Not to be seene?
> *Ouerreach.*   Still cloistered vp? Her reason,
> I hope assures her, though she make her selfe
> Close prisoner euer for her husbands losse,
> 'Twill not recouer him.
>   *Order.*   Sir, it is her will,

119. warne] *Dodsley*; warn'd 33   127. Go, follow] *editor*; You follow 33;
Follow *Dodsley*

Which we that are her seruants ought to serue it, 5
And not dispute. How ere, you are nobly welcome,
And if you please to stay, that you may thinke so,
There came not six dayes since from Hull, a pipe
Of rich Canarie, which shall spend it selfe
For my Ladies honour.
  Greedy.   Is it of the right race? 10
  Order. Yes, Master *Greedie.*
  Amble.   How his mouth runs or'e!
  Furnace. Ile make it run, and run. Saue your good worship.
  Greedy. Honest Master *Cooke,* thy hand, againe. How I loue thee:
Are the good dishes still in being? speake boy.
  Furnace. If you haue a minde to feed, there is a chine 15
Of beefe well seasoned.
  Greedy.   Good!
  Furnace.   A pheasant larded.
  Greedy. That I might now giue thanks for't!
  Furnace.   Other Kickeshawes.
Besides there came last night from the forrest of Sherwood
The fattest stagge I euer cook'd.
  Greedy.   A stagge man?
  Furnace. A stagge Sir, part of it prepar'd for dinner, 20
And bak'd in puffpast.
  Greedy.   Puffepast too, Sir *Giles*!
A ponderous chine of beefe! a pheasant larded!
And red deere too Sir *Giles,* and bak'd in puffepast!
All businesse set aside; let vs giue thankes here.
  Furnace. How the leane Sceleton's rap'd!
  Ouerreach.   You know wee cannot.
  Marrall. Your Worships are to sit on a commission, 26
And if you faile to come, you lose the cause.
  Greedy. Cause me no causes. I'le proue't, for such a dinner
We may put off a commission: you shall find it
Henrici decimo quarto.
  Ouerreach. Fie Master *Greedie.* 30
Will you loose me a thousand pounds for a dinner?
No more for shame. We must forget the belly,
When we thinke of profit.

  I. iii. 5. serue it] *33*; serve *Dodsley* 16. pheasant] *33²*; pleasant *33¹* 17. Kicke-
shawes] *Coxeter* (Kickshaws); Kukeshawes *33* 18. night] *Dodsley*; might *33*

Greedy.   Well, you shall or'erule me.
I could eu'n crie now. Doe you heare master *Cooke*,
Send but a corner of that immortall pastie,
And I, in thankefulnesse, will by your boy
Send you a brace of three-pences.
    Furnace.   Will you be so prodigall?

Enter WELBORNE.

Ouerreach. Remember me to your Lady. Who haue wee here?
Welborne. You know me.
    Ouerreach.   I did once, but now I will not,
Thou art no blood of mine. Auant thou begger,
If euer thou presume to owne me more,
Ile haue thee cag'd, and whipp'd.
    Greedy.   Ile grant the warrant,
Thinke of *Piecorner, Furnace.*
                              Exeunt OVERREACH, GREEDY, MARRALL.
    Watchall.   Will you out Sir?
I wonder how you durst creepe in.
    Order.   This is rudenesse,
And sawcie impudence.
    Amble.   Cannot you stay
To be seru'd among your fellowes from the basket,
But you must presse in to the hall?
    Furnace.   Prethee vanish
Into some outhouse, though it be the piggestie,
My skullion shall come to thee.

Enter ALWORTH.

    Welborne.   This is rare:
Oh here's *Tom Alworth. Tom.*
    Alworth.   We must be strangers,
Nor would I haue you seene here for a million.   *Exit* ALWORTH.
    Welborne. Better, and better. He contemnes mee too?

Enter WOMAN *and* CHAMBERMAID.

Woman. Foh what a smell's here! what thing's this?
    Chambermaid.   A creature
Made out of the priuie. Let vs hence for loues sake,
Or I shall sowne.

    48. though] *Dodsley*; thought *33*   50. *Tom Alworth.*] *Dodsley*; ~.~ ^ *33*

Woman. I beginne to faint already.

Exeunt WOMAN, *and* CHAMBERMAID.

Watchall. Will know your way?

Amble. Or shall wee teach it you,
By the head, and shoulders?

Welborne. No: I will not stirre.
Doe you marke, I will not. Let me see the wretch
That dares attempt to force me. Why you slaues,
Created only to make legges, and cringe;
To carrie in a dish, and shift a trencher;
That haue not soules only to hope a blessing
Beyond blacke iackes, or flagons; you that were borne
Only to consume meate, and drinke, and batten
Vpon reuersions: who aduances? who
Shewes me the way?

Enter LADY, WOMAN, CHAMBERMAID.

Order. My Lady.

Chambermaid. Here's the Monster.

Woman. Sweet Madam, keepe your gloue to your nose.

Chambermaid. Or let me
Fetch some perfumes may be predominant,
You wrong your selfe else.

Welborne. Madam, my designes
Beare me to you.

Lady. To me?

Welborne. And though I haue met with
But ragged entertainment from your groomes here,
I hope from you to receiue that noble vsage,
As may become the true friend of your husband,
And then I shall forget these.

Lady. I am amaz'd,
To see, and heare this rudenesse. Dar'st thou thinke
Though sworne, that it can euer find beleefe,
That I, who to the best men of this Countrey,
Deni'd my presence since my husbands death,
Can fall so low, as to change words with thee?
Thou Sonne of infamie, forbeare my house,
And know, and keepe the distance that's betweene vs,
Or, though it be against my gentler temper,

I shall take order you no more shall be
An eye-sore to me.
   Welborne.   Scorne me not good Lady;
But as in forme you are Angelicall
Imitate the heauenly natures, and vouchsafe
At the least awhile to heare me. You will grant
The blood that runs in this arme, is as noble
As that which fills your veines; those costly iewells,
And those rich clothes you weare; your mens obseruance,
And womens flatterie, are in you no vertues,
Nor these ragges, with my pouerty, in me vices.
You haue a faire fame, and I know deserue it,
Yet Lady I must say in nothing more,
Than in the pious sorrow you haue show'n
For your late noble husband.
   Order.   How she starts!
   Furnace. And hardly can keepe finger from the eye
To heare him nam'd.
   Lady.   Haue you ought else to say?
   Welborne. That husband Madam, was once in his fortune
Almost as low, as I. Want, debts, and quarrells
Lay heauy on him: let it not be thought
A boast in me, though I say, I releeu'd him.
'Twas I that gaue him fashion; mine the sword
That did on all occasions second his;
I brought him on, and off with honour, *Lady*:
And when in all mens iudgements he was sunke,
And in his owne hopes not to be buoy'd vp,
I step'd vnto him, tooke him by the hand,
And set him vpright.
   Furnace.   Are not wee base Rogues
That could forget this?
   Welborne.   I confesse you made him
Master of your estate, nor could your friends
Though he brought no wealth with him, blame you for't;
For he had a shape, and to that shape a minde
Made vp of all parts, either great, or noble,
So winning a behauiour, not to be
Resisted, Madam.

      107. buoy'd] *Dodsley*; bung'd 33

Lady. 'Tis most true, He had.
Welborne. For his sake then, in that I was his friend,
Doe not contemne me.
Lady. For what's past, excuse me,
I will redeeme it. *Order* giue the Gentleman
A hundred pounds.
Welborne. No Madam, on no termes: 120
I will nor begge, nor borrow six pence of you,
But be suppli'd elsewhere, or want thus euer.
Only one suite I make, which you deny not
To strangers: and 'tis this. *Whispers to her.*
Lady. Fie, nothing else?
Welborne. Nothing; vnlesse you please to charge your seruants,
To throw away a little respect vpon mee. 126
Lady. What you demand is yours.
Welborne. I thanke you, *Lady.*
Now what can be wrought out of such a suite,
Is yet in supposition; I haue said all,
When you please you may retire. Nay, all's forgotten, 130
And for a luckie *Omen* to my proiect,
Shake hands, and end all quarrells in the cellar.
Order. Agreed, agreed.
Furnace. Still merry master *Welborne.* *Exeunt.*

[II. i]

Actus secundi, Scena prima.

OVERREACH. MARRALL.

Ouerreach. HEE'S gone I warrant thee; this *Commission* crush'd him.
Marrall. Your worship haue the way on't, and ne're misse
To squeeze these vnthrifts into ayre: and yet
The chapp-falne *Iustice* did his part, returning
For your aduantage the *Certificate* 5
Against his conscience, and his knowledge too,
(With your good fauour) to the vtter ruine
Of the poore Farmer.
Ouerreach. 'Twas for these good ends
I made him a *Iustice.* He that bribes his bellie,

II. i. 2. on't] *Dodsley*; out 33

Is certaine to command his soule.
    Marrall.   I wonder
(Still with your licence) why, your Worship hauing
The power to put this thinne-gut in commission,
You are not in't your selfe?
    Ouerreach.   Thou art a foole;
In being out of Office I am out of danger,
Where if I were a *Iustice*, besides the trouble,
I might, or out of wilfulnesse, or error,
Run my selfe finely into a *Præmunire*,
And so become a prey to the Informer.
No, I'le haue none of't; 'tis enough I keepe
Greedie at my deuotion: so he serue
My purposes, let him hang, or damne, I care not.
Friend-ship is but a word.
    Marrall.   You are all wisdome.
    Ouerreach. I would be worldly wise, for the other wisdome
That does prescribe vs a well-gouern'd life,
And to doe right to others, as our selues,
I value not an Atome.
    Marrall.   What course take you,
With your good patience, to hedge in the Mannour
Of your neighbour master *Frugall*? as 'tis sayd,
He will nor sell, nor borrow, nor exchange,
And his land lying in the mid'st of your many Lordshipps,
Is a foule blemish.
    Ouerreach.   I haue thought on't, *Marrall*,
And it shall take. I must haue all men sellers,
And I the only Purchaser.
    Marrall.   'Tis most fit Sir.
    Ouerreach. I'le therefore buy some Cottage neare his Mannour,
Which done, I'le make my men breake ope his fences;
Ride o're his standing corne, and in the night
Set fire on his barnes; or breake his cattells legges.
These Trespasses draw on Suites, and Suites expences,
Which I can spare, but will soone begger Him.
When I haue harried him thus two, or three yeare,
Though he sue *in forma pauperis*, in spite
Of all his thrift, and care he'le grow behind-hand.
    Marrall. The best I euer heard; I could adore you.

Ouerreach. Then with the fauour of my man of *Law*,
I will pretend some title: Want will force him
To put it to arbitrement: then if he sell
For halfe the value, he shall haue ready money,
And I possesse his land.
   Marrall.   'Tis aboue wonder!
Welborne was apt to sell, and needed not
These fine arts Sir to hooke him in.
   Ouerreach.   Well thought on.
This varlet *Marrall* liues too long, to vpbraide me
With my close cheate put vpon him. Will nor cold,
Nor hunger kill him?
   Marrall.   I know not what to thinke on't.
I haue vs'd all meanes, and the last night I caus'd
His host the Tapster to turne him out of doores;
And haue beene since with all your friends, and tenants,
And on the forfeit of your fauour charg'd 'em,
Though a crust of mouldie bread would keep him from staruing,
Yet they should not relieue him. This is done, Sir.
   Ouerreach. That was something, *Marrall*, but thou must goe
      further,
And suddainely *Marrall.*
   Marrall.   Where, and when you please Sir.
   Ouerreach. I would haue thee seeke him out, and if thou canst,
Perswade him that 'tis better steale, than begge.
Then if I proue he has but rob'd a Henroost,
Not all the world shall saue him from the gallowes.
Doe any thing to worke him to despaire,
And 'tis thy Masterpeece.
   Marrall.   I will doe my best, Sir.
   Ouerreach. I am now on my maine worke with the Lord *Louell*,
The gallant minded, popular Lord *Louell*;
The minion of the peoples loue. I heare
Hee's come into the Country, and my aimes are
To insinuate my selfe into his knowledge,
And then inuite him to my house.
   Marrall.   I haue you.
This points at my young Mistris.
   Ouerreach.   She must part with

   57. 'em] *Brooke*; him *33*; them *Dodsley*

That humble title, and write honourable,
Right honorable *Marrall*, my right honorable daughter;
If all I haue, or e're shall get will doe it.
I will haue her well attended, there are Ladies
Of errant Knights decay'd, and brought so low,
That for cast clothes, and meate, will gladly serue her.
And 'tis my glory, though I come from the Cittie,
To haue their issue, whom I haue vndone,
To kneele to mine, as bond-slaues.
 Marrall.   'Tis fit state, Sir.
 Ouerreach. And therefore, Ile not haue a Chambermaide
That tyes her shooes, or any meaner office,
But such whose Fathers were Right worshipfull.
'Tis a rich Mans pride, there hauing euer beene
More than a Fewde, a strange Antipathie
Betweene vs, and true Gentry.

     Enter WELBORNE.

 Marrall.   See, who's here, Sir.
 Ouerreach. Hence monster; Prodigie.
 Welborne.   Sir your Wifes Nephew;
Shee, and my Father tumbled in one belly.
 Ouerreach. Auoid my sight, thy breath's infectious, Rogue.
I shun thee as a Leprosie, or the Plague.
Come hither *Marrall*, this is the time to worke him.
 Marrall. I warrant you, Sir.   *Exit* OVERREACH.
 Welborne.   By this light I thinke hee's mad.
 Marrall. Mad? had you tooke compassion on your selfe,
You long since had beene mad.
 Welborne.   You haue tooke a course
Betweene you, and my venerable Vncle,
To make me so.
 Marrall. The more pale spirited you,
That would not be instructed. I sweare deepely.
 Welborne. By what?
 Marrall.   By my Religion.
 Welborne.   Thy religion!
The Diuells Creed, but what would you haue done?
 Marrall. Had there beene but one tree in all the Shire,
Nor any hope to compasse a penny Halter,

Before, like you, I had outliu'd my fortunes,
A With had seru'd my turne to hang my selfe.
I am zealous in your cause: pray you hang your selfe,
And presently, as you loue your credit.
 Welborne.   I thanke you.
 Marrall. Will you stay till you dye in a ditch? Or lice deuoure you?
Or if you dare not doe the feate your selfe,
But that you'le put the state to charge, and trouble,
Is there no purse to bee cut? house to be broken?
Or market Women with egges that you may murther,
And so dispatch the businesse?
 Welborne.   Heer's varietie
I must confesse; but I'le accept of none
Of all your gentle offers, I assure you.
 Marrall. Why, haue you hope euer to eate againe?
Or drinke? Or be the master of three farthings?
If you like not hanging, drowne your selfe, take some course
For your reputation.
 Welborne. 'Twill not do, deare tempter,
With all the Rhetorike the fiend hath taught you.
I am as farre as thou art from despaire,
Nay, I haue Confidence, which is more than Hope,
To liue, and suddainely, better than euer.
 Marrall. Ha! Ha! these Castles you build in the aire
Will not perswade me, or to giue, or lend
A token to you.
 Welborne. Ile be more kind to thee.
Come thou shalt dine with me.
 Marrall.   With you!
 Welborne.   Nay more, dine *gratis*.
 Marrall. Vnder what hedge I pray you? Or at whose cost?
Are they *Padders*? or *Abram*-men, that are your consorts?
 Welborne. Thou art incredulous, but thou shalt dine
Not alone at her house, but with a gallant *Lady*,
With mee, and with a *Lady*.
 Marrall.   *Lady!* what *Lady?*
With the *Lady* of the *Lake*, or *Queene* of *Fairies?*
For I know, it must be an inchanted dinner.
 Welborne. With the Ladie *Alworth*, knaue.

Marrall. Nay, now there's hope
Thy braine is crack'd.
Welborne. Marke there, with what respect
I am entertain'd.
Marrall. With choice no doubt of Dogge-whippes.
Why, doest thou euer hope to passe her Porter?
Welborne. 'Tis not far off, go with me: trust thine owne eyes. 140
Marrall. Troth in my hope, or my assurance rather
To see thee curuet, and mount like a Dogge in a blanket
If euer thou presume to passe her threshold,
I will endure thy company.
Welborne. Come along then. *Exeunt.*

Actus secundi, Scena secunda.

ALWORTH. WAITING-WOMAN. CHAMBERMAID. ORDER.
AMBLE. FURNACE. WATCHALL.

Woman. Could you not command your leasure one houre longer?
Chambermaid. Or halfe an houre?
Alworth. I haue told you what my hast is:
Besides being now anothers, not mine owne,
How c're I much desire to enioy you longer,
My duty suffers, if to please my selfe 5
I should neglect my Lord.
Woman. Pray you doe me the fauour
To put these few Quince-cakes into your pocket,
They are of mine owne preseruing.
Chambermaid. And this Marmulade;
'Tis comfortable for your stomacke.
Woman. And at parting
Excuse me if I begge a farewell from you. 10
Chambermaid. You are still before me. I moue the same suite Sir.
Kisses 'em seuerally.
Furnace. How greedie these Chamberers are of a beardlesse chinne!
I thinke the Titts will rauish him.
Alworth. My seruice
To both.
Woman. Ours waites on you.

II. ii. 13. thinke] *Dodsley*; thinne 33

Chambermaid. And shall doe euer.
Order. You are my *Ladyes* charge, be therefore carefull 15
That you sustaine your parts.
Woman. We can beare I warrant you.
Exeunt WOMAN *and* CHAMBERMAID.
Furnace. Here; drinke it off, the ingredients are cordiall,
And this the true Elixir; It hath boild
Since midnight for you. 'Tis the Quintessence
Of fiue Cockes of the game, ten dozen of Sparrowes, 20
Knuckells of Veale, Potato rootes, and Marrow;
Currall, and Ambergreece: were you two yeares elder,
And I had a Wife, or gamesome Mistrisse,
I durst trust you with neither: You neede not baite
After this I warrant you; though your iourney's long, 25
You may ride on the strength of this till to morrow morning.
Alworth. Your courtesies ouerwhelme me: I much grieue
To part from such true friends, and yet find comfort;
My attendance on my honorable *Lord*
(Whose resolution holds to visit my *Lady*) 30
Will speedily bring me backe.
Knocking at the gate; MARRALL *and* WELBORNE *within.*
Marrall. Dar'st thou venture further?
Welborne. Yes, yes, and knocke againe.
Order. 'Tis he; disperse.
Amble. Performe it brauely.
Furnace. I know my Cue, nere doubt me.
They go off seuerall wayes.

[*Enter* MARRALL *and* WELBORNE.]

Watchall. Beast that I was to make you stay: most welcome,
You were long since expected.
Welborne. Say so much 35
To my friend I pray you.
Watchall. For your sake I will Sir.
Marrall. For his sake!
Welborne. Mum; this is nothing.
Marrall. More than euer
I would haue beleeu'd though I had found it in my Primer.

15. are] *33*; hear *Craik*   33 SD. Enter . . . WELBORNE] *editor*; *not in 33*;
Re-enter Watchall, *introducing* Wellborn *and* Marrall *Gifford*[1]

Alworth. When I haue giu'n you reasons for my late harshnesse,
You'le pardon, and excuse me: for, beleeue me 40
Though now I part abruptly, in my seruice
I will deserue it.
　　Marrall.　　　Seruice! with a vengeance!
　　Welborne. I am satisfied: farwell *Tom.*
　　Alworth.　　　　　　　　All ioy stay with you.
　　　　　　　　　　　　　　Exit ALWORTH.

　　　　　　　Enter AMBLE.

　　Amble. You are happily encounter'd: I yet neuer
Presented one so welcome, as I know 45
You will be to my *Lady.*
　　Marrall.　　　This is some vision;
Or sure these men are mad, to worship a Dunghill;
It cannot be a truth.
　　Welborne.　　　Be still a Pagan,
An vnbeleeuing Infidell, be so Miscreant,
And meditate on blanketts, and on dogge-whippes. 50

　　　　　　　Enter FURNACE.

　　Furnace. I am glad you are come; vntill I know your pleasure,
I knew not how to serue vp my *Ladies* dinner.
　　Marrall. His pleasure; is it possible?
　　Welborne.　　　　　　What's thy will?
　　Furnace. Marry Sir, I haue some Growse, and Turkie chicken,
Some Rayles, and Quailes, and my *Lady* will'd me aske you 55
What kind of sawces best affect your palat,
That I may vse my vtmost skill to please it.
　　Marrall. The Diuell's enter'd this cooke, sawce for his palat!
That on my knowledge, for almost this twelue month,
Durst wish but cheeseparings, and browne bread on Sundayes. 60
　　Welborne. That way I like 'em best.
　　Furnace.　　　　　　It shall be done Sir.
　　　　　　　　　　　　　　Exit FURNACE.
　　Welborne. What thinke you of the hedge we shall dine vnder?
Shall we feed *gratis*?
　　Marrall.　　　I know not what to thinke;
Pray you make me not mad.

Enter ORDER.

Order. This place becomes you not;
Pray you walke Sir, to the dining roome.
　Welborne. I am well here
'Till her *Ladiship* quitts her chamber.
　Marrall. Well here say you?
'Tis a rare change! but yesterday you thought
Your selfe well in a Barne, wrapp'd vp in Pease-straw.

Enter WOMAN, *and* CHAMBERMAID.

　Woman. O Sir, you are wish'd for.
　Chambermaid. My Lady dream't Sir of you.
　Woman. And the first command she gaue, after she rose
Was (her deuotions donne) to giue her notice
When you approch'd here.
　Chambermaid. Which is done on my vertue.
　Marrall. I shall be conuerted, I begin to grow
Into a new beleefe, which Saints, nor Angells
Could haue woone me to haue faith in.

Enter LADY.

　Woman. Sir, my *Lady.*
　Lady. I come to meete you, and languish'd till I saw you.
This first kisse is for forme; I allow a second
To such a friend.
　Marrall. To such a friend! Heau'n blesse me!
　Welborne. I am wholly yours, yet Madam, if you please
To grace this Gentleman with a salute—
　Marrall. Salute me at his bidding!
　Welborne. I shall receaue it
As a most high fauour.
　Lady. Sir, you may command me.
　Welborne. Run backward from a *Lady*? and such a *Lady*?
　Marrall. To kisse her foote is to poore me, a fauour,
I am vnworthy of— *Offers to kisse her foote.*
　Lady. Nay, pray you rise,
And since you are so humble, I'le exalt you;
You shall dine with me to day, at mine owne table.

80. salute—] *Gifford*; ∼. *33*　84. to poore me, a fauour,] *after Dodsley*; to poore, me a fauour; *33*

Marrall. Your *Ladiships* table? I am not good enough
To sit at your Stewards boord.
  Lady.   You are too modest:
I will not be deni'd.

      Enter FURNACE.

  Furnace.   Will you still be babling,   90
Till your meate freeze on the table? the old tricke still.
My Art ne're thought on.
  Lady.   Your arme, Master *Welborne*:
Nay keep vs company.
  Marrall.   I was neuer so grac'd.
    Exeunt WELBORNE, LADY, AMBLE, MARRALL,
        WOMAN [, CHAMBERMAID].
  Order. So we haue play'd our parts, and are come off well.
But if I know the mistery, why my *Lady*   95
Consented to it, or why Master *Welborne*
Desir'd it, may I perish.
  Furnace.   Would I had
The roasting of his heart, that cheated him,
And forces the poore gentleman to these shiftes.
By Fire (for Cookes are *Persians*, and sweare by it) 100
Of all the griping, and extorting tyrants
I euer heard, or read of, I ne're met
A match to Sir *Giles Ouerreach*.
  Watchall.   What will you take
To tell him so fellow *Furnace*?
  Furnace.   Iust as much
As my throate is worth, for that would be the price on't. 105
To haue a vsurer that starues himselfe,
And weares a cloke of one and twenty yeares
On a sute of fourteene groates, bought of the Hangman,
To grow rich, and then purchase, is too common:
But this Sir *Giles* feedes high, keepes many seruants, 110
Who must at his command doe any outrage;
Rich in his habit; vast in his expences;
Yet he to admiration still increases
In wealth, and Lordships.
  Order.   He frights men out of their Estates,

    93 SD. CHAMBERMAID]; *Gifford*; *not in 33*

And breakes through all Law-netts, made to curbe ill men, 115
As they were cobwebbs. No man dares reproue him.
Such a spirit to dare, and power to doe, were neuer
Lodg'd so vnluckily.

Enter AMBLE.

Amble. Ha, ha; I shall burst.
Order. Containe thy selfe man.
Furnace. Or make vs partakers
Of your suddaine mirth.
Amble. Ha, ha, my *Lady* has got 120
Such a guest at her table, this terme-driuer *Marrall*,
This snippe of an *Attourney*.
Furnace. What of him man?
Amble. The knaue thinkes still hee's at the cookes shop in *Ramme-alley*,
Where the Clarkes diuide, and the Elder is to choose;
And feedes so slouenly.
Furnace. Is this all?
Amble. My *Lady* 125
Dranke to him for fashion sake, or to please master *Welborne*.
As I liue he rises, and takes vp a dish,
In which there were some remnants of a boild capon,
And pledges her in whitebroth.
Furnace. Nay, 'tis like
The rest of his tribe.
Amble. And when I brought him wine, 130
He leaues his stoole, and after a legge or two
Most humbly thankes my worship.
Order. Rose already!
Amble. I shall be chid.

Enter LADY, WELBORNE, MARRALL.

Furnace. My *Lady* frownes.
Lady. You waite well.
Let me haue no more of this, I obseru'd your ieering.
Sirra, I'le haue you know, whom I thinke worthy 135
To sit at my table, be he ne're so meane,
When I am present, is not your companion.
Order. Nay, shee'le preserue what's due to her.

Furnace. This refreshing
Followes your flux of laughter.
   Lady. You are master
Of your owne will. I know so much of manners 140
As not to enquire your purposes, in a word
To me you are euer welcome, as to a house
That is your owne.
   Welborne. Marke that.
   Marrall. With reuerence Sir,
And it like your Worship.
   Welborne. Trouble your selfe no farther,
Deare Madam; my heart's full of zeale, and seruice, 145
How euer in my language I am sparing.
Come master *Marrall.*
   Marrall. I attend your Worship.
                      Exeunt WELBORNE, MARRALL.
   Lady. I see in your lookes you are sorry, and you know me
An easy mistris: bee merry; I haue forgot all.
Order, and *Furnace* come with me, I must giue you 150
Further directions.
   Order. What you please.
   Furnace. We are ready. [*Exeunt.*]

Actus secundi, Scena tertia.

WELBORNE. MARRALL.

   Welborne. I thinke I am in a good way.
   Marrall. Good, Sir! the best way,
The certaine best way.
   Welborne. There are casualties
That men are subiect too.
   Marrall. You are aboue 'em.
And as you are already Worshipfull,
I hope e're long you will increase in Worship, 5
And be Right worshipfull.
   Welborne. Prethee doe not flowt mee.
What I shall be, I shall be. Is't for your ease,

---

151 SD. *Exeunt.*] *Coxeter*; not in 33   II. iii. 1. Good, Sir! the best way,] *Dodsley*; Good Sir; the best way. *33*; Good! sir; the best way, *Gifford*

You keepe your hat off?
    Marrall.   Ease, and it like your Worship?
I hope *Jacke Marrall* shall not liue so long,
To proue himselfe such an vnmannerly beast,
Though it haile Hazell Nutts, as to be couer'd
When your Worshipp's present.
    Welborne.   Is not this a true Rogue?   *Aside.*
That out of meere hope of a future cosnage
Can turne thus suddainely: 'tis ranke already.
    Marrall. I know your Worshipp's wise, and needs no counsell:
Yet if in my desire to doe you seruice,
I humbly offer my aduice, (but still
Vnder correction) I hope I shall not
Incurre your high displeasure.
    Welborne.   No; speake freely.
    Marrall. Then in my iudgement Sir, my simple iudgement,
(Still with your Worshipps fauour) I could wish you
A better habit, for this cannot be
But much distastfull to the noble *Lady*,
(I say no more) that loues you, for this morning
To me (and I am but a Swine to her)
Before th'assurance of her wealth perfum'd you,
You sauour'd not of amber.
    Welborne.   I doe now then?
    Marrall. This your Battoone hath got a touch of it.
                             Kisses the end of his cudgell.
Yet if you please for change I haue twenty pounds here
Which, out of my true loue I presently
Lay downe at your Worshipps feet: 'twill serue to buy you
A riding suite.
    Welborne.   But where's the horse?
    Marrall.   My Gelding
Is at your seruice: nay, you shall ride me
Before your Worship shall be put to the trouble
To walke a foote. Alas, when you are Lord
Of this *Ladies* mannour (as I know you will be)
You may with the lease of glebe land, call'd *Knaues-acre*,
A place I would manure, requite your vassall.

    28 SD. *placed as Coxeter; opposite line 27 in 33*   29. for change] *33*; to change *conj. editor*   35. a foote] *33*; afoot *Gifford*

Welborne. I thanke thy loue: but must make no vse of it,
What's twenty pounds?
 Marrall.   'Tis all that I can make, Sir.   40
 Welborne. Doest thou thinke though I want clothes I could not
  haue 'em,
For one word to my *Lady*?
 Marrall.   As I know not that!
 Welborne. Come I'le tell thee a secret, and so leaue thee.
I'le not giue her the aduantage, though she be
A gallant minded *Lady*, after we are married   45
(There being no woman, but is sometimes froward)
To hit me in the teeth, and say she was forc'd
To buy my wedding clothes, and tooke me on
With a plaine Riding-suite, and an ambling Nagge.
No, I'le be furnish'd something like my selfe.   50
And so farewell; for thy suite touching *Knaues acre*,
When it is mine 'tis thine.
 Marrall.   I thanke your Worship.
              Exit WELBORNE.
How was I coozen'd in the calculation
Of this mans fortune, my master coozen'd too,
Whose pupill I am in the art of undoing men,   55
For that is our profession; well, well, master *Welborne*,
You are of a sweet nature, and fit againe to be cheated:
Which, if the fates please, when you are possess'd
Of the land, and *Lady*, you *sans question* shall be.
I'le presently thinke of the meanes.   *Walke by musing.*

       Enter OVERREACH.

 Ouerreach.   Sirrha, take my horse.   60
I'le walke to get me an appetite; 'tis but a mile,
And Exercise will keep me from being pursie.
Ha! *Marrall*! is he coniuring? perhaps
The knaue has wrought the prodigall to doe
Some outrage on himselfe, and now he feeles   65
Compunction in his conscience for't: no matter
So it be done. *Marrall.*
 Marrall.   Sir.
 Ouerreach.   How succeed we

   53. was I] *Dodsley*; was *33*   60 SD. musing] *Dodsley*; masing *33*

In our plot on *Welborne?*
 Marrall.   Neuer better Sir.
 Ouerreach. Has he hang'd, or drown'd himselfe?
 Marrall.   No Sir, he liues.
Liues once more to be made a prey to you,
A greater prey than euer.
 Ouerreach.   Art thou in thy witts?
If thou art reueale this miracle, and briefely.
 Marrall. A *Lady* Sir, is falne in loue with him.
 Ouerreach. With him? what *Lady?*
 Marrall.   The rich *Lady Alworth.*
 Ouerreach. Thou Dolt; how dar'st thou speake this?
 Marrall.   I speake truth;
And I doe so but once a yeare, vnlesse
It be to you Sir, we din'd with her *Ladyship,*
I thanke his Worship.
 Ouerreach.   His Worship!
 Marrall.   As I liue Sir,
I din'd with him, at the great *Ladyes* table,
Simple as I stand here, and saw when she kiss'd him,
And would at his request, haue kiss'd me too,
But I was not so audacious, as some Youths are,
And dare do any thing be it ne're so absurd,
And sad after performance.
 Ouerreach.   Why thou Rascall,
To tell me these impossibilities:
Dine, at her table? and kisse him? or thee?
Impudent Varlet. Haue not I my selfe
To whom great *Countesses* dores haue oft flew open,
Ten times attempted, since her husbands death,
In vaine to see her, though I came—a suitor;
And yet your good Sollicitor-ship, and rogue—*Welborne,*
Were brought into her presence, feasted with her.
But that I know thee a Dogge, that cannot blush,
This most incredible lye would call vp one
On thy buttermilke cheekes.
 Marrall.   Shall I not trust my eyes Sir?
Fi^r Or tast? I feele her good cheere in my belly.

  82. as some Youths] *33²*; and some Yonths *33¹* 83. And dare] *33*; Who dare *conj. Coxeter*; That dare *Gifford*

Ouerreach. You shall feele me, if you giue not ouer Sirra;
Recouer your braines agen, and be no more gull'd
With a beggers plot assisted by the aides
Of seruing men, and chambermaides, for beyound these   100
Thou neuer saw'st a Woman, or I'le quit you
From my imployments.
 Marrall.   Will you credit this yet?
On my confidence of their marriage I offer'd *Welborne*
(I would giue a crowne now, I durst say his worship) *Aside.*
My nagge, and twenty pounds.
 Ouerreach.   Did you so Ideot? *Strikes him downe.*
Was this the way to worke him to despaire   106
Or rather to crosse me?
 Marrall.   Will your worship kill me?
 Ouerreach. No, no; but driue the lying spirit out of you.
 Marrall. Hee's gone.
 Ouerreach.   I haue done then: now forgetting
Your late imaginerie feast, and *Lady*,   110
Know my Lord *Louell* dines with me to morrow,
Be carefull nought be wanting to receaue him,
And bid my daughters women trimne her vp,
Though they paint her, so she catch the Lord, I'le thanke 'em;
There's a peece for my late blowes.
 Marrall.   I must yet suffer: 115
But there may be a time—   *Aside.*
 Ouerreach.   Doe you grumble?
 Marrall.   No Sir. [*Exeunt.*]

Actus tertii, Scena prima.

LOVELL. ALWORTH. *Seruants.*

 Louell. WALKE the horses downe the hill: something in priuate,
I must impart to *Alworth.*   *Exeunt serui.*
 Alworth.   O my Lord,
What sacrifice of reuerence, dutie, watching,
Although I could put off the vse of sleepe,
And euer waite on your commands to serue 'em;   5

---

 105. Ideot] *Coxeter*; I doe *33* 116. *Exeunt.*] *Dodsley*; *not in 33* III. i. 5. to serue] *Dodsley*; serue *33*

What dangers, though in ne're so horrid shapes,
Nay death it selfe, though I should run to meet it,
Can I, and with a thankefull willingnesse suffer;
But still the retribution will fall short
Of your bounties showr'd vpon me.
    Louell.   Louing Youth;
Till what I purpose be put into act,
Doe not o're-prize it. Since you haue trusted me
With your soules nearest, nay her dearest secret,
Rest confident 'tis in a cabinet lock'd,
Treachery shall neuer open. I haue found you
(For so much to your face I must professe,
How er'e you guard your modesty with a blush for't)
More zealous in your loue, and seruice to me
Than I haue beene in my rewards.
    Alworth.   Still great ones
Aboue my merit.
    Louell.   Such your Gratitude calls 'em:
Nor am I of that harsh, and rugged temper
As some Great men are tax'd with, who imagine
They part from the respect due to their Honours,
If they vse not all such as follow 'em,
Without distinction of their births, like slaues.
I am not so condition'd: I can make
A fitting difference betweene my Foot-boy,
And a Gentleman, by want compell'd to serue me.
    Alworth. 'Tis thankefully acknowledg'd: you haue beene
More like a Father to me than a Master.
Pray you pardon the comparison.
    Louell.   I allow it;
And to giue you assurance I am pleas'd in't,
My carriage and demeanor to your Mistrisse,
Faire *Margaret*, shall truely witnesse for me
I can command my passions.
    Alworth.   'Tis a conquest
Few Lords can boast of when they are tempted. Oh!
    Louell. Why do you sigh? can you be doubtfull of mee?
By that faire name, I in the warres haue purchas'd,
And all my actions hitherto vntainted,

8. suffer;] *33*; ~? *Mason, McIlwraith*   22. tax'd with,] *Dodsley*; ~, ~∧ *33*

I will not be more true to mine owne Honour, 40
Than to my *Alworth*.
    Alworth.   As you are the braue Lord *Louell*,
Your bare word only giuen, is an assurance
Of more validity, and weight to me
Than all the othes bound vp with imprecations,
Which when they would deceiue, most Courtiers practize: 45
Yet being a man (for sure to stile you more
Would rellish of grosse flatterie) I am forc'd
Against my confidence of your worth, and vertues,
To doubt, nay more to feare.
    Louell.   So young, and iealous?
    Alworth. Were you to encounter with a single foe, 50
The victorie were certaine: but to stand
The charge of two such potent enemies,
At once assaulting you, as Wealth and Beauty,
And those too seconded with Power, is oddes
Too great for *Hercules*.
    Louell.   Speake your doubts, and feares, 55
Since you will nourish 'em, in plainer language,
That I may vnderstand 'em.
    Alworth.   What's your will,
Though I lend armes against my selfe, (prouided
They may aduantage you) must be obeyed.
My much lou'd Lord, were *Margaret* only faire, 60
The cannon of her more than earthly forme,
Though mounted high, commanding all beneath it,
And ramn'd with bullets of her sparkling eyes,
Of all the bulwarkes that defend your senses
Could batter none, but that which guards your sight. 65
But when the well tun'd accents of her tongue
Make musike to you, and with numerous sounds
Assault your hearing (such as if *Vlysses*
Now liu'd againe, how ere he stood the *Sirens*,
Could not resist) the combat must grow doubtfull 70
Betweene your Reason, and rebellious Passions.
Ad this too; when you feele her touch, and breath,
Like a soft Westerne wind, when it glides o're
Arabia, creating gummes, and spices:

    65. none] *Dodsley*; more *33*   68. as if *Vlysses*] *33*; as Ulysses, if [he] *Gifford*

And in the Van, the *Nectar* of her lippes 75
Which you must tast, bring the battalia on,
Well arm'd, and strongly lin'd with her discourse,
And knowing manners, to giue entertainement;
Hyppolitus himselfe would leaue *Diana*,
To follow such a *Venus*.
  Louell.   Loue hath made you 80
Poeticall, *Alworth*.
  Alworth. Grant all these beat off,
Which if it be in man to doe, you'le doe it;
Mammon in Sir *Giles Ouerreach* stepps in
With heapes of ill got gold, and so much land,
To make her more remarkable, as would tire 85
A Falcons winges in one day to fly ouer.
O my good Lord, these powerfull aydes, which would
Make a mishapen *Negro* beautifull,
(Yet are but ornaments to giue her lustre,
That in her selfe is all perfection) must 90
Preuaile for her. I here release your trust.
'Tis happinesse, enough, for me to serue you,
And sometimes with chast eyes to looke vpon her.
  Louell. Why, shall I sweare?
  Alworth.   O by no meanes my Lord;
And wrong not so your iudgement to the world 95
As from your fond indulgence to a boy,
Your page, your seruant, to refuse a blessing
Diuers Great men are riualls for.
  Louell.   Suspend
Your iudgement 'till the triall. How far is it
T' *Ouerreach* house?
  Alworth. At the most some halfe houres riding; 100
You'le soone be there.
  Louell. And you the sooner freed
From your iealous feares.
  Alworth. O that I durst but hope it. *Exeunt.*

77. lin'd] *Dodsley*; liu'd *33*

Actus tertii, Scena secunda.

OVERREACH. GREEDY. MARRALL.

Ouerreach. Spare for no cost, let my Dressers cracke with the weight
Of curious viands.
    Greedy. Store indeed's no sore, Sir.
    Ouerreach. That prouerbe fitts your stomacke Master *Greedie*.
And let no plate be seene, but what's pure gold,
Or such whose workemanship exceeds the matter
That it is made of, let my choicest linnen
Perfume the roome, and when we wash, the water
With pretious powders mix'd, so please my Lord,
That he may with enuie wish to bath so euer.
    Marrall. 'Twil be very chargeable.
    Ouerreach.   Auant you Drudge:
Now all my labour'd ends are at the stake,
Is't a time to thinke of thrift? call in my daughter, [*Exit* MARRALL.]
And master *Iustice*, since you loue choice dishes,
And plenty of 'em—
    Greedy.   As I doe indeed Sir,
Almost as much as to giue thankes for 'em.
    Ouerreach. I doe conferre that prouidence, with my power
Of absolute command to haue abundance,
To your best care.
    Greedy.   I'le punctually discharge it
And giue the best directions. Now am I
In mine owne conceite a Monarch, at the least
Arch-president of the boyl'd, the roast, the bak'd,
For which I will eate often, and giue thankes,
When my bellies brac'd vp like a drumme, and that's pure iustice.
                                                                  Exit GREEDY.
    Ouerreach. It must bee so: should the foolish girle proue modest,
Shee may spoile all, she had it not from me,
But from her mother, I was euer forward,
As she must bee, and therefore I'le prepare her.

III. ii. 6–7. let my choicest linnen / Perfume] 33; lay my choicest Linnen, / Perfume *Coxeter*; set my choicest linnen; / Perfume *conj. McIlwraith*   12 SD. *Exit* MARRALL.] *Gifford*² ; *not in* 33   24. It] *Dodsley*; I 33

[*Enter*] MARGARET.

Alone, and let your woemen waite without.
  Margaret. Your pleasure Sir?
  Ouerreach.   Ha, this is a neate dressing!
These orient pearles, and diamonds well plac'd too!
The Gowne affects me not, it should haue beene
Embroider'd o're, and o're with flowers of gold,
But these rich Iewells, and quaint fashion helpe it.
And how below? since oft the wanton eye,
The face obseru'd, descends vnto the foot;
Which being well proportion'd, as yours is,
Inuites as much as perfect white, and red,
Though without art. How like you your new Woman,
The Lady *Downefalne*?
  Margaret.   Well for a companion;
Not as a seruant.
  Ouerreach.   Is she humble *Meg*?
And carefull too; her Ladiship forgotten?
  Margaret. I pitty her fortune.
  Ouerreach.   Pitty her? Trample on her.
I tooke her vp in an old tamin gowne,
(Euen staru'd for want of two penny chopps) to serue thee:
And if I vnderstand, shee but repines
To doe thee any duty, though ne're so seruile,
I'le packe her to her Knight, where I haue lodg'd him,
Into the Counter, and there let 'em howle together.
  Margaret. You know your owne wayes, but for me I blush
When I command her, that was once attended
With persons, not inferior to my selfe
In birth.
  Ouerreach. In birth? Why, art thou not my daughter?
The blest child of my industrie, and wealth?
Why foolish girle, was't not to make thee great,
That I haue ran, and still pursue those wayes
That hale downe curses on mee, which I minde not?
Part with these humble thoughts, and apt thy selfe
To the noble state I labour to aduance thee,
Or by my hopes to see thee honorable,

            48. Into] *33*; In *Coxeter*

I will adopt a stranger to my heyre, 60
And throw thee from my care, doe not prouoke mee.
   Margaret. I will not Sir; mould mee which way you please.

Enter GREEDY.

   Ouerreach. How, interrupted?
   Greedy.   'Tis matter of importance.
The cooke Sir is selfe-will'd and will not learne
From my experience, there's a fawne brought in Sir, 65
And for my life I cannot make him rost it,
With a *Norfolke* dumpling in the belly of it.
And Sir, we wisemen know, without the dumpling
'Tis not worth three pence.
   Ouerreach.   Would it were whole in thy belly
To stuffe it out; Cooke it any way, prethee leaue me. 70
   Greedy. Without order for the dumpling?
   Ouerreach.   Let it be dumpl'd
Which way thou wilt, or tell him I will scalld him
In his owne Caldron.
   Greedy.   I had lost my stomake,
Had I lost my mistrisse dumpling, I'le giue thanks for't.
Exit GREEDY.
   Ouerreach. But to our businesse *Megge*, you haue heard who
    dines here? 75
   Margaret. I haue Sir.
   Ouerreach.   'Tis an honourable man.
A Lord, *Megge*, and commands a regiment
Of Souldiers, and what's rare is one himselfe,
A bold, and vnderstanding one; and to be
A Lord, and a good leader in one volume, 80
Is granted vnto few, but such as rise vp
The Kingdomes glory.

Enter GREEDY.

   Greedy.   I'le resigne my office,
If I be not better obey'd.
   Ouerreach.   Slight, art thou franticke?
   Greedy. Franticke! 'twould make me a franticke, and stark-mad,
Were I not a *Iustice of peace*, and *coram* too, 85

   74 for't] Dodsley; for 33   SD. *placed as Coxeter; opposite line 75 in 33*

Which this rebellious Cooke cares not a straw for.
There are a dozen of Woodcockes—
    Ouerreach.   Make thy selfe
Thirteene, the bakers dozen.
    Greedy.   I am contented
So they may be dress'd to my minde, he has found out
A new deuice for sawce, and will not dish 'em
With tosts, and butter; my Father was a Taylor,
And my name though a Iustice, *Greedie Woodcocke*,
And ere I'le see my linage so abus'd,
I'le giue vp my commission.
    Ouerreach.   Cooke, Rogue obey him.
I haue giuen the word, pray you now remoue your selfe,
To a coller of brawne, and trouble me no farther.
    Greedy. I will, and meditate what to eate at dinner.
                                              Exit GREEDY.
    Ouerreach. And as I said *Meg*, when this gull disturb'd vs;
This honourable Lord, this Collonell,
I would haue thy husband.
    Margaret.   There's too much disparity
Betweene his quality, and mine, to hope it.
    Ouerreach. I more then hope 't, and doubt not to effect it,
Be thou no enemy to thy selfe, my wealth
Shall weigh his titles downe, and make you equalls.
Now for the meanes to assure him thine; obserue me;
Remember hee's a Courtier, and a Soldier,
And not to be trifl'd with, and therefore when
He comes to woe you, see you doe not coye it.
This mincing modesty hath spoyl'd many a match
By a first refusall, in vaine after hop'd for.
    Margaret. You'le haue mee Sir, preserue the distance, that
Confines a Virgin?
    Ouerreach.   Virgin me no Virgins.
I must haue you lose that name, or you lose me.
I will haue you priuate, start not, I say priuate;
If thou art my true daughter, not a bastard,
Thou wilt venture alone with one man, though he came
Like *Iupiter* to *Semele*, and come off too.
And therefore when he kisses you, kisse close.

                108. you doe] *Dodsley*; ~, ~ 33

Margaret. I have heard this is the strumpetts fashion Sir,
Which I must neuer learne.
    Ouerreach.   Learne any thing,
And from any creature that may make thee great;
From the Diuell himselfe.
    Margaret.   This is but Diuelish doctrine. [*Aside.*]
    Ouerreach. Or if his blood grow hot, suppose he offer
Beyond this, doe not you stay 'till it coole,
But meete his ardor, if a couch be neare,
Sit downe on't, and inuite him.
    Margaret.   In your house?
Your owne house Sir, for heau'ns sake, what are you then?
Or what shall I be Sir?
    Ouerreach.   Stand not on forme,
Words are no substances.
    Margaret.   Though you could dispence
With your owne Honour; cast aside Religion,
The hopes of heauen, or feare of hell; excuse mee,
In worldly policie, this is not the way
To make me his wife, his whore I grant it may doe.
My maiden Honour so soone yeelded vp,
Nay prostituted, cannot but assure him
I that am light to him will not hold weight
When he is tempted by others: so in iudgement
When to his lust I haue giuen vp my honour
He must, and will forsake me.
    Ouerreach.   How? forsake thee?
Doe I weare a sword for fashion? or is this arme
Shrunke vp? or wither'd? does there liue a man
Of that large list I haue encounter'd with,
Can truly say I e're gaue inch of ground,
Not purchas'd with his blood, that did oppose me?
Forsake thee when the thing is done? he dares not.
Giue me but proofe, he has enioy'd thy person,
Though all his Captaines, Eccho's to his will,
Stood arm'd by his side to iustify the wrong,
And he himselfe in the head of his bold troope,
Spite of his Lordship, and his Collonelship,

   122 SD. *Aside.*] *Coxeter*; *not in 33*   137. When he is] *33*; When *Dodsley*;
Whene'er *Gifford*; When his, *Craik*

Or the Iudges fauour, I will make him render
A bloody and a strict accompt, and force him
By marrying thee, to cure thy wounded honour;
I haue said it.

Enter MARRALL.

Marrall.   Sir, the man of Honors come,
Newly alighted.
   Ouerreach.   In; without reply   155
And doe as I command, or thou art lost.   *Exit* MARGARET.
Is the lowd musicke I gaue order for
Readie to receiue him?
   Marrall.   'Tis Sir.
   Ouerreach.   Let 'em sound
A princely welcome.   [*Exit* MARRALL.]
           Roughnesse a while leaue me,
For fawning now, a stranger to my nature,   160
Must make way for mee.   *Loud musicke.*

Enter LOVELL, GREEDY, ALWORTH, MARRALL.

Louell.   Sir, you meete your trouble.
   Ouerreach. What you are pleas'd to stile so is an honor
Aboue my worth, and fortunes.
   Alworth.   Strange, so humble.
   Ouerreach. A iustice of peace my Lord.   *Presents* GREEDY *to him.*
   Louell.   Your hand good Sir.
   Greedy. This is a Lord; and some thinke this a fauour; [*Aside.*]
But I had rather haue my hand in my dumpling.   166
   Ouerreach. Roome for my Lord.
   Louell.   I misse Sir your faire daughter,
To crowne my welcome.
   Ouerreach.   May it please my Lord
To taste a glasse of Greeke wine first, and suddainely
She shall attend my Lord.
   Louell.   You'le be obey'd Sir.   170
           Exeunt omnes preter OVERREACH.
   Ouerreach. 'Tis to my wish; assoone as come aske for her!
Why, *Megge? Megge Ouerreach.*

159. Exit MARRALL.] *Gifford*²; *not in* 33.   165 SD. *Aside.*] *Dodsley; not in* 33

[*Enter* MARGARET.]

How! teares in your eies!
Ha! drie 'em quickely, or I'le digge 'em out.
Is this a time to whimper? meete that Greatnesse
That flies into thy bosome, thinke what 'tis   175
For me to say, *My honorable daughter*,
And thou, when I stand bare, to say put on,
Or father you forget your selfe, no more,
But be instructed, or expect—he comes.

Enter LOVELL, GREEDY, ALWORTH, MARRALL.

A blacke-brow'd girle my Lord.
   Louell.   As I liue a rare one. *They salute.*
   Alworth. Hee's tooke already: I am lost.
   Ouerreach.   That kisse,   181
Came twanging off, I like it, quit the roome: *The rest off.*
A little bashfull my good Lord, but you
I hope will teach her boldnesse.
   Louell.   I am happy
In such a scholler: but—
   Ouerreach.   I am past learning,   185
And therefore leaue you to your selues: remember—*To his daughter.*
                                Exit OVERREACH.
   Louell. You see faire Lady, your father is sollicitous
To haue you change the barren name of Virgin
Into a hopefull wife.
   Margaret.   His haste my Lord,
Holds no power o're my will.
   Louell.   But o're your duty.   190
   Margaret. Which forc'd too much may breake.
   Louell.   Bend rather sweetest:
Thinke of your yeares.
   Margaret.   Too few to match with yours:
And choicest fruites too soone plucked, rot, and wither.
   Louell. Doe you thinke I am old?
   Margaret.   I am sure I am too young.
   Louell. I can aduance you.
   Margaret.   To a hill of sorrow,   195

172 SD. *Enter* MARGARET.] *Coxeter*; *not in* 33   189. His haste] *Dodsley*; He hast 33

Where euery houre I may expect to fall,
But neuer hope firme footing. You are noble,
I of a low descent, how euer rich;
And tissues match'd with skarlet suite but ill.
O my good Lord I could say more, but that   200
I dare not trust these walls.
   Louell.   Pray you trust my eare then.

Enter OVERREACH *listning.*

   Ouerreach. Close at it! whispering! this is excellent!
And by their postures, a consent on both parts.

Enter GREEDY.

   Greedy. Sir *Giles*, Sir *Giles*.
   Ouerreach.   The great fiend stop that clapper.
   Greedy. It must ring out Sir, when my belly rings noone.   205
The bak'd meates are run out, the rost turn'd powder.
   Ouerreach. I shall powder you.
   Greedy.   Beate me to dust I care not.
In such a cause as this, I'le dye a martyr.
   Ouerreach. Marry and shall: you *Barathrum* of the shambells.
Strikes him.
   Greedy. How! strike a *Iustice of peace*? 'tis pettie treason,   210
Edwardi quinto; but that you are my friend
I could commit you without bayle or maine-prise.
   Ouerreach. Leaue your balling Sir, or I shall commit you
Where you shall not dine to day; disturbe my Lord,
When he is in discourse?
   Greedy.   Is't a time to talke   215
When we should be munching?
   Louell.   Ha! I heard some noise.
   Ouerreach. Mum, villaine, vanish: shall we breake a bargaine
Almost made vp?   *Thrust* GREEDY *off.*
   Louell.   Lady, I vnderstand you,
And rest most happy in your choice; beleeue it,
I'le be a carefull pilot to direct   220
Your yet vncertaine barke to a port of safety.
   Margaret. So shall your Honor saue two liues, and bind vs
Your slaues for euer.

206. bak'd] *Dodsley*; back'd 33

Louell.   I am in the act rewarded,
Since it is good; how e're, you must put on
An amorous carriage towards me, to delude   225
Your subtle father.
    Margaret.   I am prone to that.
    Louell. Now breake wee off our conference. Sir *Giles*.
Where is Sir *Giles*?

            Enter OVERREACH, *and the rest.*

    Ouerreach.   My noble Lord; and how
Does your Lordship find her?
    Louell.   Apt Sir *Giles*, and comming,
And I like her the better.
    Ouerreach.   So doe I too.   230
    Louell. Yet should we take forts at the first assault
'Twere poore in the defendant, I must confirme her
With a loue letter or two, which I must haue
Deliuer'd by my page, and you giue way too't.
    Ouerreach. With all my soule, a towardly Gentleman, 235
Your hand good master *Alworth*, know my house
Is euer open to you.
    Alworth.   'Twas shut 'till now.   *Aside.*
    Ouerreach. Well done, well done, my honorable daughter:
Th'art so already: know this gentle youth,
And cherish him my honorable daughter.   240
    Margaret. I shall with my best care.   *Noise within as of a coch.*
    Ouerreach.   A Coch.
    Greedy.   More stops
Before we goe to dinner! o my gutts!

            Enter LADY, *and* WELBORNE.

    Lady.   If I find welcome
You share in it; if not I'le backe againe,
Now I know your ends, for I come arm'd for all
Can be obiected.
    Louell.   How! the Lady *Alworth*!   245
    Ouerreach. And thus attended!
    Marrall.   No, I am a dolt;
        LOVELL *salutes the* LADY, *the* LADY *salutes* MARGARET.
            225. An] *Dodsley*; And *33*

The spirit of lyes had entred me.
  Ouerreach.   Peace Patch,
'Tis more than wonder! an astonishment
That does possesse me wholly!
  Louell.   Noble Lady,
This is a fauour, to preuent my visit,   250
The seruice of my life can neuer equall.
  Lady. My Lord, I lay'd waite for you, and much hop'd
You would haue made my poore house your first Inne:
And therefore doubting that you might forget me,
Or too long dwell here hauing such ample cause   255
In this vnequall'd beauty for your stay;
And fearing to trust any but my selfe
With the relation of my seruice to you,
I borrow'd so much from my long restraint,
And tooke the ayre in person to inuite you.   260
  Louell. Your bounties are so great they robbe me, Madam,
Of words to giue you thankes.
  Lady.   Good Sir *Giles Ouerreach.* *Salutes him.*
How doest thou *Marrall*? lik'd you my meate so ill,
You'le dine no more with me?
  Greedy.   I will when you please
And it like your Ladiship.
  Lady.   When you please master *Greedie*; 265
If meat can doe it, you shall be satisfied.
And now my Lord, pray take into your knowledge
This Gentleman; how e're his outside's course, *Presents*
His inward linings are as fine, and faire,   WELBORNE.
As any mans: wonder not I speake at large: 270
And howsoe're his humor carries him
To be thus accoutred; or what taint soeuer
For his wild life hath stucke vpon his fame,
He may e're long, with boldnesse, rancke himselfe
With some that haue contemn'd him. Sir *Giles Ouerreach*, 275
If I am welcome, bid him so.
  Ouerreach.   My nephew.
He has beene too long a stranger: faith you haue:
Pray let it bee mended.   LOVELL *conferring with* WELBORNE.
  Marrall.   Why Sir, what doe you meane?
This is rogue *Welborne*, Monster, Prodigie.

That should hang, or drowne himselfe, no man of Worship,   280
Much lesse your Nephew.
    Ouerreach.   Well Sirra, we shall reckon
For this hereafter.
    Marrall.   I'le not lose my ieere
Though I be beaten dead for't.
    Welborne.   Let my silence plead
In my excuse my Lord, till better leasure
Offer it selfe to heare a full relation   285
Of my poore fortunes.
    Louell.   I would heare, and helpe 'em.
    Ouerreach. Your dinner waites you.
    Louell.   Pray you lead, we follow.
    Lady. Nay you are my ghest, come deere master *Welborne.*
    Exeunt, manet GREEDY.
    Greedy. Deare master *Welborne*! So shee said; Heau'n! heau'n!
If my belly would giue me leaue I could ruminate   290
All day on this: I haue granted twenty warrants
To haue him committed, from all prisons in the Shire,
To Nottingham iayle; and now deare master *Welborne*!
And my good nephew! but I play the foole
To stand here prating, and forget my dinner.   295

    Enter MARRALL.

Are they set *Marrall*?
    Marrall.   Long since, pray you a word Sir.
    Greedy. No wording now.
    Marrall.   In troth, I must; my master
Knowing you are his good friend, makes bold with you,
And does intreat you, more ghests being come in,
Then he expected, especially his nephew,   300
The table being full too, you would excuse him
And suppe with him on the cold meate.
    Greedy.   How! no dinner
After all my care?
    Marrall.   'Tis but a pennance for
A meale; besides, you broke your fast.
    Greedy.   That was
But a bit to stay my stomacke: a man in Commission   305
Giue place to a tatterdemallion?

Marrall.   No bugge words Sir,
Should his Worship heare you—
    Greedy.   Lose my dumpling too?
And butter'd tosts, and woodcocks?
    Marrall.   Come, haue patience.
If you will dispense a little with your Worship,
And sit with the waiting woemen, you'll haue dumpling,   310
Woodcocke, and butter'd tosts too.
    Greedy.   This reuiues me,
I will gorge there sufficiently.
    Marrall.   This is the way Sir.   *Exeunt.*

Actus tertii, Scena tertia.

OVERREACH *as from dinner.*

Ouerreach. Shee's caught! O woemen! she neglects my Lord,
And all her complements appli'd to *Welborne*!
The garments of her widdowhood lay'd by,
She now appeares as glorious as the spring.
Her eyes fix'd on him; in the wine shee drinkes,   5
He being her pledge, she sends him burning kisses,
And sitts on thornes, till she be priuate with him.
She leaues my meate to feed vpon his lookes;
And if in our discourse he be but nam'd
From her a deepe sigh followes; but why grieue I   10
At this? it makes for me, if she proue his,
All that is hers is mine, as I will worke him.

Enter MARRALL.

    Marrall. Sir the whole boord is troubled at your rising.
    Ouerreach. No matter, I'le excuse it, prethee *Marrall*,
Watch an occasion to inuite my Nephew   15
To speake with me in priuate.
    Marrall.   Who? the rogue,
The Lady scorn'd to looke on?
    Ouerreach.   You are a Wagge.

    307. you—] *Dodsley;* ~? *33*   310. you'll] *Dodsley;* you *33*

Enter LADY *and* WELBORNE.

Marrall. See Sir shee's come, and cannot be without him.
Lady. With your fauour Sir, after a plenteous dinner,
I shall make bold to walke, a turne, or two
In your rare garden.
    Ouerreach.   There's an arbor too
If your Ladieship please to vse it.
    Lady.   Come master *Welborne.*
                Exeunt LADY *and* WELBORNE.
    Ouerreach. Grosser, and grosser, now I beleeue the Poet
Fain'd not but was historicall, when he wrot,
Pasiphae was enamour'd of a bull,
This Ladies lust's more monstrous.
        Enter LOVELL, MARGARET *and the rest.*
                My good Lord,
Excuse my manners.
    Louell.   There needes none Sir *Giles,*
I may ere long say Father, when it pleases
My dearest mistresse to giue warrant to it.
    Ouerreach. She shall seale to it my Lord, and make me happy.
    Margaret. My Lady is return'd.
        Enter WELBORNE *and the* LADY.
    Lady.   Prouide my coach,
I'le instantly away: my thanks Sir *Giles*
For my entertainment.
    Ouerreach.   'Tis your Noblenesse
To thinke it such.
    Lady.   I must doe you a further wrong
In taking away your honorable Ghest.
    Louell. I waite on you Madam, farwell good Sir *Giles.*
    Lady. Good mistresse *Margaret*: nay come master *Welborne,*
I must not leaue you behind, in sooth I must not.
    Ouerreach. Robbe me not Madam, of all ioyes at once;
Let my Nephew stay behind: he shall haue my coach,
(And after some small conference betweene vs)
Soone ouertake your Ladyship.
    Lady.   Stay not long Sir.
    Louell. This parting kisse: you shall euery day heare from me
By my faithfull page.

Alworth. 'Tis a seruice I am proud of.
                    Exeunt LOVELL, LADY, ALWORTH, MARRALL.
  Ouerreach. Daughter to your chamber. You may wonder Nephew,
After so long an enmity betweene vs   [*Exit* MARGARET.]
I should desire your friendship?
  Welborne.   So I doe Sir.
'Tis strange to me.
  Ouerreach.   But I'le make it no wonder,
And what is more vnfold my nature to you.
We worldly men, when wee see friends, and kinsmen,   50
Past hope suncke in their fortunes, lend no hand
To lift 'em vp, but rather set our feet
Vpon their heads, to presse 'em to the bottome;
As I must yeeld, with you I practis'd it.
But now I see you in a way to rise,   55
I can and will assist you, this rich Lady
(And I am glad of't) is enamour'd of you;
'Tis too apparent Nephew.
  Welborne.   No such thing:
Compassion rather Sir.
  Ouerreach.   Well in a word,
Because your stay is short, I'le haue you seene   60
No more in this base shape; nor shall shee say
She married you like a begger, or in debt.
  Welborne. Hee'le run into the noose, and saue my labour. *Aside.*
  Ouerreach. You haue a trunke of rich clothes, not far hence
In pawne, I will redeeme 'em, and that no clamor   65
May taint your credit for your petty debts,
You shall haue a thousand pounds to cut 'em off,
And goe a freeman to the wealthy Lady.
  Welborne. This done Sir out of loue, and no ends else—
  Ouerreach. As it is Nephew.
  Welborne.   Bindes me still your seruant.   70
  Ouerreach. No complements; you are stay'd for; e're y'aue supp'd
You shall heare from me, my coach Knaues for my Nephew:
To morrow I will visit you.
  Welborne.   Heer's an Vncle

III. iii. 44 SD. ALWORTH, MARRALL.] *after* Gifford; *Alworth. Margaret. Marrall.* 33
46 SD. *Exit* MARGARET.] *Gifford; not in* 33   47. *Welborne.*] *after Dodsley;* Well: 33
70. me] *Dodsley;* my 33

In a mans extreames! how much they doe belye you
That say you are hard-harted.
 Ouerreach.   My deeds nephew 75
Shall speake my loue, what men report, I waigh not. *Exeunt.*

Finis Actus tertii.

Actus quarti, Scena prima.

LOVELL. ALWORTH.

 Louell. 'T IS well: giue me my cloke: I now discharge you
From further seruice. Minde your owne affaires,
I hope they will proue successefull.
 Alworth.   What is blest
With your good wish my Lord, cannot but prosper.
Let after-times report, and to your Honor, 5
How much I stand engag'd, for I want language
To speake my debt: yet if a teare, or two
Of ioy for your much goodnesse, can supply
My tongues defects I could—
 Louell.   Nay, doe not melt:
This ceremoniall thankes to mee's superfluous. 10
 Ouerreach within. Is my Lord stirring?
 Louell. 'Tis he, oh here's your letter: let him in.

Enter OVERREACH, GREEDY, MARRALL.

 Ouerreach. A good day to my Lord.
 Louell.   You are an early riser,
Sir *Giles.*
 Ouerreach. And reason to attend your Lordship.
 Louell. And you too master *Greedie*, vp so soone? 15
 Greedy. In troth my Lord after the Sun is vp
I cannot sleep, for I haue a foolish stomacke
That croakes for breakefast. With your Lordships fauour,
I haue a serious question to demand
Of my worthy friend Sir *Giles.*
 Louell.   Pray you vse your pleasure. 20
 Greedy. How far Sir *Giles*, and pray you answer me
Vpon your credit, hold you it to be

From your Mannor house, to this of my Lady *Alworths*?
   Ouerreach. Why some foure mile.
   Greedy.   How! foure mile? good Sir *Giles*.
Vpon your reputation thinke better,   25
For if you doe abate but one halfe quarter
Of fiue you doe your selfe the greatest wrong
That can be in the world: for foure miles riding
Could not haue rais'd so huge an appetite
As I feele gnawing on me.
   Marrall.   Whither you ride,   30
Or goe a foote, you are that way still prouided
And it please your Worship.
   Ouerreach.   How now Sirra? prating
Before my Lord: no difference? go to my Nephew;
See all his debts discharg'd, and help his Worship
To fit on his rich suite.
   Marrall.   I may fit you too;   35
Toss'd like a dogge still.   *Exit* MARRALL.
   Louell.   I haue writt this morning
A few lines to my mistresse your faire daughter.
   Ouerreach. 'Twill fire her, for shee's wholy yours already:
Sweet master *Alworth*, take my ring, 'twill carry you
To her presence I dare warrant you, and there pleade   40
For my good Lord, if you shall find occasion.
That done, pray ride to *Nottingham*, get a licence,
Still by this token, I'le haue it dispatch'd,
And suddainely my Lord, that I may say
My honorable, nay, right honorable daughter.   45
   Greedy. Take my aduice young Gentleman: get your breakefast.
'Tis vnholsome to ride fasting, I'le eate with you
And eate to purpose.
   Ouerreach.   Some Furies in that gut:
Hungry againe! did you not deuoure this morning,
A shield of Brawne, and a barrell of *Colchester* oysters?   50
   Greedy. Why that was Sir, only to scoure my stomacke,
A kind of a preparatiue. Come Gentleman,
I will not haue you feed like the Hangman of *Vllushing*
Alone, while I am here.
   Louell.   Hast your returne.

    IV. i. 33. no difference?] *33*; No deference? *Mason*; no difference! *Gifford*

Alworth. I will not faile my Lord.
Greedy.   Nor I to line
My Christmas coffer.   *Exeunt* GREEDY *and* ALWORTH.
  Ouerreach.   To my wish, we are priuate.
I come not to make offer with my daughter
A certaine portion, that were poore, and triuiall:
In one word I pronounce all that is mine,
In lands, or leases, ready coine, or goods,
With her, my Lord comes to you; nor shall you haue
One motiue to induce you to beleeue,
I liue too long, since euery yeare I'le add
Something vnto the heape, which shall be yours too.
  Louell. You are a right kind father.
  Ouerreach.   You shall haue reason
To thinke me such; how doe you like this seate?
It is well wooded, and well water'd, the Acres
Fertile, and rich; would it not serue for change
To entertaine your friends in a Sommer progresse?
What thinkes my noble Lord?
  Louell.   'Tis a wholesome aire,
And well built pile, and she that's mistresse of it
Worthy the large reuennue.
  Ouerreach.   Shee the mistresse?
It may be so for a time: but let my Lord
Say only that he likes it, and would haue it,
I say ere long 'tis his.
  Louell.   Impossible.
  Ouerreach. You doe conclude too fast, not knowing me,
Nor the engines that I worke by; 'tis not alone
The Lady *Alworths* Lands, for those once *Welbornes*,
(As by her dotage on him, I know they will be,)
Shall soone be mine, but point out any mans
In all the Shire, and say they lie conuenient,
And vsefull for your Lordship, and once more
I say aloud, They are yours.
  Louell.   I dare not owne
What's by vniust, and cruell meanes extorted:
My fame, and credit are more deare to me,
Than so to expose 'em to be censur'd by
The publike voice.

Ouerreach. You run my Lord no hazard.
Your reputation shall stand as faire
In all good mens opinions as now:
Nor can my actions, though condemn'd for ill,
Cast any foule aspersion vpon yours;
For though I doe contemne report my selfe,
As a meere sound, I still will be so tender
Of what concernes you in all points of Honour,
That the immaculate whitenesse of your Fame,
Nor your vnquestion'd integrity
Shall e're be sullied with one taint, or spot
That may take from your innocence, and candor.
All my ambition is to haue my daughter
Right honorable, which my Lord can make her.
And might I liue to dance vpon my knee
A young Lord *Louell*, borne by her vnto you,
I write *nil vltra* to my proudest hopes.
As for possessions, and annuall rents
Equiualent to maintaine you in the port,
Your noble birth, and present state requires,
I doe remoue that burthen from your shoulders,
And take it on mine owne: for though I ruine
The Country to supply your riotous wast,
The scourge of prodigalls, want, shall neuer find you.
   Louell. Are you not frighted with the imprecations,
And curses, of whole families made wretched
By your sinister practises?
   Ouerreach. Yes as rocks are
When foamie billowes split themselues against
Their flinty ribbes; or as the Moone is mou'd,
When wolues with hunger pin'd, howle at her brightnesse.
I am of a solid temper, and like these
Steere on a constant course: with mine owne sword
If call'd into the field, I can make that right,
Which fearefull enemies murmur'd at as wrong.
Now, for these other pidling complaints
Breath'd out in bitternesse, as when they call me
Extortioner, Tyrant, Cormorant, or Intruder
On my poore Neighbours right, or grand incloser
Of what was common, to my priuate vse;

Nay, when my eares are pierc'd with Widdowes cries,
And vndon Orphants wash with teares my threshold;
I only thinke what 'tis to haue my daughter
Right honorable; and 'tis a powerfull charme
Makes me insensible of remorse, or pitty,   130
Or the least sting of Conscience.
    Louell.   I admire
The toughnesse of your nature.
    Ouerreach.   'Tis for you
My Lord, and for my daughter, I am marble;
Nay more, more, if you will haue my character
In little, I enioy more true delight   135
In my arriuall to my wealth, these darke,
And crooked wayes, than you shall e're take pleasure
In spending what my industry hath compass'd.
My hast commands me hence, In one word therefore
Is it a Match?
    Louell.   I hope that is past doubt now.   140
    Ouerreach. Then rest secure, not the hate of all mankind here;
Nor feare of what can fall on me hereafter,
Shall make me studie ought but your aduancement,
One story higher. An Earle! if gold can do it.
Dispute not my religion, nor my faith,   145
Though I am borne thus headlong by my will;
You may make choice of what beleefe you please,
To me they are equall, so my Lord good morrow.   *Exit.*
    Louell. Hee's gone, I wonder how the Earth can beare
Such a portent! I, that haue liu'd a Souldier,   150
And stood the enemies violent charge vndaunted,
To heare this blasphemous beast, am bath'd all ouer
In a cold sweat: yet like a mountaine he,
Confirm'd in Atheisticall assertions,
Is no more shaken, than *Olimpus* is   155
When angry *Boreas* loades his double head
With suddaine drifts of snow.

               Enter AMBLE, LADY, WOMAN.
    Lady.   Saue you my Lord.
Disturbe I not your priuacie?

126. eares] *Dodsley*; cares *33*   134. more, more,] *editor*; more more *33*; more, *Dodsley*

Louell. No good Madam;
For your owne sake I am glad you came no sooner.
Since this bold, bad man, Sir *Giles Ouerreach*
Made such a plaine discouerie of himselfe,
And read this morning such a diuellish Matins,
That I should thinke it a sinne next to his,
But to repeat it.
   Lady. I ne're press'd my Lord
On others priuacies, yet against my will,
Walking, for health sake, in the gallerie
Adioyning to your lodgings, I was made
(So vehement, and loud he was) partaker
Of his tempting offers.
   Louell. Please you to command
Your seruants hence, and I shall gladly heare
Your wiser counsell.
   Lady. 'Tis my Lord a womans,
But true, and hearty; wait in the next roome,
But be within call: yet not so neere to force me
To whisper my intents.
   Amble. We are taught better
By you good Madam.
   Woman. And well know our distance.
   Lady. Doe so, and talke not, 'twill become your breeding.
                               Exeunt AMBLE *and* WOMAN.
Now my good Lord; if I may vse my freedome,
As to an honour'd friend?
   Louell. You lessen else
Your fauour to me.
   Lady. I dare then say thus;
As you are Noble (how e're common men
Make sordid wealth the obiect, and sole end
Of their industrious aimes) 'twill not agree
With those of eminent blood (who are ingag'd
More to prefer their Honours, than to increase
The State left to 'em, by their Ancestours)
To study large additions to their fortunes
And quite neglect their births: though I must grant
Riches well got to be a vsefull Seruant,

           169. *Louell.*] *Dodsley*; *Lad.* 33

But a bad Master.
  Louell.   Madam, 'tis confessed;
But what infer you from it?
  Lady.   This my Lord;
That as all wrongs, though thrust into one scale
Slide of themselues off, when right fills the other,
And cannot bide the triall: so all wealth
(I meane if ill acquir'd) cemented to Honor
By vertuous wayes atchieu'd, and brauely purchas'd,
Is but as rubbage powr'd into a riuer
(How e're intended to make good the bancke)
Rendring the water that was pure before,
Polluted, and vnholsome. I allow
The heire of Sir *Giles Ouerreach, Margaret,*
A maide well qualified, and the richest match
Our North part can make boast of, yet she cannot
With all that she brings with her fill their mouthes,
That neuer will forget who was her father;
Or that my husband *Alworths* lands, and *Welbornes*
(How wrunge from both needs now no repetition)
Were reall motiues, that more work'd your Lordship
To ioyne your families, than her forme, and vertues.
You may conceaue the rest.
  Louell.   I doe sweet Madam;
And long since haue consider'd it. I know
The summe of all that makes a iust man happy
Consists in the well choosing of his wife,
And there well to discharge it, does require
Equality of yeares, of birth, of fortune,
For beauty being poore, and not cried vp
By birth or wealth, can truely mixe with neither.
And wealth, where there's such difference in yeares,
And faire descent, must make the yoke vneasie:
But I come neerer.
  Lady.   Pray you doe my Lord.
  Louell. Were *Ouerreach*' states thrice centupl'd; his daughter
Millions of degrees, much fairer than she is,
(How e're I might vrge presidents to excuse me)

---

207. motiues] *Dodsley*; motiue *33*   220. *Ouerreach*' states] *Gifford*; *Ouerreach,* stat's *33*

I would not so adulterate my blood
By marrying *Margaret*, and so leaue my issue
Made vp of seuerall peeces, one part skarlet   225
And the other *London*-blew. In my owne tombe
I will interre my name first.
    Lady.   I am glad to heare this: *Aside.*
Why then my Lord pretend you marriage to her?
Dissimulation but tyes false knots
On that straite line, by which you hitherto   230
Haue measur'd all your actions.
    Louell.   I make answer
And aptly, with a question. Wherefore haue you,
That since your Husbands death, haue liu'd a strict,
And chaste *Nuns* life, on the suddaine giu'n your selfe
To visits, and entertainments? thinke you Madam   235
'Tis not growne publike conference? or the fauours
Which you too prodigally haue throwne on *Welborne*,
Being too reseru'd before, incurre not censure?
    Lady. I am innocent heere, and on my life I sweare
My ends are good.
    Louell.   On my soule so are mine   240
To *Margaret*: but leaue both to the euent;
And since this friendly priuacie does serue
But as an offer'd meanes vnto our selues
To search each other farther; you hauing showne
Your care of mee, I, my respect to you;   245
Denie me not, but still in chaste words Madam
An after-noones discourse.
    Lady.   So I shall heare you.   [*Exeunt.*]

[IV. ii]   *Actus quarti, Scena secunda.*

TAPWELL. FROTH.

  Tapwell. Vndone, vndone! this was your counsaile, *Froth*.
  Froth. Mine! I defie thee, did not master *Marrall*
(He has marr'd all I am sure) strictly command vs
(On paine of Sir *Giles Ouerreach* displeasure)
To turne the Gentleman out of dores?

    236. growne] *Dodsley*; growge 33   247. Exeunt.] *Dodsley*; *not in* 33

Tapwell. 'Tis true,
But now hee's his Vncles darling, and has got
Master *Iustice Greedy* (since he fill'd his belly)
At his commandement, to doe any thing;
Woe, woe to vs.
 Froth. He may proue mercifull.
 Tapwell. Troth, we do not deserue it at his hands:
Though he knew all the passages of our house,
As the receiuing of stolne goods, and bawdrie,
When he was rogue *Welborne*, no man would beleeue him,
And then his information could not hurt vs.
But now he is right Worshipfull againe,
Who dares but doubt his testimonie? me thinkes
I see thee *Froth* already in a cart
For a close Bawde, thine eyes eu'n pelted out
With durt, and rotten egges, and my hand hissing
(If I scape the halter) with the letter *R*.
Printed vpon it.
 Froth. Would that were the worst:
That were but nine dayes wonder, as for credit
We haue none to lose; but we shall lose the money
He owes vs and his custome, there's the hell on't.
 Tapwell. He has summon'd all his Creditours by the drum,
And they swarme about him like so many souldiers
On the pay day, and has found out such a new way
To pay his old debts, as 'tis very likely
He shall be chronicl'd for it.
 Froth. He deserues it
More than ten Pageants. But are you sure his Worship
Comes this way to my Ladies?
    A cry within, Braue Master Welborne.
 Tapwell. Yes I heare him.
 Froth. Be ready with your petition and present it
To his good Grace.

  Enter WELBORNE *in a rich habit,* GREEDY, [MARRALL,]
  ORDER, FURNACE, *three* CREDITORS. TAPWELL *kneeling
    deliuers his bill of debt.*

 Welborne. How's this! petition'd too?
  IV. ii. 33 SD. MARRALL] *Gifford; not in* 33

But note what miracles, the payment of
A little trash, and a rich suite of clothes
Can worke vpon these Rascalls. I shall be
I thinke prince *Welborne.*
    Marrall. When your Worships married
You may be, I know what I hope to see you.
    Welborne. Then looke thou for aduancement.
    Marrall. To be knowne
Your Worships Bayliffe is the marke I shoot at.
    Welborne. And thou shalt hit it.
    Marrall. Pray you Sir dispatch
These needie followers, and for my admittance
Prouided you'l defend   *This interim,* TAPWELL *and* FROTH
  me from Sir *Giles,*   *flattering and bribing Iustice* GREEDY.
Whose seruice I am weary of, I'le say something
You shall giue thankes for.
    Welborne. Feare me not Sir *Giles.*
    Greedy. Who? *Tapwell?* I remember thy wife brought me
Last new yeares tide, a couple of fat turkies.
    Tapwell. And shall doe euery Christmas, let your Worship
But stand my friend now.
    Greedy. How? with master *Welborne?*
I can doe any thing with him, on such termes;
See you this honest couple: they are good soules
As euer drew out fosset, haue they not
A payre of honest faces?
    Welborne. I o're heard you,
And the bribe he promis'd, you are cousend in 'em,
For of all the scumme that grew rich by my riots
This for a most vnthankefull knaue, and this
For a base bawde, and whore, haue worst deseru'd me,
And therefore speake not for 'em, by your place
You are rather to do me iustice; lend me your eare,
Forget his Turkies, and call in his Licence,
And at the next Faire, I'le giue you a yoke of Oxen
Worth all his Poultry.
    Greedy. I am chang'd on the suddaine
In my opinion! come neere; neerer Rascall.
And now I view him better; did you e're see
One looke so like an arch-knaue? his very countenance,

Should an vnderstanding iudge but looke vpon him,
Would hang him, though he were innocent.
   Tapwell, Froth.   Worshipfull Sir.
   Greedy. No though the great Turke came insteed of Turkies,
To begge my fauour, I am inexorable:
Thou hast an ill name: besides thy musty Ale   70
That hath destroy'd many of the Kings leige people
Thou neuer hadst in thy house to stay mens stomackes
A peece of *Suffolke* cheese, or Gammon of Bacon,
Or any esculent, as the learned call it,
For their emolument, but sheere drinke only.   75
For which grosse fault, I heere doe damne thy licence,
Forbidding thee euer to tap, or draw.
For instantly, I will in mine owne person
Command the Constable to pull downe thy Signe;
And doe it before I eate.
   Froth.   No mercie?
   Greedy.   Vanish.   80
If I shew any, may my promis'd Oxen gore me.
   Tapwell. Vnthankefull knaues are euer so rewarded.
                         Exeunt GREEDY, TAPWELL, FROTH.
   Welborne. Speake; what are you?
   1. *Creditor.*   A decay'd Vintner Sir,
That might haue thriued but that your worship broke me
With trusting you with Muskadine and Egges,   85
And fiue pound Suppers, with your after drinkings,
When you lodg'd vpon the *Banckside*.
   Welborne.   I remember.
   1. *Creditor.* I haue not beene hasty, nor e're layd to arrest you.
And therefore Sir—
   Welborne.   Thou art an honest fellow:
I'le set thee vp againe, see his bill pay'd.   90
What are you?
   2. *Creditor.*   A Taylor once, but now meere Botcher.
I gaue you credit for a suite of clothes,
Which was all my stocke, but you failing in payment,
I was remou'd from the Shop-boord, and confin'd
Vnder a Stall.
   Welborne.   See him pay'd, and botch no more.   95

     69. my] *Dodsley*; any 33   87. I remember] *Dodsley*; Remember 33

2. *Creditor.* I aske no interest Sir.
 Welborne.   Such Taylors need not,
If their bills are pay'd in one and twenty yeare
They are seldome losers. O, I know thy face,
Thou were't my Surgeon: you must tell no tales.
Those dayes are done. I will pay you in priuate.
 Order. A royall Gentleman.
 Furnace.   Royall as an Emperour!
He'le proue a braue master, my good *Lady* knew
To choose a man.
 Welborne. See all men else discharg'd,
And since *Old debts are clear'd by a new way*,
A little bountie, will not misbecome mee;
There's something honest Cooke for thy good breakefasts,
And this for your respect, take't, 'tis good gold
And I able to spare it.
 Order.   You are too munificent.
 Furnace. Hee was euer so.
 Welborne.   Pray you on before.
 3. *Creditor.*   Heauen blesse you.
 Marrall. At foure a clocke the rest know where to meet me.
       Exeunt ORDER, FURNACE, CREDITORS.
 Welborne. Now master *Marrall*, what's the weightie secret
You promis'd to impart?
 Marrall.   Sir, time, nor place
Allow me to relate each circumstance;
This only in a word: I know Sir *Giles*
Will come vpon you for security
For his thousand pounds, which you must not consent to.
As he growes in heat, as I am sure hee will,
Be you but rough, and say Hee's in your debt
Ten times the summe, vpon sale of your land;
I had a hand in't (I speake it to my shame)
When you were defeated of it.
 Welborne.   That's forgiuen.
 Marrall. I shall deserue't; then vrge him to produce
The deed in which you pass'd it ouer to him,
Which I know Hee'le haue about him to deliuer

---

110 SD. *Exeunt* ... CREDITORS.] *Dodsley; Exeunt Ord. Furn. | Furn. Credit. 33*
122 deserue't; then] *Gifford;* ~∧ ~; 33

To the Lord *Louell*, with many other writings,   125
And present moneys; I'le instruct you further,
As I waite on your Worship; if I play not my price
To your full content, and your Vncles much vexation,
Hang vp *Jacke Marrall*.
   Welborne.   I relie vpon thee.   *Exeunt.*

Actus quarti, Scena vltima.

ALWORTH. MARGARET.

   Alworth. Whither to yeeld the first praise to my Lord's
Vnequall'd temperance, or your constant sweetnesse,
That I yet liue, my weake hands fasten'd on
Hopes anchor, spite of all stormes of Despaire,
I yet rest doubtfull.
   Margaret.   Giue it to Lord *Louell.*   5
For what in him was bounty, in mee's duty.
I make but payment of a debt, to which
My vowes in that high office registred,
Are faithfull witnesses.
   Alworth.   'Tis true my dearest,
Yet when I call to mind how many faire ones   10
Make wilfull shipwracke of their faiths, and oathes
To God, and Man, to fill the armes of Greatnesse,
And you rise vp no lesse than a glorious starre
To the amazement of the world, that hold out
Against the sterne authority of a Father,   15
And spurne at honour when it comes to court you,
I am so tender of your good, that faintly
With your wrong I can wish my selfe that right
You yet are pleas'd to do mee.
   Margaret.   Yet, and euer.
To me what's title, when content is wanting?   20
Or wealth rak'd vp together with much care,
And to be kept with more, when the heart pines,
In being dispossest of what it longs for,
Beyond the Indian mines; or the smooth brow

   IV. iii. 13. And you rise vp no lesse] *Gifford, after Dodsley*; And you, rise vp lesse *33*; Can you rise vp lesse *conj. McIlwraith*

Of a pleas'd Sire, that slaues me to his will? 25
And so his rauenous humour may bee feasted
By my obedience, and he see me great,
Leaues to my soule nor faculties, nor power
To make her owne election.
 Alworth.   But the dangers
That follow the repulse.
 Margaret.   To me they are nothing: 30
Let *Alworth* loue, I cannot be vnhappy.
Suppose the worst, that in his rage he kill me;
A teare, or two, by you dropt on my hearse
In sorrow for my fate, will call backe life
So far, as but to say that I die yours, 35
I then shall rest in peace; or should he proue
So cruell, as one death would not suffize
His thirst of vengeance, but with lingring torments
In mind, and body, I must wast to ayre,
In pouerty, ioyn'd with banishment, so you share 40
In my afflictions, (which I dare not wish you,
So high I prize you) I could vndergoe 'em,
With such a patience as should looke downe
With scorne on his worst malice.
 Alworth.   Heauen auert
Such trialls of your true affection to me, 45
Nor will it vnto you that are all mercie
Shew so much rigour: but since wee must run
Such desperate hazards, let vs doe our best
To steere betweene 'em.
 Margaret.   Your Lord's ours, and sure,
And though but a young actor second me 50
In doing to the life, what he has plotted,

    Enter OVERREACH.

The end may yet proue happy: now my *Alworth*.
 Alworth. To your letter, and put on a seeming anger.
 Margaret. I'le pay my Lord all debts due to his title,
And when with termes, not taking from his Honour, 55
He does sollicite me, I shall gladly heare him.
But in this peremptory, nay commanding way,
T'appoint a meeting, and without my knowledge,

A Priest to tye the knot, can ne're be vndone
'Till death vnloose it, is a confidence   60
In his Lordship, will deceiue him.
    Alworth.   I hope better,
Good Lady.
    Margaret. Hope Sir what you please: for me
I must take a safe and secure course; I haue
A father, and without his full consent,
Though all Lords of the land kneel'd for my fauour, 65
I can grant nothing.
    Ouerreach.   I like this obedience.
But whatsoeuer my Lord writes, must, and shall bee
Accepted, and embrac'd. Sweet master *Alworth*,
You shew your selfe a true, and faithfull seruant
To your good Lord, he has a iewell of you.   70
How? frowning *Meg*? are these lookes to receiue
A messenger from my Lord? what's this? giue me it.
    Margaret. A peece of arrogant paper like th'inscriptions.
                            OVERREACH *read the letter.*
    Ouerreach. Faire mistrisse from your seruant learne, all ioyes
That we can hope for, if deferr'd, proue toyes; 75
Therefore this instant, and in priuate meete
A Husband, that will gladly at your feet
Lay downe his Honours, tendring them to you
With all content, the Church being payd her due.
Is this the arrogant peece of paper? Foole,   80
Will you still be one? in the name of madnesse, what
Could his good Honour write more to content you?
Is there ought else to be wisht after these two,
That are already offer'd? Marriage first,
And lawfull pleasure after: what would you more? 85
    Margaret. Why Sir, I would be married like your daughter;
Nor hurried away i'th night I know not whither,
Without all ceremonie: no friends inuited
To honour the sollemnity.
    Alworth.   An't please your Honour,
For so before to morrow I must stile you,   90
My Lord desires this priuacie in respect
His honourable kinsmen are far off,

                1. desires] *Dodsley*; desire *33*

And his desires to haue it done brooke not
So long delay as to expect their comming;
And yet He stands resolu'd, with all due pompe,   95
As running at the ring, playes, masques, and tilting,
To haue his marriage at Court celebrated
When he has brought your Honour vp to *London*.
   Ouerreach. He tells you true; 'tis the fashion on my knowledge,
Yet the good Lord to please your peeuishnes   100
Must put it off forsooth, and lose a night
In which perhaps he might get two boyes on thee.
Tempt me no farther, if you do, this goad
Shall pricke you to him.
   Margaret.   I could be contented,
Were you but by to do a fathers part,   105
And giue me in the Church.
   Ouerreach.   So my Lord haue you
What do I care who giues you? Since my Lord
Does purpose to be priuate, I'le not crosse him.
I know not master *Alworth* how my Lord
May be prouided, and therefore there's a purse   110
Of gold, 'twill serue this nights expence, to morrow
I'le furnish him with any summes: in the meane time
Vse my ring to my Chaplaine; he is benefic'd
At my Mannor of *Gotam*, and call'd parson *Will-doe*.
'Tis no matter for a licence, I'le beare him out in't.   115
   Margaret. With your fauour Sir, what warrant is your ring?
He may suppose I got that twenty wayes
Without your knowledge, and then to be refus'd,
Were such a staine vpon me; if you pleas'd Sir
Your presence would do better.
   Ouerreach.   Still peruerse?   120
I say againe I will not crosse my Lord,
Yet I'le preuent you too. Paper and incke there?
   Alworth. I can furnish you.
   Ouerreach.   I thanke you, I can write then.
                                          Writes on his booke.
   Alworth. You may if you please, put out the name of my Lord,
In respect he comes disguis'd, and only write,   125
Marry her to this Gentleman.

        103. goad] *Dodsley*; good 33   107. you?] *Dodsley*; ∼∧ 33

Ouerreach.   Well aduis'd,   MARGARET *kneeles.*
'Tis done, away! my blessing Girle? thou hast it.
Nay, no reply, begone, good master *Alworth*,
This shall be the best nights worke, you euer made.
   Alworth. I hope so Sir.   *Exeunt* ALWORTH *and* MARGARET.
   Ouerreach.   Farewell; now all's cocke-sure: 130
Me thinkes I heare already, Knights, and Ladies,
Say Sir *Giles Ouerreach*, how is it with
Your Honourable daughter? has her Honour
Slept well to night? or will her Honour please
To accept this Monkey? Dog? or Paraquit?   135
(This is state in Ladies) or my eldest sonne
To be her page, and wait vpon her trencher?
My ends! my ends are compass'd! then for *Welborne*
And the lands; were he once married to the widdow,
I haue him here, I can scarce containe my selfe,   140
I am so full of ioy; nay ioy all ouer.   *Exit.*

        The end of the fourth Act.

Actus quinti, Scena prima.

LOVELL. LADY. AMBLE.

   Lady. BY this you know, how strong the motiues were
That did, my Lord, induce me to dispence
A little with my grauity, to aduance
(In personating some few fauours to him)
The plots, and proiects of the downe-trod *Welborne.*   5
Nor shall I e're repent (although I suffer
In some few mens opinions for't) the action.
For he, that ventur'd all for my deare Husband,
Might iustly claime an obligation from me
To pay him such a courtesie: which had I   10
Coiley, or ouer-curiously denied,
It might haue argu'd me of little loue
To the deceas'd.

---

136. (This ... Ladies)] *Dodsley*; ⁓ This ... Ladies. 33   141 SD. *Exit.* / *The*
end ... *Act.*] *Coxeter*; *Exit the end of the fourth* / *Act.* 33   V. i. *prima*] *Coxeter*
(Scene I.); *quinta* 33

Louell. What you intended Madam
For the poore Gentleman, hath found good successe,
For as I vnderstand, his debts are pay'd,
And he once more furnish'd for faire imployment.
But all the arts that I haue vs'd to raise
The fortunes of your ioy, and mine, young *Alworth*,
Stand yet in supposition; though I hope well,
For the young louers are in wit more pregnant,
Than their yeares can promise; and for their desires,
On my knowledge they are equall.
 Lady.   As my wishes
Are with yours my Lord, yet giue me leaue to feare
The building, though well grounded: to deceiue
Sir *Giles*, that's both a Lyon, and a Fox
In his proceedings, were a worke beyond
The strongest vndertakers, not the triall
Of two weake innocents.
 Louell.   Despaire not Madam:
Hard things are compass'd oft by easie meanes,
And iudgement, being a gift deriu'd from heauen,
Though sometimes lodg'd i'th hearts of worldly men
(That ne're consider from whom they receiue it)
Forsakes such as abuse the giuer of it.
Which is the reason, that the politicke,
And cunning Statesman, that beleeues he fathomes
The counsels of all Kingdomes on the earth
Is by simplicity oft ouerreach'd.
 Lady. May he be so, yet in his name to expresse it
Is a good Omen.
 Louell.   May it to my selfe
Proue so good Lady in my suite to you:
What thinke you of the motion?
 Lady.   Troth my Lord
My owne vnworthinesse may answer for me;
For had you, when that I was in my prime,
My virgin-flower vncropp'd, presented me
With this great fauour, looking on my lownesse
Not in a glasse of selfe-loue, but of truth,
I could not but haue thought it, as a blessing

37. ouerreach'd] *Dodsley*; ouerreach 33

Far, far beyond my merit.
  Louell.   You are too modest,
And vnderualue that which is aboue
My title, or what euer I call mine.   50
I grant, were I a *Spaniard* to marry
A widdow might disparage me, but being
A true-borne *Englishman*, I cannot find
How it can taint my Honour; nay what's more,
That which you thinke a blemish is to me   55
The fairest lustre. You alreadie Madam
Haue giuen sure proofes how dearely you can cherish
A Husband that deserues you: which confirmes me,
That if I am not wanting in my care
To doe you seruice, you'le be still the same   60
That you were to your *Alworth*; in a word
Our yeares, our states, our births are not vnequall,
You being descended nobly and alli'd so;
If then you may be wonne to make me happy,
But ioyne your lipps to mine, and that shall be   65
A solemne contract.
  Lady.   I were blind to my owne good
Should I refuse it, yet my Lord receiue me
As such a one, the studie of whose whole life
Shall know no other obiect but to please you.
  Louell. If I returne not with all tendernesse,   70
Equall respect to you, may I die wretched.
  Lady. There needs no protestation my Lord
To her that cannot doubt,

       Enter WELBORNE.

        you are welcome Sir.
Now you looke like your selfe.
  Welborne.   And will continue
Such in my free acknowledgement, that I am   75
Your creature Madam, and will neuer hold
My life mine owne, when you please to command it.
  Louell. It is a thankefulnesse that well becomes you;
You could not make choice of a better shape,
To dresse your mind in.
  Lady.   For me I am happy   80

That my endeuours prosper'd; saw you of late
Sir *Giles*, your Vncle?
    Welborne. I heard of him, Madam,
By his minister *Marrall*, he's growne into strange passions
About his daughter, this last night he look'd for
Your Lordship at his house, but missing you,   85
And she not yet appearing, his wise-head
Is much perplex'd, and troubl'd.
    Louell. It may be
Sweet heart, my proiect tooke.
    Lady. I strongly hope.

    Enter OVERREACH *with distracted lookes,*
    driuing in MARRALL *before him.*

    Ouerreach. Ha! find her Boobie, thou huge lumpe of nothing,
I'le bore thine eyes out else.
    Welborne. May it please your Lordship   90
For some ends of mine owne but to withdraw
A little out of sight, though not of hearing,
You may perhaps haue sport.
    Louell. You shall direct me.   *Stepps aside.*
    Ouerreach. I shall sol fa you Rogue.
    Marrall. Sir, for what cause
Doe you vse me thus?
    Ouerreach. Cause slaue? why I am angrie,   95
And thou a subiect only fit for beating,
And so to coole my choler; looke to the writing,
Let but the seale be broke vpon the box,
That has slepp'd in my cabinet these three yeares,
I'le racke thy soule for't.
    Marrall. I may yet crie quittance,   100
Though now I suffer, and dare not resist.   *Aside.*
    Ouerreach. Lady, by your leaue, did you see my Daughter Lady?
And the Lord her husband? Are they in your house?
If they are, discouer, that I may bid 'em ioy;
And as an entrance to her place of Honour,   105
Set your Ladyship on her left hand, and make coursies
When she nodds on you; which you must receiue
As a speciall fauour.

    106. Set] *editor*; See *33*   coursies] *editor*; courseis *33*; cour'tsies *Dodsley*

Lady. When I know, Sir *Giles*,
Her state requires such ceremony, I shall pay it,
But in the meane time, as I am my selfe,
I giue you to vnderstand, I neither know,
Nor care where her Honour is.
    Ouerreach. When you once see her
Supported, and led by the Lord her Husband,
You'le be taught better. Nephew.
    Welborne. Sir.
    Ouerreach. No more?
    Welborne. 'Tis all I owe you.
    Ouerreach. Haue your redeem'd ragges
Made you thus insolent?
    Welborne. Insolent to you? *In scorne.*
Why what are you Sir, vnlesse in your yeares,
At the best, more than my selfe?
    Ouerreach. His fortune swells him,
'Tis rancke he's married.
    Lady. This is excellent!
    Ouerreach. Sir, in calme language (though I seldome vse it)
I am familiar with the cause, that makes you
Beare vp thus brauely, there's a certaine buz
Of a stolne marriage, do you heare? of a stolne marriage,
In which 'tis said there's some body hath beene coozin'd.
I name no parties.
    Welborne. Well Sir, and what followes?
    Ouerreach. Marry this; since you are peremptory: remember,
Vpon meere hope of your great match, I lent you
A thousand pounds: put me in good security,
And suddainely, by *Mortgage*, or by *Statute*
Of some of your new possessions, or I'le haue you
Dragg'd in your lauender robes to the Gaole, you know me,
And therefore do not trifle.
    Welborne. Can you be
So cruell to your Nephew, now hee's in
The way to rise? was this the courtesie
You did me in pure loue, and no ends else?
    Ouerreach. End me no ends: ingage the whole estate,

---

115. *Ouerreach.*] Dodsley; *Welb.* 33   123. heare? of a stolne marriage,] Dodsley; heare of a stolne marriage? 33   129. by *Mortgage*] Dodsley; my ~ 33

And force your Spouse to signe it, you shall haue
Three, or foure thousand more to rore, and swagger,
And reuell in bawdy tauernes.
 Welborne.   And begge after:
Meane you not so?
 Ouerreach.   My thoughts are mine, and free.
Shall I haue security?
 Welborne.   No: indeed you shall not:
Nor bond, nor bill, nor bare acknowledgement,
Your great looks fright not me.
 Ouerreach.   But my deeds shall:
Outbrau'd?   *They both draw, the seruants enter.*
 Lady. Helpe murther, murther.
 Welborne.   Let him come on,
With all his wrongs, and iniuries about him,
Arm'd with his cut-throate practises to guard him;
The right that I bring with me, will defend me,
And punish his extortion.
 Ouerreach.   That I had thee
But single in the field.
 Lady.   You may, but make not
My house your quarrelling Scene.
 Ouerreach.   Were't in a Church,
By heauen, and hell, I'le do't.
 Marrall.   Now put him to
The shewing of the deed.
 Welborne.   This rage is vaine Sir,
For fighting, feare not, you shall haue your hands full,
Vpon the least incitement; and whereas
You charge me with a debt of a thousand pounds,
If there be law, (how e're you haue no conscience)
Either restore my land, or I'le recouer
A debt, that's truely due to me, from you,
In value ten times more than what you challenge.
 Ouerreach. I in thy debt! O impudence! did I not purchase
The land left by thy father? that rich land,
That had continued in *Welbornes* name
Twenty descents; which like a riotous foole
Thou did'st make sale of? is not here inclos'd
The deed that does confirme it mine?

Marrall. Now, now!
Welborne. I doe acknowledge none, I ne're pass'd o're
Any such land; I grant for a yeare, or two,
You had it in trust, which if you doe discharge,
Surrendring the possession, you shall ease
Your selfe, and me, of chargeable suits in law,
Which if you proue not honest, (as I doubt it)
Must of necessity follow.
    Lady. In my iudgement
He does aduise you well.
    Ouerreach. Good! Good! conspire
With your new Husband Lady; second him
In his dishonest practises; but when
This Mannor is extended to my vse,
You'le speake in an humbler key, and sue for fauour.
    Lady. Neuer: do not hope it.
    Welborne. Let despaire first sease me.
    Ouerreach. Yet to shut up thy mouth, and make thee giue
Thy selfe the lye, the lowd lye: I draw out
The precious euidence; if thou canst forsweare
Thy hand, and seale, and make a forfeit of   *Opens the box.*
Thy eares to the pillory: see here's that will make
My interrest cleare. Ha!
    Lady. A faire skinne of parchment!
    Welborne. Indented I confesse, and labells too,
But neither wax, nor words. How! thunder-strooke?
Not a syllable to insult with? my wise Vncle,
Is this your precious euidence? is this that makes
Your interest cleare?
    Ouerreach. I am o'rewhelm'd with wonder!
What prodigie is this? what subtle diuell
Hath raz'd out the inscription? the wax
Turn'd into dust! the rest of my deedes whole,
As when they were deliuer'd! and this onely
Made nothing! doe you deale with witches Raskall?
There is a *statute* for you, which will bring
Your necke in a hempen circle, yes there is.
And now 'tis better thought for, Cheater know
This iuggling shall not saue you.

        197. thought for,] *Gifford;* ~, ~ ∧ 33

Welborne.   To saue thee
Would begger the stocke of mercy.
    Ouerreach.   *Marrall.*
    Marrall.   Sir.
    Ouerreach. Though the witnesses are dead, your testimony
Helpe with an oath or two, and for thy master,   *Flattering him.*
Thy liberall master, my good honest seruant,
I know, you will sweare any thing to dash
This cunning slight: besides, I know thou art
A publike notarie, and such stand in law
For a dozen witnesses; the deed being drawne too
By thee, my carefull *Marrall*, and deliuer'd
When thou wert present will make good my title;
Wilt thou not sweare this?
    Marrall.   I? no I assure you.
I haue a conscience, not sear'd vp like yours,
I know no deeds.
    Ouerreach.   Wilt thou betray me?
    Marrall.   Keepe him
From vsing of his hands, I'le vse my tongue
To his no little torment.
    Ouerreach.   Mine owne Varlet
Rebell against me?
    Marrall.   Yes, and vncase you too.
The Ideot; the Patch; the Slaue; the Boobie;
The propertie fit only to be beaten
For your morning exercise; your Footeball, or
Th'vnprofitable lumpe of flesh; your Drudge,
Can now anatomize you, and lay open
All your blacke plotts; and leuell with the earth
Your hill of pride; and with these gabions guarded,
Vnloade my great artillerie, and shake,
Nay puluerize the walls you thinke defend you.
    Lady. How he foames at the mouth with rage.
    Welborne.   To him againe.
    Ouerreach. O that I had thee in my gripe, I would teare thee
Ioint, after ioint.
    Marrall.   I know you are a tearer,
But I'le haue first your fangs par'd off, and then
Come nearer to you, when I haue discouer'd,

And made it good before the Iudge, what wayes
And diuelish practises you vs'd to coozen 230
With an armie of whole families, who yet liue,
And but enrol'd for souldiers were able
To take in *Dunkerke*.
    Welborne.   All will come out.
    Lady.   The better.
    Ouerreach. But that I will liue, Rogue, to torture thee,
And make thee wish, and kneele in vaine to dye, 235
These swords that keepe thee from me, should fix here
Although they made my body but one wound,
But I would reach thee.
    Louell.   Heau'ns hand is in this,
One Ban-dogge worrie the other.   *Aside.*
    Ouerreach.   I play the foole,
And make my anger but ridiculous. 240
There will be a time, and place, there will be, cowards,
When you shall feele what I dare do.
    Welborne.   I thinke so:
You dare do any ill, yet want true valour
To be honest, and repent.
    Ouerreach.   They are words I know not,
Nor e're will learne. Patience, the beggers vertue, 245
Shall find no harbour here.

        Enter GREEDY *and Person* WILL-DOE.

                   After these stormes
At length a calme appeares. Welcome, most welcome:
There's comfort in thy lookes, is the deed done?
Is my daughter married? say but so my Chaplaine
And I am tame.
    Will-doe.   Married? yes I assure you. 250
    Ouerreach. Then vanish all sad thoughts; there's more gold for thee,
My doubts, and feares are in the titles drown'd
Of my right honorable, my right honorable daughter.
    Greedy. Here will I be feasting; at least for a month
I am prouided: emptie gutts croke no more, 255
You shall be stuff'd like baggepipes, not with wind

    246 SD. *Enter* ... WILL-DOE.] *editor; opposite line 245 in 33*

But bearing dishes.
    Ouerreach.   Instantly be here?   *Whispring to* WILL-DOE.
To my wish, to my wish, now you that plot against me
And hop'd to trippe my heeles vp; that contemn'd me;
                                              Loud musicke.
Thinke on't and tremble, they come, I heare the musicke.
A lane there for my Lord.
    Welborne.   This sodaine heate
May yet be cool'd Sir.
    Ouerreach.   Make way there for my Lord.

        Enter ALWORTH *and* MARGARET.

    Margaret. Sir, first your pardon, then your blessing, with
Your full allowance of the choice I haue made: *Kneeling.*
As euer you could make vse of your reason,
Grow not in passion: since you may as well
Call backe the day that's past, as vntie the knot
Which is too strongly fasten'd; not to dwell
Too long on words, this's my Husband.
    Ouerreach.   How!
    Alworth. So I assure you: all the rites of marriage
With euery circumstance are past; alas Sir,
Although I am no Lord, but a Lords page,
Your daughter, and my lou'd wife mournes not for it,
And for Right honourable sonne in Law, you may say
Your dutifull daughter.
    Ouerreach.   Diuell: are they married?
    Will-doe. Doe a fathers part, and say heau'n giue 'em ioy.
    Ouerreach. Confusion, and ruine, speake, and speake quickly,
Or thou art dead.
    Will-doe.   They are married.
    Ouerreach.   Thou had'st better
Haue made a contract with the King of fiends
Than these, my braine turnes!
    Will-doe.   Why this rage to me?
Is not this your letter Sir? and these the words?
Marry her to this Gentleman.
    Ouerreach.   It cannot:
Nor will I e're beleeue it, 's death I will not,

        283. it, 's death] *after Dodsley;* it's death 33

That I, that in all passages I touch'd
At worldly profit, haue not left a print
Where I haue trod for the most curious search
To trace my footstepps, should be gull'd by children,
Baffull'd, and fool'd, and all my hopes, and labours,
Defeated, and made void.
    Welborne.   As it appeares,
You are so my graue Vncle.
    Ouerreach.   Village Nurses
Reuenge their wrongs with curses, I'le not wast
A syllable, but thus I take the life
Which wretched I gaue to thee.   *Offers to kill* MARGARET.
    Louell.   Hold for your owne sake!
Though charity to your daughter hath quite left you,
Will you do an act, though in your hopes lost here,
Can leaue no hope for peace, or rest hereafter?
Consider; at the best you are but a man,
And cannot so create your aimes, but that
They may be cross'd.
    Ouerreach.   Lord, thus I spit at thee,
And at thy counsaile; and againe desire thee
And as thou art a souldier, if thy valour
Dares shew it selfe where multitude, and example
Lead not the way, lets quit the house, and change
Six words in priuate.
    Louell.   I am ready.
    Lady.   Stay Sir,
Contest with one distracted?
    Welborne.   You'le grow like him
Should you answer his vaine challenge.
    Ouerreach.   Are you pale?
Borrow his help, though *Hercules* call it oddes
I'le stand against both, as I am hem'd in thus.
Since like the *Libian* Lyon in the toyle,
My fury cannot reach the coward hunters
And only spends it selfe, I'le quit the place,
Alone I can do nothing: but I haue seruants
And friends to second me, and if I make not

---

308. both, as I am] *33*; both as I am, *Gifford Dodsley*; like *Libian-Lyon 33*;   309. like the *Libian* Lyon]

This house a heape of ashes (by my wrongs,
What I haue spoke I will make good) or leaue
One throat vncut, if it be possible
Hell ad to my afflictions.   *Exit* OVERREACH.
   Marrall.   Is't not braue sport?
   Greedy. Braue sport? I am sure it has tane away my stomacke,
I do not like the sawce.
   Alworth.   Nay, weep not dearest:
Though it expresse your pittie, what's decreed
Aboue, wee cannot alter.
   Lady.   His threats moue mee
No scruple, Madam.
   Marrall.   Was it not a rare tricke
(And it please your Worship) to make the deed nothing?
I can do twenty neater, if you please
To purchase, and grow rich, for I will be
Such a sollicitor, and steward for you,
As neuer Worshipfull had.
   Welborne.   I do beleeue thee.
But first discouer the quaint meanes you vs'd
To raze out the conueyance?
   Marrall.   They are mysteries
Not to be spoke in publike: certaine mineralls
Incorporated in the incke, and wax.
Besides he gaue me nothing, but still fed me
With hopes, and blowes; and that was the inducement
To this *Conumbrum.* If it please your Worship
To call to memorie, this mad beast once caus'd me
To vrge you, or to drowne, or hang, your selfe,
I'le doe the like to him if you command me.
   Welborne. You are a Raskall, he that dares be false
To a master, though vniust, will ne're be true
To any other: looke not for reward,
Or fauour from me, I will shun thy sight
As I would doe a basiliskes. Thanke my pittie
If thou keep thy eares, how e're I will take order
Your practise shall be silenc'd.
   Greedy.   I'le commit him,
If you'le haue me Sir?

        315. leaue] *Dodsley*; leau'd *33*

Welborne. That were to little purpose, 345
His conscience be his prison, not a word
But instantly begone.
   Order. Take this kicke with you.
   Amble. And this.
   Furnace. If that I had my cleuer here
I would diuide your Knaues head.
   Marrall. This is the hauen,
False seruants still arriue at.   *Exit* MARRALL.

              Enter OVERREACH.

   Lady. Come agen! 350
   Louell. Feare not I am your guard.
   Welborne. His lookes are ghastly.
   Will-doe. Some little time I haue spent vnder your fauours
In physicall studies, and if my iudgement erre not
Hee's mad beyond recouery: but obserue him,
And looke to your selues.
   Ouerreach. Why is not the whole world 355
Included in my selfe? to what vse then
Are friends, and seruants? say there were a squadron
Of pikes, lined through with shot, when I am mounted
Vpon my iniuries, shall I feare to charge 'em? 359
No: I'le through the battalia, and that routed,   *Flourishing his*
I'le fall to execution. Ha! I am feeble: *sword ensheathed.*
Some vndone widdow sitts vpon mine arme,
And takes away the vse of't; and my sword
Glew'd to my scabberd with wrong'd orphans teares
Will not be drawne. Ha! what are these? sure hangmen, 365
That come to bind my hands, and then to dragge me
Before the iudgement seate! now they are new shapes
And do appeare like furies, with steele whippes
To scourge my vlcerous soule! shall I then fall
Ingloriously, and yeeld? no, spite of fate 370
I will be forc'd to hell like to my selfe;
Though you were legions of accursed spiritts,
Thus would I flie among you.
   Welborne. There's no helpe,

   360 SD. *ensheathed*] *editor*; *vnsheathed 33*; *in the Sheath Coxeter*; *sheathed Gifford*
   373. *Thus*] *Dodsley*; *Welb.* Thus *33*   *Welborne.* There's] *Dodsley*; There's *33*

  Disarme him first, then bind him.
   Greedy.   Take a *Mittimus*
And carry him to *Bedlam*.
    Louell.   How he fomes!
   Welborne. And bites the earth.
   Will-doe.   Carry him to some darke roome,
There try what Art can do for his recouery.
   Margaret. O my deare father! *They force* OVERREACH *off.*
   Alworth.   You must be patient mistresse.
   Louell. Here is a president to teach wicked men,
That when they leaue Religion, and turne Atheists
Their owne abilities leaue 'em. Pray you take comfort,
I will endeuour you shall be his guardians
In his distractions: and for your land master *Welborne*,
Be it good, or ill in law, I'le be an vmpire,
Betweene you, and this, th'vndoubted heire
Of Sir *Giles Ouerreach*; for me, here's the anchor
That I must fix on.
   Alworth. What you shall determine,
My lord, I will allow of.
   Welborne.   'Tis the language
That I speake too; but there is something else
Beside the repossession of my land,
And payment of my debts, that I must practise.
I had a reputation, but 'twas lost
In my loose course; and 'till I redeeme it
Some noble way, I am but halfe made vp.
It is a time of Action, if your Lordship
Will please to conferre a company vpon mee
In your command, I doubt not in my seruice
To my King, and Country, but I shall do something
That may make me right agen.
   Louell.   Your suite is granted,
And you lou'd for the motion.
   Welborne.   Nothing wants then
But your allowance—

THE EPILOGVE.

But your allowance, and in that, our all
Is comprehended; it being knowne, **nor we,**
Nor he that wrot the Comedie can be free
Without your Mannumission, *which if you*
Grant willingly, as a faire fauour due 5
To the Poets, and our labours, (as you may,
For we despaire not Gentlemen of the Play)
We iointly shall professe your grace hath might
To teach vs action, and him how to write.

FINIS.

APPENDIX

ABRAHAM WRIGHT'S EXCERPTS AND COMMENTS (*c.* 1640)

(See General Introduction, vol. i, pp. xlii–xliii)

From British Museum Add. MS. 22608, 'Excerpta quaedam per A. W. Adolescentem.'

fol. 93

    Out ye new way to pay old debts, a Comedie by Philip Massenger.

Act: 1. Noe bouze? nor noe Tobacco? xx some curate pend this inuectiue, and you studied it.

Mr Tapwell if I owe you anything shew it in chalke or Ile pay nothing, and you are to haue noe other register

S^rrah, haue not I made purses for thee? then thou lickd my bootes: and thought your holy-day cloake too course to cleane them.

fol. 93^v A page. One y^t is scarce manumizd from ye porters lodge (ie, yt is still subiect to ye porters lash) and yet sworne seruant to ye pantofle. xx ye queene of flowers, ye glory of ye spring, ye sweetest comfort to our smell, ye rose / sprang from an enuious brier; soe may a kind daughter from a churlish father.

My ladies goe-beefore. Ie, a gentleman vsher.

If such fortifications (Ie, such as cookes make.) had binne practisd at Breda, spinola might haue thrown his cap at it and nere tooke [it.]

good s^r, doe soe much as remember pie-corner, and help mee to a peice of yt. (Ie ye corner of ye pie.

Why you slaues / created onely to make leggs, and cringe: / to carry a dish, and shift a trencher; yt haue noe soules onely to hope a blessing / beeyond blacke iacks and flagons.

Act: 2 My duety suffers, if to please my selfe I should neglect my lord

sorrow followes ye flux of laughture.

Act: 3 Hee eates till his belly's bracd vp like a drumme. xx this is granted vnto few, but such as rise vp ye Kdomes glory.
Thou barathrum of ye shambles. Ie, a great eater. xx shees very willing, yet should wee take forts at ye first assaulte; twere poore in ye defendant. xx your bounties are soe great they rob mee, madam, of words to giue you thankes. (The rest not worth ye reading

A new way to pay old debts.

A silly play. ye plot but ordinary wch is ye cheating of an vsurer beeing ye plot of a great many plaies, at least a maine passage in them. but for ye lines they are very poore, noe expressions, but onely plaine downright relating ye matter; wthout any new dress either of language or fancy.